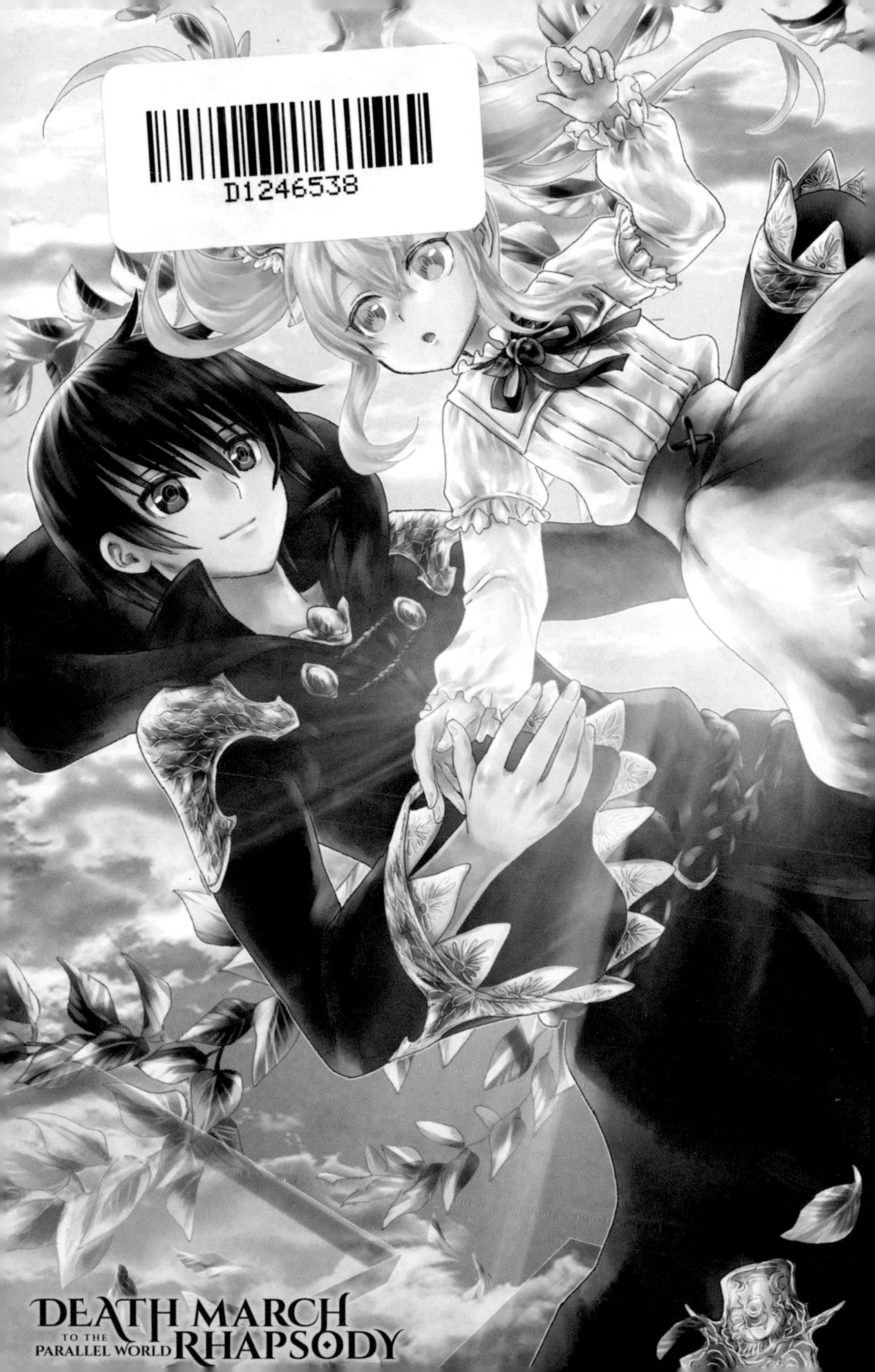

DEATH MARCH TO THE PARALLEL WORLD RHAPSODY

CONTENTS

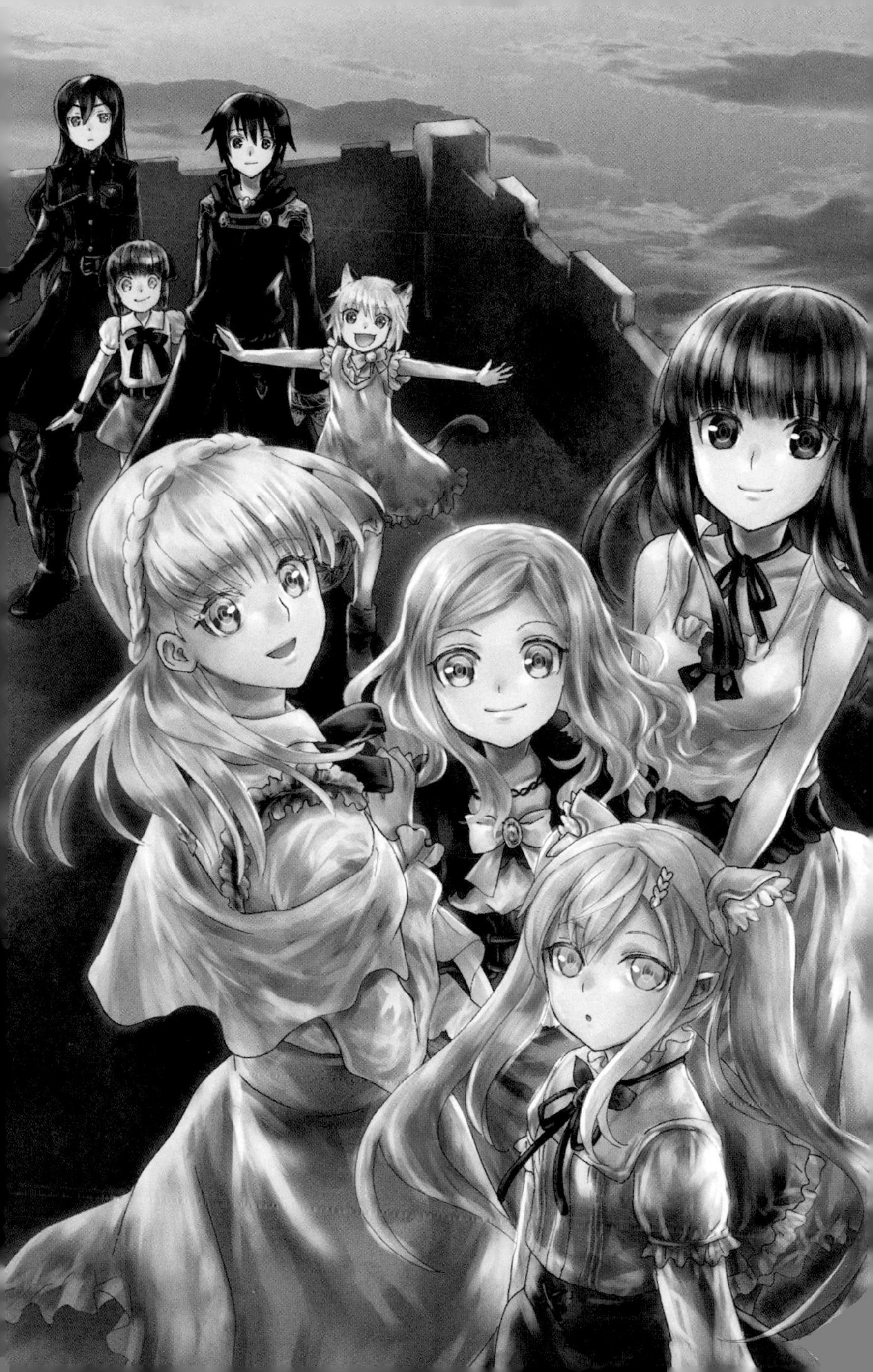

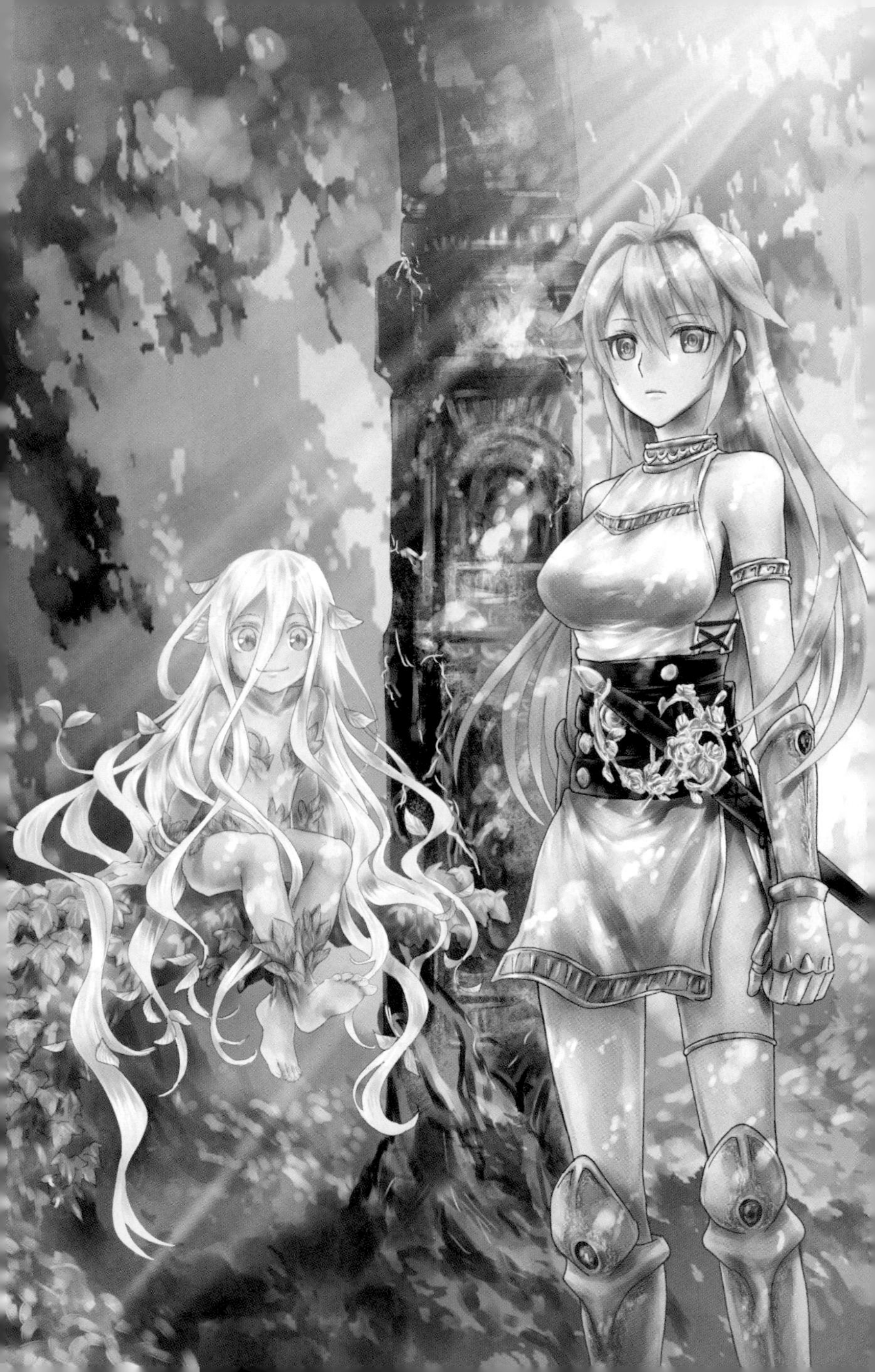

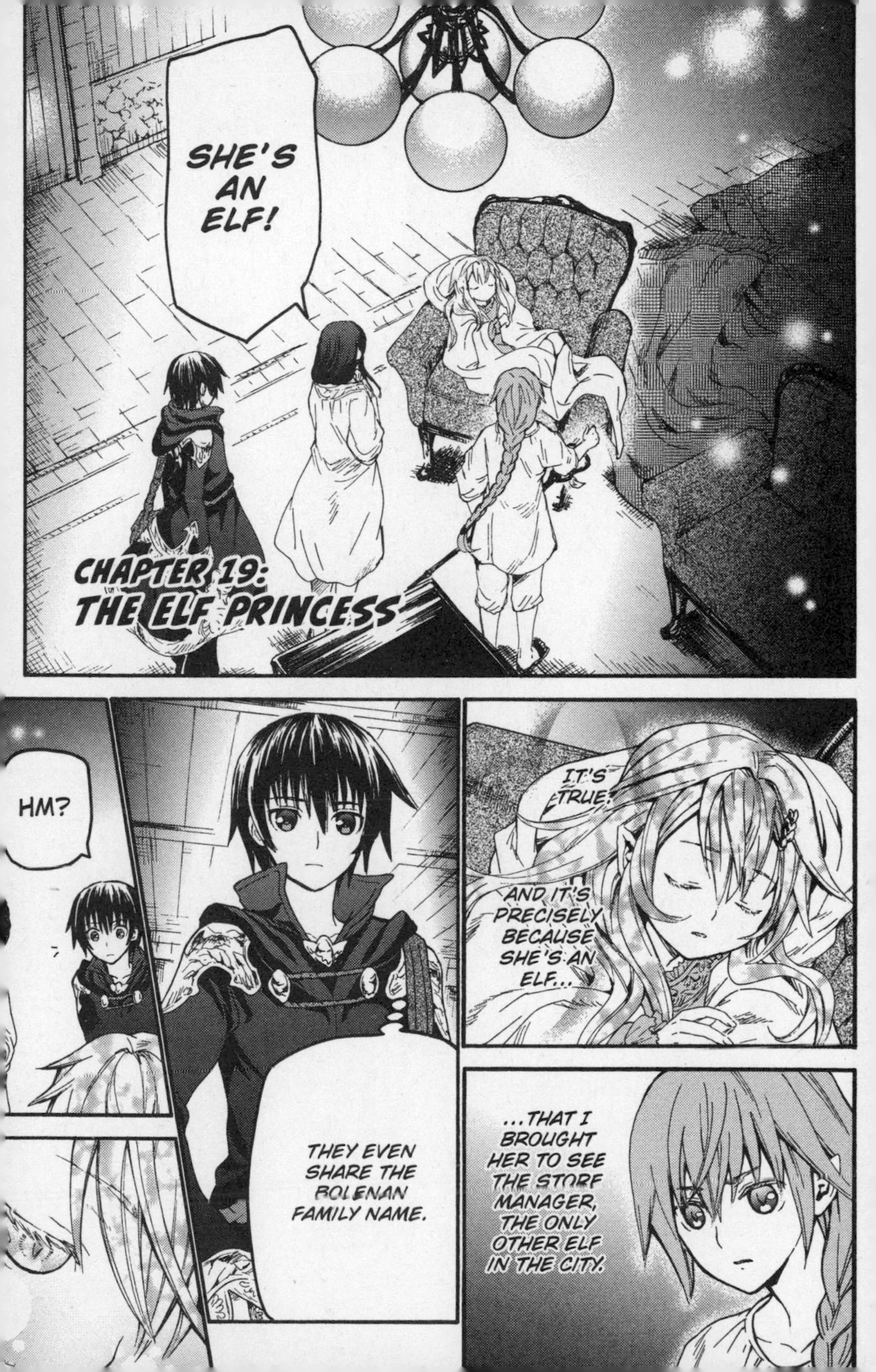
SHE'S AN ELF!
CHAPTER 19: THE ELF PRINCESS
IT'S TRUE.
AND IT'S PRECISELY BECAUSE SHE'S AN ELF...
...THAT I BROUGHT HER TO SEE THE STORE MANAGER, THE ONLY OTHER ELF IN THE CITY.
THEY EVEN SHARE THE BOLENAN FAMILY NAME.
HM?

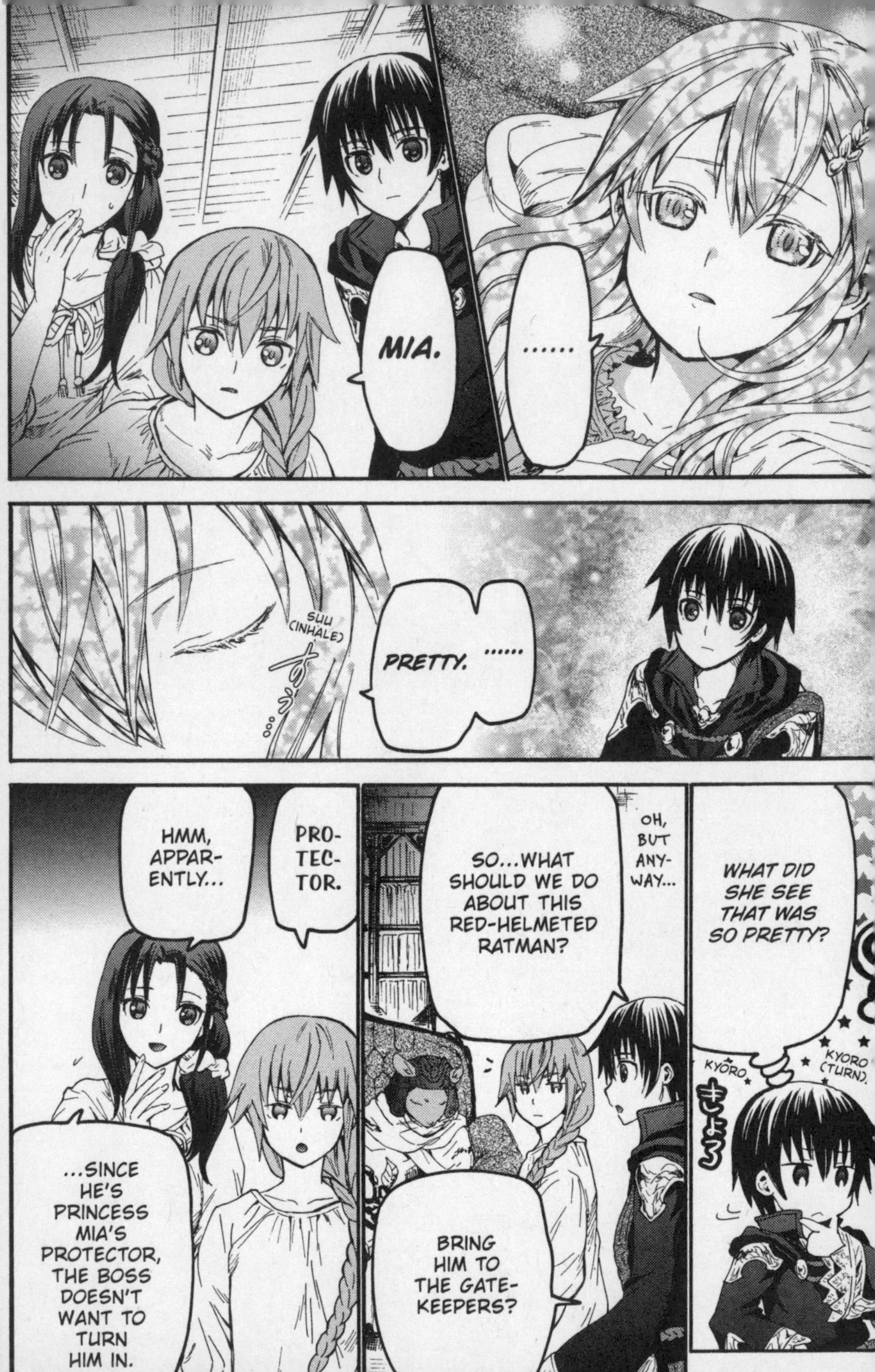
......
MIA.
......
PRETTY.
SUU (INHALE)
WHAT DID SHE SEE THAT WAS SO PRETTY?
KYORO (TURN).
KYORO
きょろ
OH, BUT ANYWAY...
SO...WHAT SHOULD WE DO ABOUT THIS RED-HELMETED RATMAN?
BRING HIM TO THE GATE-KEEPERS?
PRO-TEC-TOR.
HMM, APPAR-ENTLY...
...SINCE HE'S PRINCESS MIA'S PROTECTOR, THE BOSS DOESN'T WANT TO TURN HIM IN.

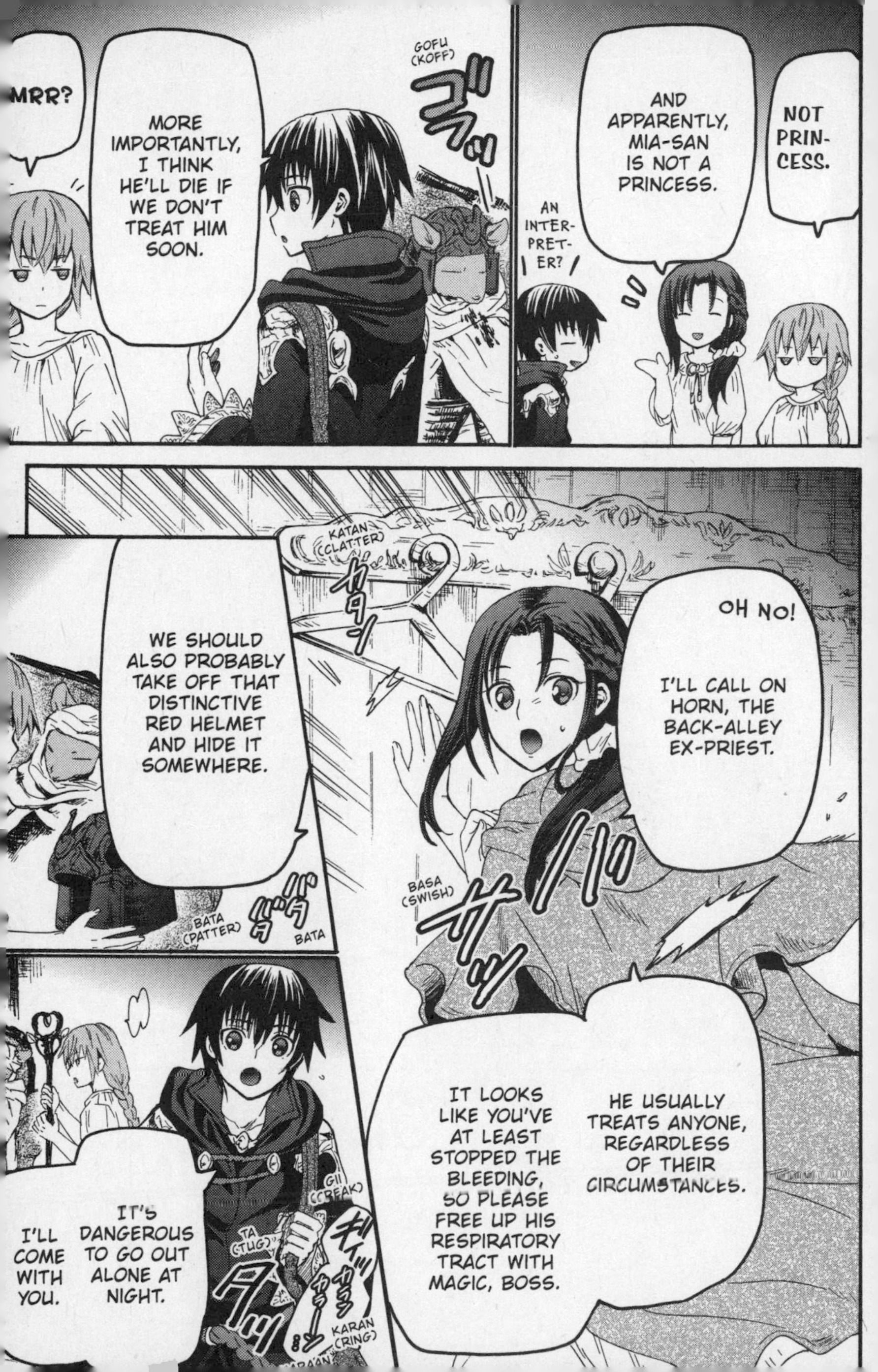
NOT PRINCESS.
AND APPARENTLY, MIA-SAN IS NOT A PRINCESS.
AN INTERPRETER?
GOFU (KOFF)
MORE IMPORTANTLY, I THINK HE'LL DIE IF WE DON'T TREAT HIM SOON.
MRR?
KATAN (CLATTER)
OH NO!
I'LL CALL ON HORN, THE BACK-ALLEY EX-PRIEST.
BASA (SWISH)
HE USUALLY TREATS ANYONE, REGARDLESS OF THEIR CIRCUMSTANCES.
IT LOOKS LIKE YOU'VE AT LEAST STOPPED THE BLEEDING, SO PLEASE FREE UP HIS RESPIRATORY TRACT WITH MAGIC, BOSS.
WE SHOULD ALSO PROBABLY TAKE OFF THAT DISTINCTIVE RED HELMET AND HIDE IT SOMEWHERE.
BATA (PATTER)
BATA
GII (CREAK)
TA (TUG)
KARAN (RING)
IT'S DANGEROUS TO GO OUT ALONE AT NIGHT.
I'LL COME WITH YOU.

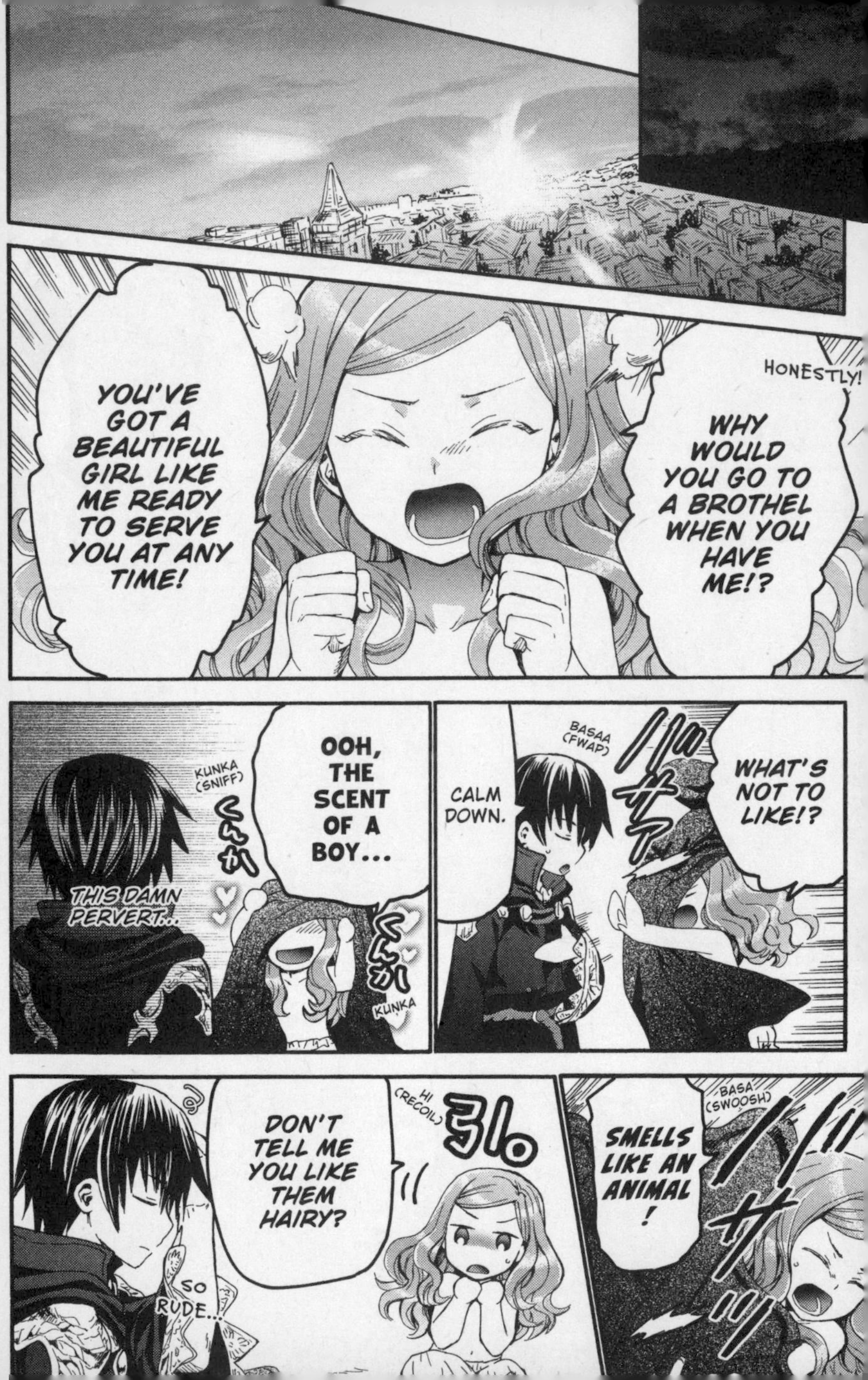
HONESTLY!
WHY WOULD YOU GO TO A BROTHEL WHEN YOU HAVE ME!?
YOU'VE GOT A BEAUTIFUL GIRL LIKE ME READY TO SERVE YOU AT ANY TIME!
WHAT'S NOT TO LIKE!?
BASAA (FWAP)
CALM DOWN.
OOH, THE SCENT OF A BOY...
KUNKA (SNIFF)
KUNKA
THIS DAMN PERVERT...
BASA (SWOOSH)
SMELLS LIKE AN ANIMAL!
HI (RECOIL)
DON'T TELL ME YOU LIKE THEM HAIRY?
SO RUDE...

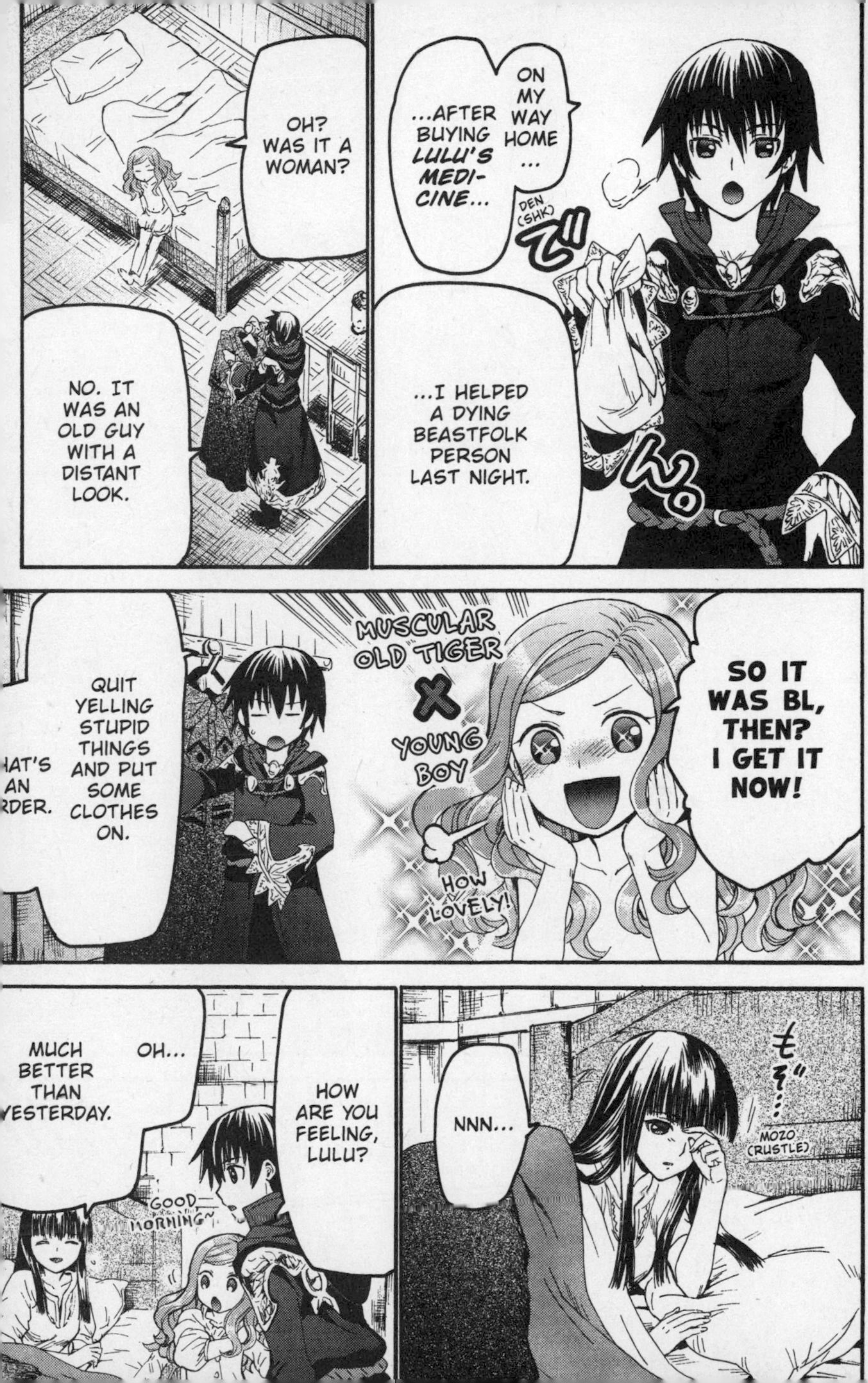
ON MY WAY HOME...
...AFTER BUYING LULU'S MEDICINE...
DEN (SHK)
...I HELPED A DYING BEASTFOLK PERSON LAST NIGHT.
OH? WAS IT A WOMAN?
NO. IT WAS AN OLD GUY WITH A DISTANT LOOK.
SO IT WAS BL, THEN? I GET IT NOW!
MUSCULAR OLD TIGER
YOUNG BOY
HOW LOVELY!
QUIT YELLING STUPID THINGS AND PUT SOME CLOTHES ON.
HAT'S AN RDER.
MOZO (RUSTLE)
NNN...
HOW ARE YOU FEELING, LULU?
OH...
MUCH BETTER THAN YESTERDAY.
GOOD MORNING~

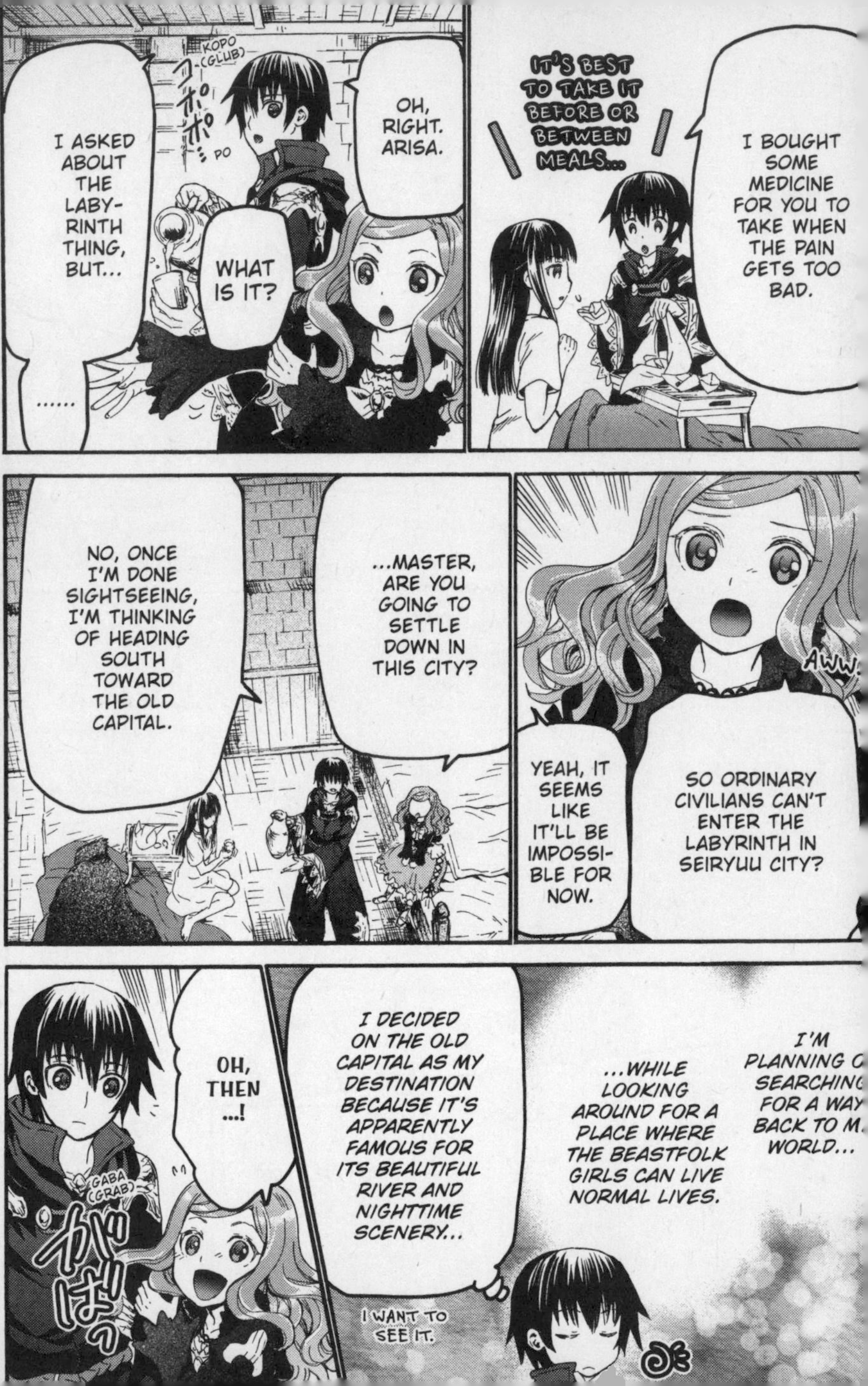
I BOUGHT SOME MEDICINE FOR YOU TO TAKE WHEN THE PAIN GETS TOO BAD.
IT'S BEST TO TAKE IT BEFORE OR BETWEEN MEALS...
OH, RIGHT. ARISA.
WHAT IS IT?
KOPO (GLUB)
PO
I ASKED ABOUT THE LABY-RINTH THING, BUT...
......
AWW
SO ORDINARY CIVILIANS CAN'T ENTER THE LABYRINTH IN SEIRYUU CITY?
YEAH, IT SEEMS LIKE IT'LL BE IMPOSSI-BLE FOR NOW.
...MASTER, ARE YOU GOING TO SETTLE DOWN IN THIS CITY?
NO, ONCE I'M DONE SIGHTSEEING, I'M THINKING OF HEADING SOUTH TOWARD THE OLD CAPITAL.
I'M PLANNING O SEARCHING FOR A WAY BACK TO M WORLD...
...WHILE LOOKING AROUND FOR A PLACE WHERE THE BEASTFOLK GIRLS CAN LIVE NORMAL LIVES.
I DECIDED ON THE OLD CAPITAL AS MY DESTINATION BECAUSE IT'S APPARENTLY FAMOUS FOR ITS BEAUTIFUL RIVER AND NIGHTTIME SCENERY...
I WANT TO SEE IT.
OH, THEN ...!
GABA (GRAB)

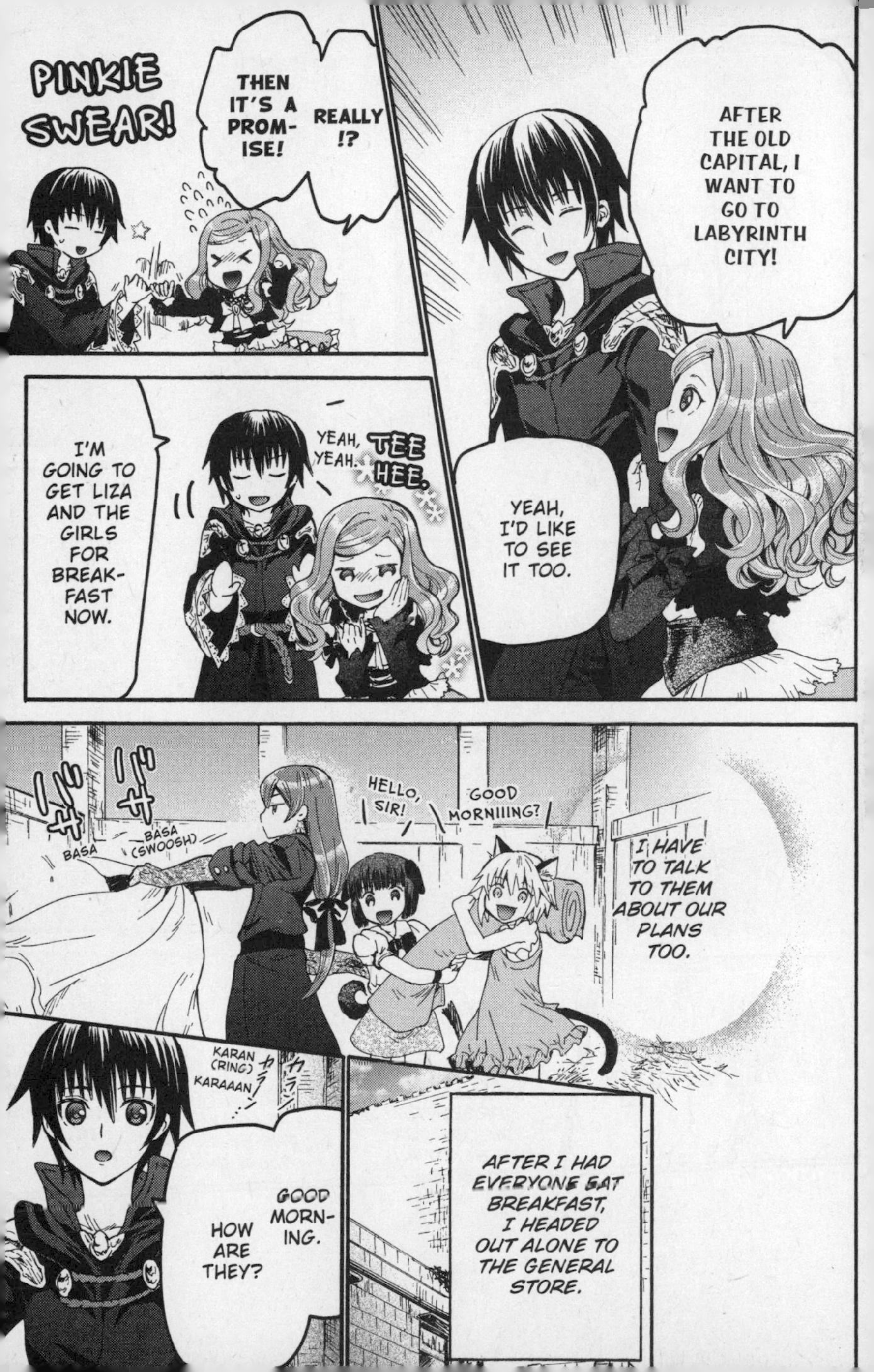
AFTER THE OLD CAPITAL, I WANT TO GO TO LABYRINTH CITY!
YEAH, I'D LIKE TO SEE IT TOO.
REALLY !?
THEN IT'S A PROMISE!
PINKIE SWEAR!
TEE HEE.
YEAH, YEAH.
I'M GOING TO GET LIZA AND THE GIRLS FOR BREAKFAST NOW.
I HAVE TO TALK TO THEM ABOUT OUR PLANS TOO.
GOOD MORNIIING?
HELLO, SIR!
BASA (SWOOSH)
BASA
AFTER I HAD EVERYONE EAT BREAKFAST, I HEADED OUT ALONE TO THE GENERAL STORE.
KARAN (RING) KARAAAN
GOOD MORNING.
HOW ARE THEY?

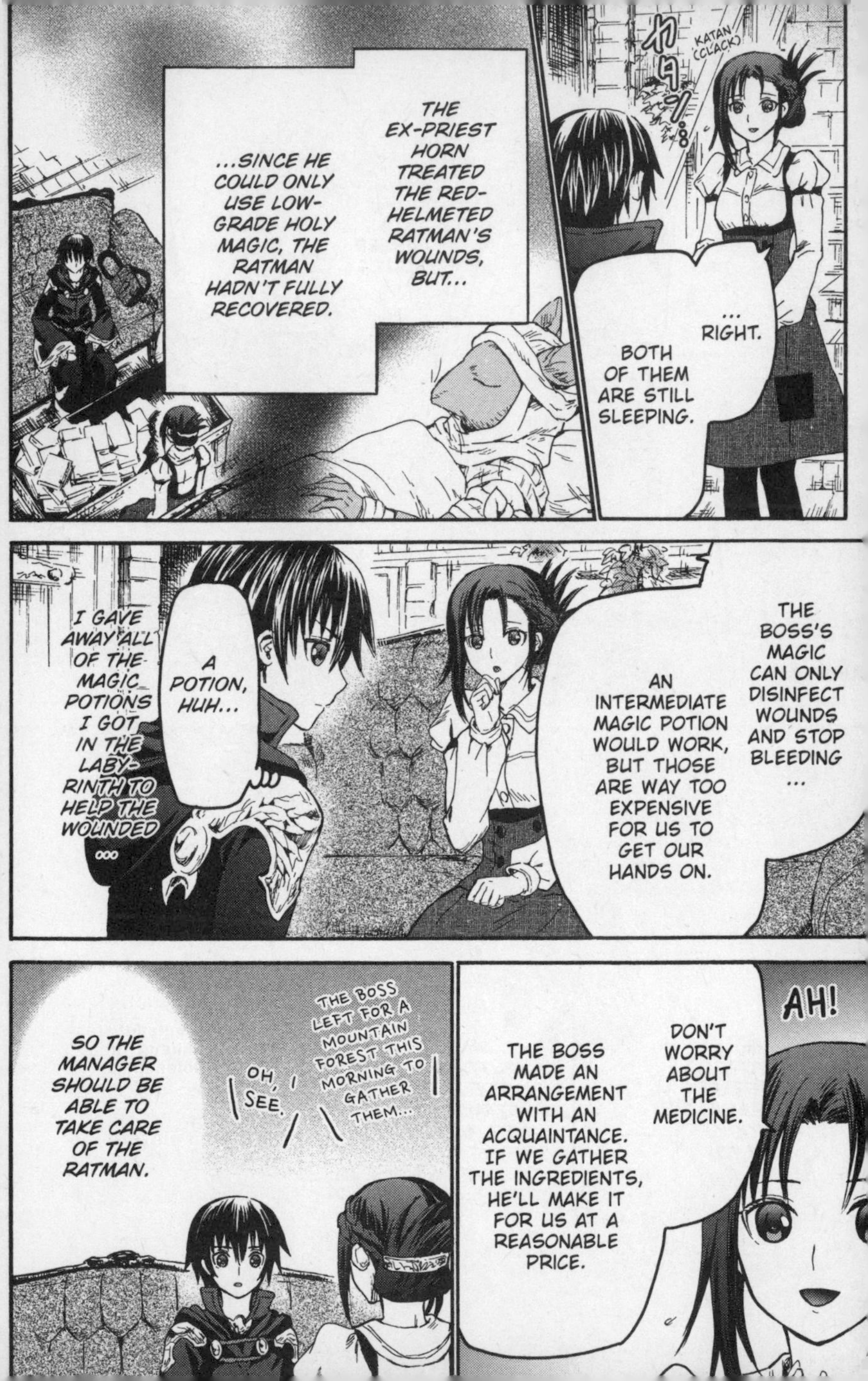
KATAN (CLACK)
...RIGHT.
BOTH OF THEM ARE STILL SLEEPING.
THE EX-PRIEST HORN TREATED THE RED-HELMETED RATMAN'S WOUNDS, BUT...
...SINCE HE COULD ONLY USE LOW-GRADE HOLY MAGIC, THE RATMAN HADN'T FULLY RECOVERED.
THE BOSS'S MAGIC CAN ONLY DISINFECT WOUNDS AND STOP BLEEDING...
AN INTERMEDIATE MAGIC POTION WOULD WORK, BUT THOSE ARE WAY TOO EXPENSIVE FOR US TO GET OUR HANDS ON.
A POTION, HUH...
I GAVE AWAY ALL OF THE MAGIC POTIONS I GOT IN THE LABYRINTH TO HELP THE WOUNDED...
AH!
DON'T WORRY ABOUT THE MEDICINE.
THE BOSS MADE AN ARRANGEMENT WITH AN ACQUAINTANCE. IF WE GATHER THE INGREDIENTS, HE'LL MAKE IT FOR US AT A REASONABLE PRICE.
THE BOSS LEFT FOR A MOUNTAIN FOREST THIS MORNING TO GATHER THEM...
OH, I SEE.
SO THE MANAGER SHOULD BE ABLE TO TAKE CARE OF THE RATMAN.

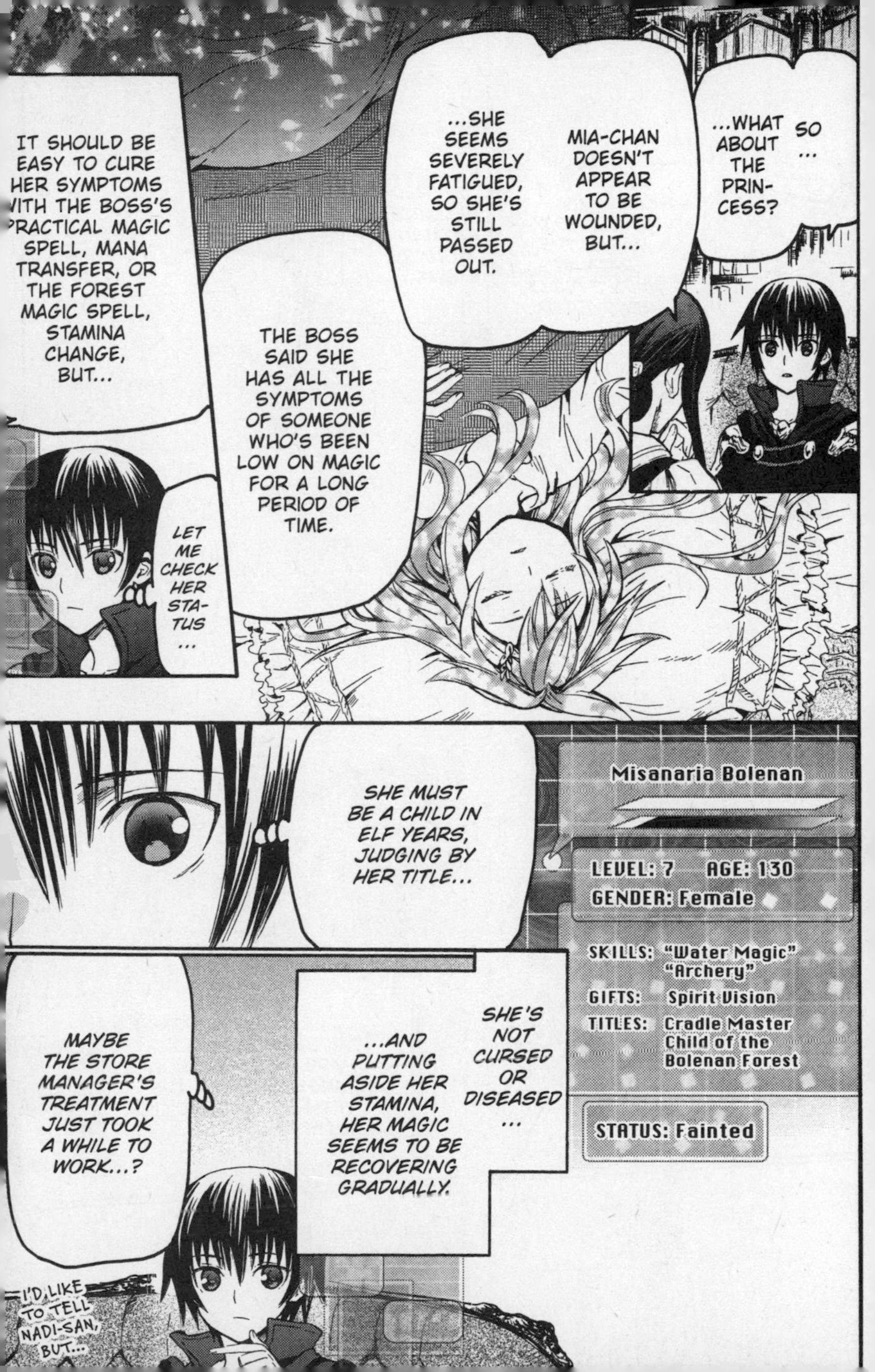
SO...
...WHAT ABOUT THE PRINCESS?
MIA-CHAN DOESN'T APPEAR TO BE WOUNDED, BUT...
...SHE SEEMS SEVERELY FATIGUED, SO SHE'S STILL PASSED OUT.
THE BOSS SAID SHE HAS ALL THE SYMPTOMS OF SOMEONE WHO'S BEEN LOW ON MAGIC FOR A LONG PERIOD OF TIME.
IT SHOULD BE EASY TO CURE HER SYMPTOMS WITH THE BOSS'S PRACTICAL MAGIC SPELL, MANA TRANSFER, OR THE FOREST MAGIC SPELL, STAMINA CHANGE, BUT...
LET ME CHECK HER STATUS...
Misanaria Bolenan
LEVEL: 7 AGE: 130
GENDER: Female
SKILLS: "Water Magic" "Archery"
GIFTS: Spirit Vision
TITLES: Cradle Master
Child of the Bolenan Forest
STATUS: Fainted
SHE MUST BE A CHILD IN ELF YEARS, JUDGING BY HER TITLE...
SHE'S NOT CURSED OR DISEASED...
...AND PUTTING ASIDE HER STAMINA, HER MAGIC SEEMS TO BE RECOVERING GRADUALLY.
MAYBE THE STORE MANAGER'S TREATMENT JUST TOOK A WHILE TO WORK...?
I'D LIKE TO TELL NADI-SAN, BUT...

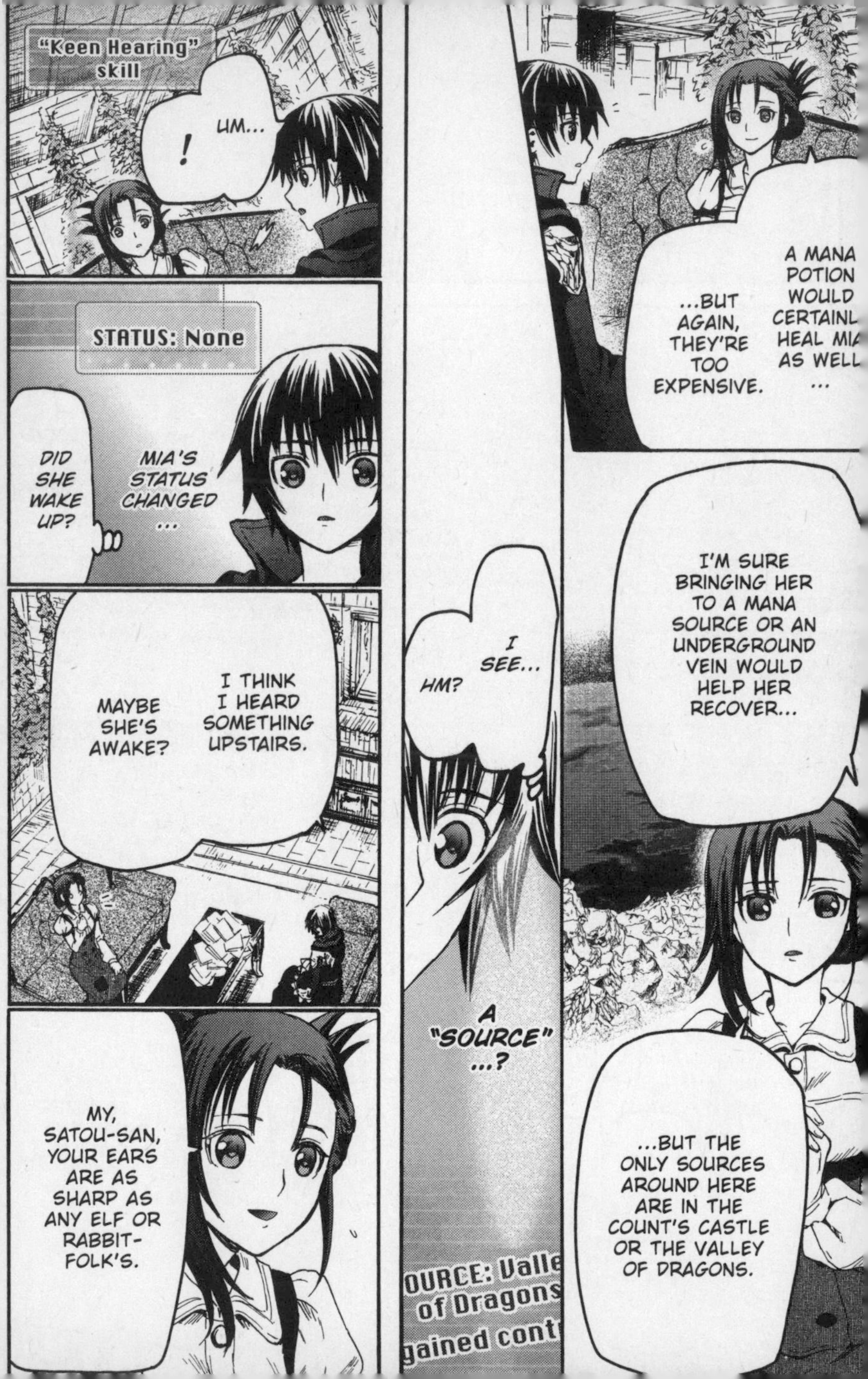
A MANA POTION WOULD CERTAINL HEAL MIA AS WELL ...
...BUT AGAIN, THEY'RE TOO EXPENSIVE.
I'M SURE BRINGING HER TO A MANA SOURCE OR AN UNDERGROUND VEIN WOULD HELP HER RECOVER...
...BUT THE ONLY SOURCES AROUND HERE ARE IN THE COUNT'S CASTLE OR THE VALLEY OF DRAGONS.
I SEE...
HM?
A "SOURCE" ...?
OURCE: Valle
of Dragons
gained contr
“Keen Hearing” skill
UM...
!
STATUS: None
MIA'S STATUS CHANGED ...
DID SHE WAKE UP?
I THINK I HEARD SOMETHING UPSTAIRS.
MAYBE SHE'S AWAKE?
MY, SATOU-SAN, YOUR EARS ARE AS SHARP AS ANY ELF OR RABBIT-FOLK'S.

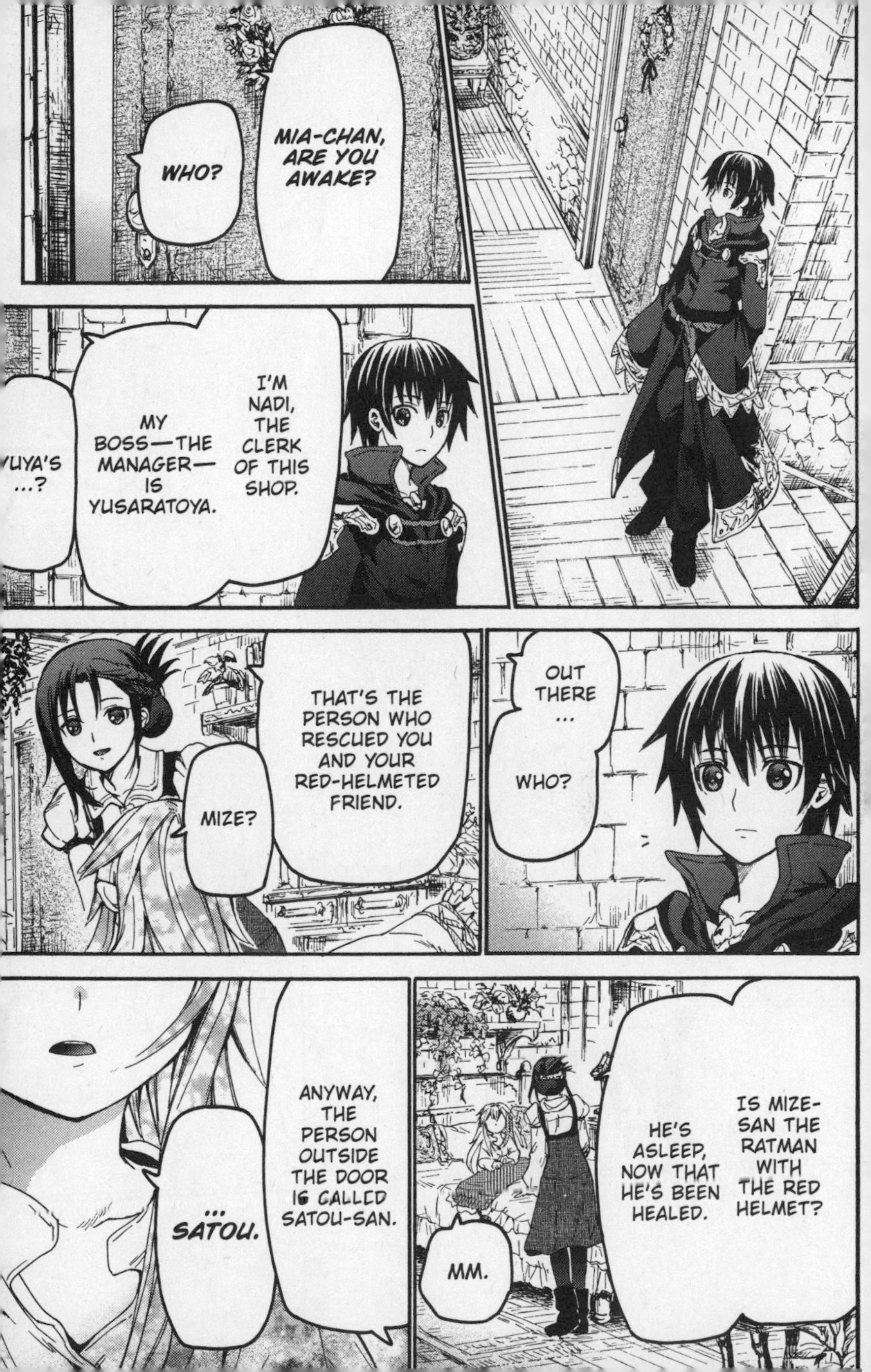
MIA-CHAN, ARE YOU AWAKE?
WHO?
I'M NADI, THE CLERK OF THIS SHOP.
MY BOSS—THE MANAGER—IS YUSARATOYA.
UYA'S ...?
OUT THERE ... WHO?
THAT'S THE PERSON WHO RESCUED YOU AND YOUR RED-HELMETED FRIEND.
MIZE?
IS MIZE-SAN THE RATMAN WITH THE RED HELMET?
HE'S ASLEEP, NOW THAT HE'S BEEN HEALED.
MM.
ANYWAY, THE PERSON OUTSIDE THE DOOR IS CALLED SATOU-SAN.
... SATOU.

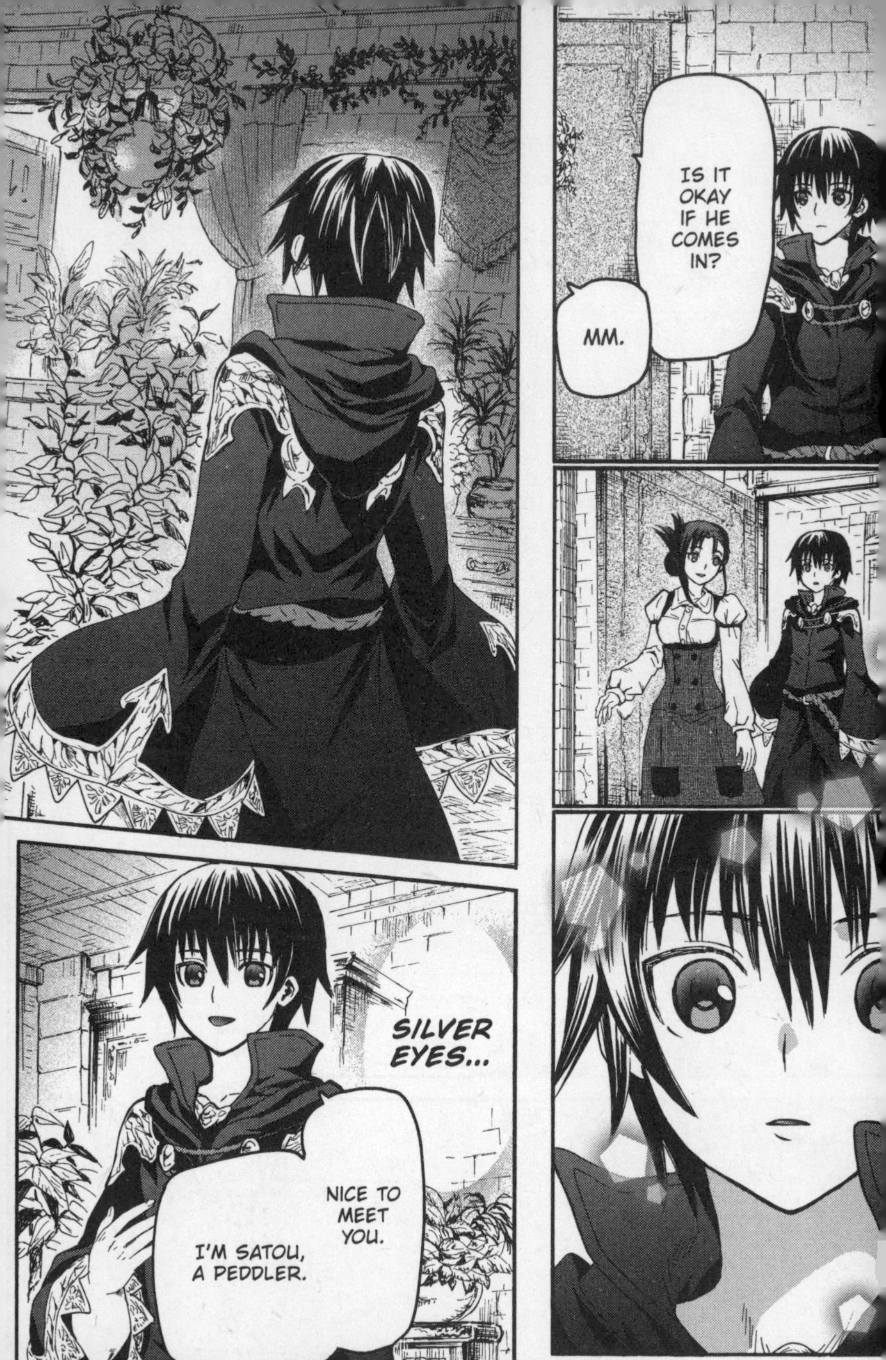
IS IT OKAY IF HE COMES IN?
MM.
SILVER EYES...
NICE TO MEET YOU.
I'M SATOU, A PEDDLER.

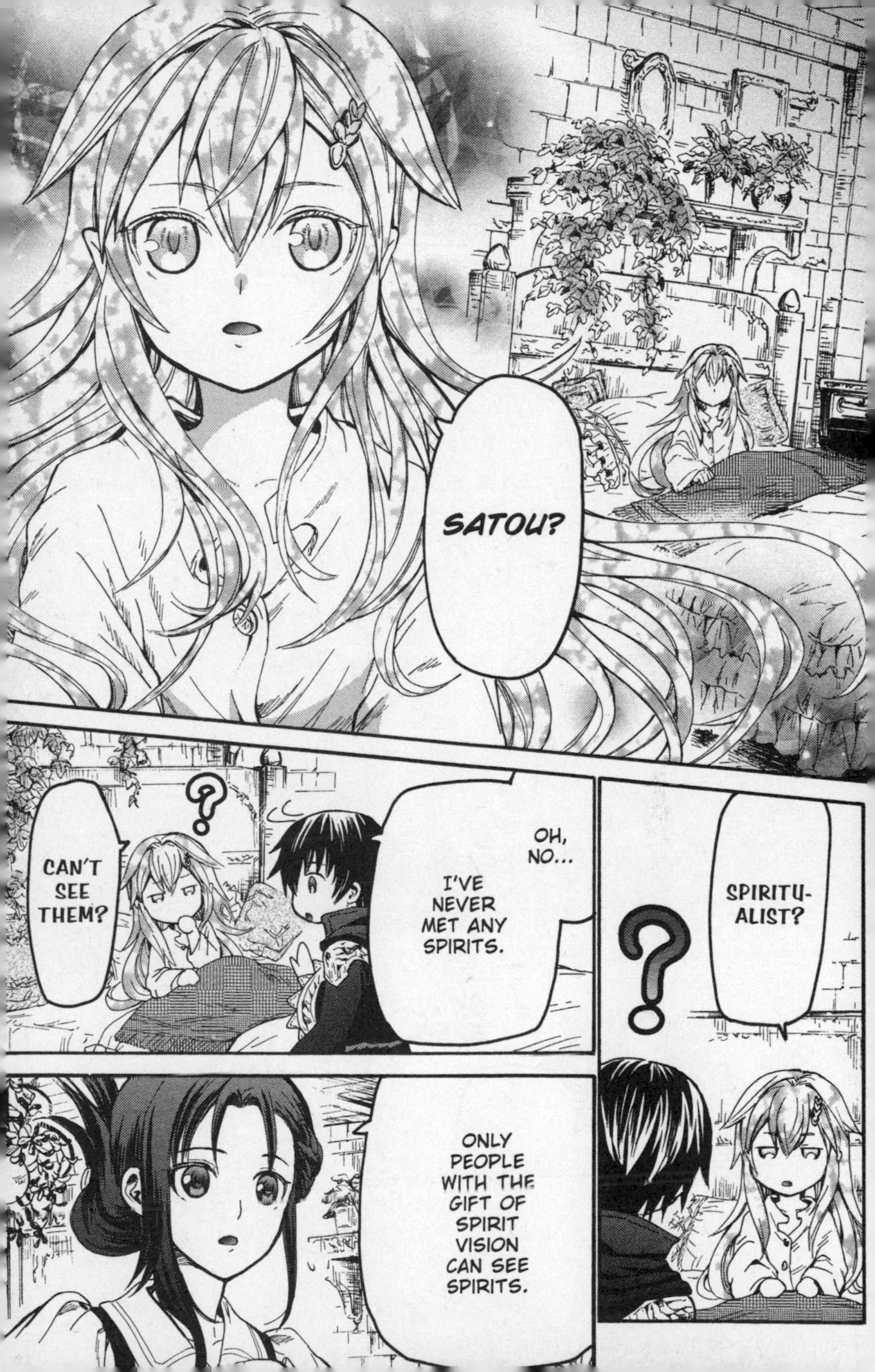
SATOU?
SPIRITU-ALIST?
OH, NO... I'VE NEVER MET ANY SPIRITS.
CAN'T SEE THEM?
ONLY PEOPLE WITH THE GIFT OF SPIRIT VISION CAN SEE SPIRITS.

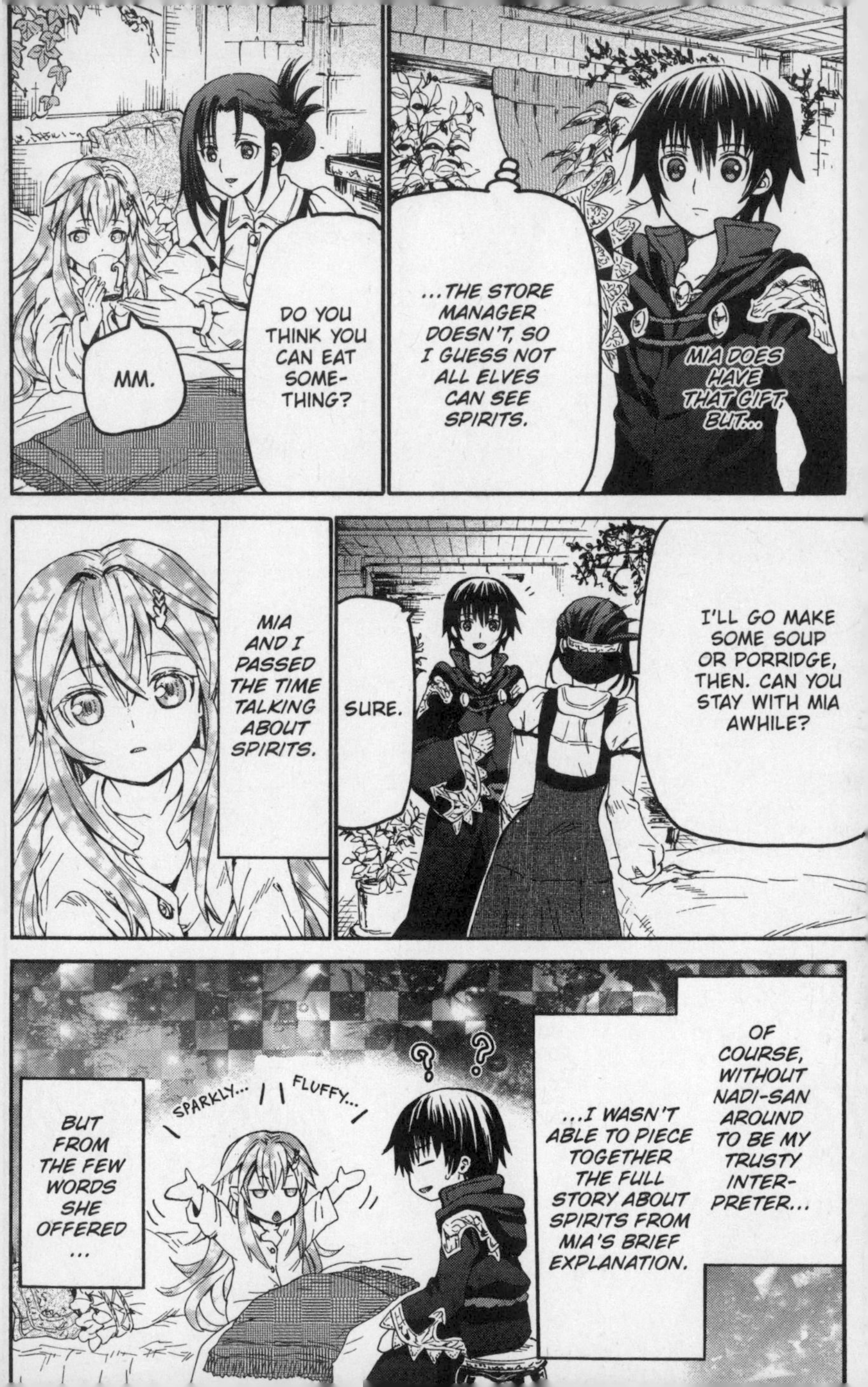
MIA DOES HAVE THAT GIFT, BUT...
...THE STORE MANAGER DOESN'T, SO I GUESS NOT ALL ELVES CAN SEE SPIRITS.
DO YOU THINK YOU CAN EAT SOMETHING?
MM.
I'LL GO MAKE SOME SOUP OR PORRIDGE, THEN. CAN YOU STAY WITH MIA AWHILE?
SURE.
MIA AND I PASSED THE TIME TALKING ABOUT SPIRITS.
OF COURSE, WITHOUT NADI-SAN AROUND TO BE MY TRUSTY INTERPRETER...
...I WASN'T ABLE TO PIECE TOGETHER THE FULL STORY ABOUT SPIRITS FROM MIA'S BRIEF EXPLANATION.
? ?
FLUFFY...
SPARKLY...
BUT FROM THE FEW WORDS SHE OFFERED...

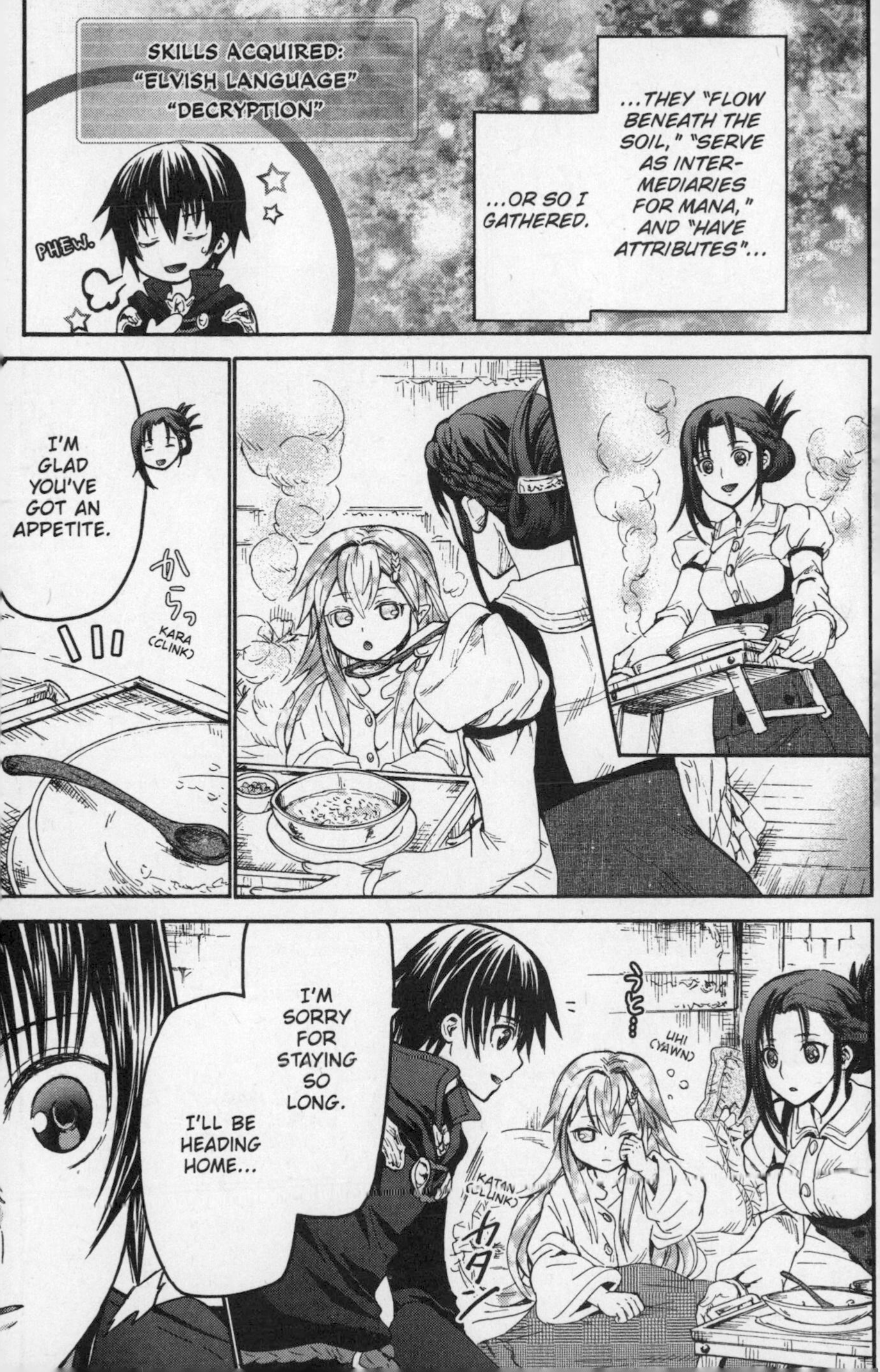
...THEY "FLOW BENEATH THE SOIL," "SERVE AS INTER-MEDIARIES FOR MANA," AND "HAVE ATTRIBUTES"...
...OR SO I GATHERED.
SKILLS ACQUIRED: "ELVISH LANGUAGE" "DECRYPTION"
PHEW.
I'M GLAD YOU'VE GOT AN APPETITE.
からっ
KARA (CLINK)
UHI (YAWN)
KATAN (CLINK)
I'M SORRY FOR STAYING SO LONG.
I'LL BE HEADING HOME...

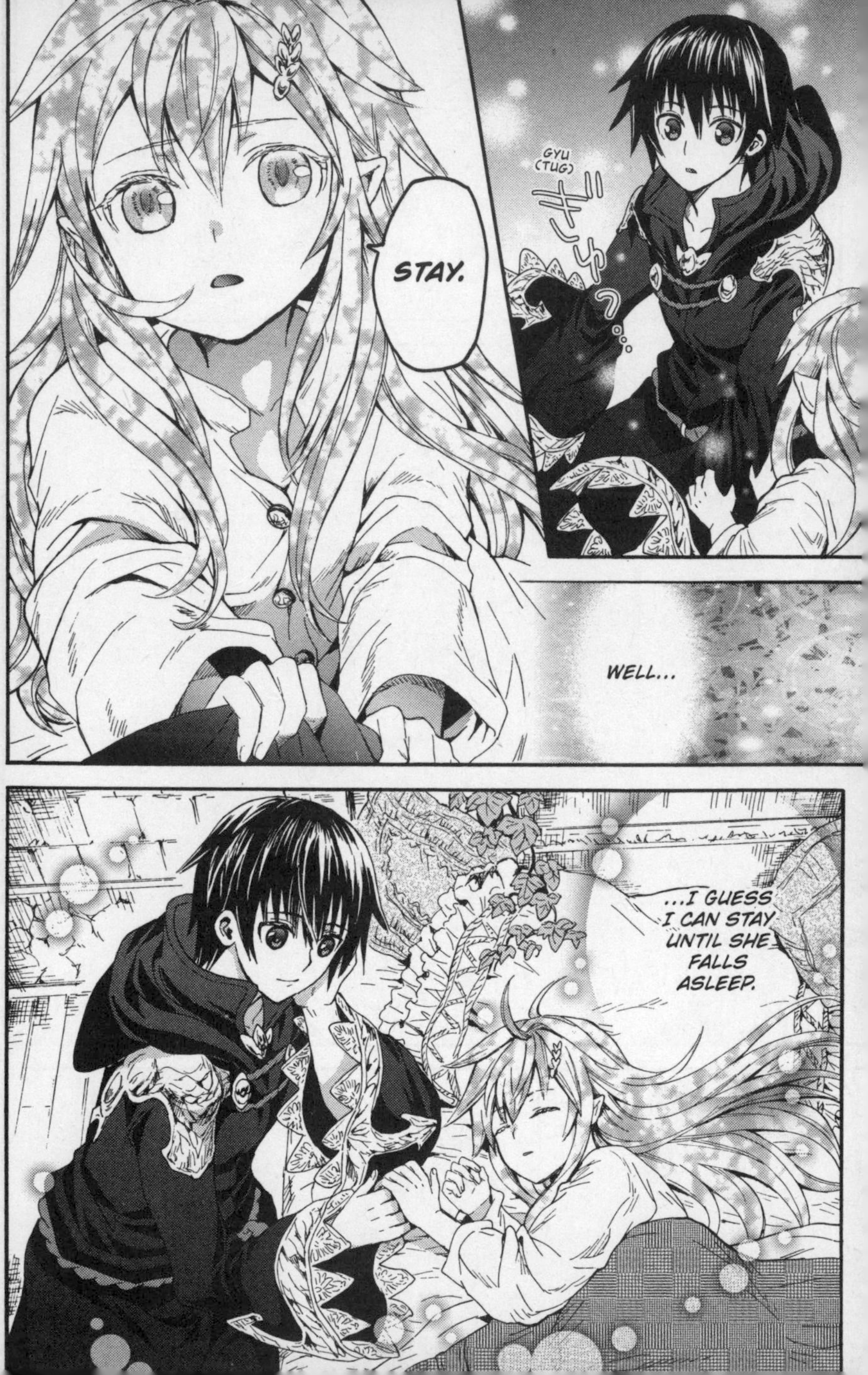
GYU (TUG)
ぎゅっ
WELL...
STAY.
...I GUESS I CAN STAY UNTIL SHE FALLS ASLEEP.

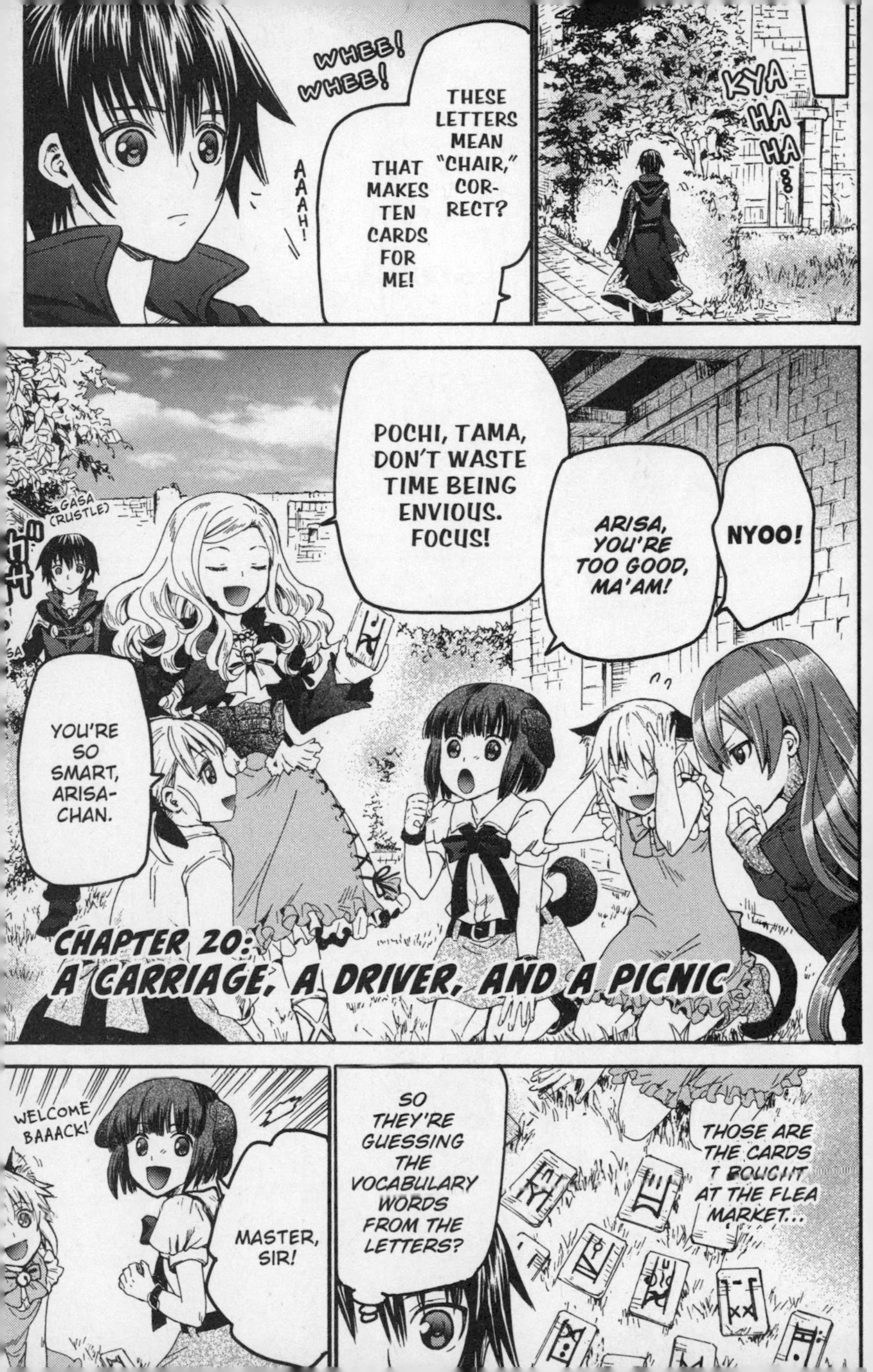
KYA HA HA...
THESE LETTERS MEAN "CHAIR," CORRECT?
THAT MAKES TEN CARDS FOR ME!
WHEE! WHEE!
AAAAH!
NYOO!
ARISA, YOU'RE TOO GOOD, MA'AM!
POCHI, TAMA, DON'T WASTE TIME BEING ENVIOUS. FOCUS!
GASA (RUSTLE)
YOU'RE SO SMART, ARISA-CHAN.
CHAPTER 20: A CARRIAGE, A DRIVER, AND A PICNIC
THOSE ARE THE CARDS I BOUGHT AT THE FLEA MARKET...
SO THEY'RE GUESSING THE VOCABULARY WORDS FROM THE LETTERS?
WELCOME BAAACK!
MASTER, SIR!

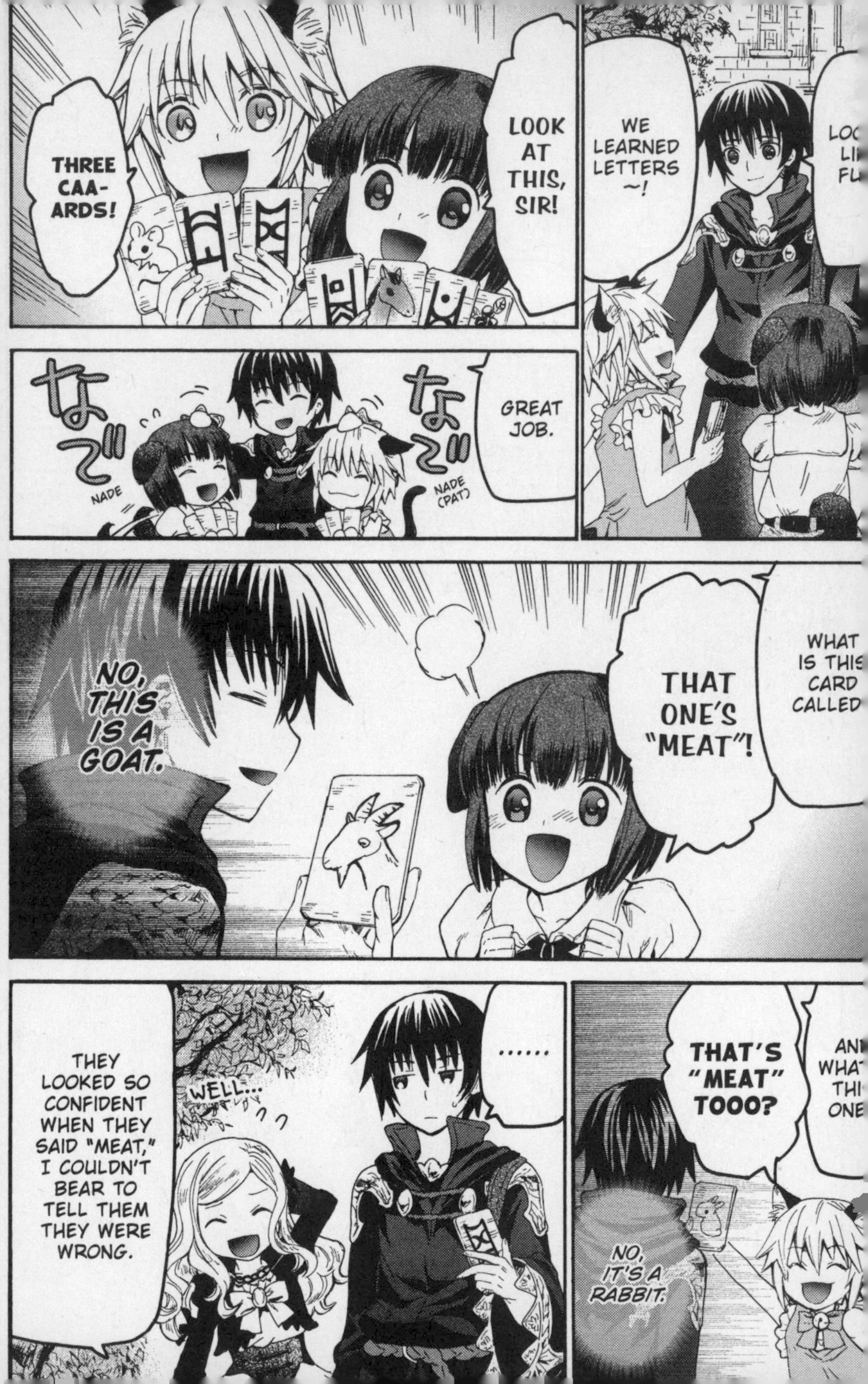
WE LEARNED LETTERS ~!
LOOK AT THIS, SIR!
THREE CAA-ARDS!
GREAT JOB.
なで
NADE (PAT)
なで
NADE
WHAT IS THIS CARD CALLED
THAT ONE'S "MEAT"!
NO, THIS IS A GOAT.
THAT'S "MEAT" TOOO?
NO, IT'S A RABBIT.
......
WELL...
THEY LOOKED SO CONFIDENT WHEN THEY SAID "MEAT," I COULDN'T BEAR TO TELL THEM THEY WERE WRONG.

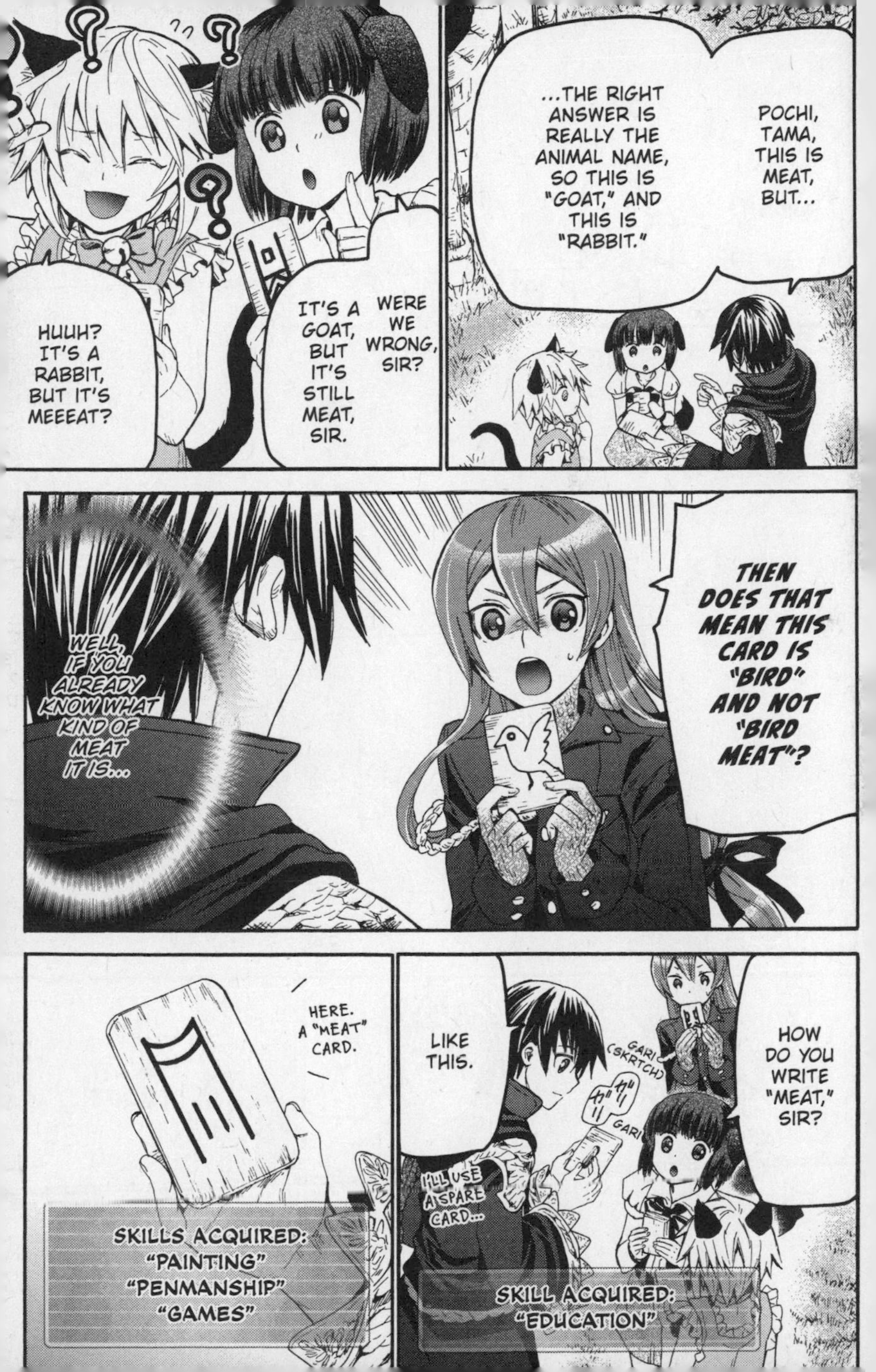
POCHI, TAMA, THIS IS MEAT, BUT...
...THE RIGHT ANSWER IS REALLY THE ANIMAL NAME, SO THIS IS "GOAT," AND THIS IS "RABBIT."
WERE WE WRONG, SIR?
IT'S A GOAT, BUT IT'S STILL MEAT, SIR.
HUUH? IT'S A RABBIT, BUT IT'S MEEEAT?
THEN DOES THAT MEAN THIS CARD IS "BIRD" AND NOT "BIRD MEAT"?
WELL, IF YOU ALREADY KNOW WHAT KIND OF MEAT IT IS...
HOW DO YOU WRITE "MEAT," SIR?
GARI (SKRTCH)
GARI
LIKE THIS.
I'LL USE A SPARE CARD...
SKILL ACQUIRED: "EDUCATION"
HERE. A "MEAT" CARD.
SKILLS ACQUIRED: "PAINTING" "PENMANSHIP" "GAMES"

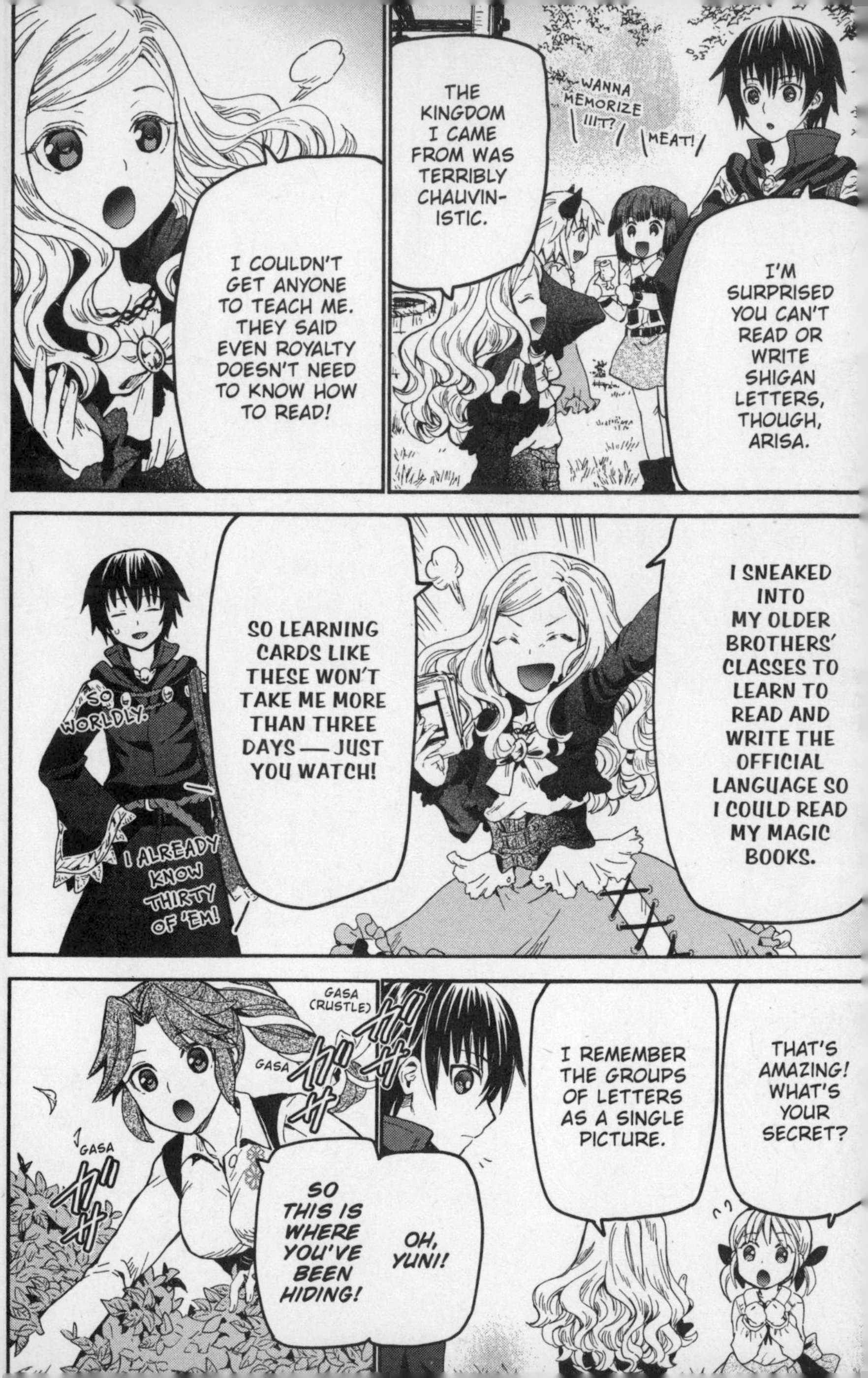
I'M SURPRISED YOU CAN'T READ OR WRITE SHIGAN LETTERS, THOUGH, ARISA.
MEAT!
WANNA MEMORIZE IIIT?
THE KINGDOM I CAME FROM WAS TERRIBLY CHAUVIN-ISTIC.
I COULDN'T GET ANYONE TO TEACH ME. THEY SAID EVEN ROYALTY DOESN'T NEED TO KNOW HOW TO READ!
I SNEAKED INTO MY OLDER BROTHERS' CLASSES TO LEARN TO READ AND WRITE THE OFFICIAL LANGUAGE SO I COULD READ MY MAGIC BOOKS.
SO LEARNING CARDS LIKE THESE WON'T TAKE ME MORE THAN THREE DAYS — JUST YOU WATCH!
SO WORLDLY.
I ALREADY KNOW THIRTY OF 'EM!
THAT'S AMAZING! WHAT'S YOUR SECRET?
I REMEMBER THE GROUPS OF LETTERS AS A SINGLE PICTURE.
GASA (RUSTLE)
GASA
OH, YUNI!
SO THIS IS WHERE YOU'VE BEEN HIDING!
GASA

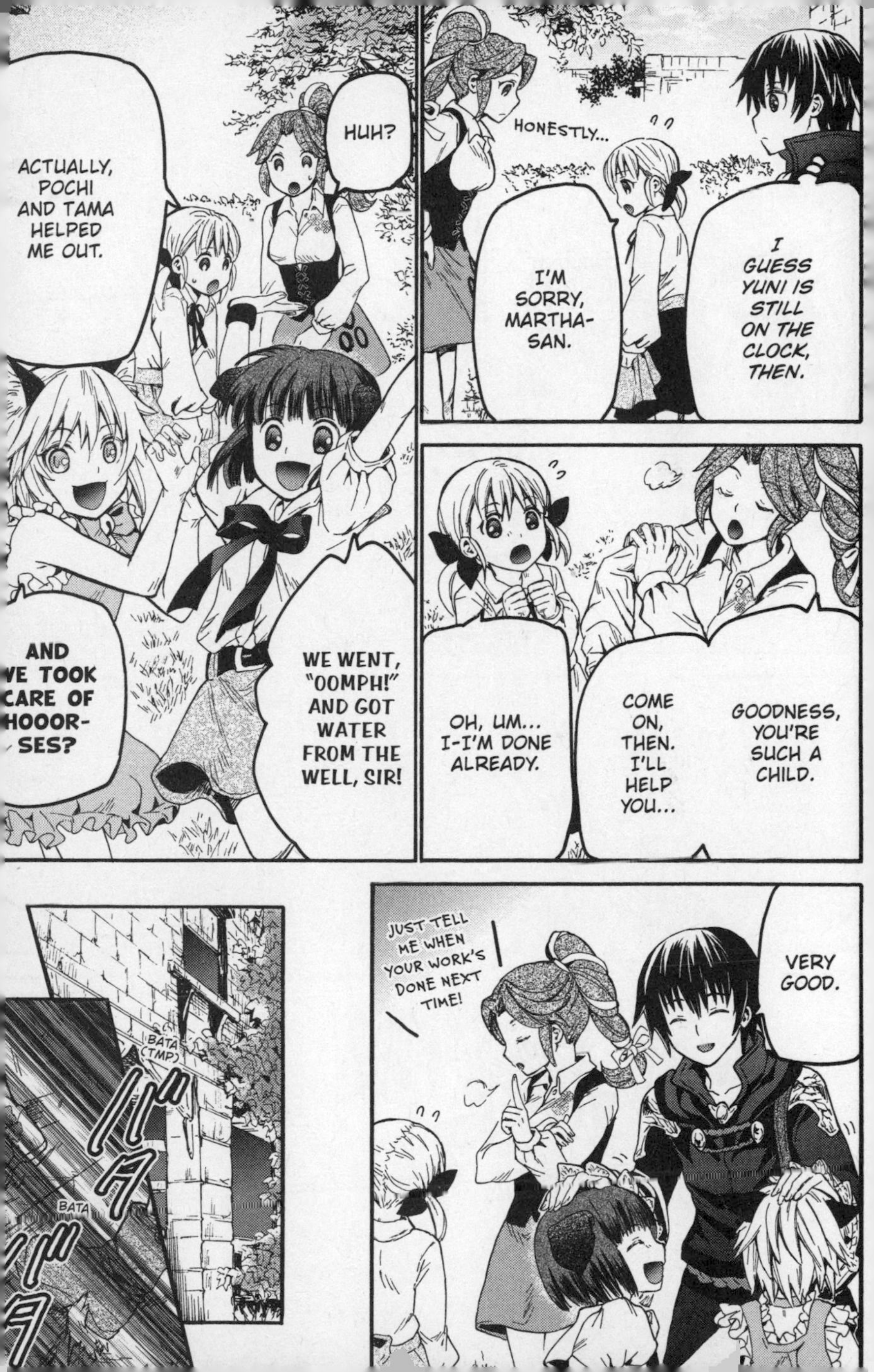
I GUESS YUNI IS STILL ON THE CLOCK, THEN.
HONESTLY...
I'M SORRY, MARTHA-SAN.
GOODNESS, YOU'RE SUCH A CHILD.
COME ON, THEN. I'LL HELP YOU...
OH, UM... I-I'M DONE ALREADY.
HUH?
ACTUALLY, POCHI AND TAMA HELPED ME OUT.
WE WENT, "OOMPH!" AND GOT WATER FROM THE WELL, SIR!
AND WE TOOK CARE OF HOOOR-SES?
VERY GOOD.
JUST TELL ME WHEN YOUR WORK'S DONE NEXT TIME!
BATA (TMP)
BATA

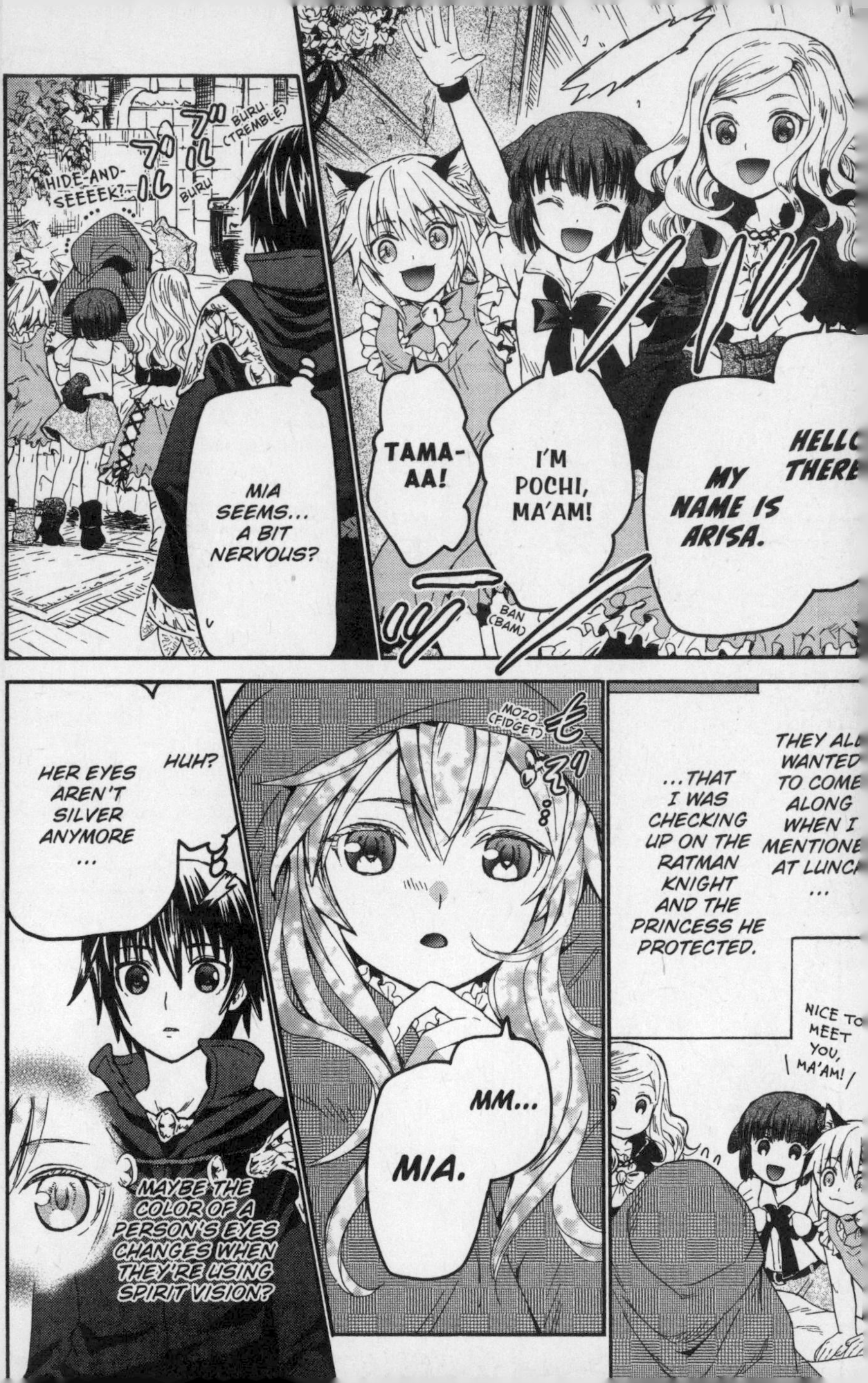
HELLO THERE
MY NAME IS ARISA.
I'M POCHI, MA'AM!
TAMA-AA!
BAN (BAM)
BURU (TREMBLE)
BURU
HIDE-AND-SEEEEK?
MIA SEEMS... A BIT NERVOUS?
THEY ALL WANTED TO COME ALONG WHEN I MENTIONE AT LUNC ...
...THAT I WAS CHECKING UP ON THE RATMAN KNIGHT AND THE PRINCESS HE PROTECTED.
NICE TO MEET YOU, MA'AM!
MOZO (FIDGET)
MM...
MIA.
HUH?
HER EYES AREN'T SILVER ANYMORE ...
MAYBE THE COLOR OF A PERSON'S EYES CHANGES WHEN THEY'RE USING SPIRIT VISION?

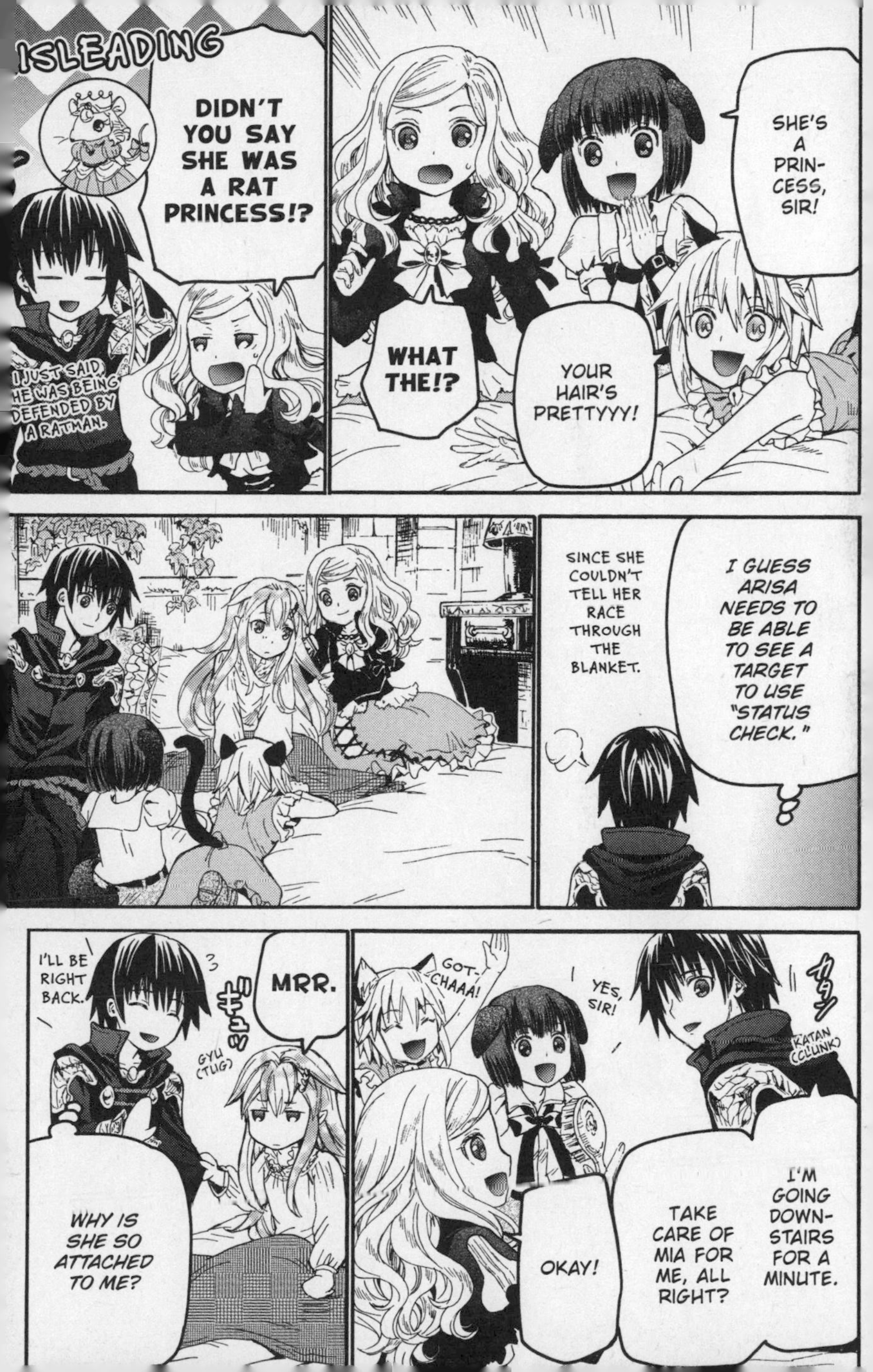
SHE'S A PRIN-CESS, SIR!
YOUR HAIR'S PRETTYYY!
WHAT THE!?
ISLEADING
DIDN'T YOU SAY SHE WAS A RAT PRINCESS!?
I JUST SAID HE WAS BEING DEFENDED BY A RATMAN.
I GUESS ARISA NEEDS TO BE ABLE TO SEE A TARGET TO USE "STATUS CHECK."
SINCE SHE COULDN'T TELL HER RACE THROUGH THE BLANKET.
KATAN (CLUNK)
I'M GOING DOWN-STAIRS FOR A MINUTE.
TAKE CARE OF MIA FOR ME, ALL RIGHT?
YES, SIR!
GOT-CHAAA!
OKAY!
MRR.
GYU (TUG)
I'LL BE RIGHT BACK.
WHY IS SHE SO ATTACHED TO ME?

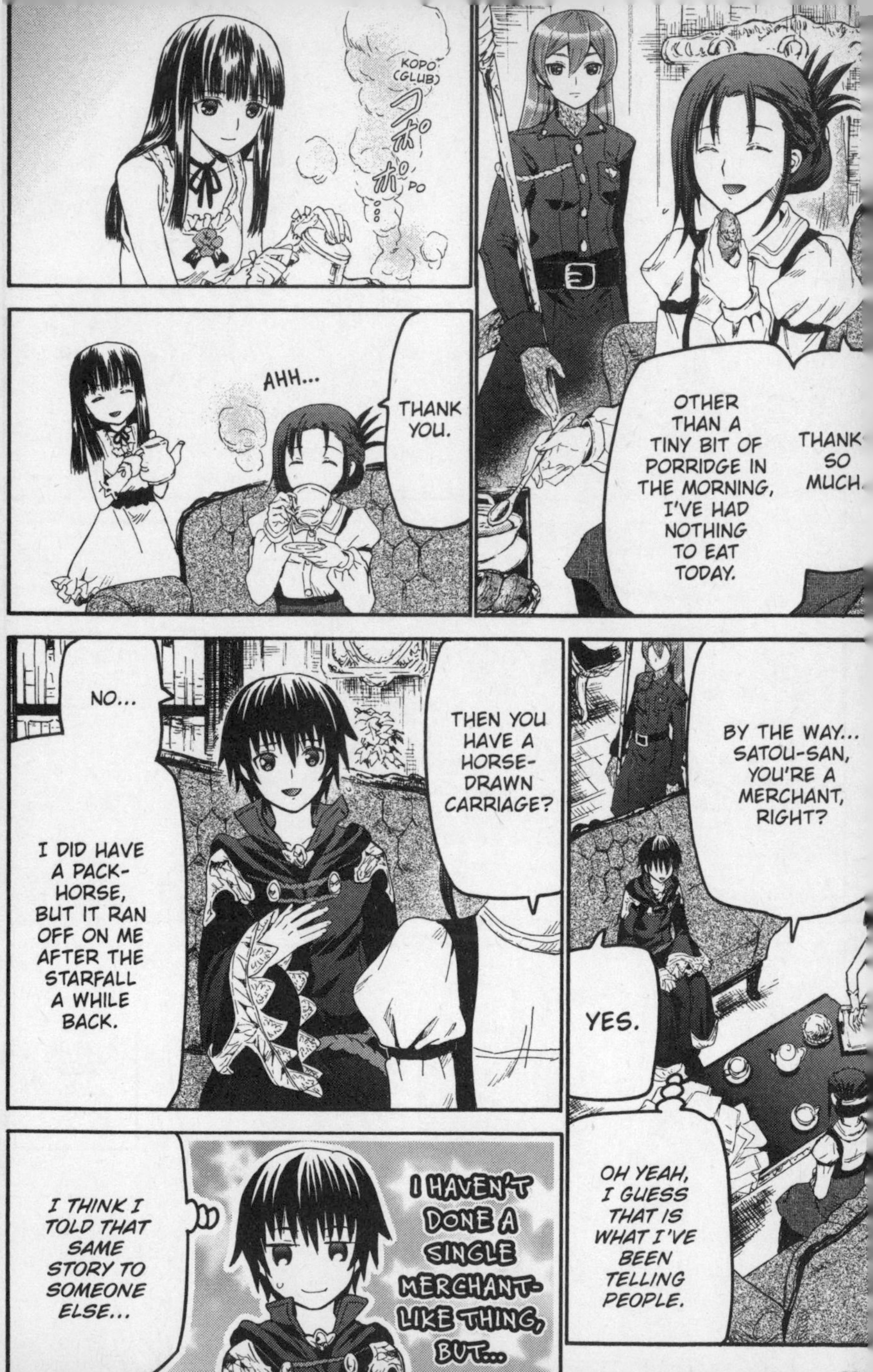
THANK SO MUCH.
OTHER THAN A TINY BIT OF PORRIDGE IN THE MORNING, I'VE HAD NOTHING TO EAT TODAY.
KOPO (GLUB)
PO
THANK YOU.
AHH...
BY THE WAY... SATOU-SAN, YOU'RE A MERCHANT, RIGHT?
YES.
THEN YOU HAVE A HORSE-DRAWN CARRIAGE?
NO...
I DID HAVE A PACK-HORSE, BUT IT RAN OFF ON ME AFTER THE STARFALL A WHILE BACK.
OH YEAH, I GUESS THAT IS WHAT I'VE BEEN TELLING PEOPLE.
I HAVEN'T DONE A SINGLE MERCHANT-LIKE THING, BUT...
I THINK I TOLD THAT SAME STORY TO SOMEONE ELSE...

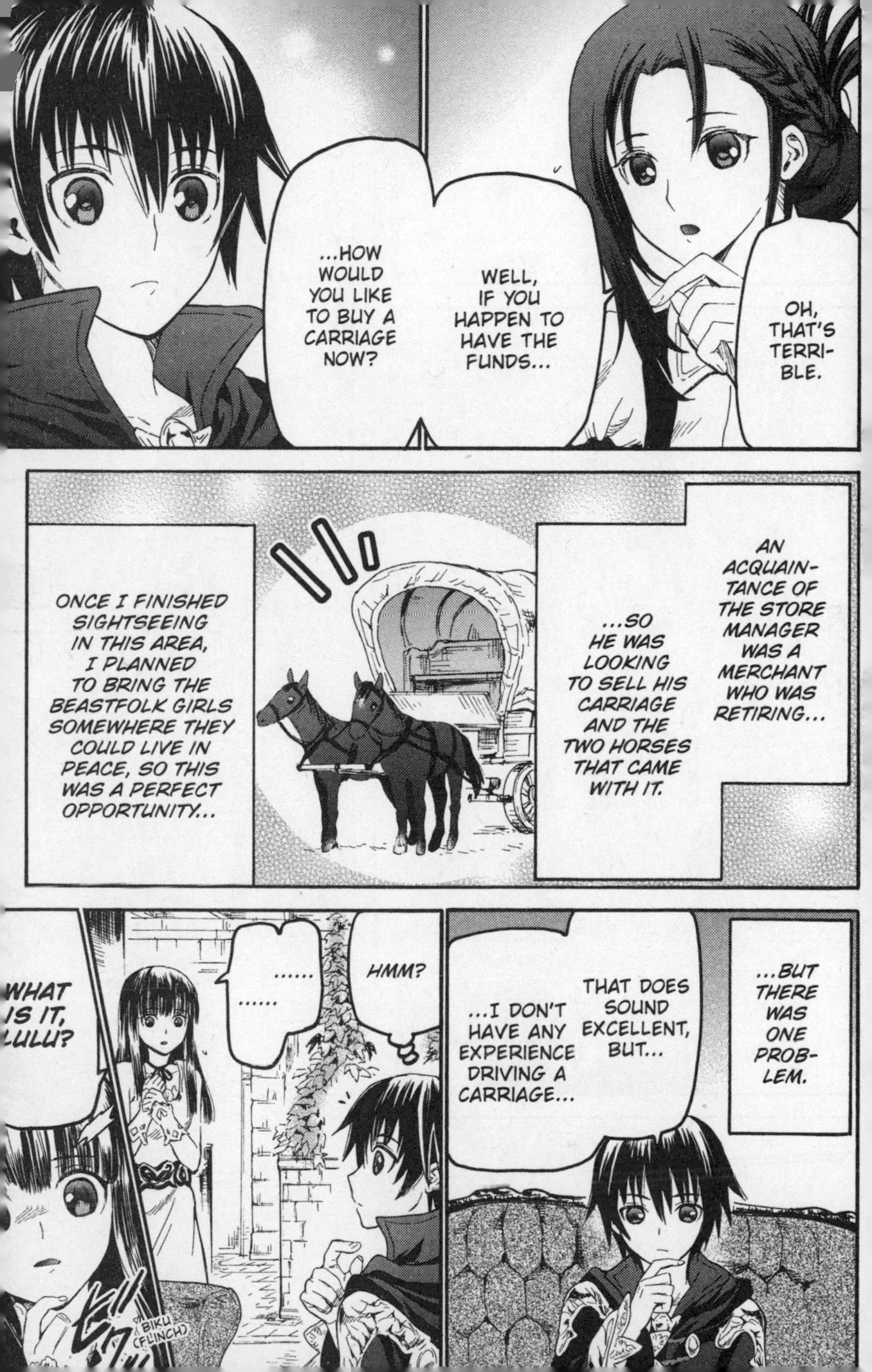
OH, THAT'S TERRIBLE.
WELL, IF YOU HAPPEN TO HAVE THE FUNDS...
...HOW WOULD YOU LIKE TO BUY A CARRIAGE NOW?
AN ACQUAINTANCE OF THE STORE MANAGER WAS A MERCHANT WHO WAS RETIRING...
...SO HE WAS LOOKING TO SELL HIS CARRIAGE AND THE TWO HORSES THAT CAME WITH IT.
ONCE I FINISHED SIGHTSEEING IN THIS AREA, I PLANNED TO BRING THE BEASTFOLK GIRLS SOMEWHERE THEY COULD LIVE IN PEACE, SO THIS WAS A PERFECT OPPORTUNITY...
...BUT THERE WAS ONE PROBLEM.
THAT DOES SOUND EXCELLENT, BUT...
...I DON'T HAVE ANY EXPERIENCE DRIVING A CARRIAGE...
HMM?
......
......
WHAT IS IT, LULU?
BIKU (FLINCH)

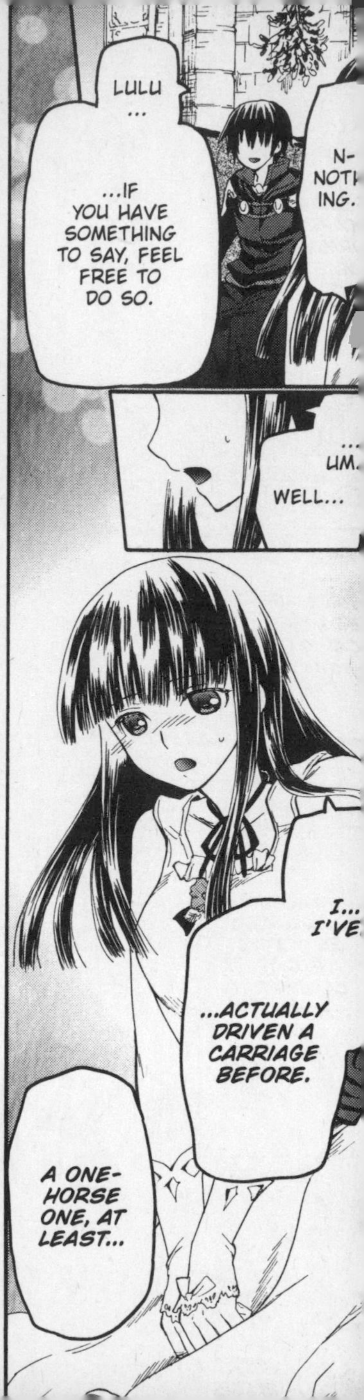
LULU ...
...IF YOU HAVE SOMETHING TO SAY, FEEL FREE TO DO SO.
N- NOTH ING.
... UM. WELL...
I... I'VE
...ACTUALLY DRIVEN A CARRIAGE BEFORE.
A ONE-HORSE ONE, AT LEAST...

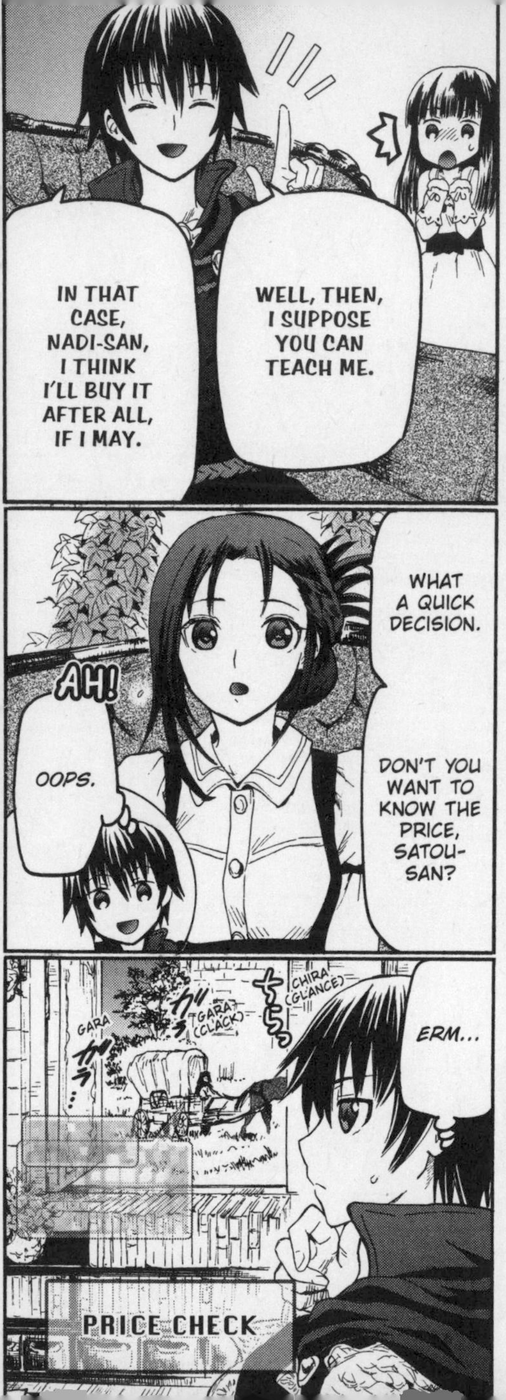
WELL, THEN, I SUPPOSE YOU CAN TEACH ME.
IN THAT CASE, NADI-SAN, I THINK I'LL BUY IT AFTER ALL, IF I MAY.
WHAT A QUICK DECISION.
DON'T YOU WANT TO KNOW THE PRICE, SATOU-SAN?
AH!
OOPS.
CHIRA (GLANCE)
GARA (CLACK)
GARA
ERM...
PRICE CHECK

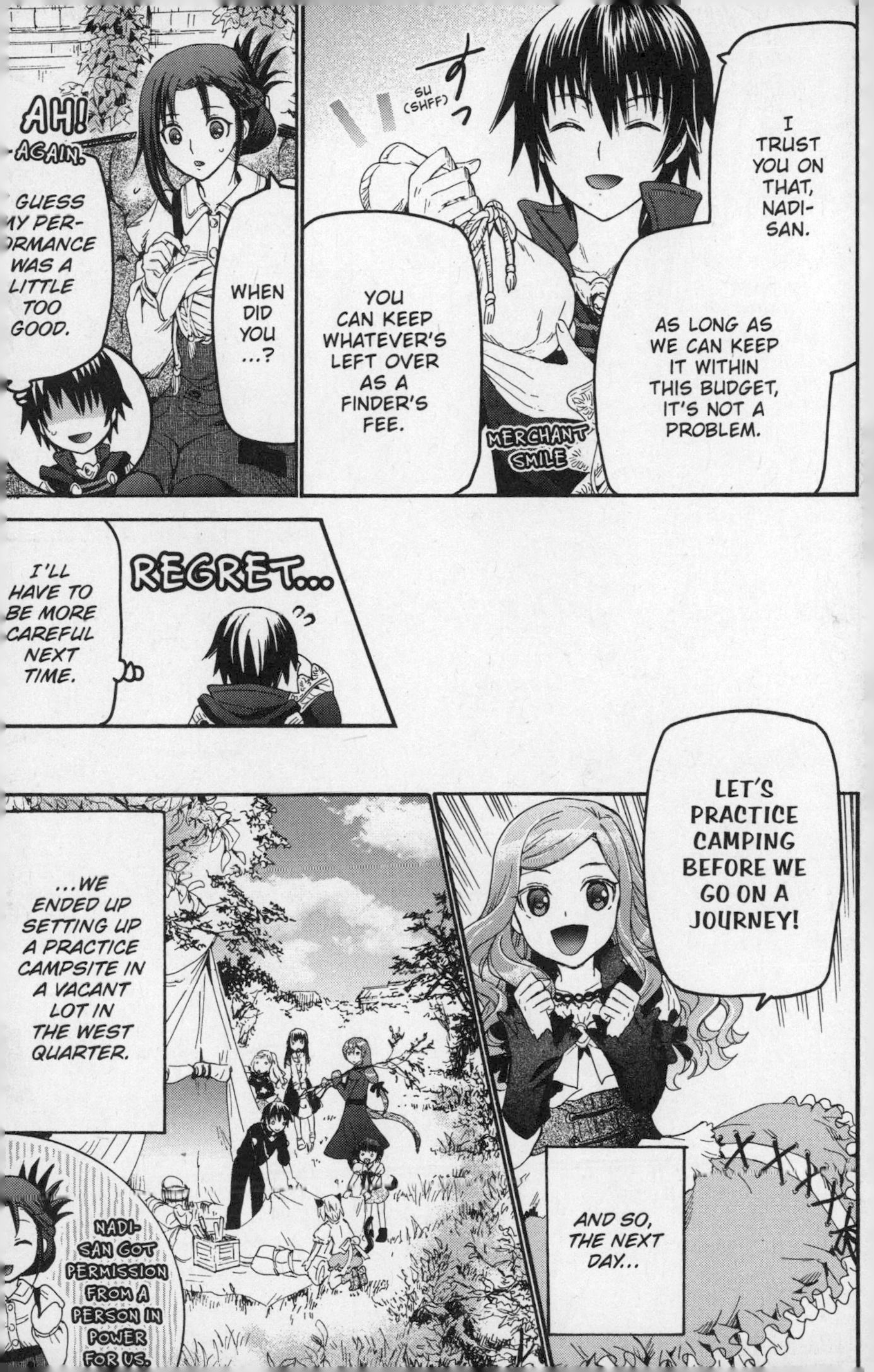
I TRUST YOU ON THAT, NADI-SAN.
AS LONG AS WE CAN KEEP IT WITHIN THIS BUDGET, IT'S NOT A PROBLEM.
SU (SHFF)
YOU CAN KEEP WHATEVER'S LEFT OVER AS A FINDER'S FEE.
MERCHANT SMILE
WHEN DID YOU ...?
AH! -AGAIN.
GUESS MY PERFORMANCE WAS A LITTLE TOO GOOD.
REGRET...
I'LL HAVE TO BE MORE CAREFUL NEXT TIME.
LET'S PRACTICE CAMPING BEFORE WE GO ON A JOURNEY!
AND SO, THE NEXT DAY...
...WE ENDED UP SETTING UP A PRACTICE CAMPSITE IN A VACANT LOT IN THE WEST QUARTER.
NADI-SAN GOT PERMISSION FROM A PERSON IN POWER FOR US.

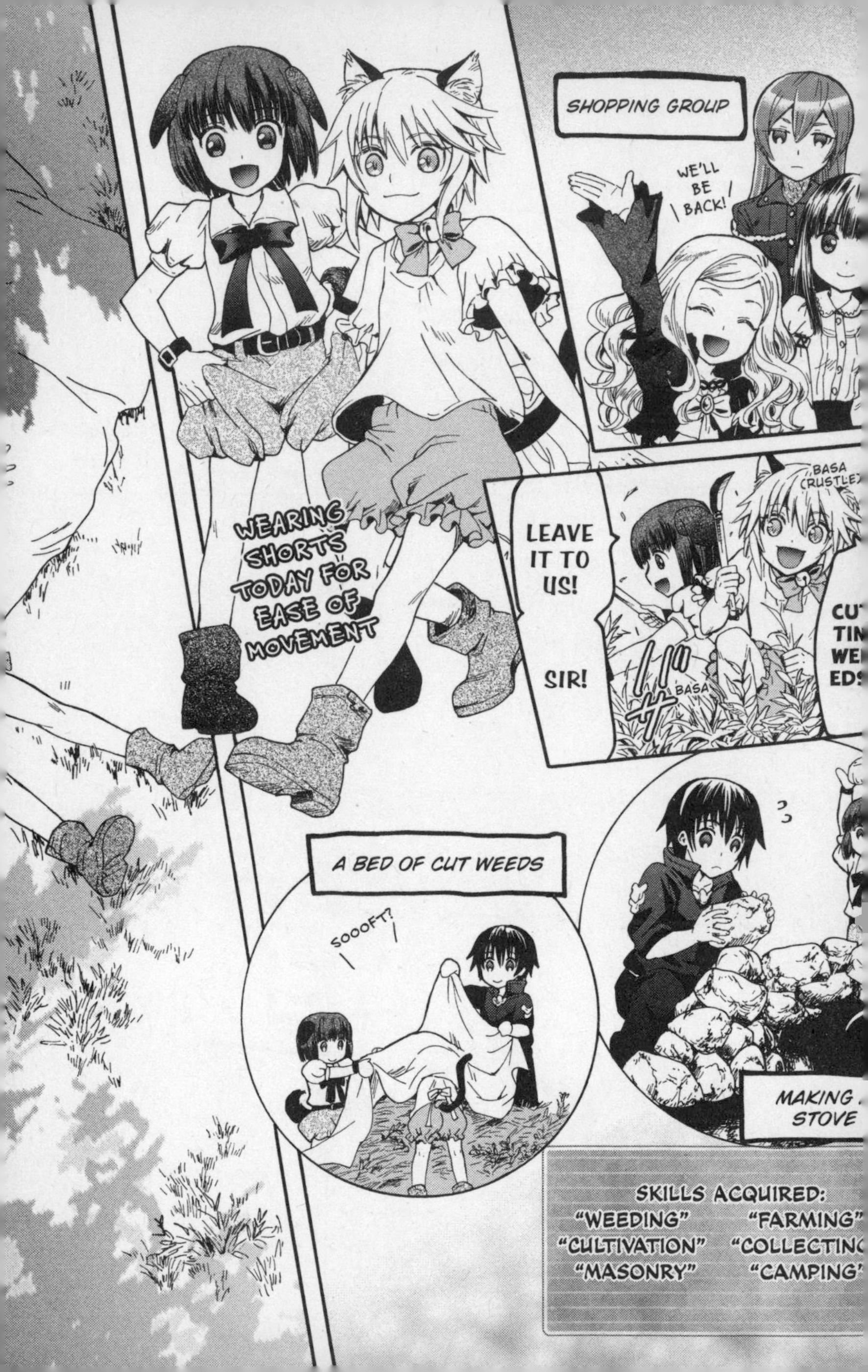
SHOPPING GROUP
WE'LL BE BACK!
BASA (RUSTLE)
CUT TIN WE EDS
LEAVE IT TO US!
SIR!
BASA
MAKING
STOVE
A BED OF CUT WEEDS
SOOOFT?
SKILLS ACQUIRED:
"WEEDING" "FARMING"
"CULTIVATION" "COLLECTING
"MASONRY" "CAMPING"
WEARING SHORTS TODAY FOR EASE OF MOVEMENT

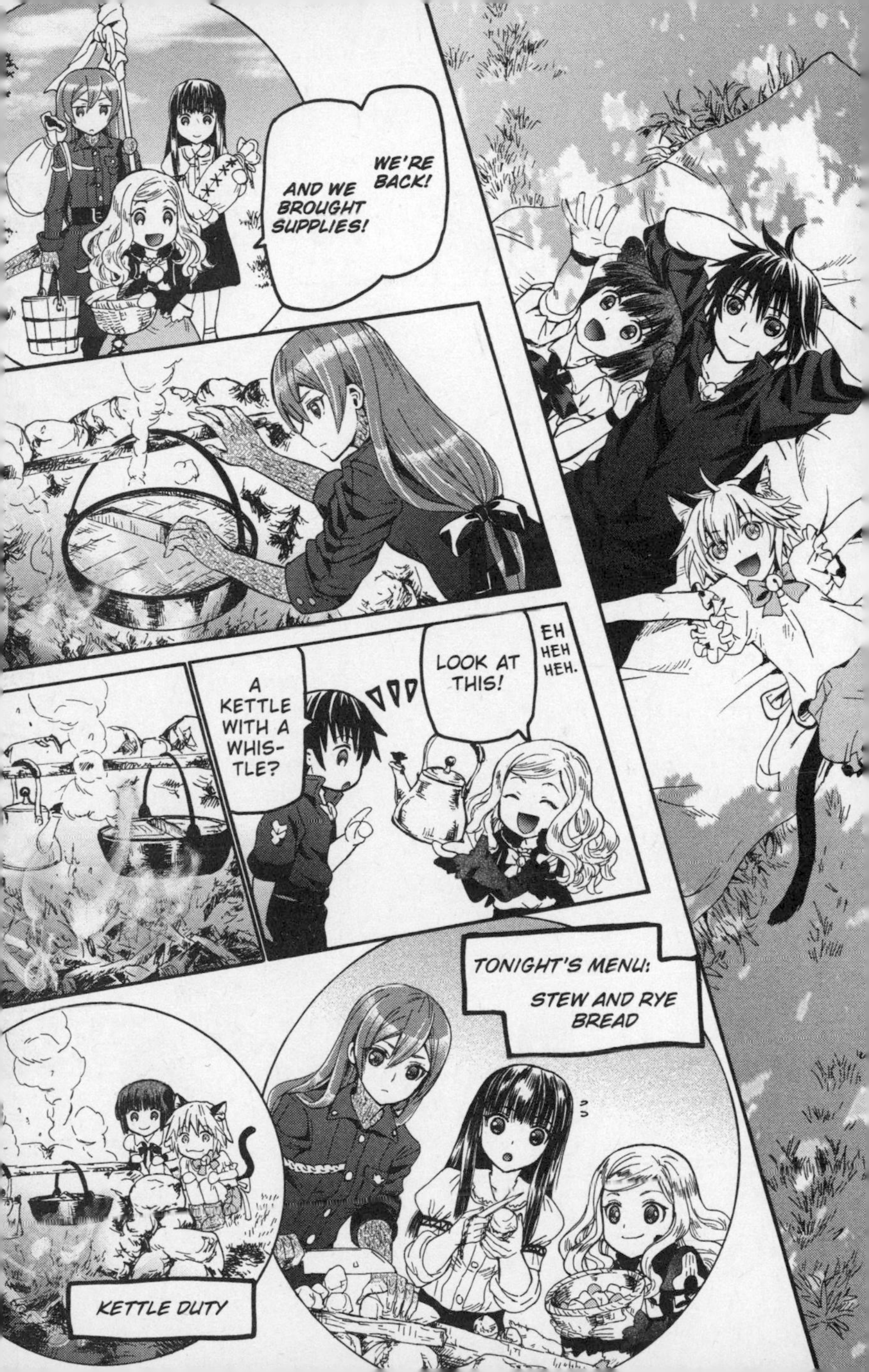
WE'RE BACK!
AND WE BROUGHT SUPPLIES!
EH HEH HEH.
LOOK AT THIS!
A KETTLE WITH A WHISTLE?
TONIGHT'S MENU: STEW AND RYE BREAD
KETTLE DUTY

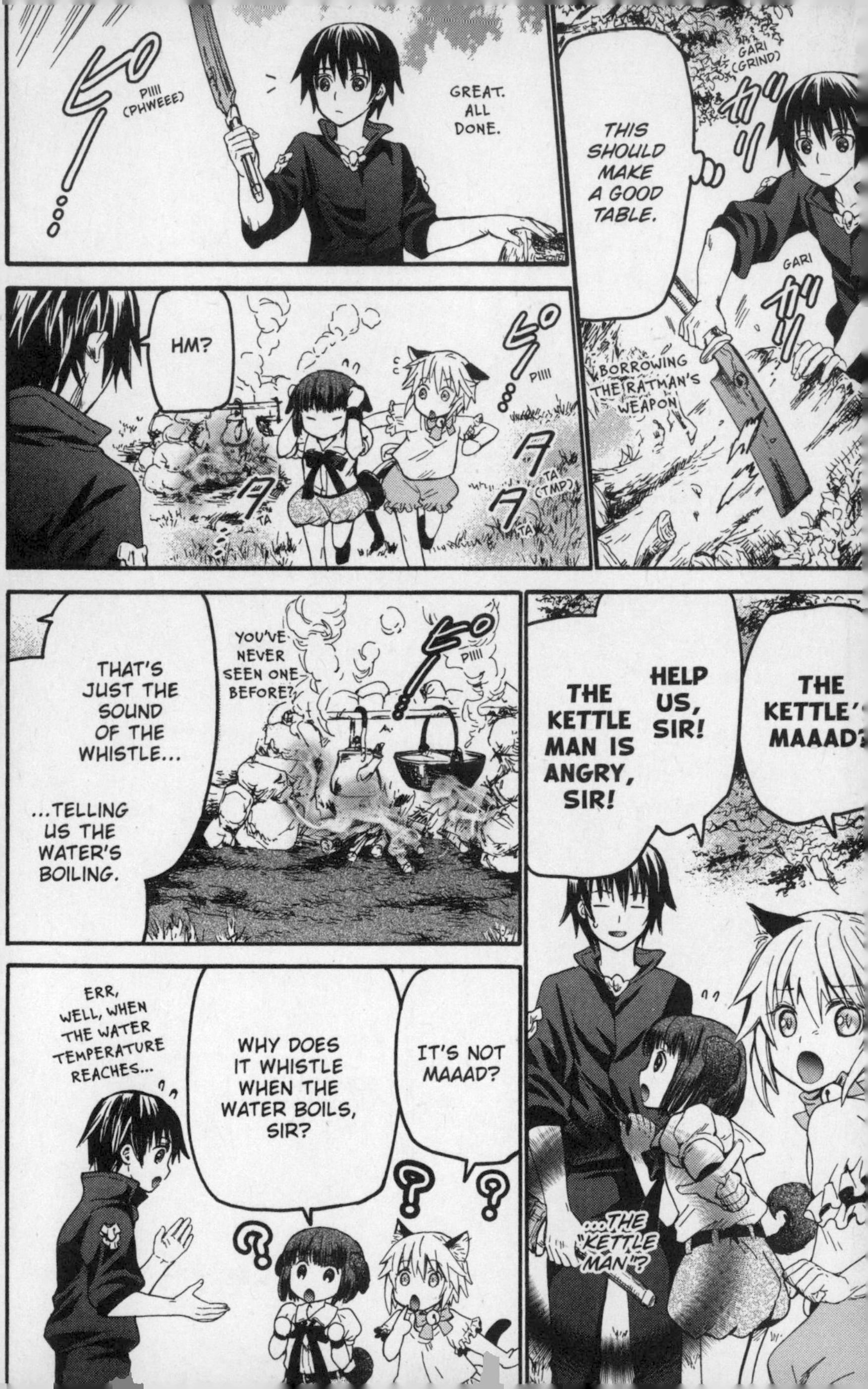
GARI (GRIND)
THIS SHOULD MAKE A GOOD TABLE.
GARI
BORROWING THE RATMAN'S WEAPON
GREAT. ALL DONE.
PIIII (PHWEEE)
PIIII
TA (TMP)
TA
HM?
TA
THE KETTLE' MAAAD
HELP US, SIR!
THE KETTLE MAN IS ANGRY, SIR!
...THE "KETTLE MAN"?
PIIII
YOU'VE NEVER SEEN ONE BEFORE?
THAT'S JUST THE SOUND OF THE WHISTLE...
...TELLING US THE WATER'S BOILING.
IT'S NOT MAAAD?
WHY DOES IT WHISTLE WHEN THE WATER BOILS, SIR?
ERR, WELL, WHEN THE WATER TEMPERATURE REACHES...

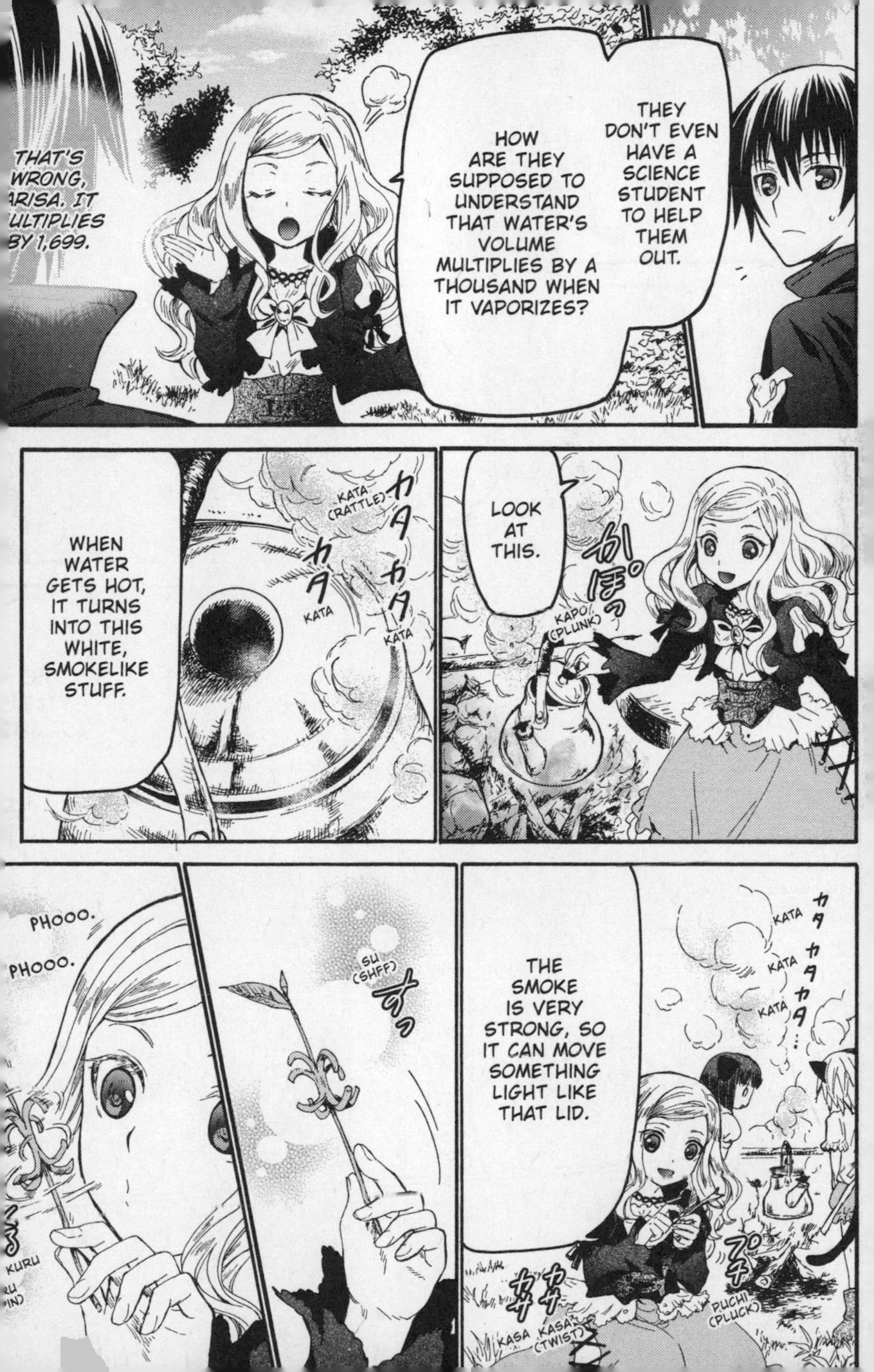
THEY DON'T EVEN HAVE A SCIENCE STUDENT TO HELP THEM OUT.
HOW ARE THEY SUPPOSED TO UNDERSTAND THAT WATER'S VOLUME MULTIPLIES BY A THOUSAND WHEN IT VAPORIZES?
THAT'S WRONG, ARISA. IT ULTIPLIES BY 1,699.
LOOK AT THIS.
KAPO (PLUNK)
KATA (RATTLE)
KATA
KATA
WHEN WATER GETS HOT, IT TURNS INTO THIS WHITE, SMOKELIKE STUFF.
KATA
KATA
KATA
THE SMOKE IS VERY STRONG, SO IT CAN MOVE SOMETHING LIGHT LIKE THAT LID.
PUCHI (PLUCK)
KASA KASA (TWIST)
SU (SHFF)
PHOOO.
PHOOO.
KURU

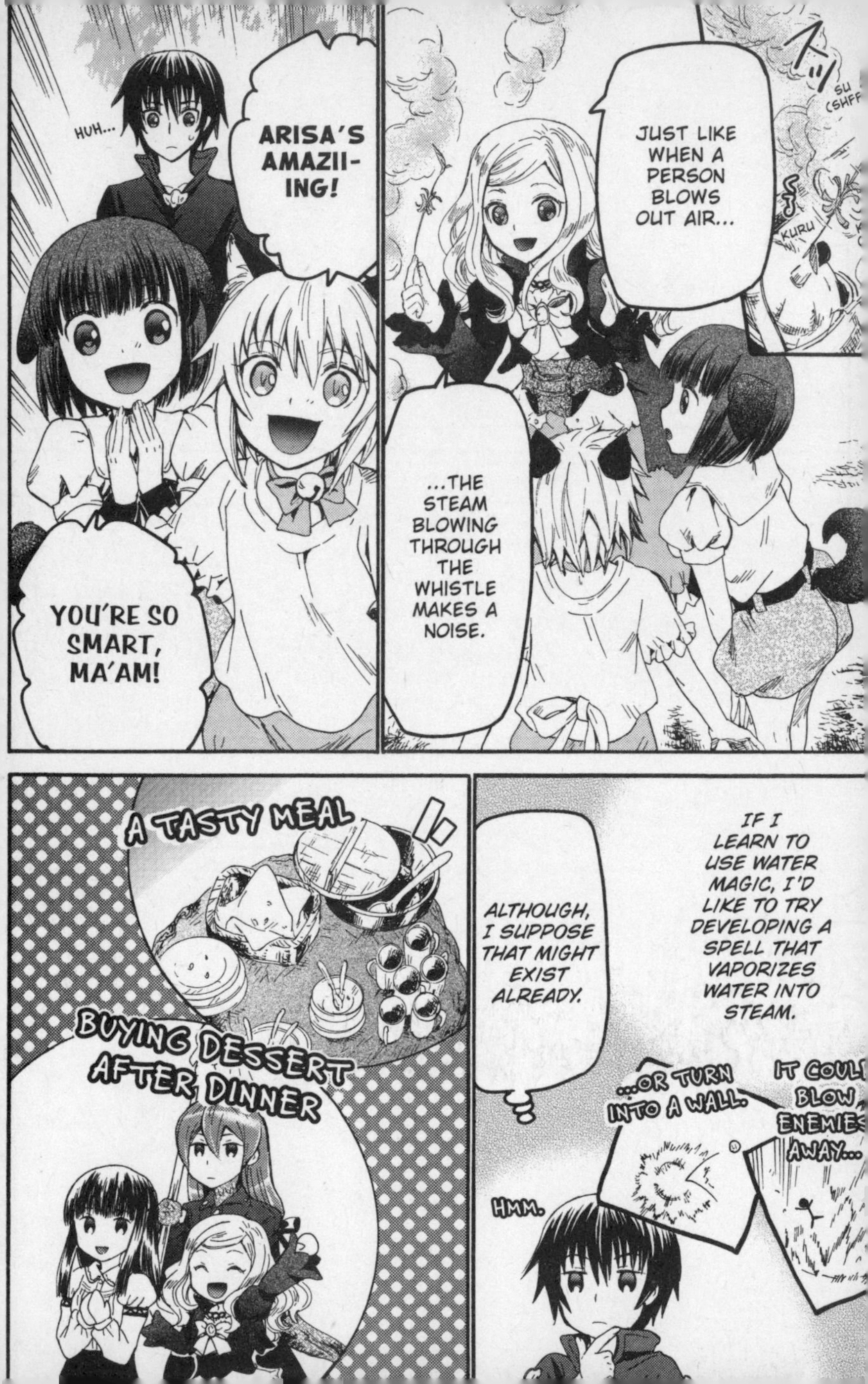
SU
(SHFF
KURU
JUST LIKE WHEN A PERSON BLOWS OUT AIR...
...THE STEAM BLOWING THROUGH THE WHISTLE MAKES A NOISE.
HUH...
ARISA'S AMAZII-ING!
YOU'RE SO SMART, MA'AM!
IF I LEARN TO USE WATER MAGIC, I'D LIKE TO TRY DEVELOPING A SPELL THAT VAPORIZES WATER INTO STEAM.
ALTHOUGH, I SUPPOSE THAT MIGHT EXIST ALREADY.
IT COUL BLOW ENEMIES AWAY...
...OR TURN INTO A WALL.
HMM.
A TASTY MEAL
BUYING DESSERT AFTER DINNER

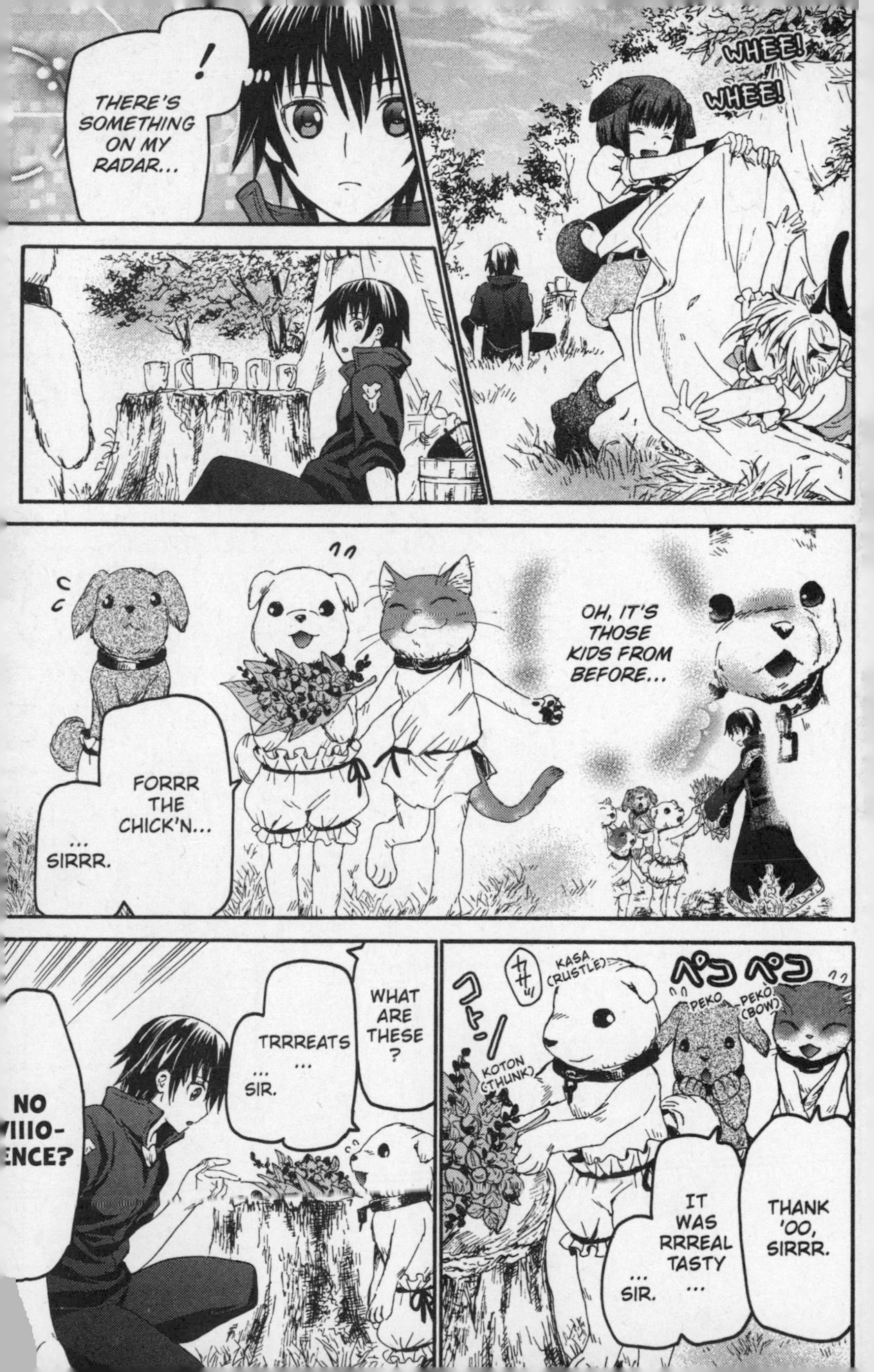
WHEE!
WHEE!
!
THERE'S SOMETHING ON MY RADAR...
OH, IT'S THOSE KIDS FROM BEFORE...
FORRR THE CHICK'N...
... SIRRR.
ペコ ペコ
PEKO
PEKO (BOW)
KASA (RUSTLE)
カサ
コトン
KOTON (THUNK)
THANK 'OO, SIRRR.
IT WAS RRREAL TASTY ...
... SIR.
WHAT ARE THESE?
TRRREATS ...
... SIR.
NO VIIIO-ENCE?

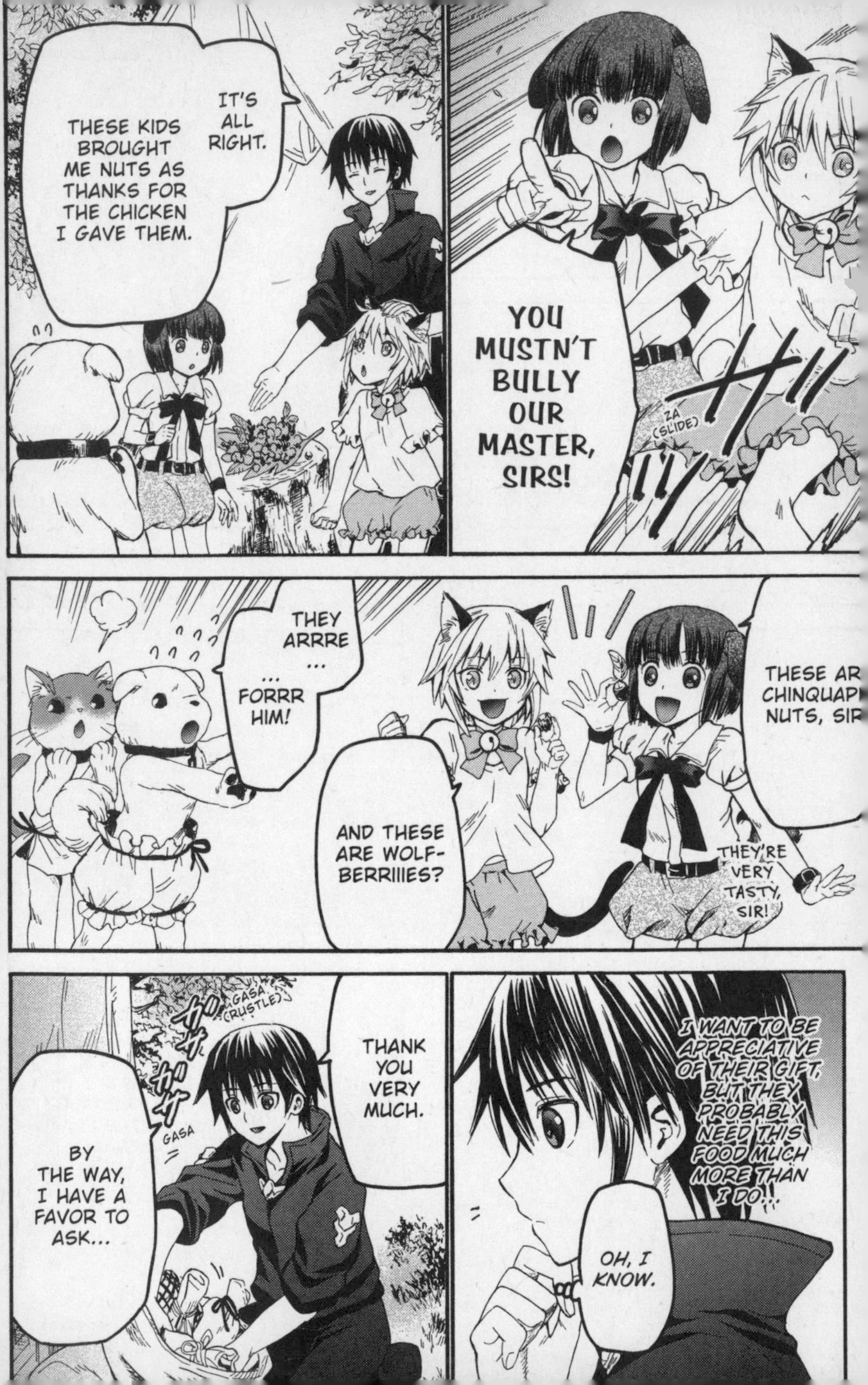
YOU MUSTN'T BULLY OUR MASTER, SIRS!
ZA (SLIDE)
IT'S ALL RIGHT.
THESE KIDS BROUGHT ME NUTS AS THANKS FOR THE CHICKEN I GAVE THEM.
THESE AR CHINQUAP NUTS, SIR
THEY'RE VERY TASTY, SIR!
AND THESE ARE WOLF-BERRIIIES?
THEY ARRRE ... FORRR HIM!
I WANT TO BE APPRECIATIVE OF THEIR GIFT, BUT THEY PROBABLY NEED THIS FOOD MUCH MORE THAN I DO...
OH, I KNOW.
THANK YOU VERY MUCH.
GASA (RUSTLE)
GASA
BY THE WAY, I HAVE A FAVOR TO ASK...

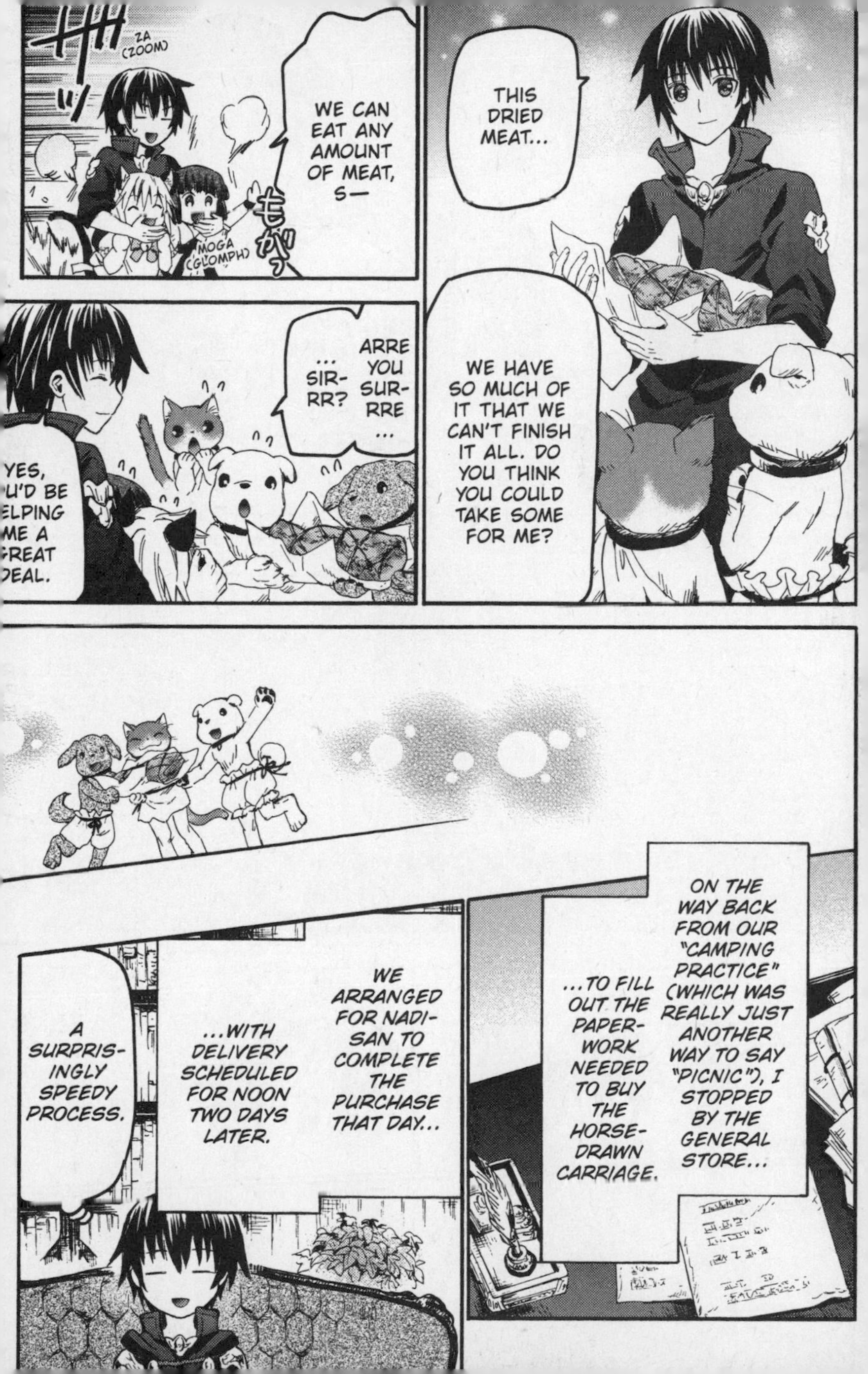
THIS DRIED MEAT...
WE HAVE SO MUCH OF IT THAT WE CAN'T FINISH IT ALL. DO YOU THINK YOU COULD TAKE SOME FOR ME?
WE CAN EAT ANY AMOUNT OF MEAT, S—
ZA (ZOOM)
もがっ
MOGA (GLOMPH)
ARRE YOU SURRRE ...
... SIRRR?
YES, U'D BE ELPING ME A REAT DEAL.
ON THE WAY BACK FROM OUR "CAMPING PRACTICE" (WHICH WAS REALLY JUST ANOTHER WAY TO SAY "PICNIC"), I STOPPED BY THE GENERAL STORE...
...TO FILL OUT THE PAPERWORK NEEDED TO BUY THE HORSE-DRAWN CARRIAGE.
WE ARRANGED FOR NADI-SAN TO COMPLETE THE PURCHASE THAT DAY...
...WITH DELIVERY SCHEDULED FOR NOON TWO DAYS LATER.
A SURPRISINGLY SPEEDY PROCESS.

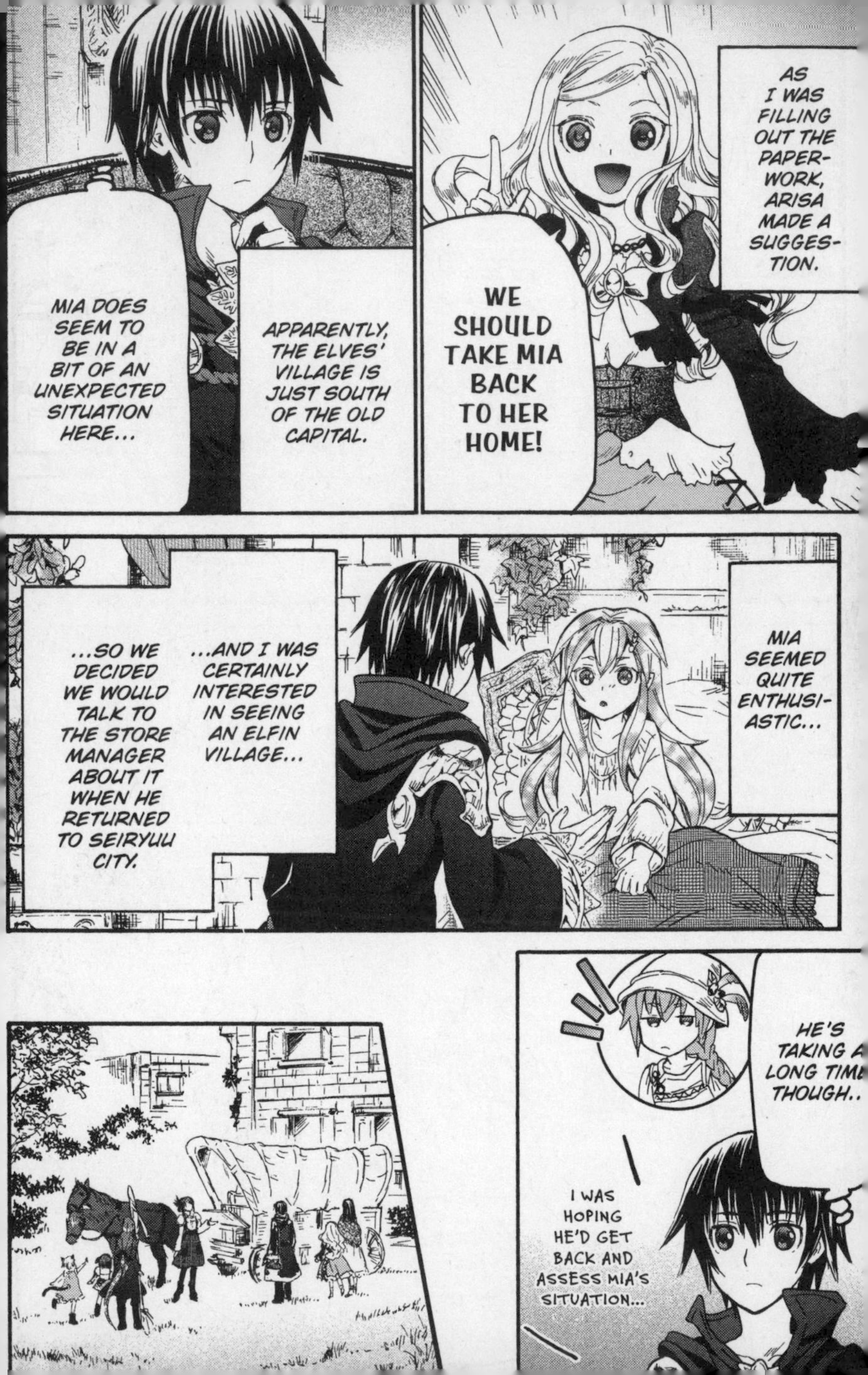
AS I WAS FILLING OUT THE PAPERWORK, ARISA MADE A SUGGESTION.
WE SHOULD TAKE MIA BACK TO HER HOME!
APPARENTLY, THE ELVES' VILLAGE IS JUST SOUTH OF THE OLD CAPITAL.
MIA DOES SEEM TO BE IN A BIT OF AN UNEXPECTED SITUATION HERE...
MIA SEEMED QUITE ENTHUSIASTIC...
...AND I WAS CERTAINLY INTERESTED IN SEEING AN ELFIN VILLAGE...
...SO WE DECIDED WE WOULD TALK TO THE STORE MANAGER ABOUT IT WHEN HE RETURNED TO SEIRYUU CITY.
HE'S TAKING A LONG TIME THOUGH..
I WAS HOPING HE'D GET BACK AND ASSESS MIA'S SITUATION...

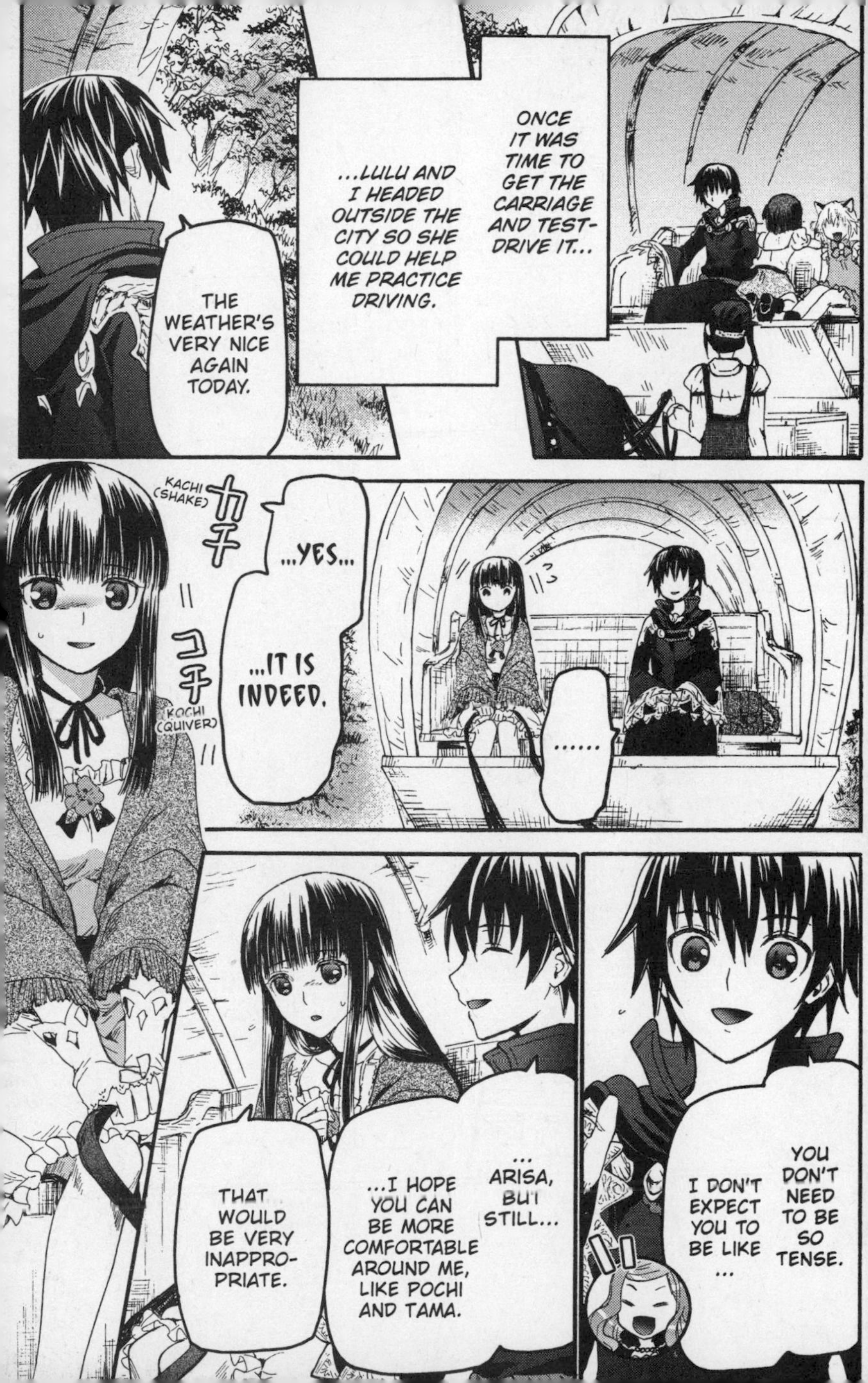
ONCE IT WAS TIME TO GET THE CARRIAGE AND TEST-DRIVE IT...
...LULU AND I HEADED OUTSIDE THE CITY SO SHE COULD HELP ME PRACTICE DRIVING.
THE WEATHER'S VERY NICE AGAIN TODAY.
......
YOU DON'T NEED TO BE SO TENSE.
I DON'T EXPECT YOU TO BE LIKE ...
... ARISA, BUT STILL...
...I HOPE YOU CAN BE MORE COMFORTABLE AROUND ME, LIKE POCHI AND TAMA.
THAT WOULD BE VERY INAPPROPRIATE.
カチ KACHI (SHAKE)
コチ KOCHI (QUIVER)
...YES...
...IT IS INDEED.

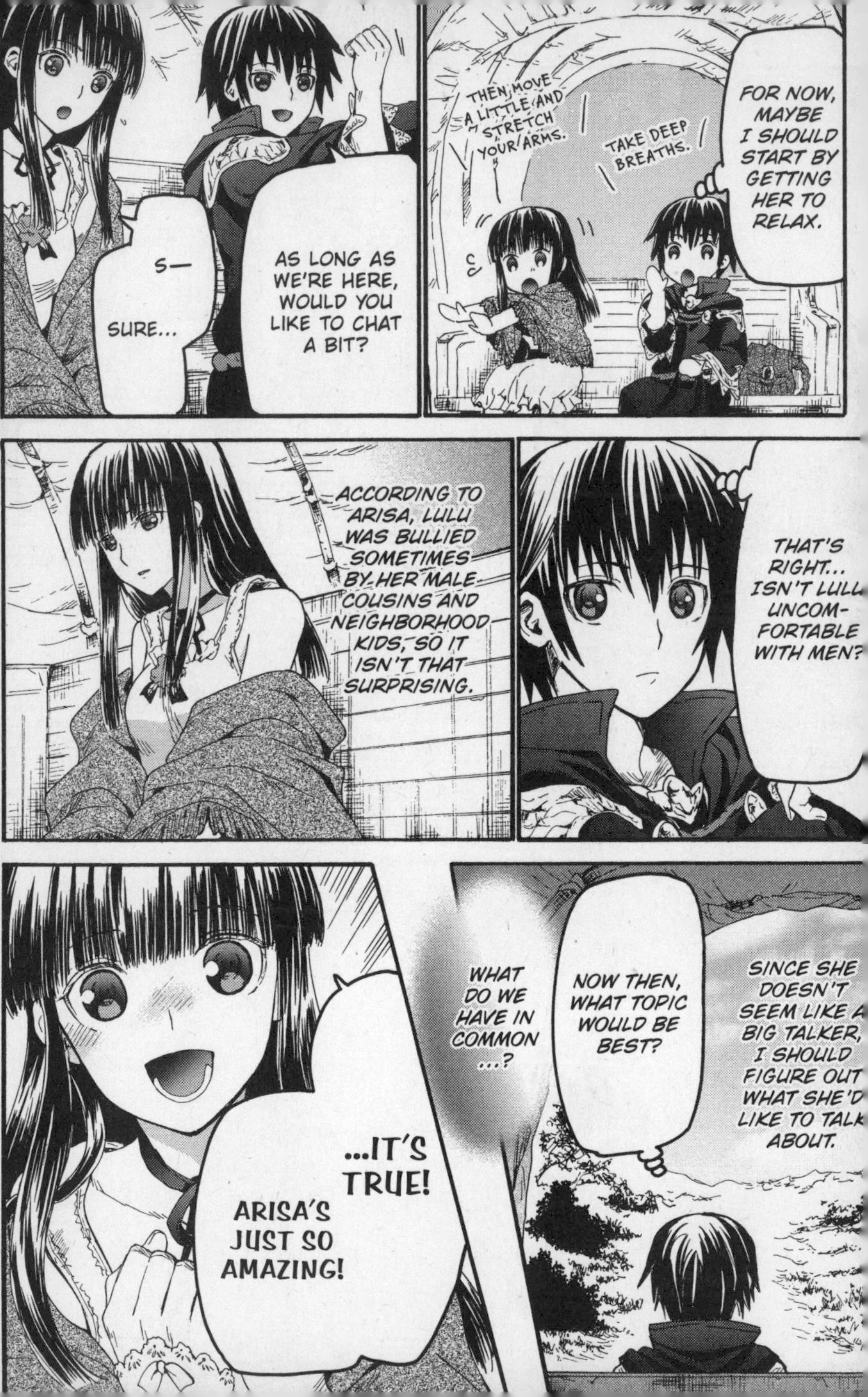
FOR NOW, MAYBE I SHOULD START BY GETTING HER TO RELAX.
TAKE DEEP BREATHS.
THEN, MOVE A LITTLE AND STRETCH YOUR ARMS.
AS LONG AS WE'RE HERE, WOULD YOU LIKE TO CHAT A BIT?
S— SURE...
THAT'S RIGHT... ISN'T LULU UNCOMFORTABLE WITH MEN?
ACCORDING TO ARISA, LULU WAS BULLIED SOMETIMES BY HER MALE COUSINS AND NEIGHBORHOOD KIDS, SO IT ISN'T THAT SURPRISING.
SINCE SHE DOESN'T SEEM LIKE A BIG TALKER, I SHOULD FIGURE OUT WHAT SHE'D LIKE TO TALK ABOUT.
NOW THEN, WHAT TOPIC WOULD BE BEST?
WHAT DO WE HAVE IN COMMON ...?
...IT'S TRUE! ARISA'S JUST SO AMAZING!

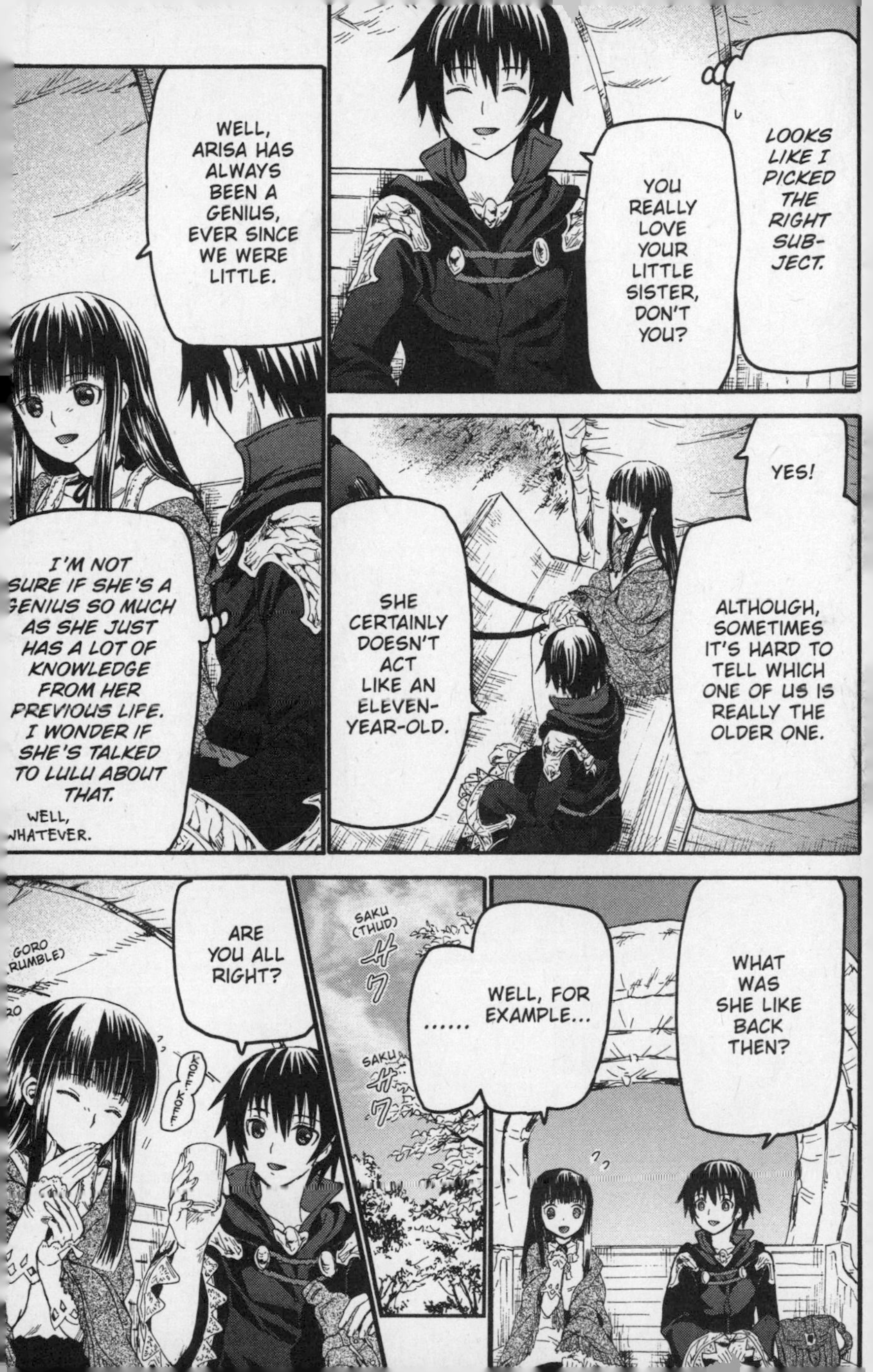
LOOKS LIKE I PICKED THE RIGHT SUB-JECT.
YOU REALLY LOVE YOUR LITTLE SISTER, DON'T YOU?
YES!
ALTHOUGH, SOMETIMES IT'S HARD TO TELL WHICH ONE OF US IS REALLY THE OLDER ONE.
SHE CERTAINLY DOESN'T ACT LIKE AN ELEVEN-YEAR-OLD.
WELL, ARISA HAS ALWAYS BEEN A GENIUS, EVER SINCE WE WERE LITTLE.
I'M NOT SURE IF SHE'S A GENIUS SO MUCH AS SHE JUST HAS A LOT OF KNOWLEDGE FROM HER PREVIOUS LIFE. I WONDER IF SHE'S TALKED TO LULU ABOUT THAT.
WELL, WHATEVER.
WHAT WAS SHE LIKE BACK THEN?
WELL, FOR EXAMPLE...
......
SAKU (THUD)
サク
SAKU
サク
ARE YOU ALL RIGHT?
GORO (RUMBLE)
RO
KOFF. KOFF

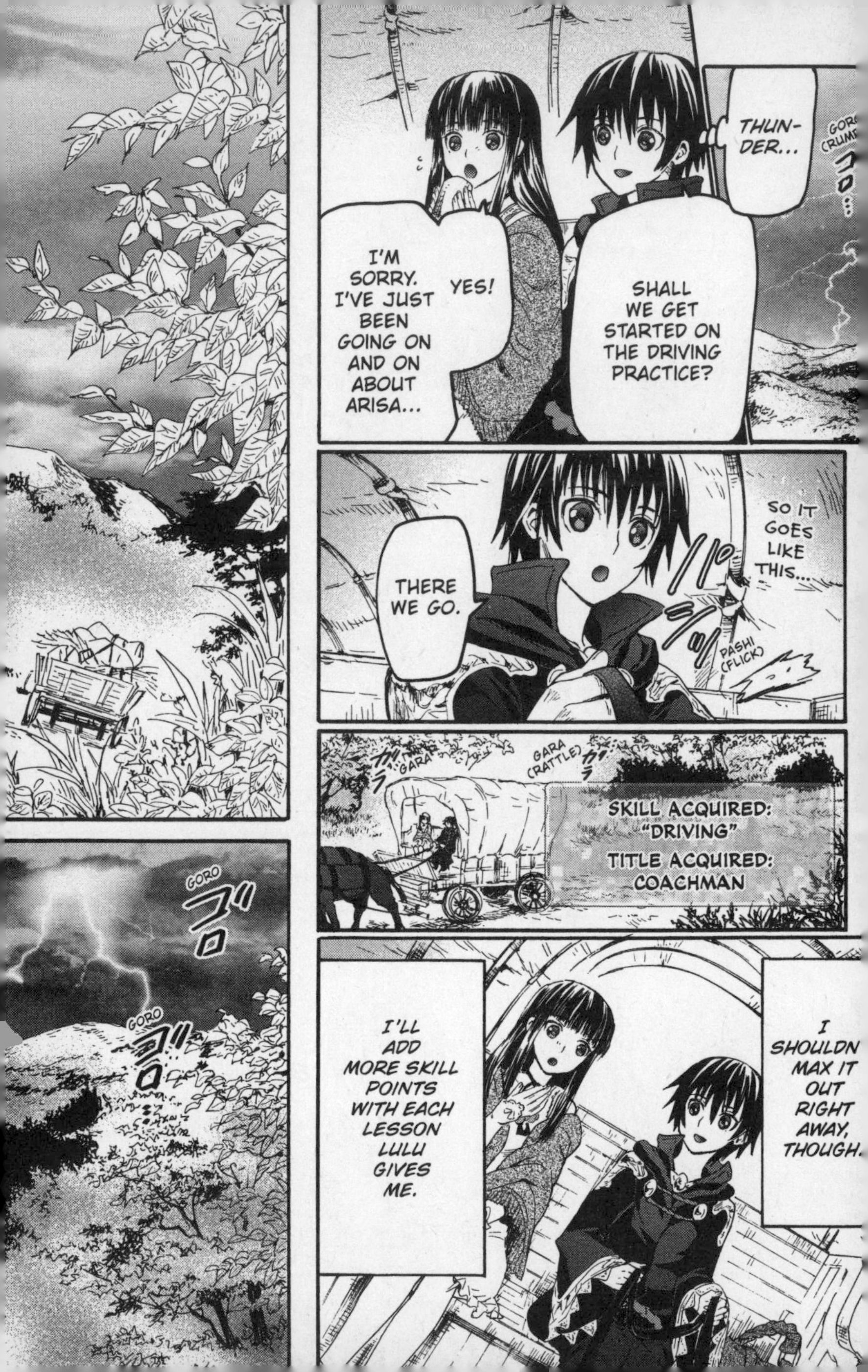
THUNDER...
GORO (RUMB
SHALL WE GET STARTED ON THE DRIVING PRACTICE?
YES!
I'M SORRY. I'VE JUST BEEN GOING ON AND ON ABOUT ARISA...
SO IT GOES LIKE THIS...
PASHI (FLICK)
THERE WE GO.
GARA (RATTLE)
GARA
SKILL ACQUIRED: "DRIVING"
TITLE ACQUIRED: COACHMAN
I SHOULDN MAX IT OUT RIGHT AWAY, THOUGH.
I'LL ADD MORE SKILL POINTS WITH EACH LESSON LULU GIVES ME.
GORO
GORO

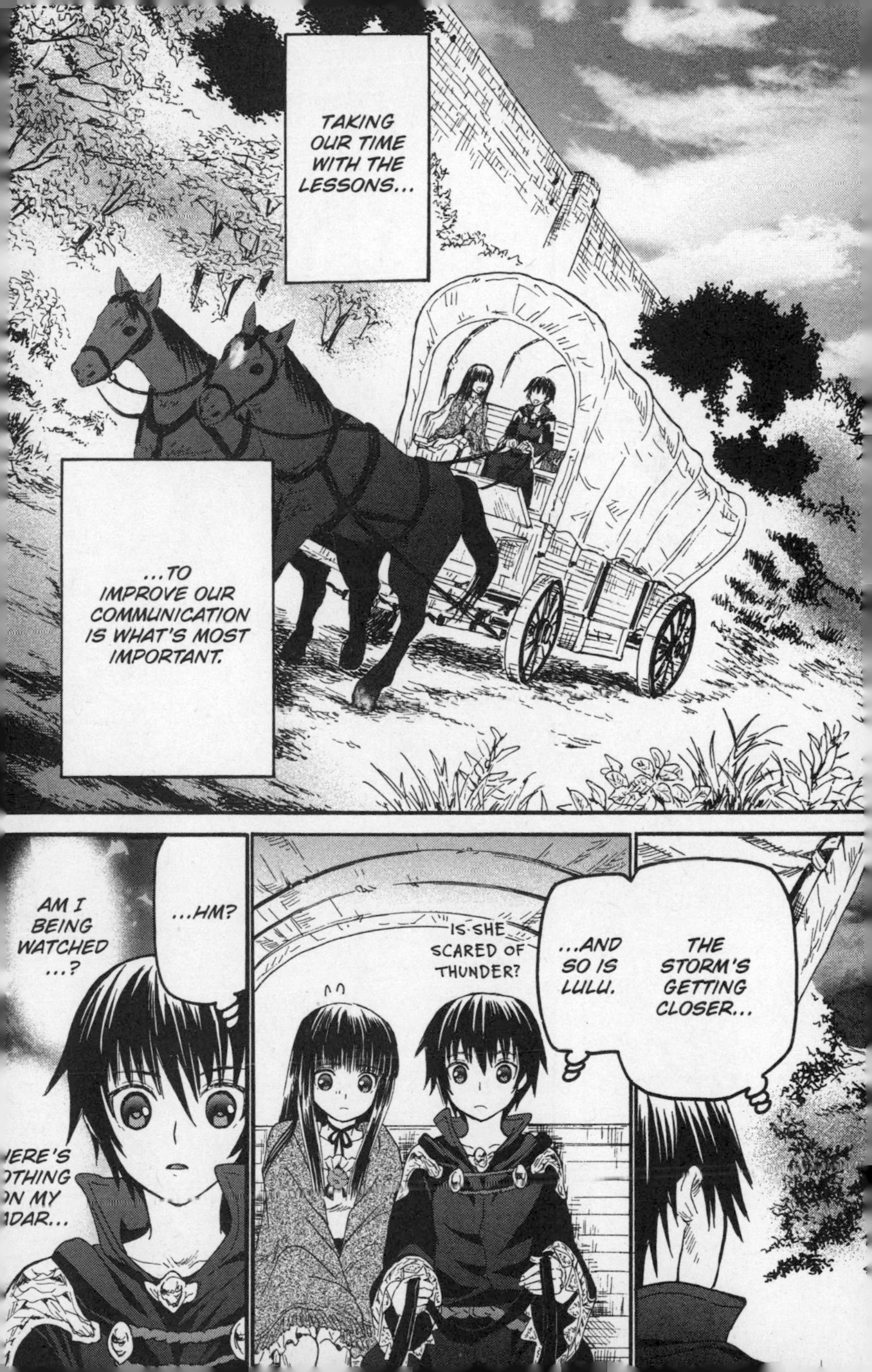
TAKING OUR TIME WITH THE LESSONS...
...TO IMPROVE OUR COMMUNICATION IS WHAT'S MOST IMPORTANT.
THE STORM'S GETTING CLOSER...
...AND SO IS LULU.
IS SHE SCARED OF THUNDER?
...HM?
AM I BEING WATCHED...?

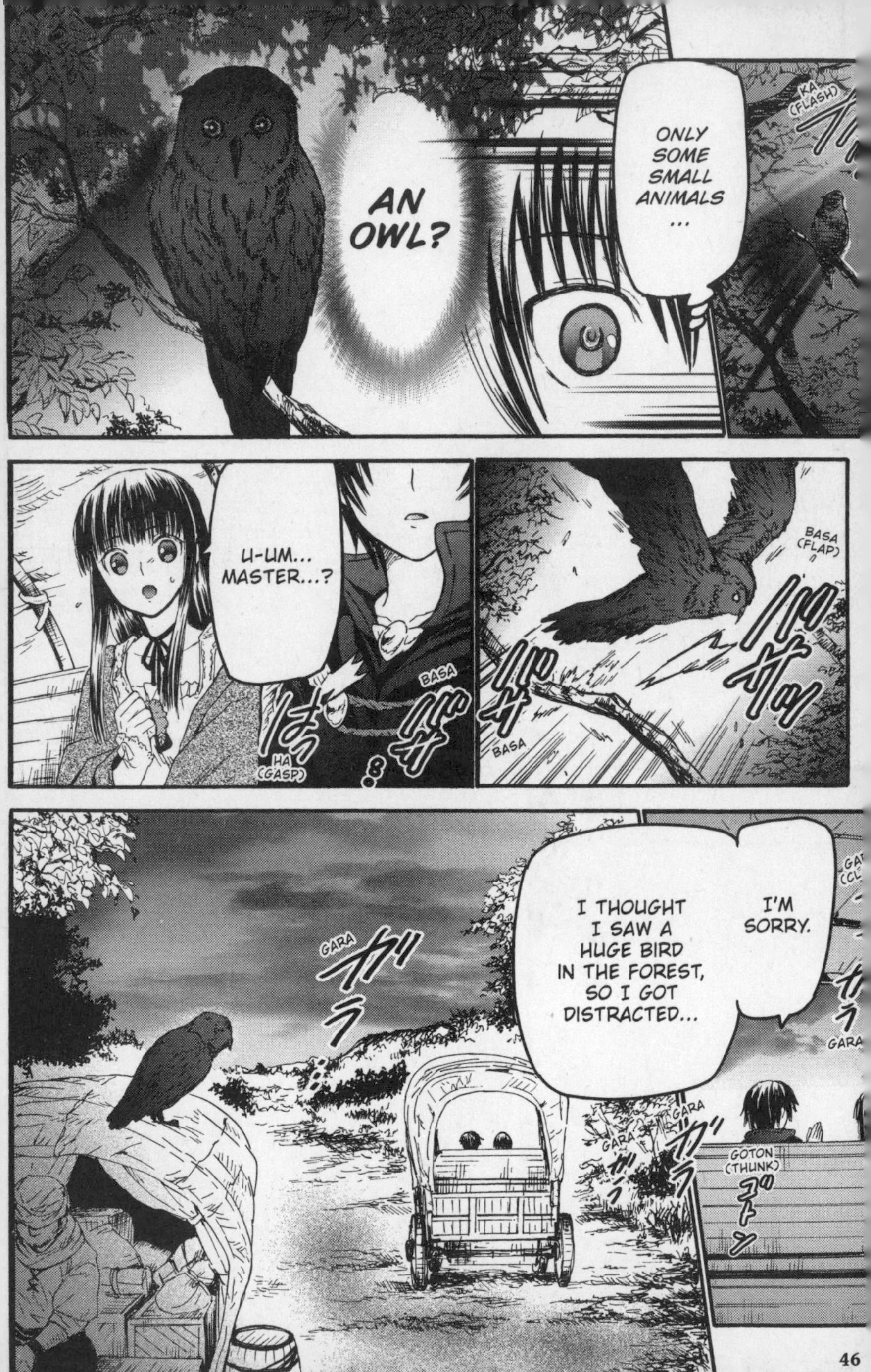
KA (FLASH)
ONLY SOME SMALL ANIMALS...
AN OWL?
BASA (FLAP)
BASA
U-UM... MASTER...?
BASA
HA (GASP)
I'M SORRY.
I THOUGHT I SAW A HUGE BIRD IN THE FOREST, SO I GOT DISTRACTED...
GARA
GOTON (THUNK)
GARA
GARA
GARA

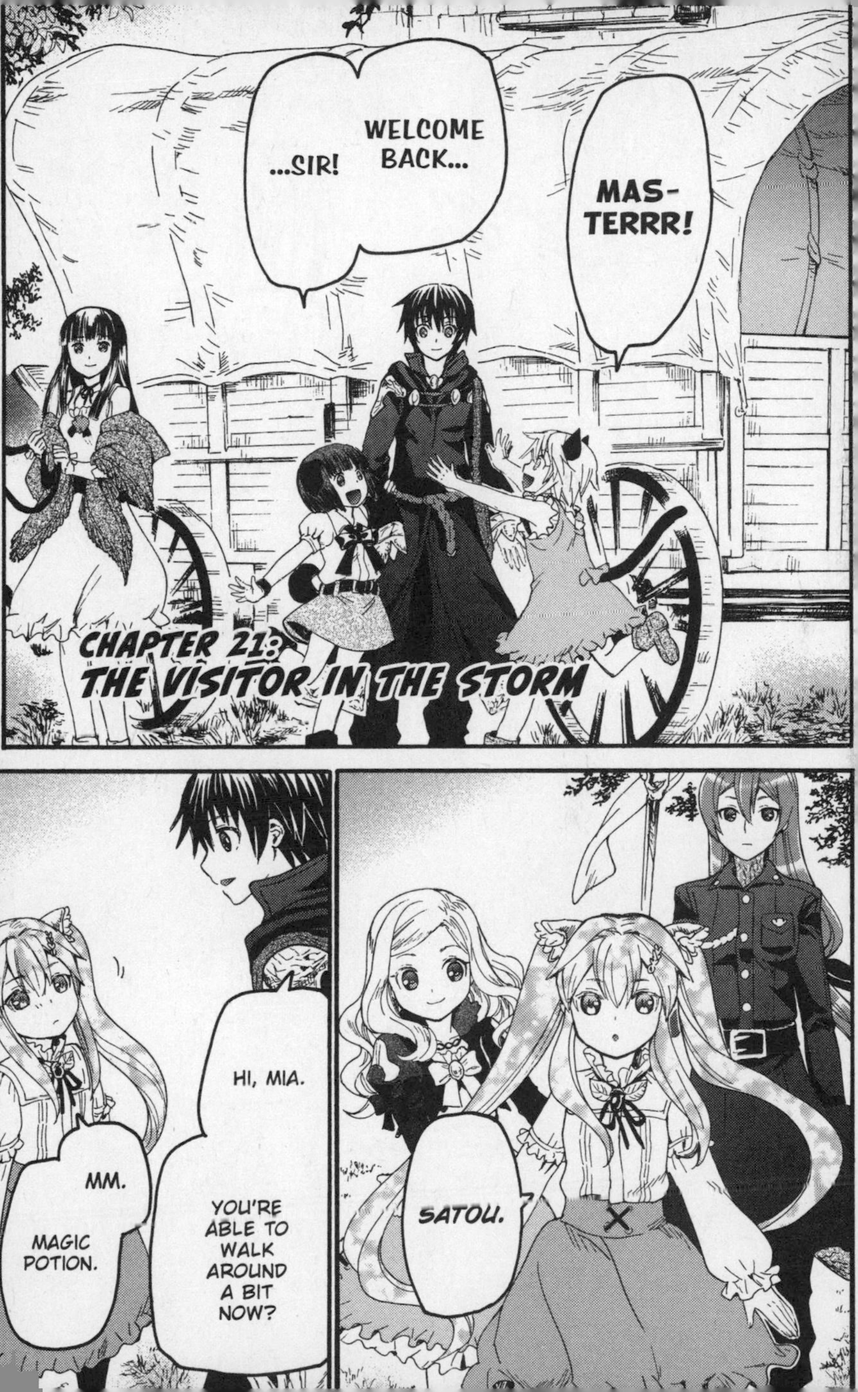
MAS-TERRR!
WELCOME BACK...
...SIR!
CHAPTER 21: THE VISITOR IN THE STORM
SATOU.
HI, MIA.
YOU'RE ABLE TO WALK AROUND A BIT NOW?
MM.
MAGIC POTION.

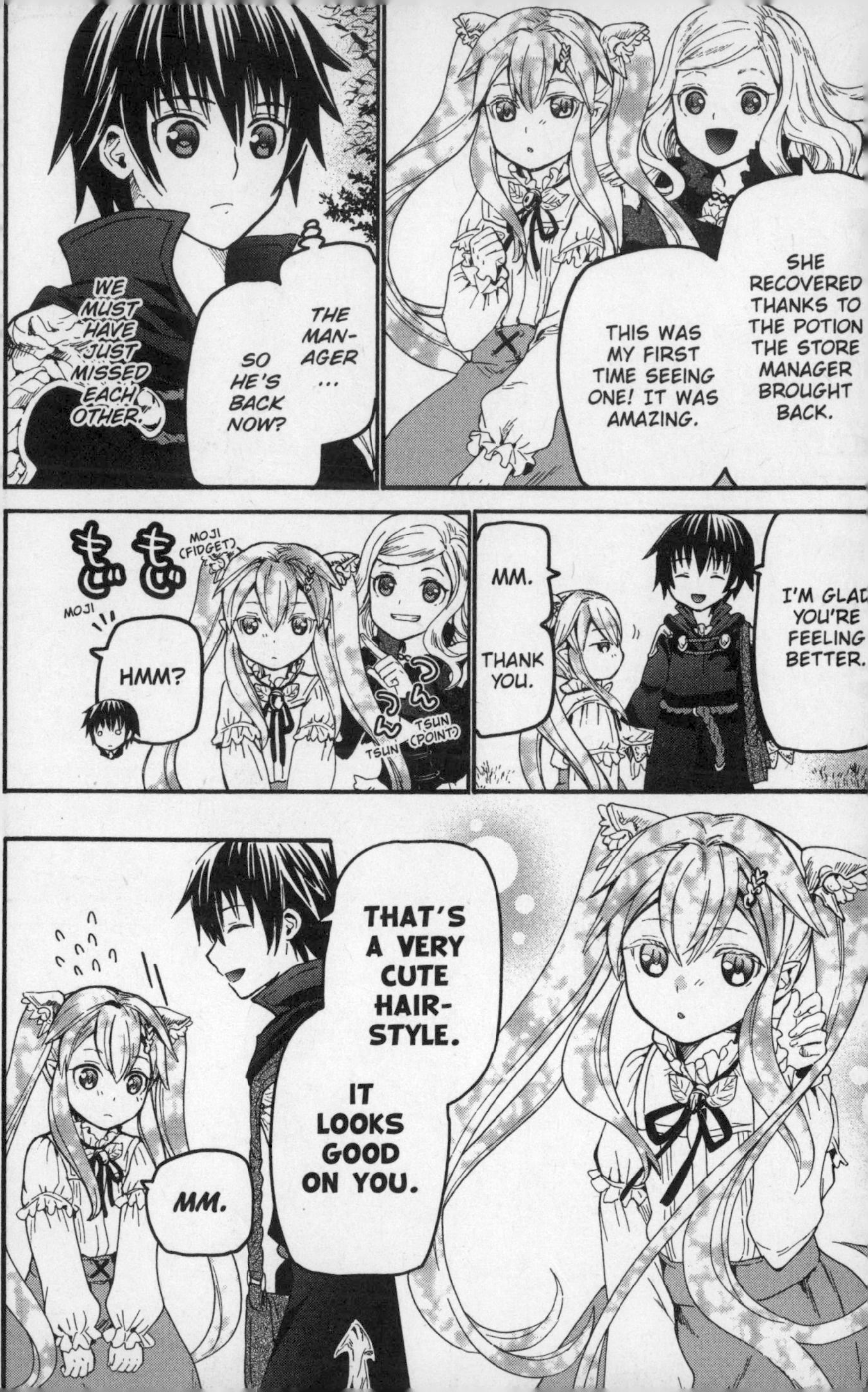
SHE RECOVERED THANKS TO THE POTION THE STORE MANAGER BROUGHT BACK.
THIS WAS MY FIRST TIME SEEING ONE! IT WAS AMAZING.
THE MAN-AGER ...
SO HE'S BACK NOW?
WE MUST HAVE JUST MISSED EACH OTHER.
I'M GLAD YOU'RE FEELING BETTER.
MM.
THANK YOU.
もじ もじ
MOJI (FIDGET)
MOJI
HMM?
つん つん
TSUN (POINT)
TSUN
THAT'S A VERY CUTE HAIR-STYLE.
IT LOOKS GOOD ON YOU.
MM.

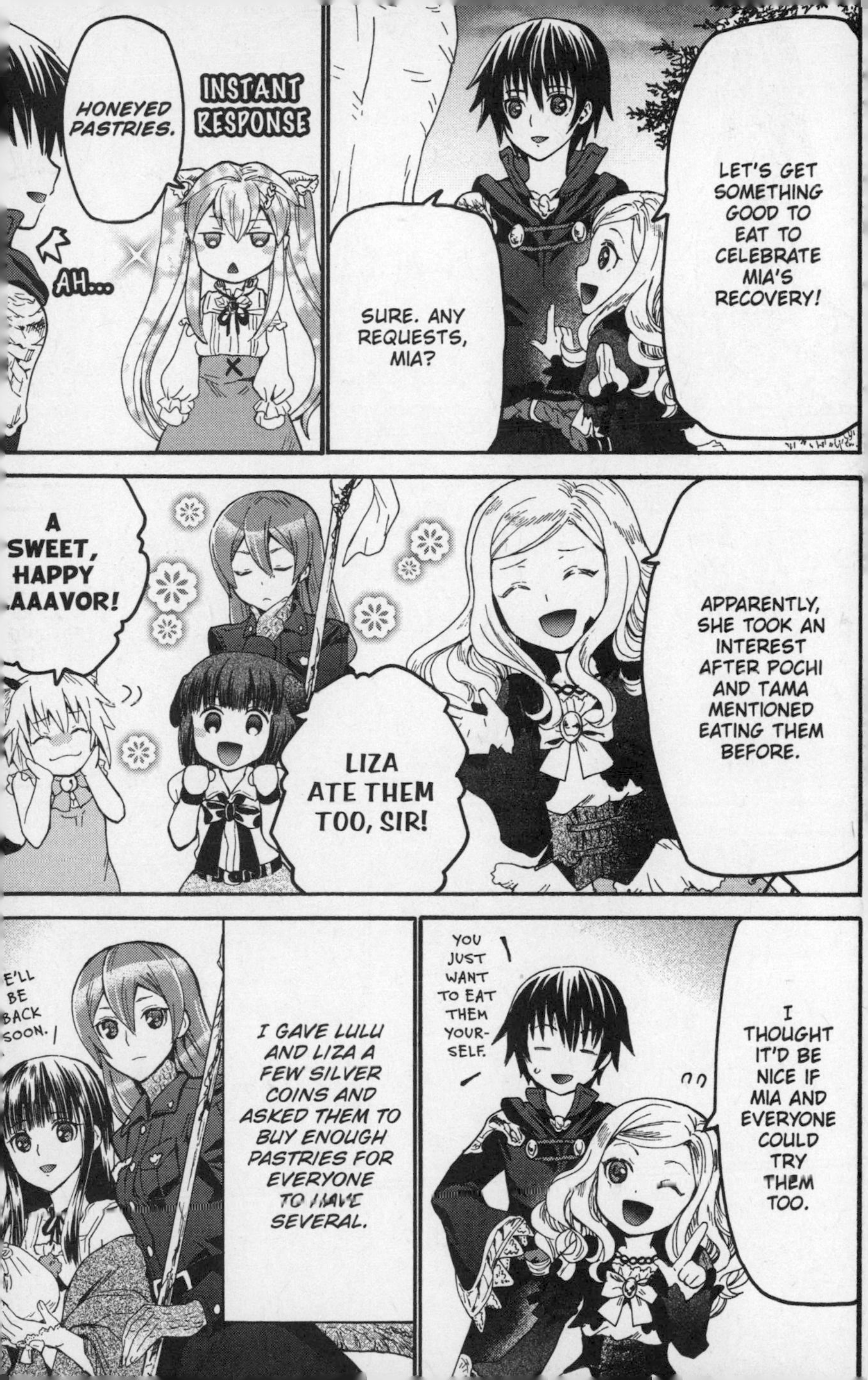
LET'S GET SOMETHING GOOD TO EAT TO CELEBRATE MIA'S RECOVERY!
SURE. ANY REQUESTS, MIA?
HONEYED PASTRIES.
INSTANT RESPONSE
AH...
APPARENTLY, SHE TOOK AN INTEREST AFTER POCHI AND TAMA MENTIONED EATING THEM BEFORE.
LIZA ATE THEM TOO, SIR!
A SWEET, HAPPY AAAVOR!
I THOUGHT IT'D BE NICE IF MIA AND EVERYONE COULD TRY THEM TOO.
YOU JUST WANT TO EAT THEM YOURSELF.
I GAVE LULU AND LIZA A FEW SILVER COINS AND ASKED THEM TO BUY ENOUGH PASTRIES FOR EVERYONE TO HAVE SEVERAL.
E'LL BE BACK SOON.

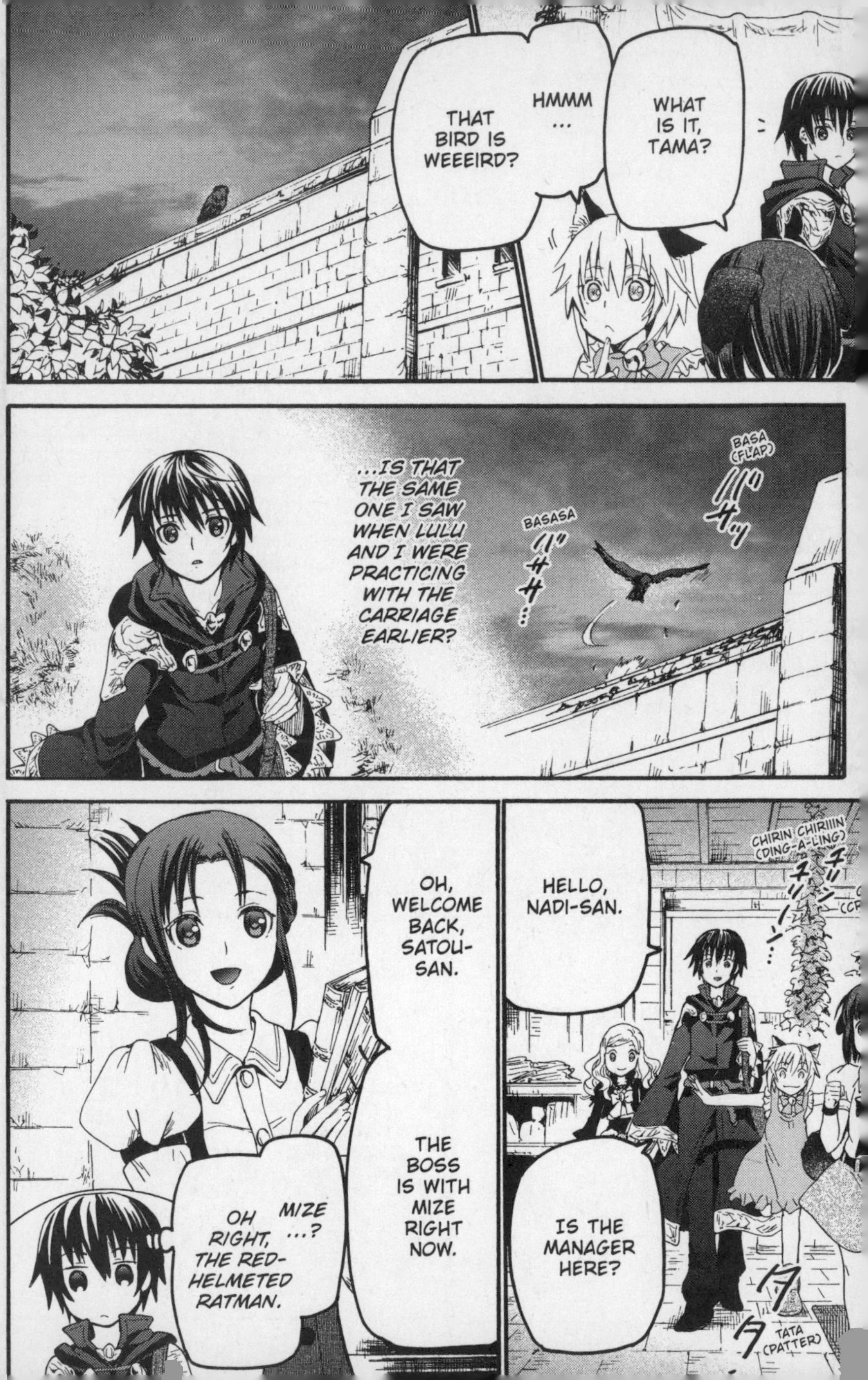
WHAT IS IT, TAMA?
HMMM ...
THAT BIRD IS WEEEIRD?
BASA (FLAP)
BASASA
...IS THAT THE SAME ONE I SAW WHEN LULU AND I WERE PRACTICING WITH THE CARRIAGE EARLIER?
CHIRIN CHIRIIIN (DING-A-LING)
HELLO, NADI-SAN.
IS THE MANAGER HERE?
TATA (PATTER)
OH, WELCOME BACK, SATOU-SAN.
THE BOSS IS WITH MIZE RIGHT NOW.
MIZE ...?
OH RIGHT, THE RED-HELMETED RATMAN.

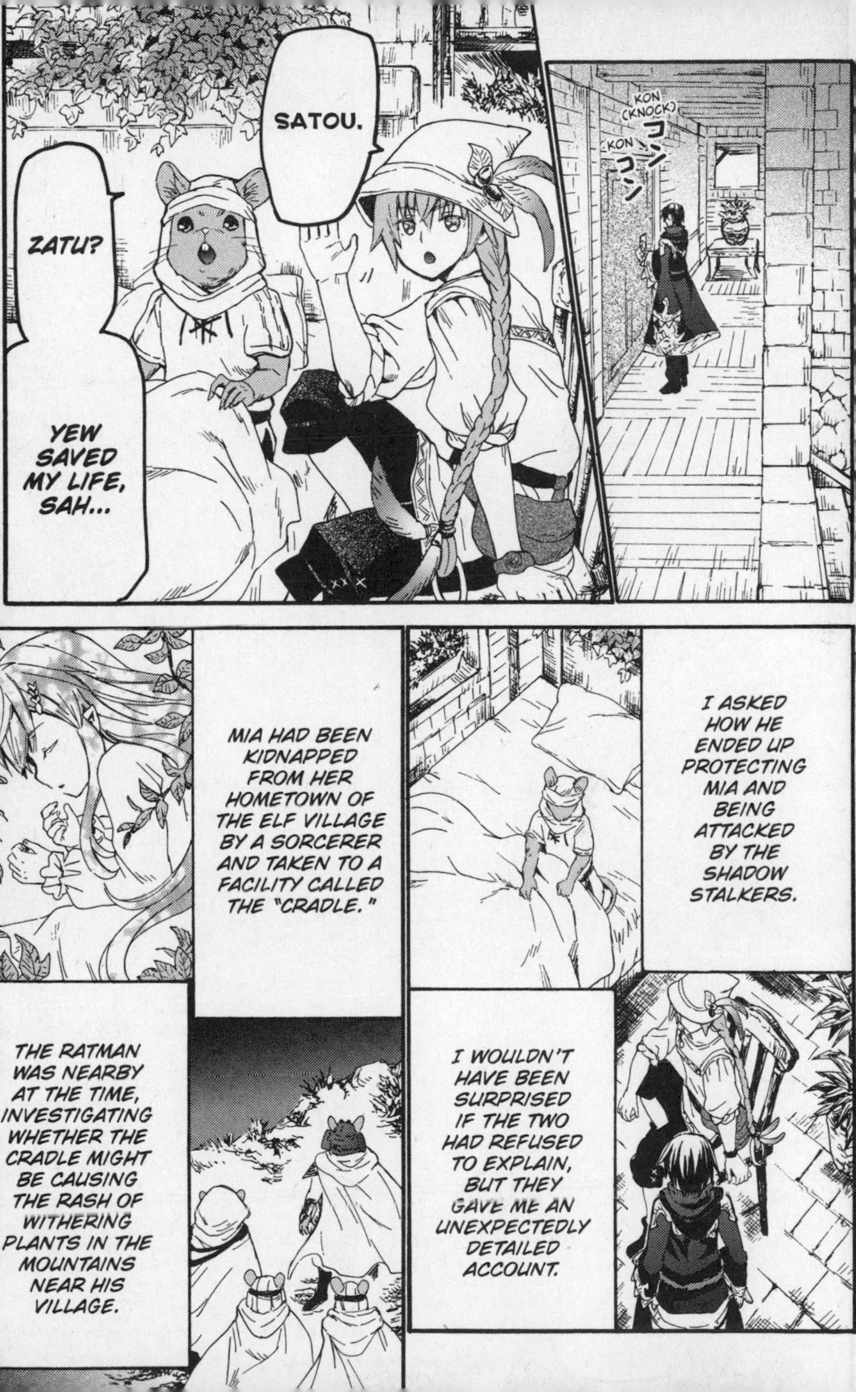
KON (KNOCK)
コン
KON
コン
SATOU.
ZATU?
YEW SAVED MY LIFE, SAH...
I ASKED HOW HE ENDED UP PROTECTING MIA AND BEING ATTACKED BY THE SHADOW STALKERS.
I WOULDN'T HAVE BEEN SURPRISED IF THE TWO HAD REFUSED TO EXPLAIN, BUT THEY GAVE ME AN UNEXPECTEDLY DETAILED ACCOUNT.
MIA HAD BEEN KIDNAPPED FROM HER HOMETOWN OF THE ELF VILLAGE BY A SORCERER AND TAKEN TO A FACILITY CALLED THE "CRADLE."
THE RATMAN WAS NEARBY AT THE TIME, INVESTIGATING WHETHER THE CRADLE MIGHT BE CAUSING THE RASH OF WITHERING PLANTS IN THE MOUNTAINS NEAR HIS VILLAGE.

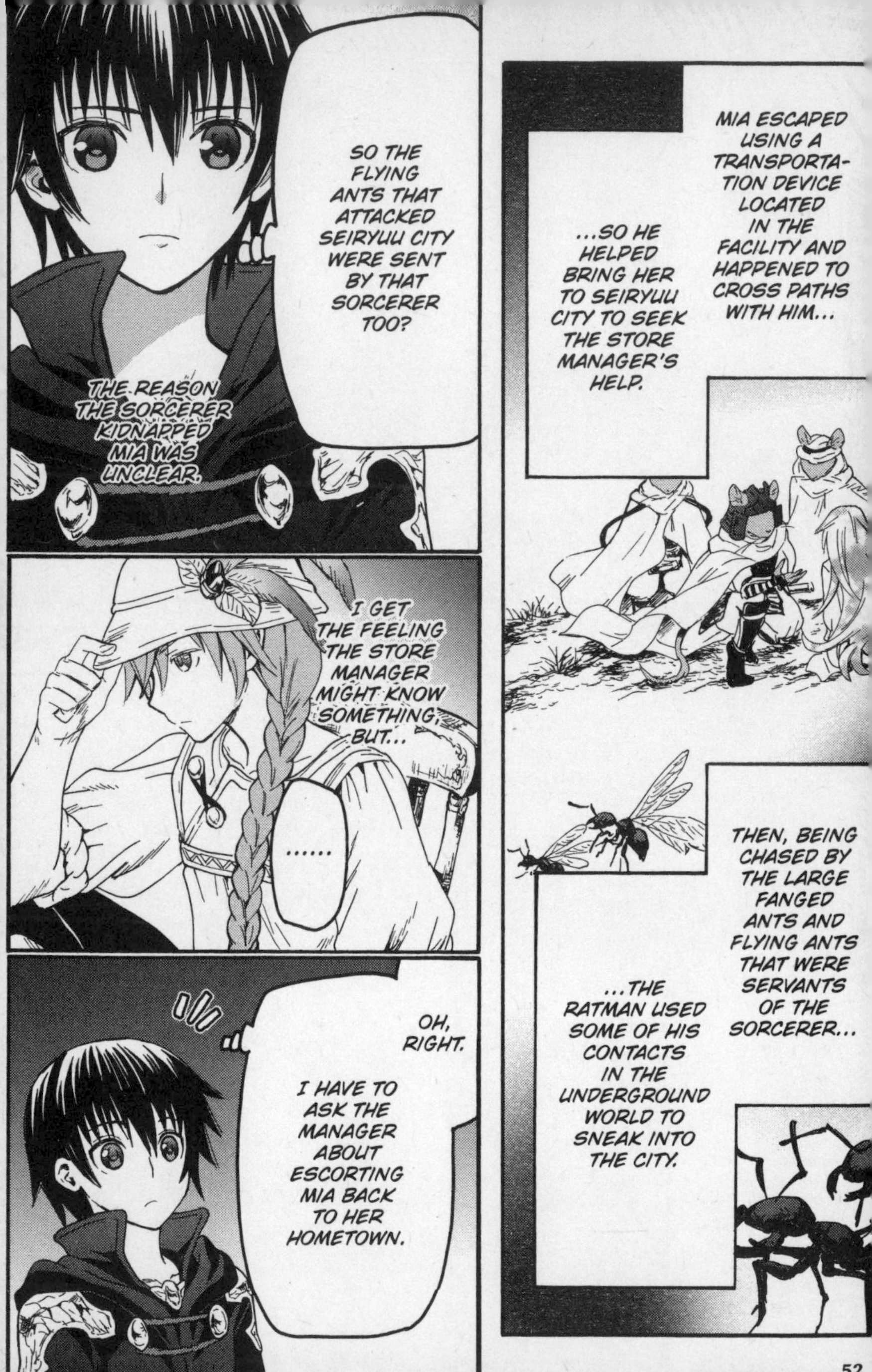
MIA ESCAPED USING A TRANSPORTATION DEVICE LOCATED IN THE FACILITY AND HAPPENED TO CROSS PATHS WITH HIM...
...SO HE HELPED BRING HER TO SEIRYUU CITY TO SEEK THE STORE MANAGER'S HELP.
THEN, BEING CHASED BY THE LARGE FANGED ANTS AND FLYING ANTS THAT WERE SERVANTS OF THE SORCERER...
...THE RATMAN USED SOME OF HIS CONTACTS IN THE UNDERGROUND WORLD TO SNEAK INTO THE CITY.
SO THE FLYING ANTS THAT ATTACKED SEIRYUU CITY WERE SENT BY THAT SORCERER TOO?
THE REASON THE SORCERER KIDNAPPED MIA WAS UNCLEAR.
I GET THE FEELING THE STORE MANAGER MIGHT KNOW SOMETHING, BUT...
......
OH, RIGHT.
I HAVE TO ASK THE MANAGER ABOUT ESCORTING MIA BACK TO HER HOMETOWN.

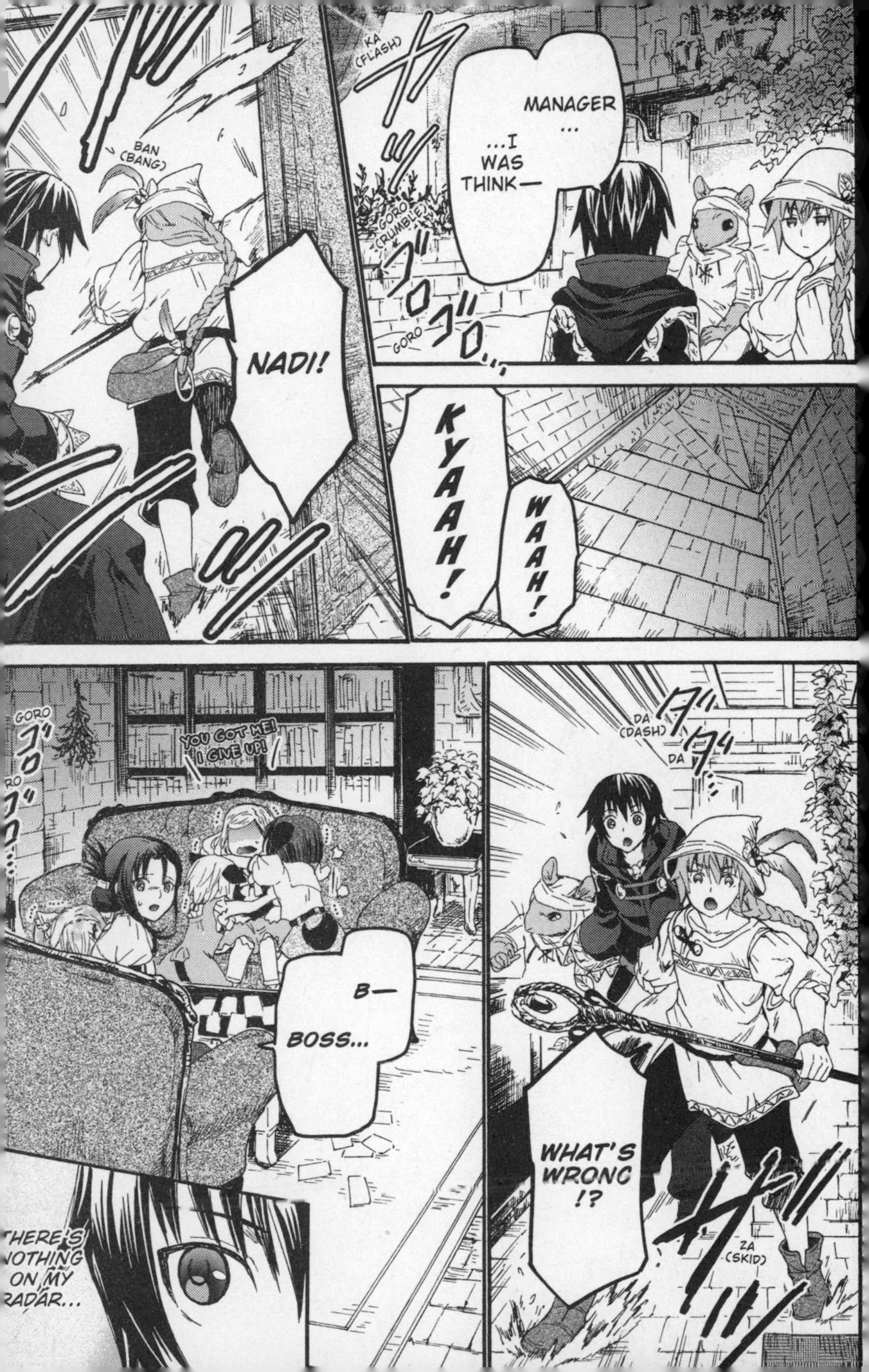
MANAGER ... ...I WAS THINK—
KA (FLASH)
GORO (CRUMBLE)
GORO
KYAAAH!
WAAAH!
BAN (BANG)
NADI!
DA (DASH)
DA
WHAT'S WRONG !?
ZA (SKID)
GORO
RO
YOU GOT ME! I GIVE UP!
B— BOSS...
THERE'S NOTHING ON MY RADAR...

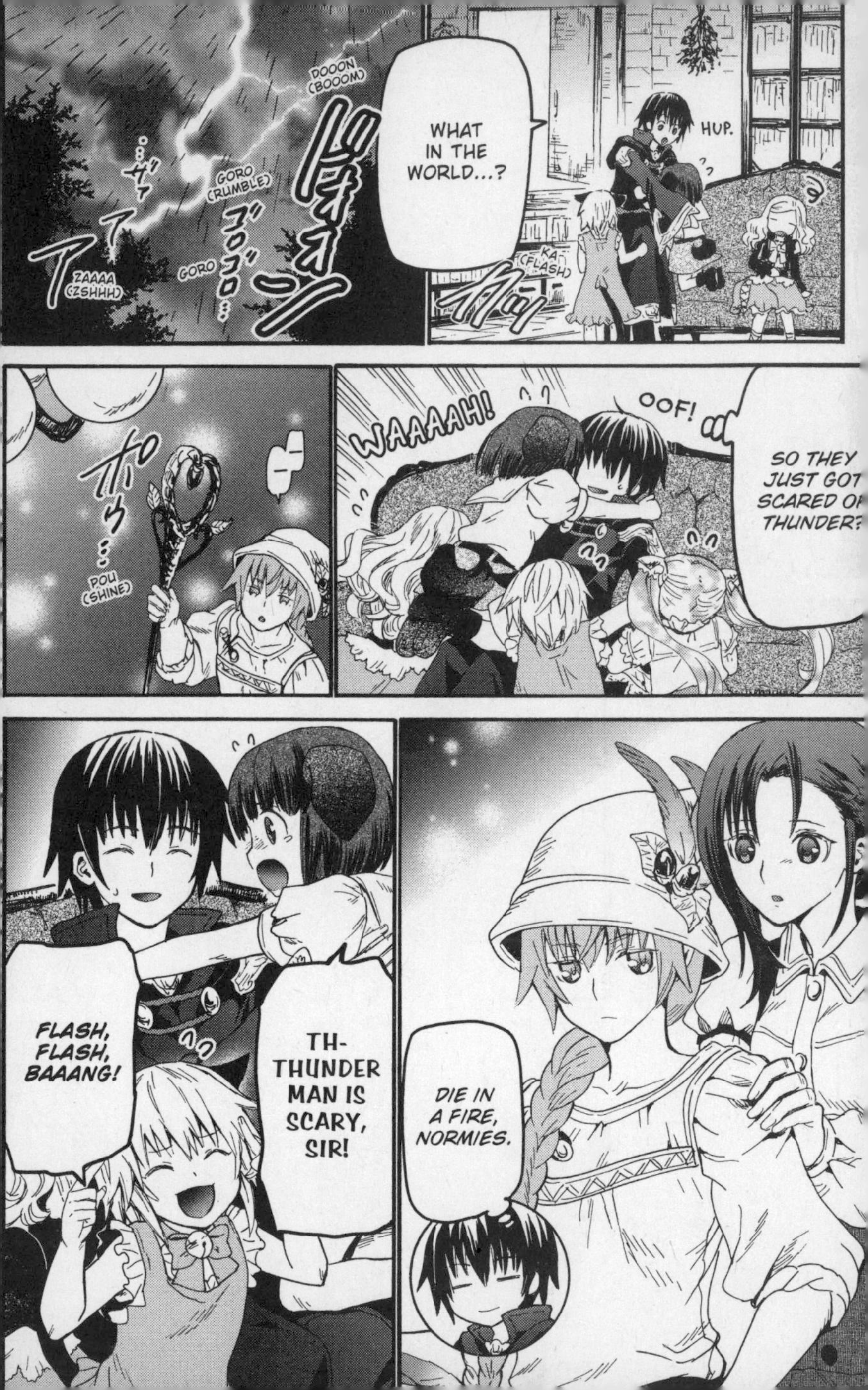
WHAT IN THE WORLD...?
HUP.
KA (FLASH)
DOOON (BOOOM)
GORO (RUMBLE)
ゴロゴロ…
GORO
ZAAAA (ZSHHH)
SO THEY JUST GOT SCARED OF THUNDER?
OOF!
WAAAAH!
POU (SHINE)
DIE IN A FIRE, NORMIES.
TH-THUNDER MAN IS SCARY, SIR!
FLASH, FLASH, BAAANG!

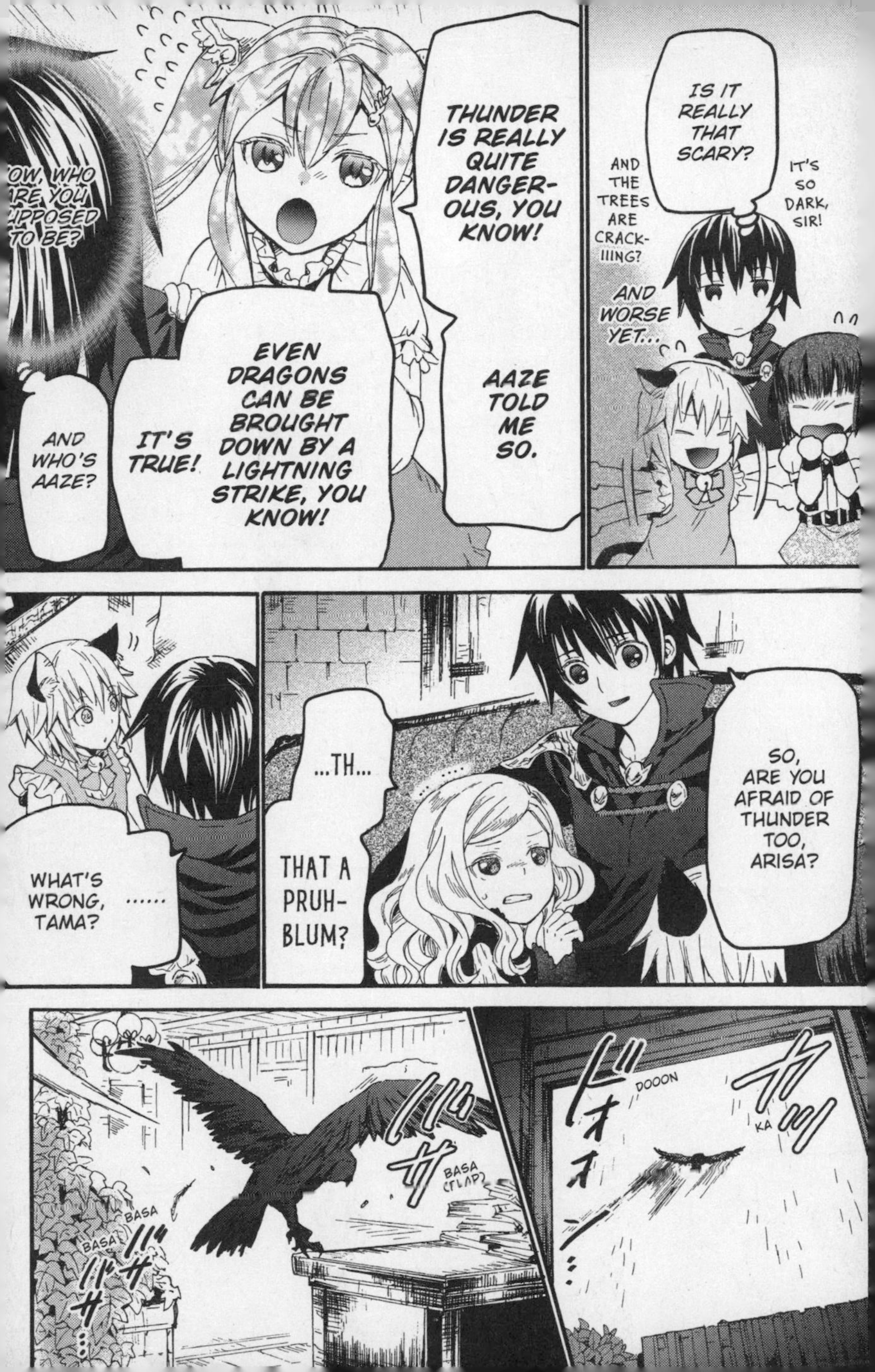
IS IT REALLY THAT SCARY?
IT'S SO DARK, SIR!
AND THE TREES ARE CRACK-IIING?
AND WORSE YET...
THUNDER IS REALLY QUITE DANGER-OUS, YOU KNOW!
AAZE TOLD ME SO.
EVEN DRAGONS CAN BE BROUGHT DOWN BY A LIGHTNING STRIKE, YOU KNOW!
IT'S TRUE!
AND WHO'S AAZE?
OW, WHO ARE YOU UPPOSED TO BE?
SO, ARE YOU AFRAID OF THUNDER TOO, ARISA?
...TH...
THAT A PRUH-BLUM?
......
WHAT'S WRONG, TAMA?
DOOON
KA
BASA (FLAP)
BASA
BASA

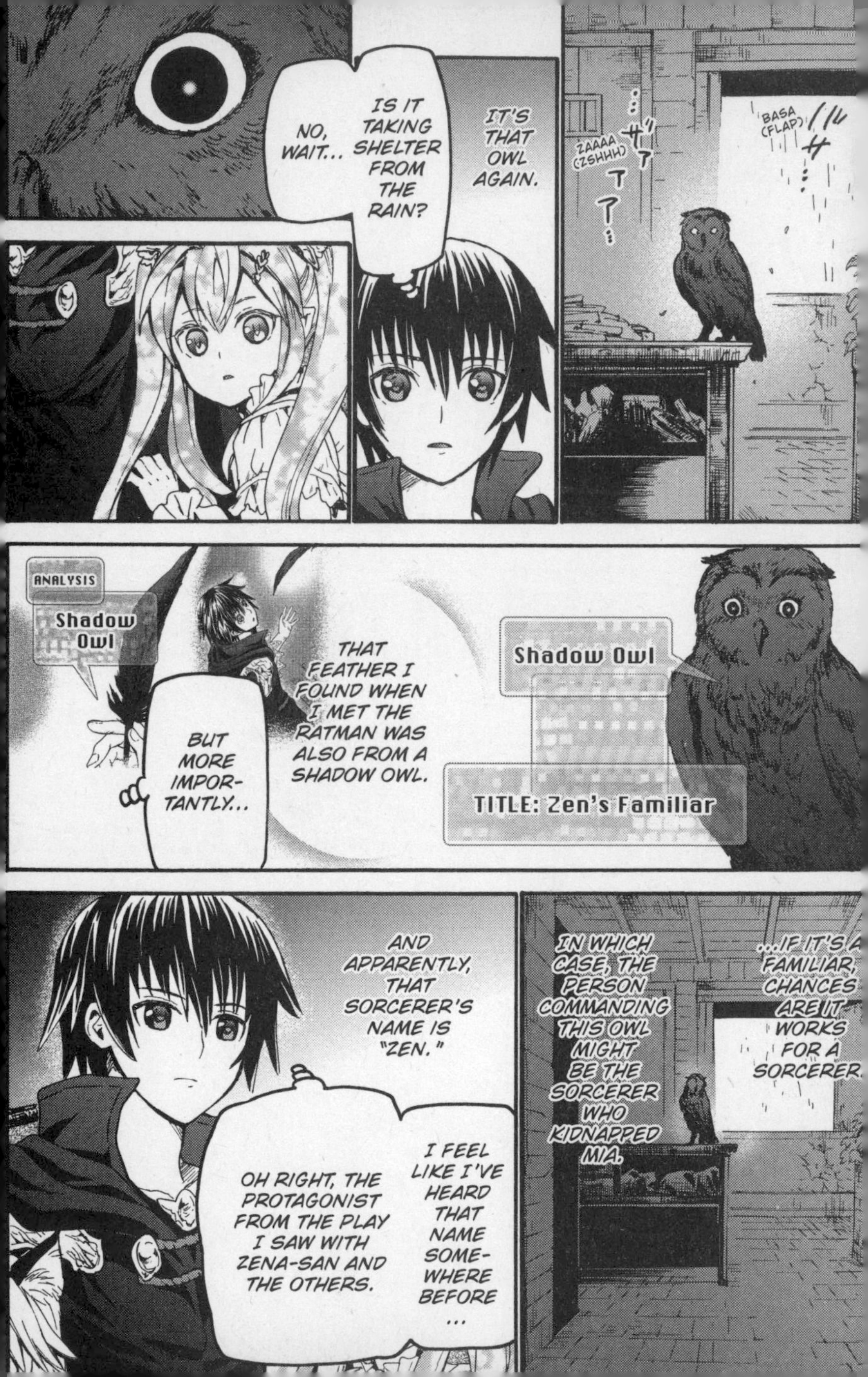
BASA (FLAP)
ZAAAA (ZSHHH)
IT'S THAT OWL AGAIN.
IS IT TAKING SHELTER FROM THE RAIN?
NO, WAIT...
Shadow Owl
TITLE: Zen's Familiar
THAT FEATHER I FOUND WHEN I MET THE RATMAN WAS ALSO FROM A SHADOW OWL.
BUT MORE IMPOR-TANTLY...
ANALYSIS
Shadow Owl
...IF IT'S A FAMILIAR, CHANCES ARE IT WORKS FOR A SORCERER.
IN WHICH CASE, THE PERSON COMMANDING THIS OWL MIGHT BE THE SORCERER WHO KIDNAPPED MIA.
AND APPARENTLY, THAT SORCERER'S NAME IS "ZEN."
I FEEL LIKE I'VE HEARD THAT NAME SOME-WHERE BEFORE...
OH RIGHT, THE PROTAGONIST FROM THE PLAY I SAW WITH ZENA-SAN AND THE OTHERS.

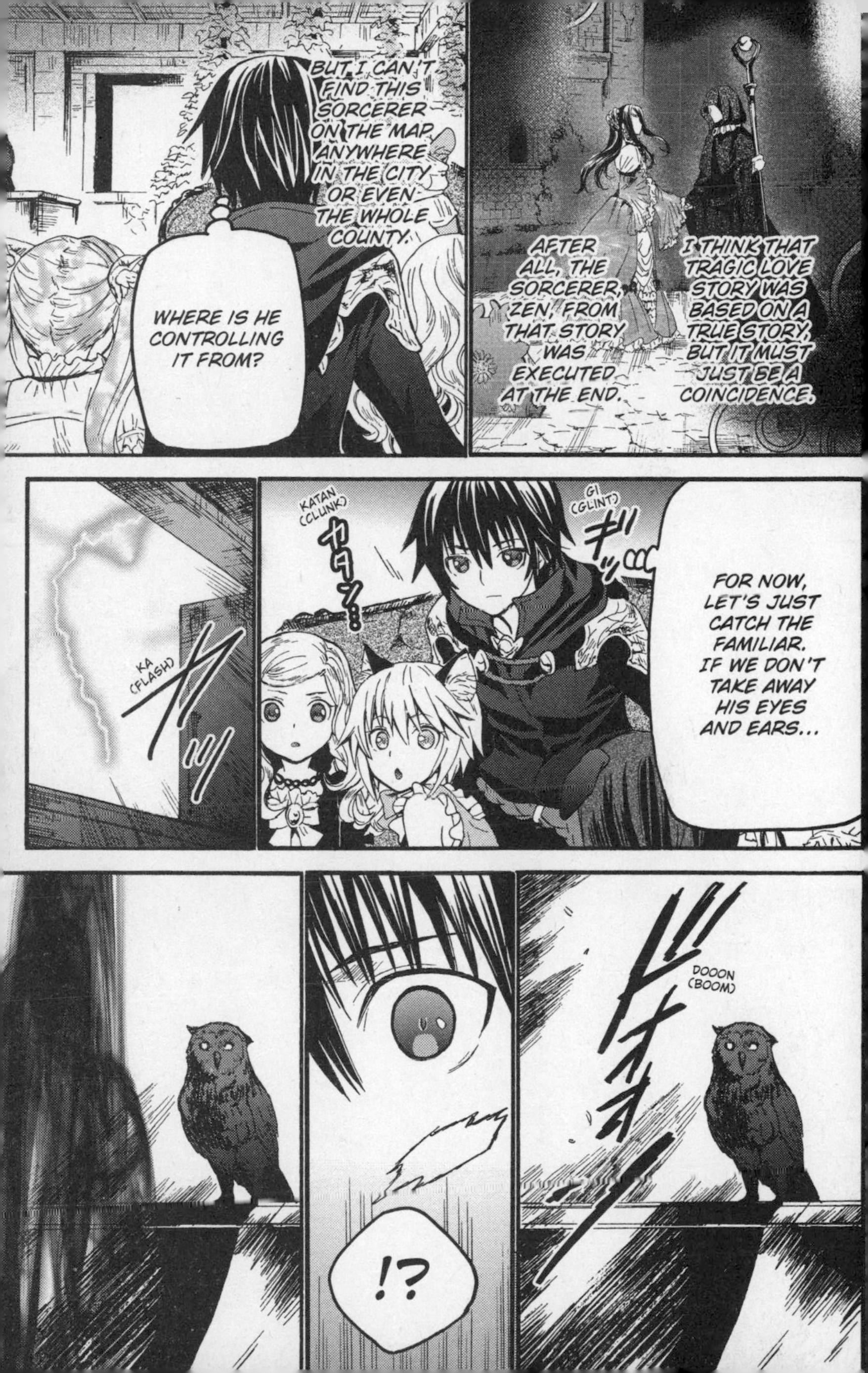
I THINK THAT TRAGIC LOVE STORY WAS BASED ON A TRUE STORY, BUT IT MUST JUST BE A COINCIDENCE.
AFTER ALL, THE SORCERER, ZEN, FROM THAT STORY WAS EXECUTED AT THE END.
BUT I CAN'T FIND THIS SORCERER ON THE MAP ANYWHERE IN THE CITY OR EVEN THE WHOLE COUNTY.
WHERE IS HE CONTROLLING IT FROM?
FOR NOW, LET'S JUST CATCH THE FAMILIAR. IF WE DON'T TAKE AWAY HIS EYES AND EARS...
GI (GLINT)
KATAN (CLUNK)
KA (FLASH)
DOOON (BOOM)
!?

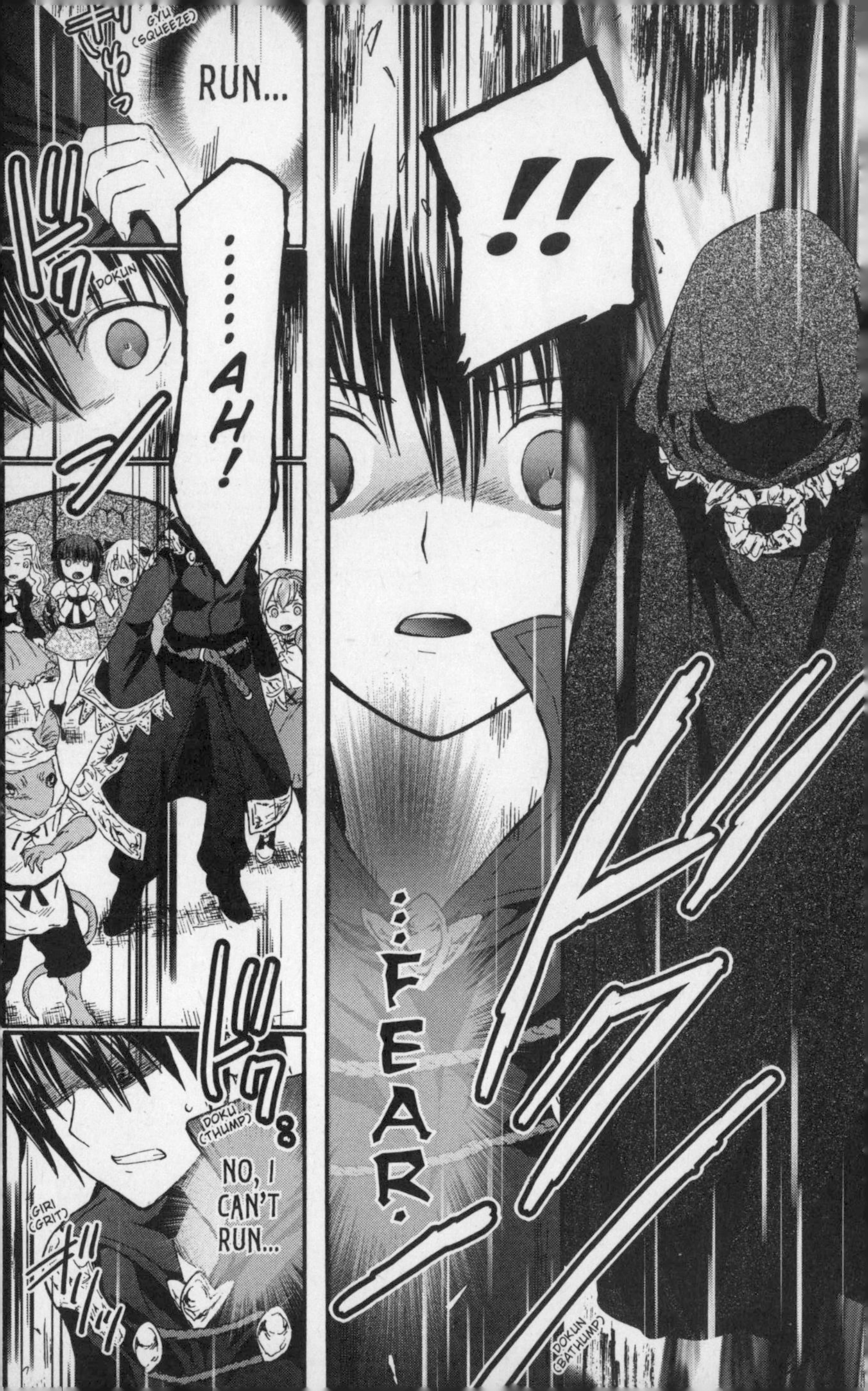
!!
...FEAR.
DOKUN (BATHUMP)
GYU (SQUEEZE)
RUN...
......AH!
DOKUN
DOKU (THUMP)
NO, I CAN'T RUN...
GIRI (GRIT)

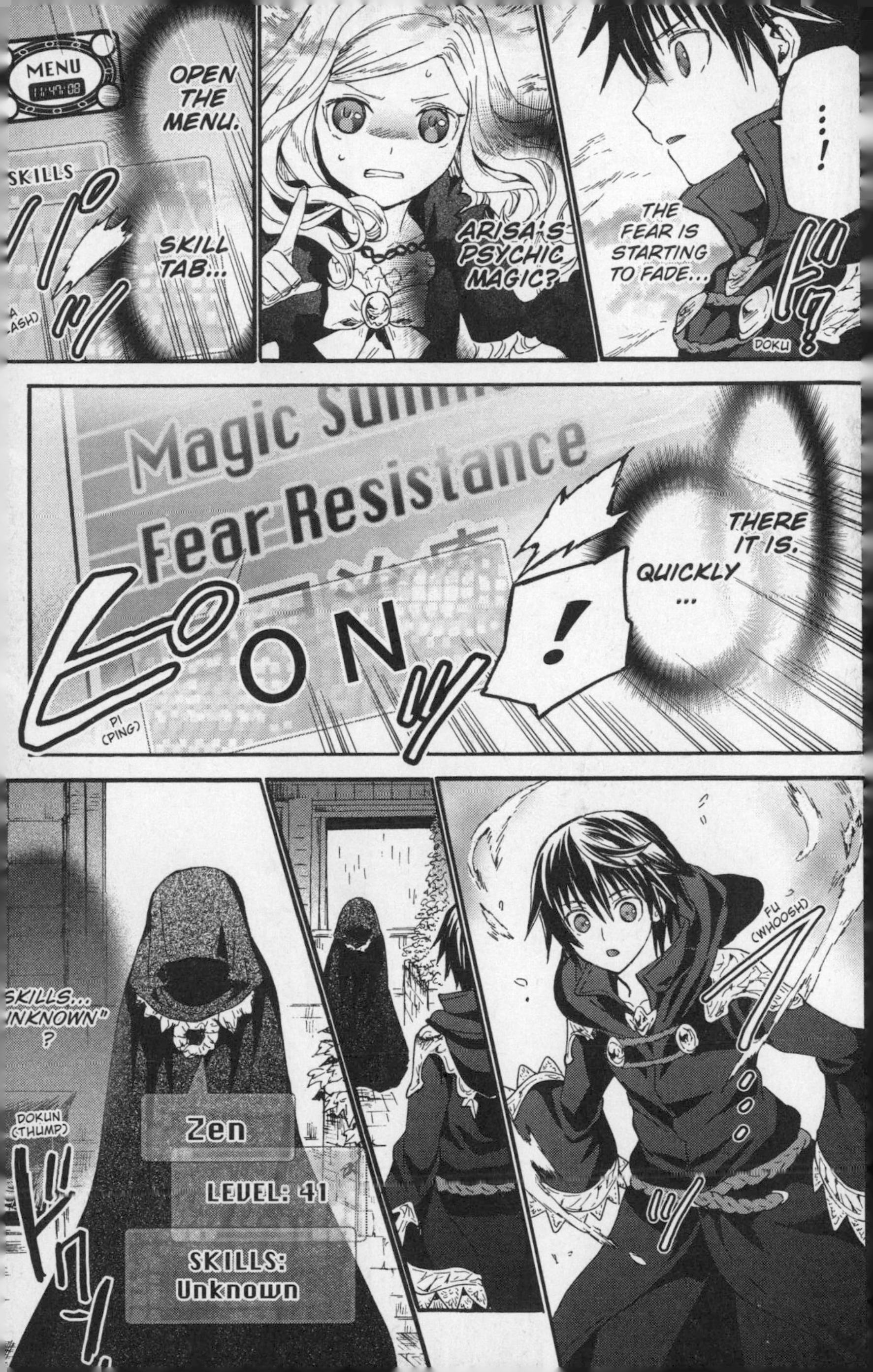
...!
THE FEAR IS STARTING TO FADE...
DOKU
ARISA'S PSYCHIC MAGIC?
MENU
11:47:08
OPEN THE MENU.
SKILLS
SKILL TAB...
THERE IT IS.
QUICKLY ...
Fear Resistance
ON
!
PI (PING)
FU (WHOOSH)
Zen
LEVEL: 41
SKILLS: Unknown
DOKUN (THUMP)

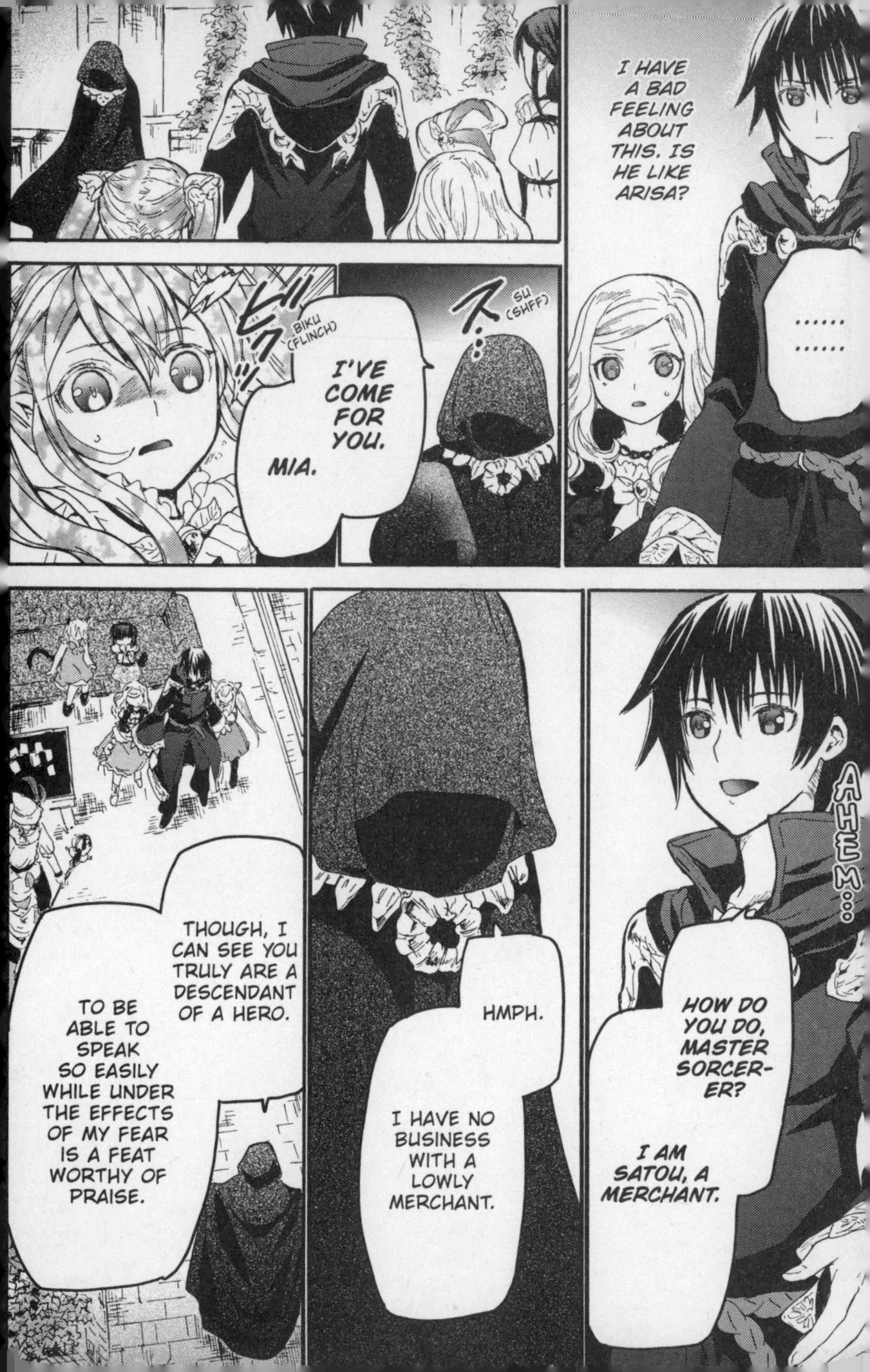
I HAVE A BAD FEELING ABOUT THIS. IS HE LIKE ARISA?
......
......
SU (SHFF)
I'VE COME FOR YOU.
MIA.
BIKU (FLINCH)
AHEM...
HOW DO YOU DO, MASTER SORCERER?
I AM SATOU, A MERCHANT.
HMPH.
I HAVE NO BUSINESS WITH A LOWLY MERCHANT.
THOUGH, I CAN SEE YOU TRULY ARE A DESCENDANT OF A HERO.
TO BE ABLE TO SPEAK SO EASILY WHILE UNDER THE EFFECTS OF MY FEAR IS A FEAT WORTHY OF PRAISE.

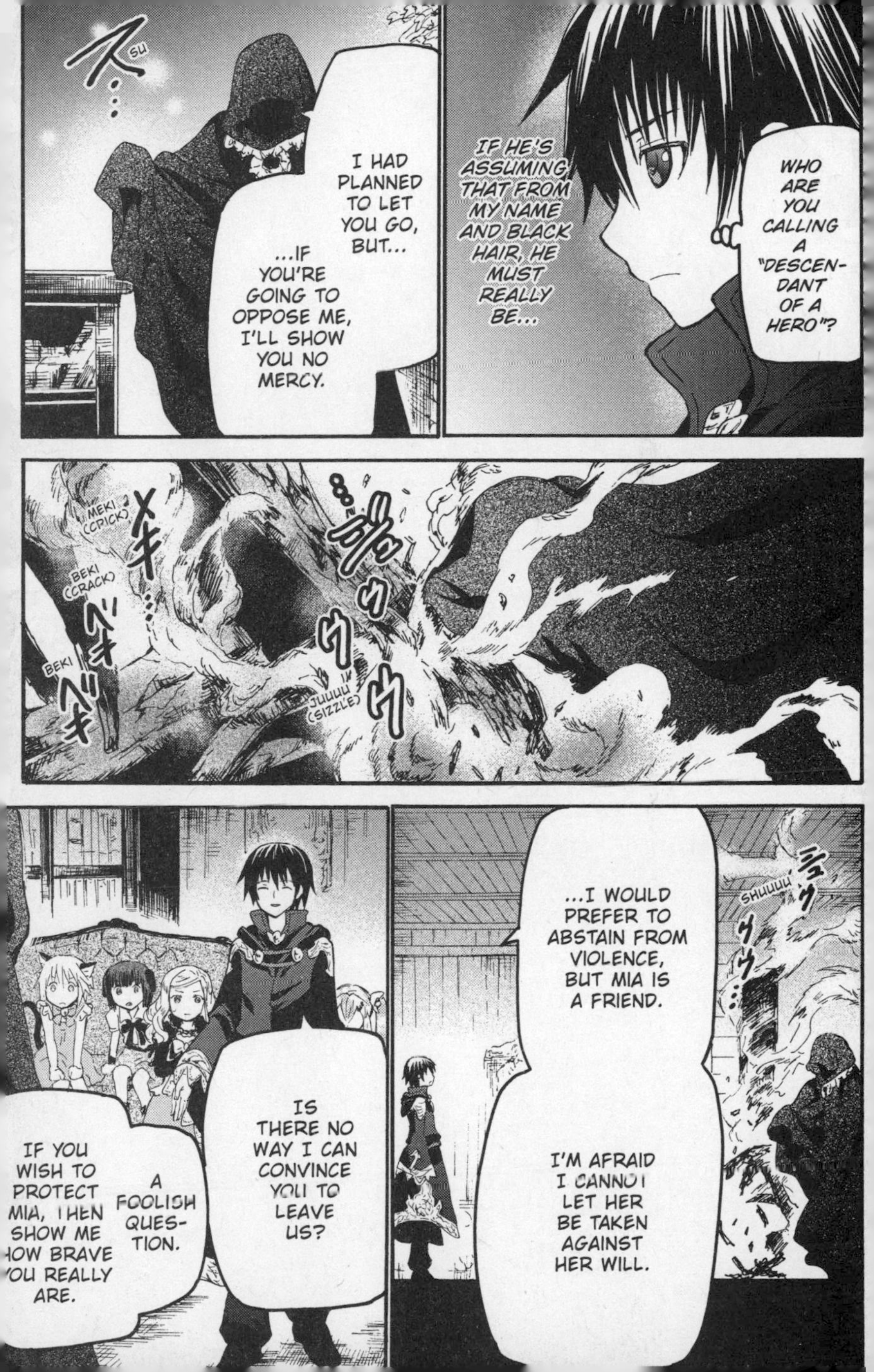
WHO ARE YOU CALLING A "DESCENDANT OF A HERO"?
IF HE'S ASSUMING THAT FROM MY NAME AND BLACK HAIR, HE MUST REALLY BE...
SU
I HAD PLANNED TO LET YOU GO, BUT...
...IF YOU'RE GOING TO OPPOSE ME, I'LL SHOW YOU NO MERCY.
JUUUU (SIZZLE)
MEKI (CRICK)
BEKI (CRACK)
BEKI
SHUUUU
...I WOULD PREFER TO ABSTAIN FROM VIOLENCE, BUT MIA IS A FRIEND.
I'M AFRAID I CANNOT LET HER BE TAKEN AGAINST HER WILL.
IS THERE NO WAY I CAN CONVINCE YOU TO LEAVE US?
A FOOLISH QUESTION.
IF YOU WISH TO PROTECT MIA, THEN SHOW ME HOW BRAVE YOU REALLY ARE.

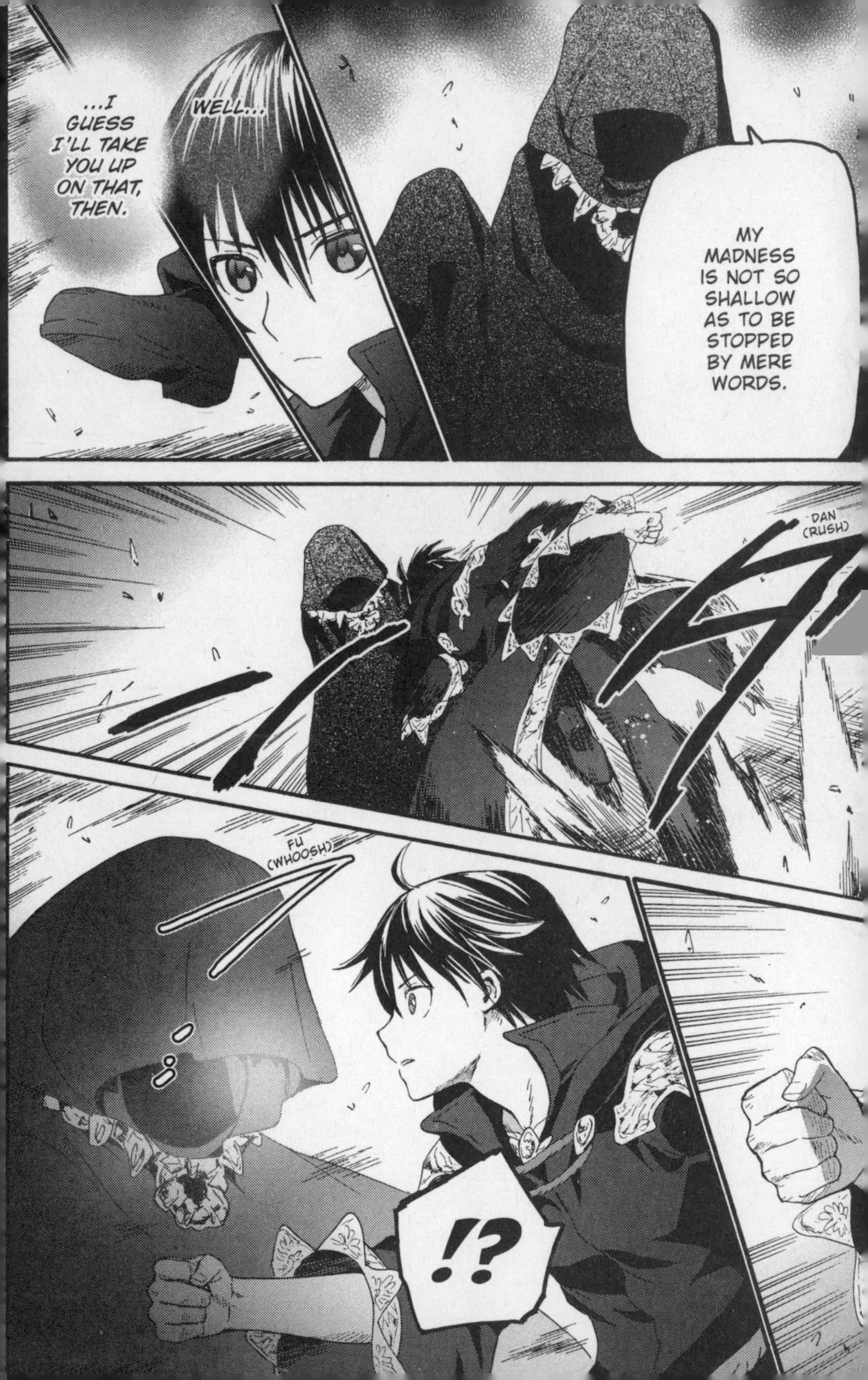
MY MADNESS IS NOT SO SHALLOW AS TO BE STOPPED BY MERE WORDS.
WELL...
...I GUESS I'LL TAKE YOU UP ON THAT, THEN.
DAN (RUSH)
FU (WHOOSH)
!?

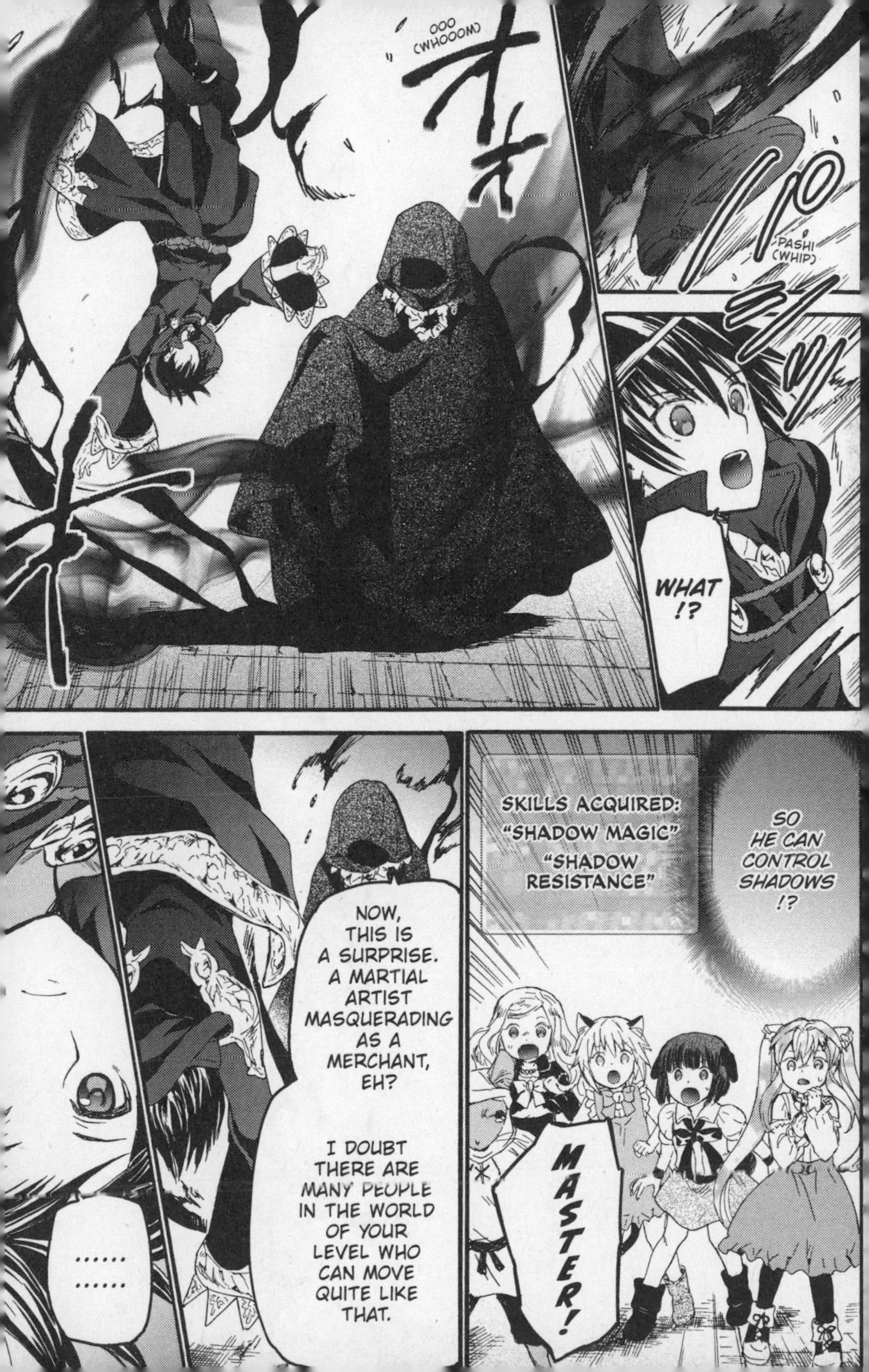
PASHI (WHIP)
WHAT !?
OOO (WHOOOM)
SO HE CAN CONTROL SHADOWS !?
SKILLS ACQUIRED: "SHADOW MAGIC" "SHADOW RESISTANCE"
MASTER!
NOW, THIS IS A SURPRISE. A MARTIAL ARTIST MASQUERADING AS A MERCHANT, EH?
I DOUBT THERE ARE MANY PEOPLE IN THE WORLD OF YOUR LEVEL WHO CAN MOVE QUITE LIKE THAT.
......
......

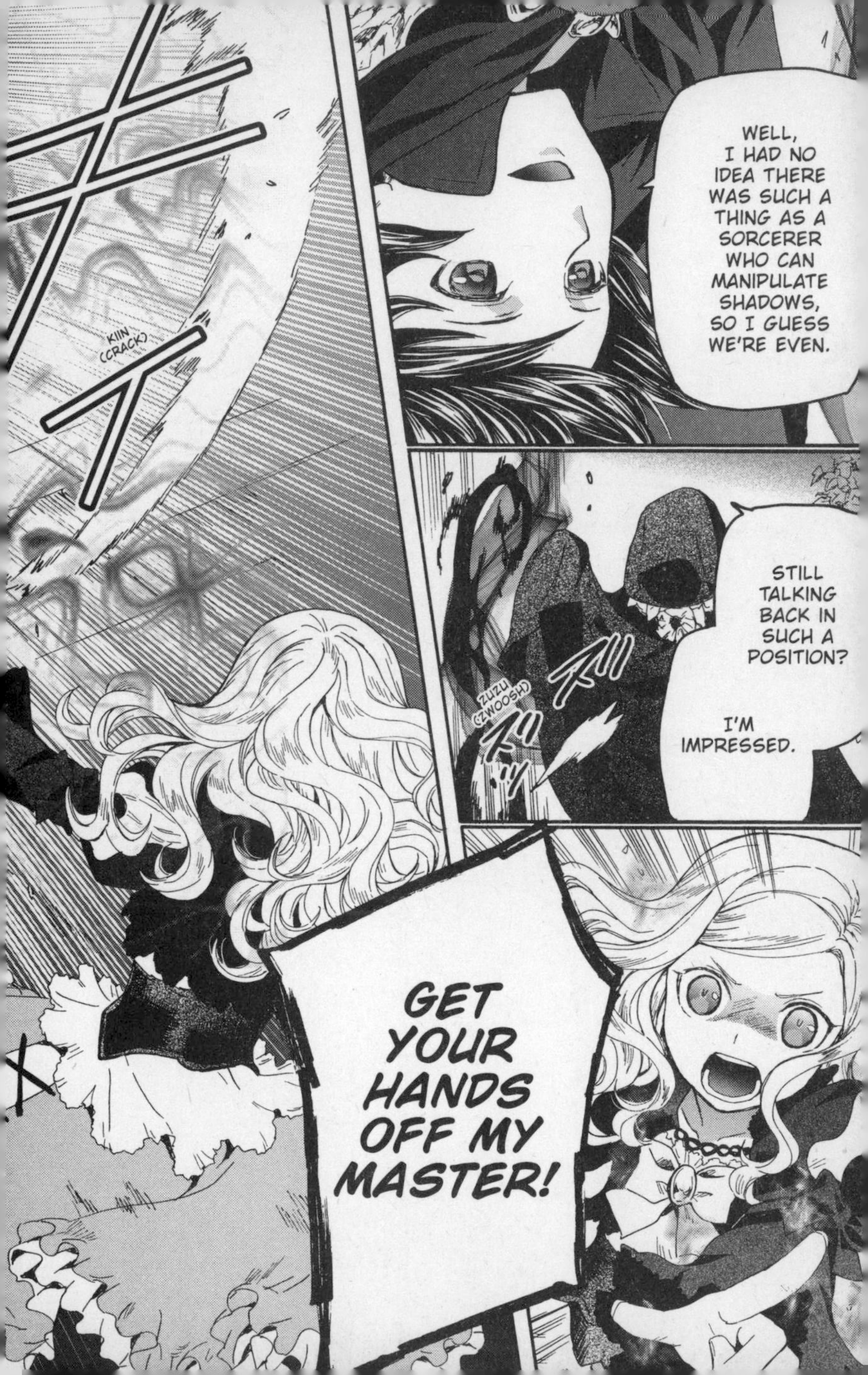
WELL, I HAD NO IDEA THERE WAS SUCH A THING AS A SORCERER WHO CAN MANIPULATE SHADOWS, SO I GUESS WE'RE EVEN.
STILL TALKING BACK IN SUCH A POSITION?
I'M IMPRESSED.
ZUZU (ZWOOSH)
GET YOUR HANDS OFF MY MASTER!
KIIN (CRACK)

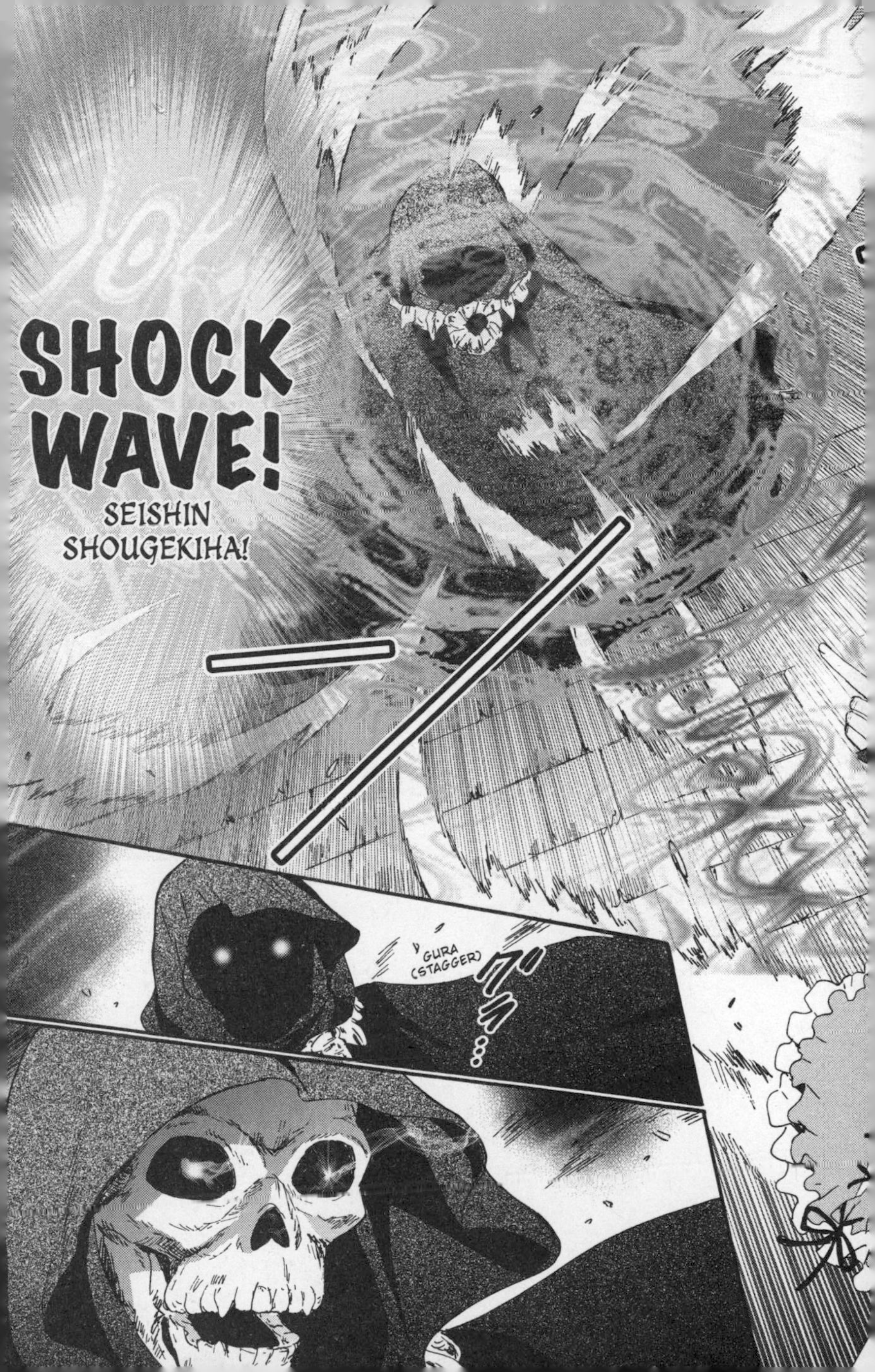
SHOCK WAVE!
SEISHIN SHOUGEKIHA!
GURA (STAGGER)

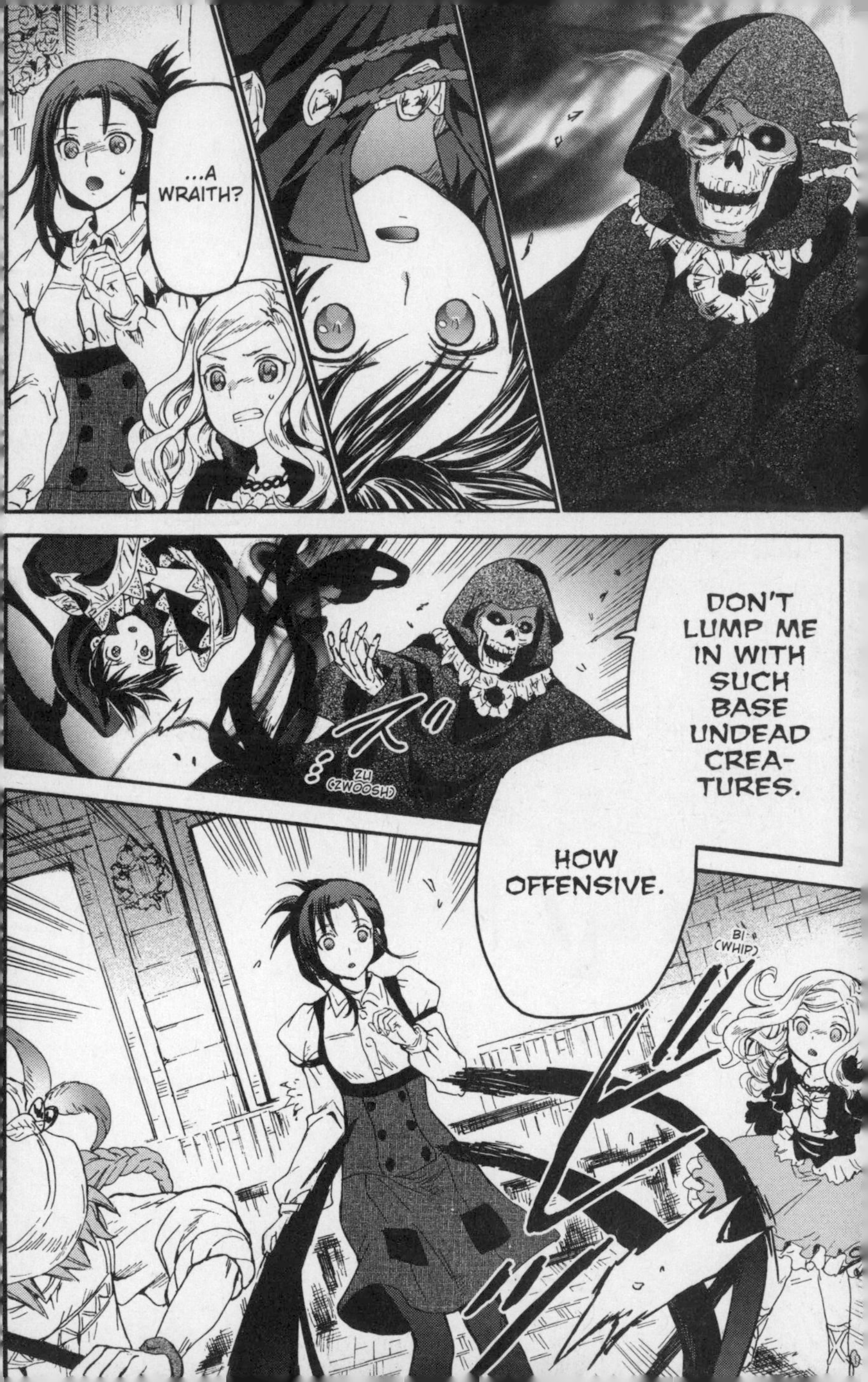
...A WRAITH?
DON'T LUMP ME IN WITH SUCH BASE UNDEAD CREATURES.
ZU (ZWOOSH)
HOW OFFENSIVE.
BI (WHIP)

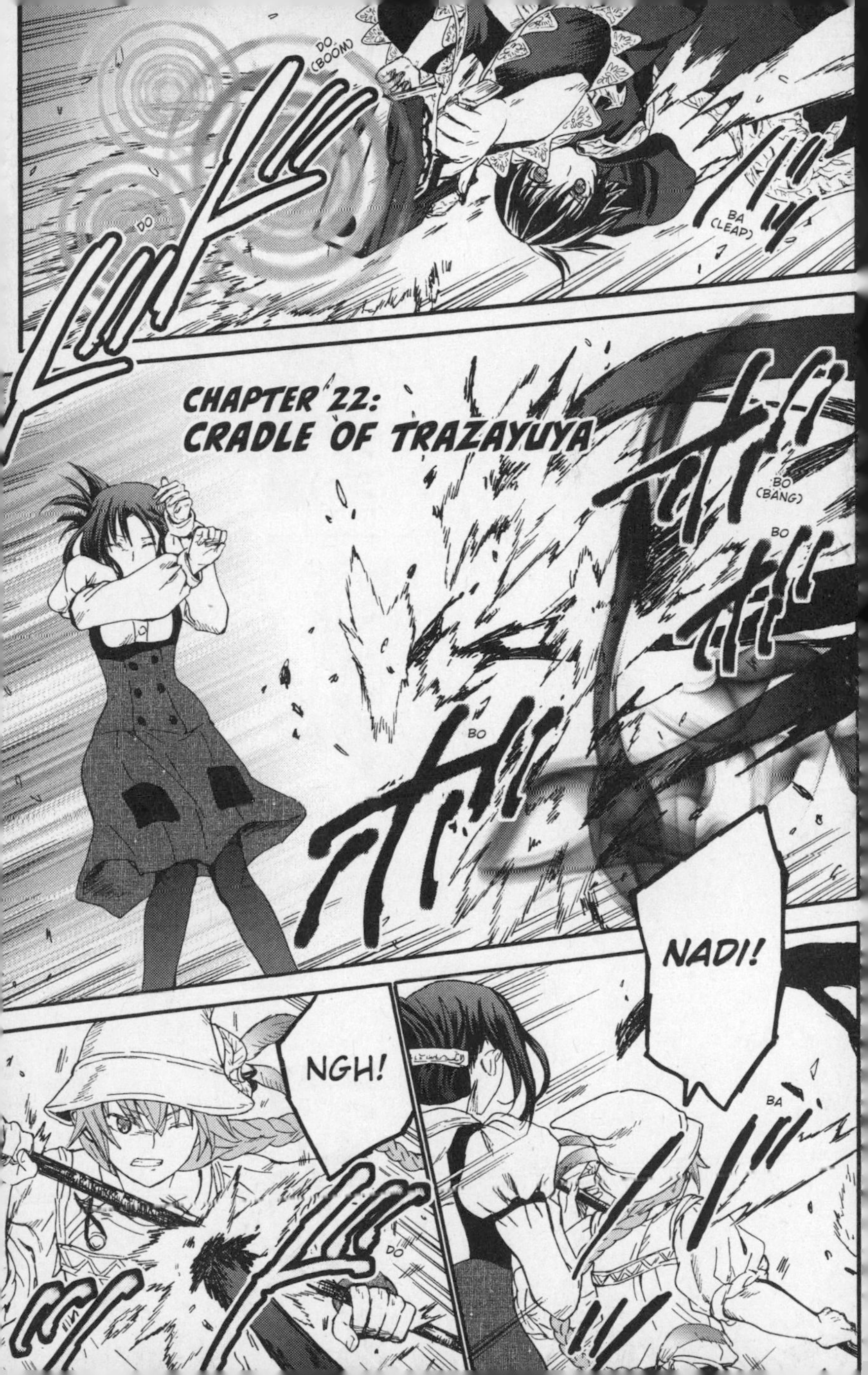
DO (BOOM)
BA (LEAP)
DO
CHAPTER 22: CRADLE OF TRAZAYUYA
BO (BANG)
BO
BO
NADI!
BA
DO
NGH!

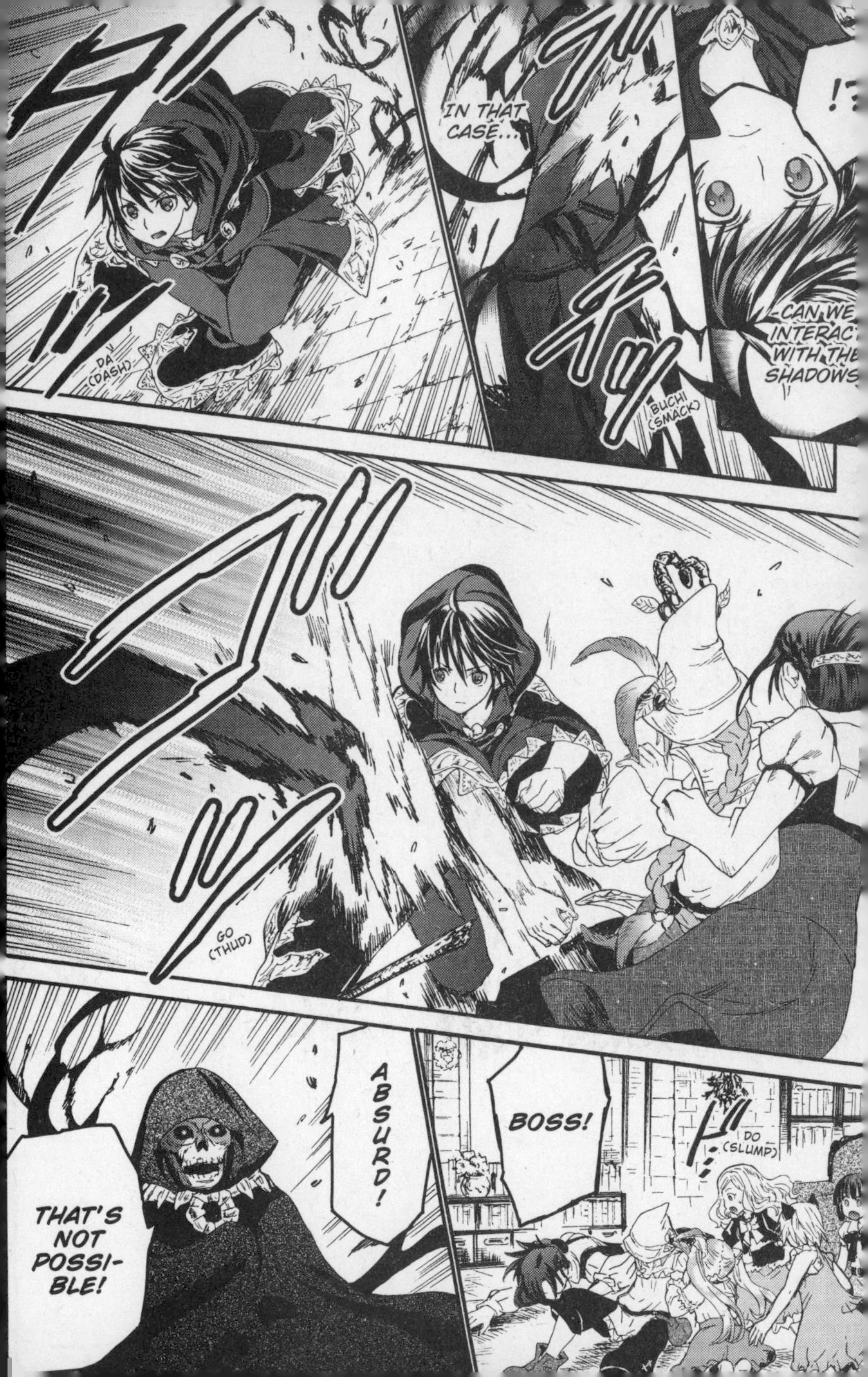
!?
CAN WE INTERAC WITH THE SHADOWS
IN THAT CASE...
BUCHI (SMACK)
DA (DASH)
GO (THUD)
BOSS!
DO (SLUMP)
ABSURD!
THAT'S NOT POSSI-BLE!

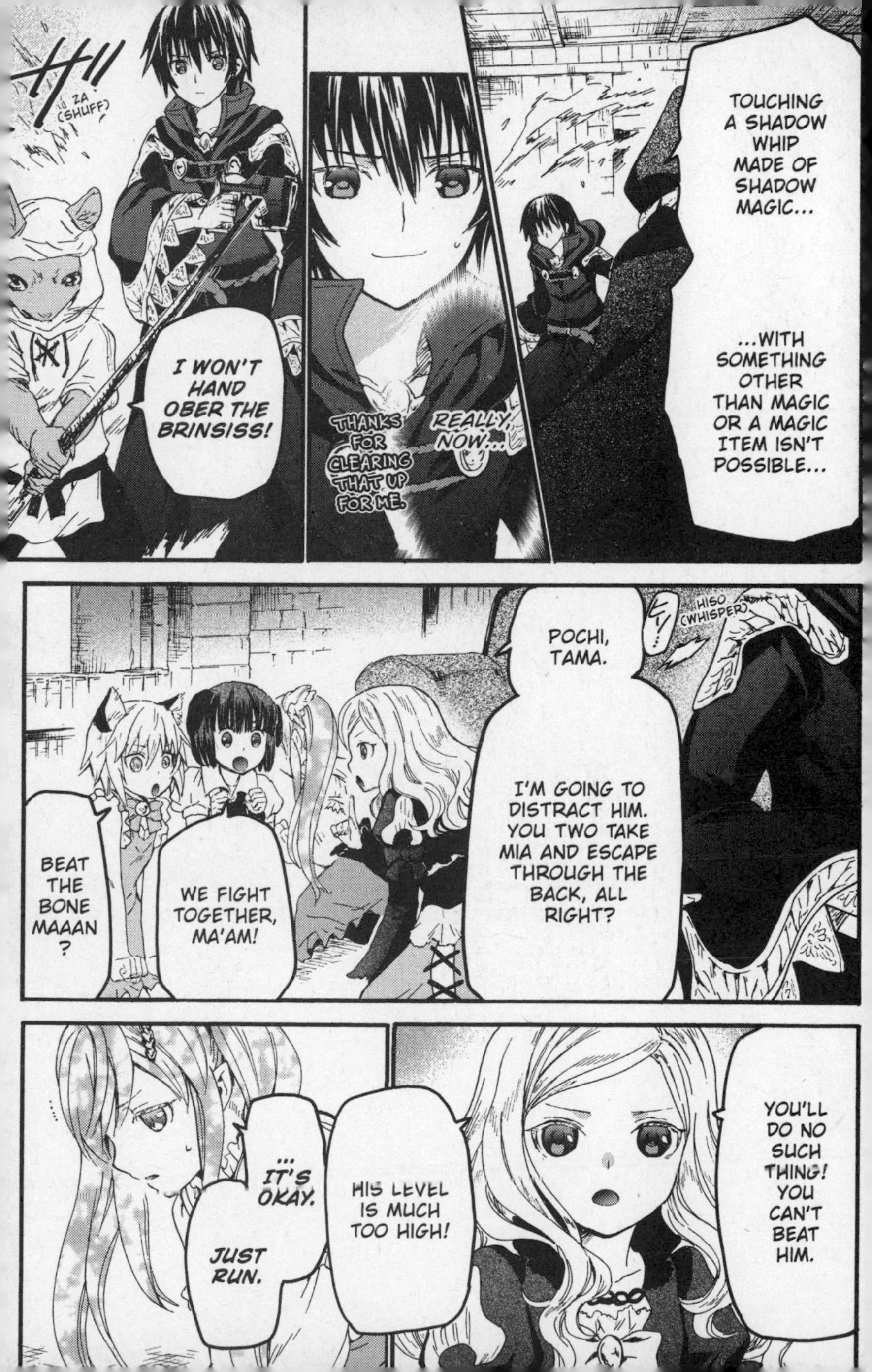
TOUCHING A SHADOW WHIP MADE OF SHADOW MAGIC...
...WITH SOMETHING OTHER THAN MAGIC OR A MAGIC ITEM ISN'T POSSIBLE...
REALLY, NOW...
THANKS FOR CLEARING THAT UP FOR ME.
ZA (SHUFF)
I WON'T HAND OBER THE BRINSISS!
HISO (WHISPER)
POCHI, TAMA.
I'M GOING TO DISTRACT HIM. YOU TWO TAKE MIA AND ESCAPE THROUGH THE BACK, ALL RIGHT?
WE FIGHT TOGETHER, MA'AM!
BEAT THE BONE MAAAN?
YOU'LL DO NO SUCH THING! YOU CAN'T BEAT HIM.
HIS LEVEL IS MUCH TOO HIGH!
... IT'S OKAY.
JUST RUN.
....

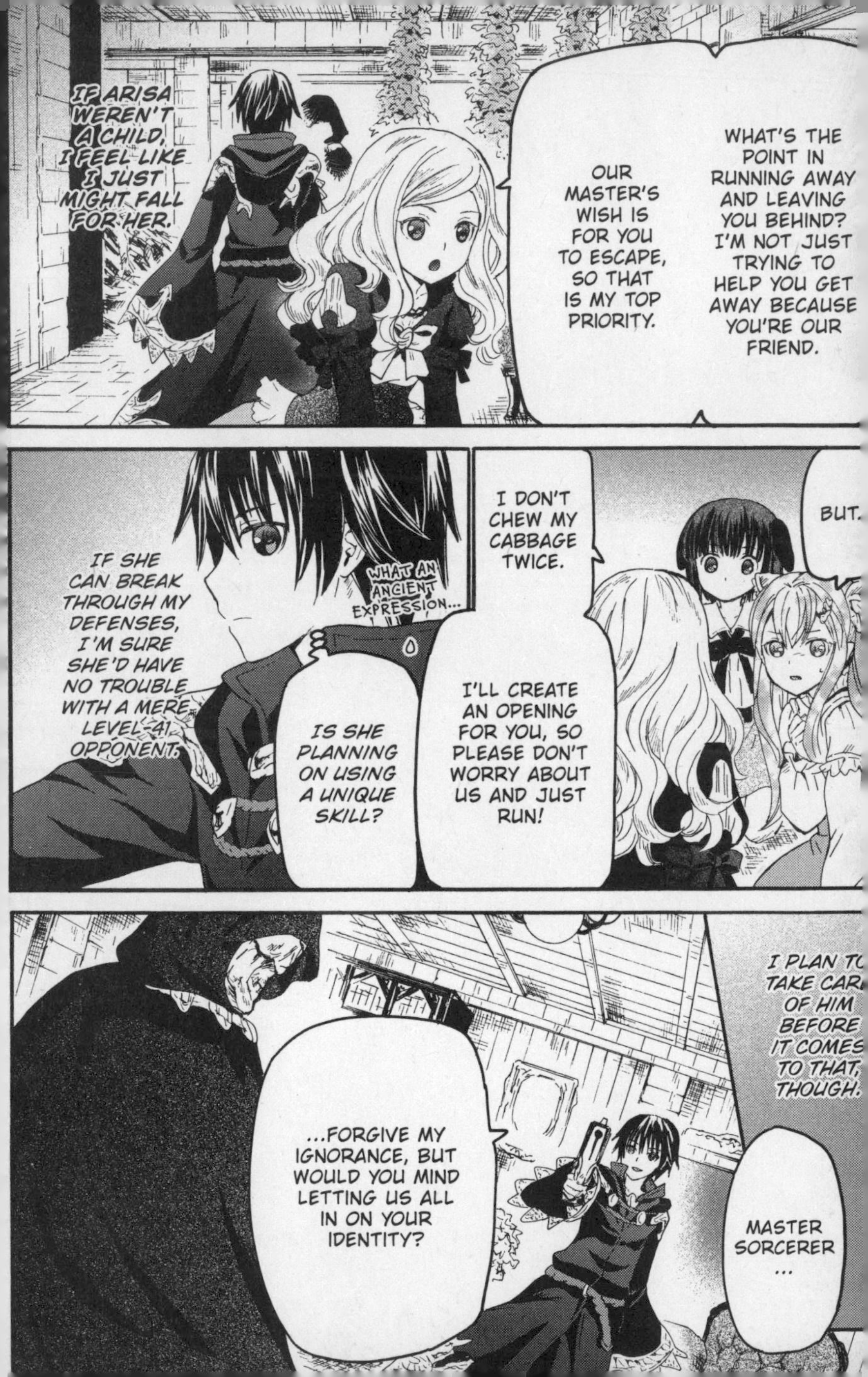
WHAT'S THE POINT IN RUNNING AWAY AND LEAVING YOU BEHIND? I'M NOT JUST TRYING TO HELP YOU GET AWAY BECAUSE YOU'RE OUR FRIEND.
OUR MASTER'S WISH IS FOR YOU TO ESCAPE, SO THAT IS MY TOP PRIORITY.
IF ARISA WEREN'T A CHILD, I FEEL LIKE I JUST MIGHT FALL FOR HER.
BUT.
I DON'T CHEW MY CABBAGE TWICE.
I'LL CREATE AN OPENING FOR YOU, SO PLEASE DON'T WORRY ABOUT US AND JUST RUN!
WHAT AN ANCIENT EXPRESSION...
IS SHE PLANNING ON USING A UNIQUE SKILL?
IF SHE CAN BREAK THROUGH MY DEFENSES, I'M SURE SHE'D HAVE NO TROUBLE WITH A MERE LEVEL-41 OPPONENT.
I PLAN TO TAKE CAR OF HIM BEFORE IT COMES TO THAT, THOUGH.
MASTER SORCERER ...
...FORGIVE MY IGNORANCE, BUT WOULD YOU MIND LETTING US ALL IN ON YOUR IDENTITY?

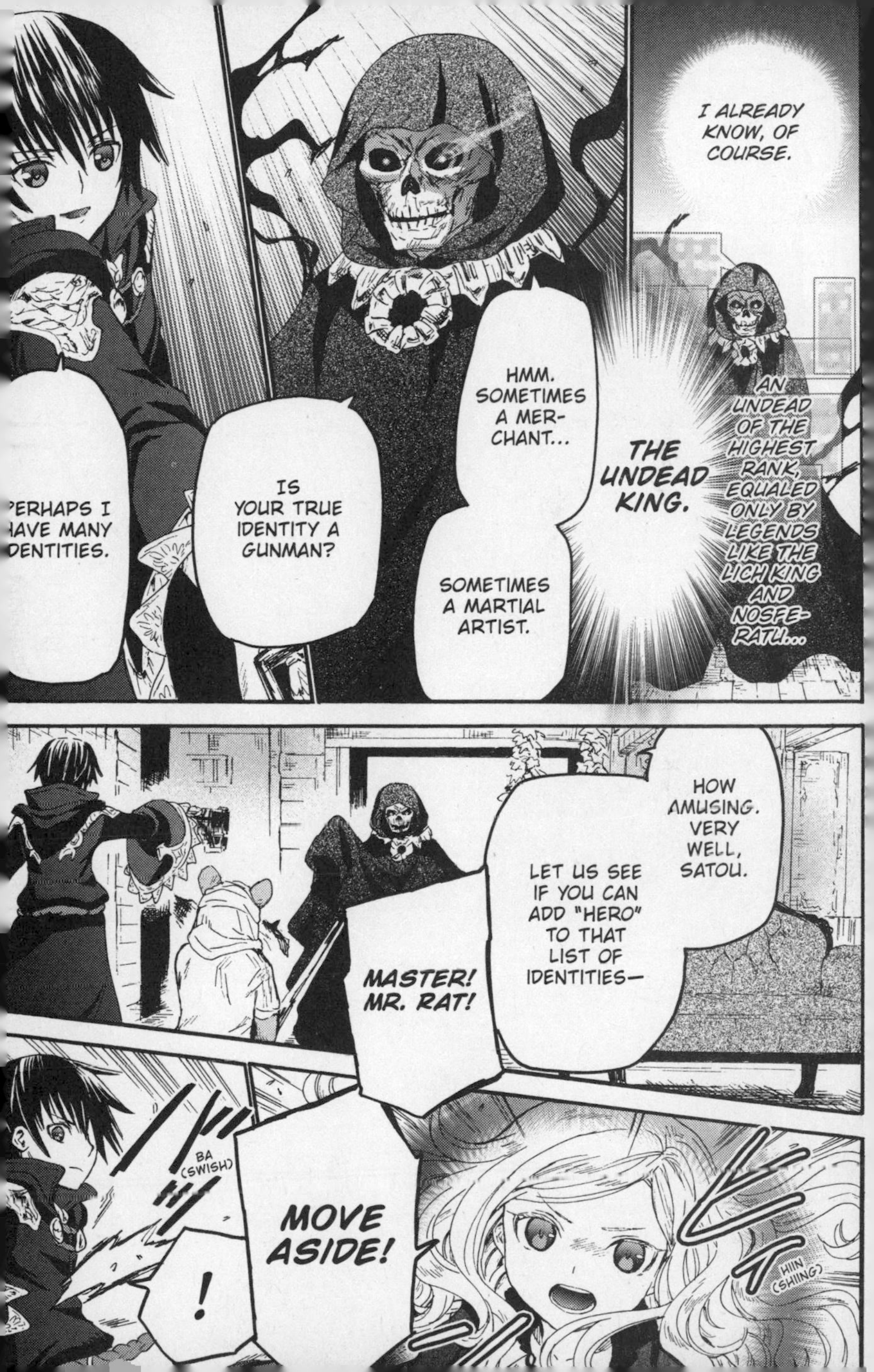
I ALREADY KNOW, OF COURSE.
AN UNDEAD OF THE HIGHEST RANK, EQUALED ONLY BY LEGENDS LIKE THE LICH KING AND NOSFE-RATU...
THE UNDEAD KING.
HMM. SOMETIMES A MER-CHANT...
SOMETIMES A MARTIAL ARTIST.
IS YOUR TRUE IDENTITY A GUNMAN?
PERHAPS I AVE MANY DENTITIES.
HOW AMUSING. VERY WELL, SATOU.
LET US SEE IF YOU CAN ADD "HERO" TO THAT LIST OF IDENTITIES—
MASTER! MR. RAT!
HIIN (SHIING)
MOVE ASIDE!
BA (SWISH)
!

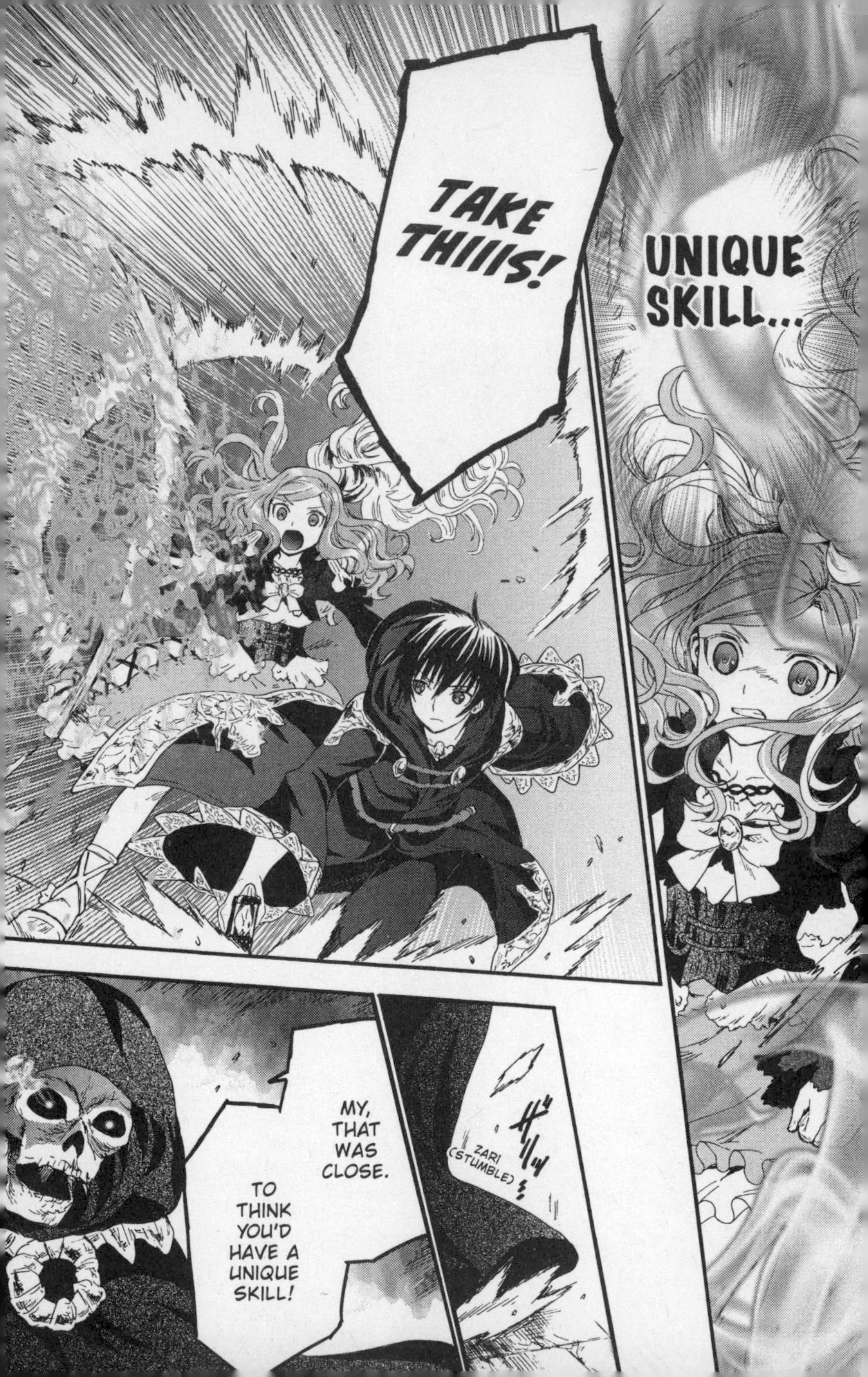
UNIQUE SKILL...
TAKE THIIIS!
ZARI (STUMBLE)
MY, THAT WAS CLOSE.
TO THINK YOU'D HAVE A UNIQUE SKILL!

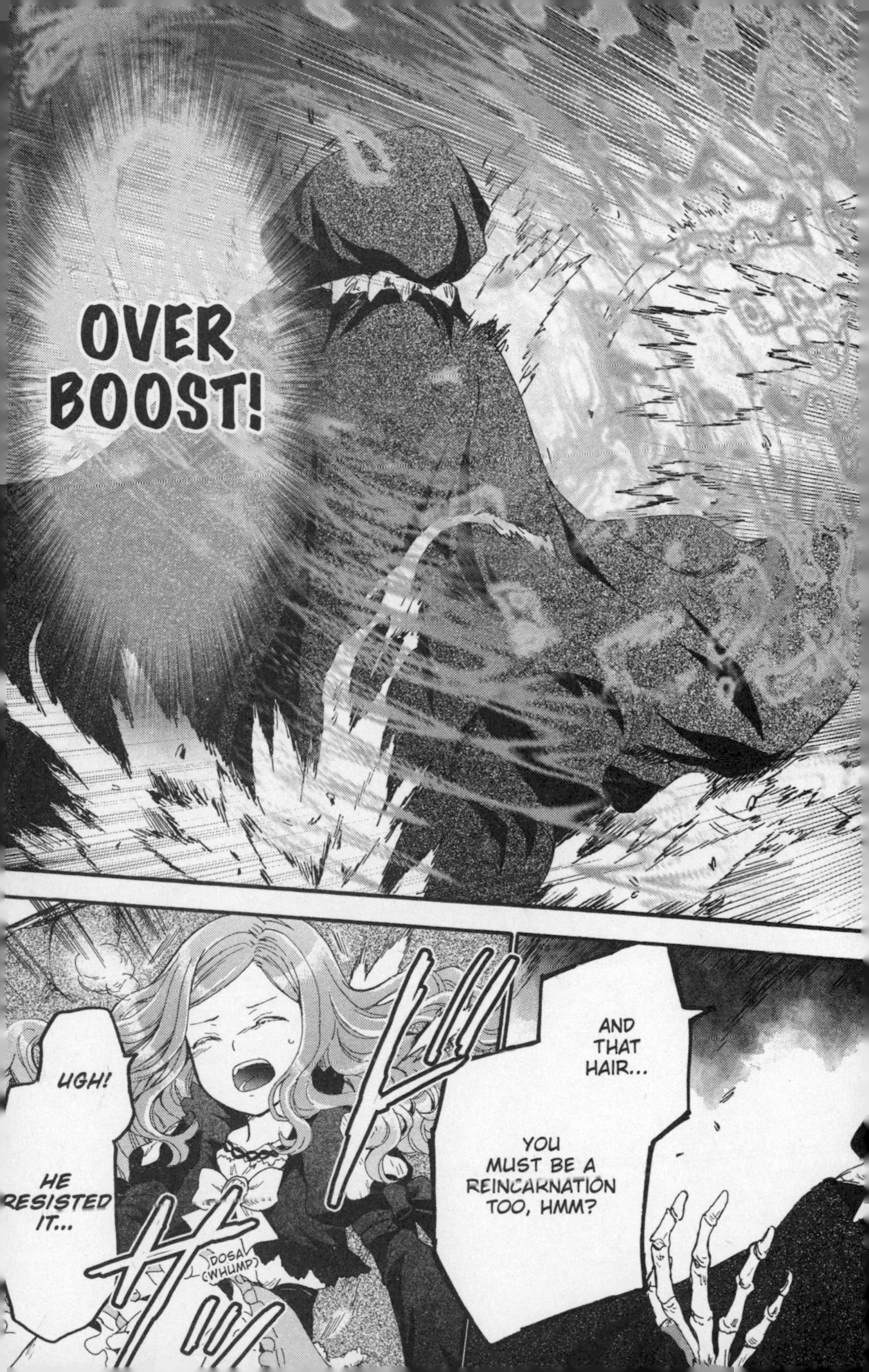
OVER BOOST!
AND THAT HAIR...
YOU MUST BE A REINCARNATION TOO, HMM?
UGH!
HE RESISTED IT...
DOSA (WHUMP)

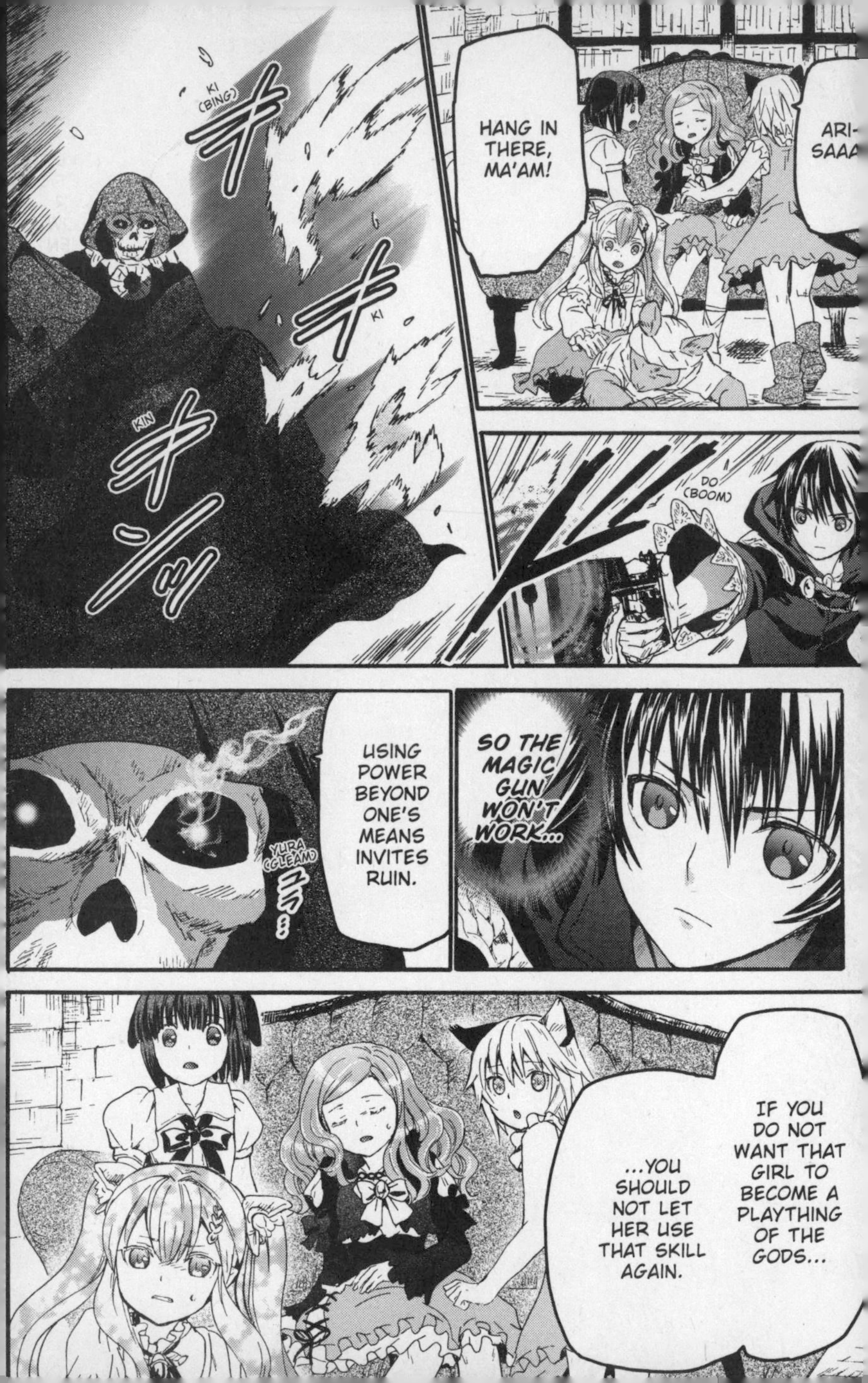
ARI-SAAA
HANG IN THERE, MA'AM!
DO (BOOM)
KI (BING)
KI
KIN
SO THE MAGIC GUN WON'T WORK...
USING POWER BEYOND ONE'S MEANS INVITES RUIN.
YURA (GLEAM)
IF YOU DO NOT WANT THAT GIRL TO BECOME A PLAYTHING OF THE GODS...
...YOU SHOULD NOT LET HER USE THAT SKILL AGAIN.

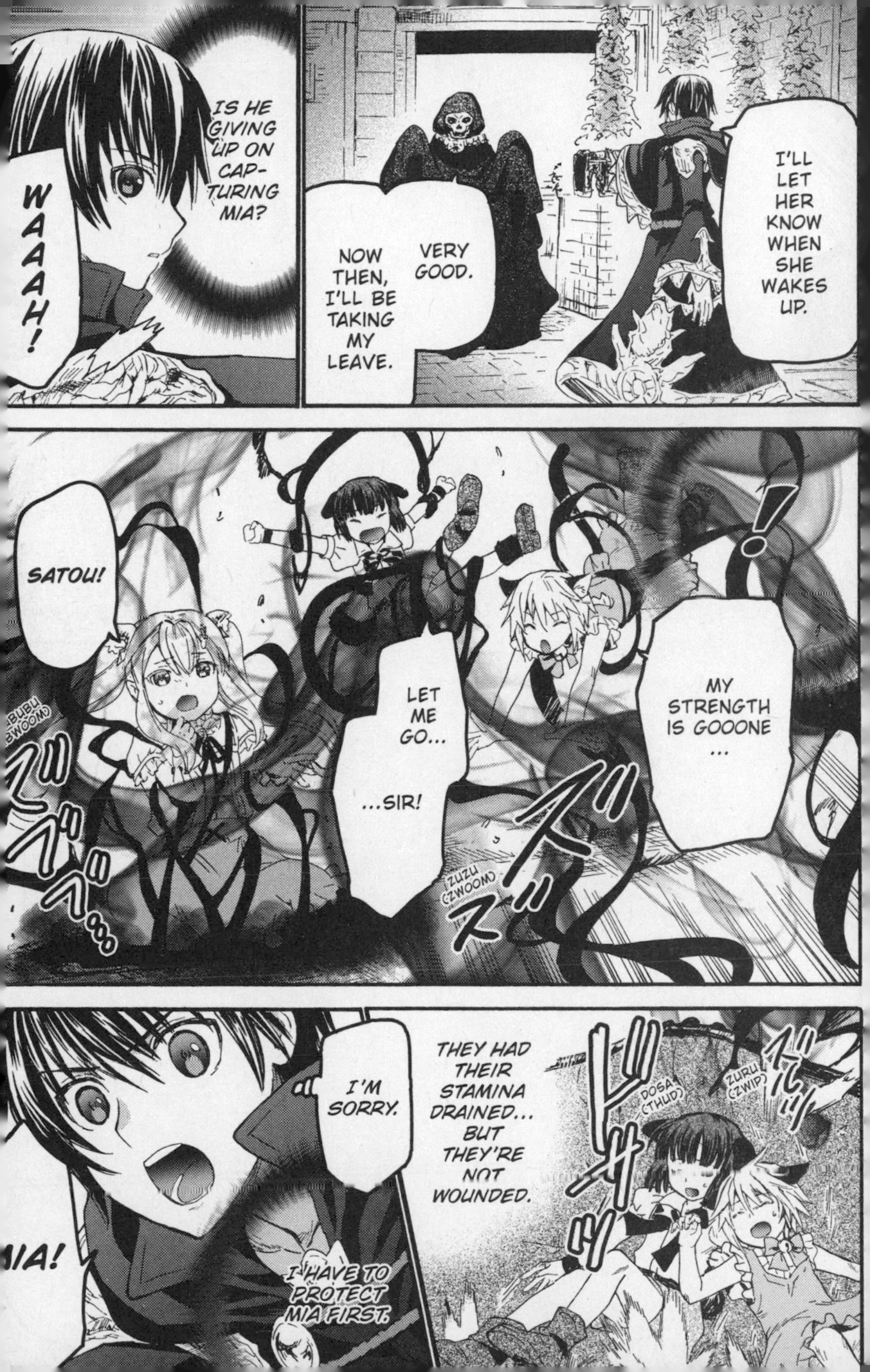
I'LL LET HER KNOW WHEN SHE WAKES UP.
VERY GOOD.
NOW THEN, I'LL BE TAKING MY LEAVE.
IS HE GIVING UP ON CAP-TURING MIA?
WAAAAH!
!
MY STRENGTH IS GOOONE ...
ZUZU (ZWOOM)
LET ME GO...
...SIR!
SATOU!
ZURU (ZWIP)
DOSA (THUD)
THEY HAD THEIR STAMINA DRAINED... BUT THEY'RE NOT WOUNDED.
I'M SORRY.
I HAVE TO PROTECT MIA FIRST.

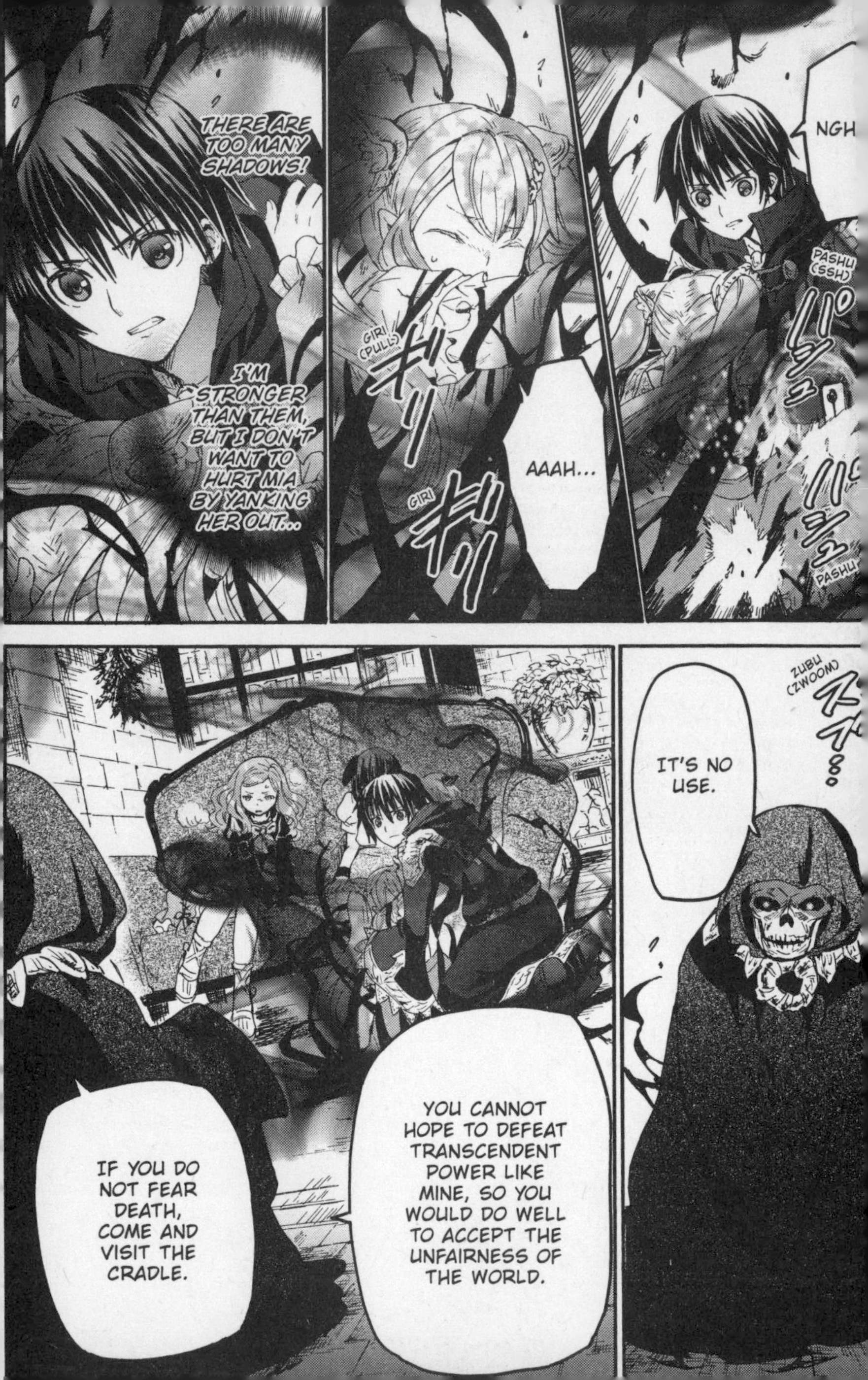
NGH
PASHU (SSH)
PASHU
GIRI (PULL)
GIRI
AAAH...
THERE ARE TOO MANY SHADOWS!
I'M STRONGER THAN THEM, BUT I DON'T WANT TO HURT MIA BY YANKING HER OUT...
ZUBU (ZWOOM)
IT'S NO USE.
YOU CANNOT HOPE TO DEFEAT TRANSCENDENT POWER LIKE MINE, SO YOU WOULD DO WELL TO ACCEPT THE UNFAIRNESS OF THE WORLD.
IF YOU DO NOT FEAR DEATH, COME AND VISIT THE CRADLE.

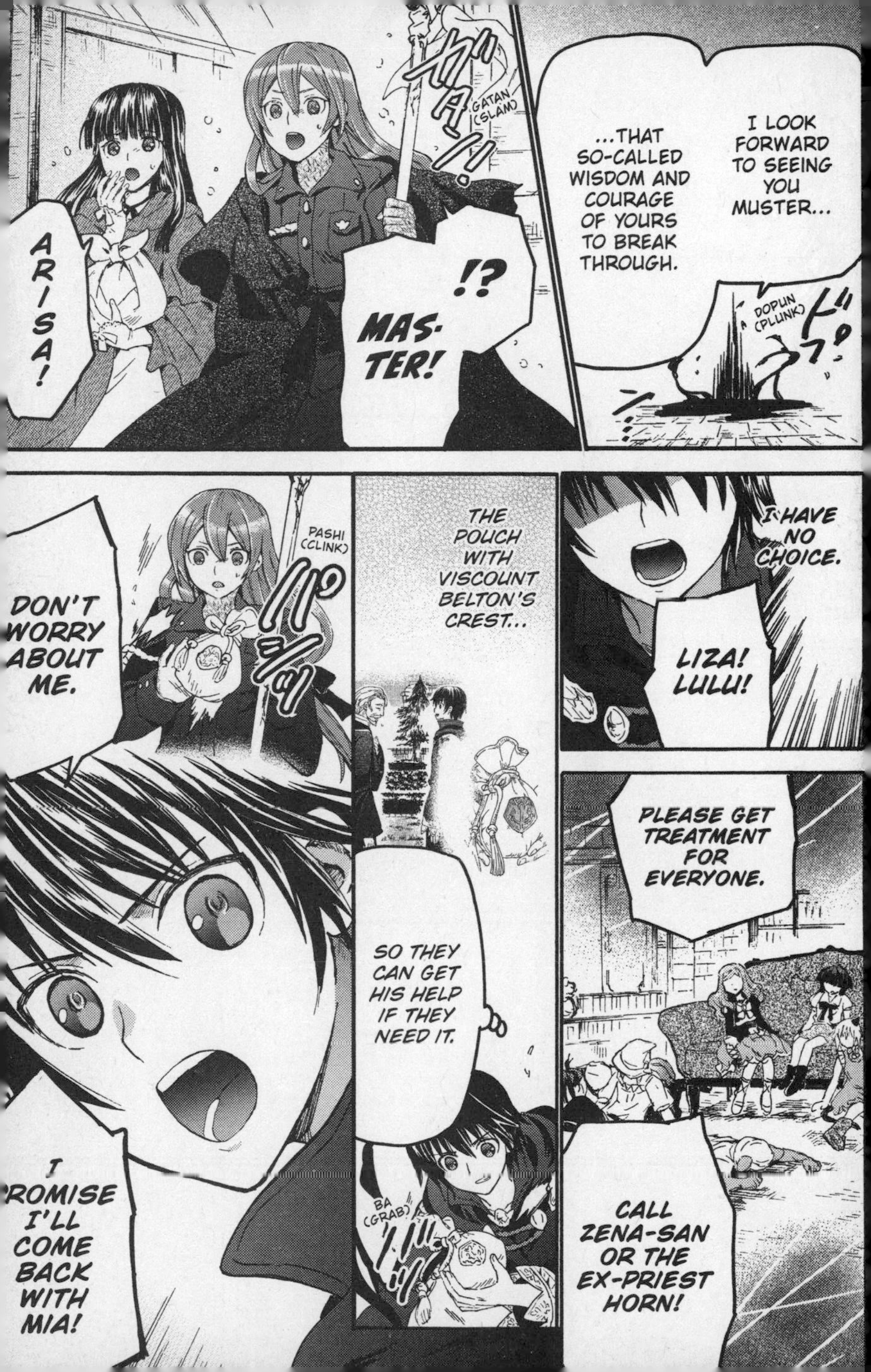
I LOOK FORWARD TO SEEING YOU MUSTER...
...THAT SO-CALLED WISDOM AND COURAGE OF YOURS TO BREAK THROUGH.
DOPUN (PLUNK)
GATAN (SLAM)
!?
MAS-TER!
ARISA!
I HAVE NO CHOICE.
LIZA! LULU!
PLEASE GET TREATMENT FOR EVERYONE.
CALL ZENA-SAN OR THE EX-PRIEST HORN!
THE POUCH WITH VISCOUNT BELTON'S CREST...
SO THEY CAN GET HIS HELP IF THEY NEED IT.
BA (GRAB)
PASHI (CLINK)
DON'T WORRY ABOUT ME.
I PROMISE I'LL COME BACK WITH MIA!

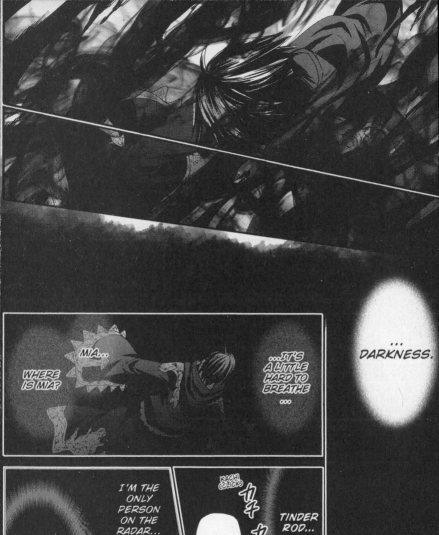

...DARKNESS.
NO LIGHT OR SOUND... I CAN'T EVEN SEE MY OWN BODY.
...IT'S A LITTLE HARD TO BREATHE...
MIA...
WHERE IS MIA?
TINDER ROD...
KACHI (CLICK)
カチ
カチ
KACHI
IT'S NOT WORKING.
I'M THE ONLY PERSON ON THE RADAR...
I'LL USE "SEARCH ENTIRE MAP."
N
W

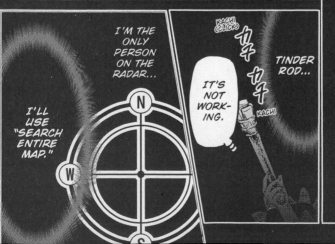

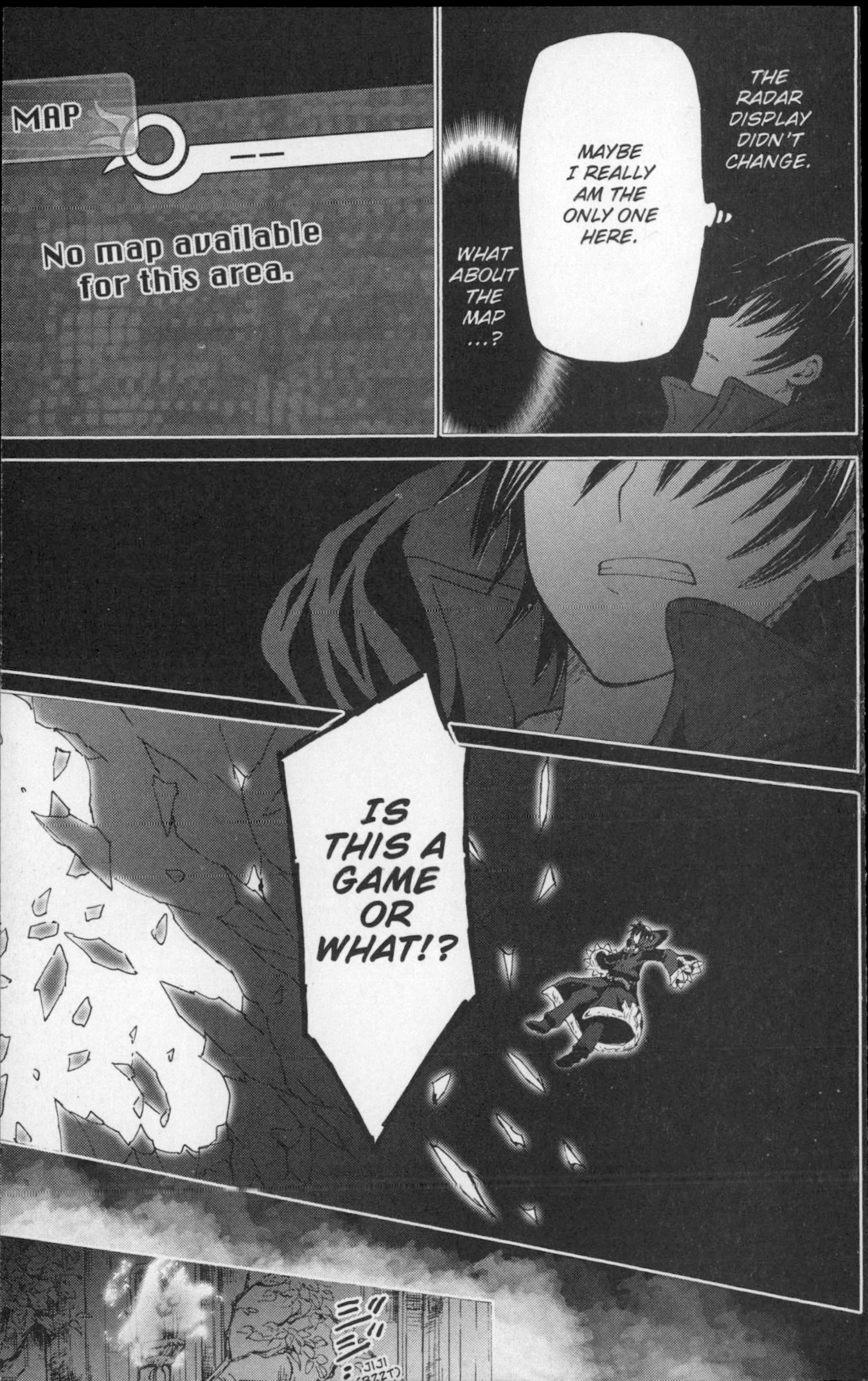
THE RADAR DISPLAY DIDN'T CHANGE.
MAYBE I REALLY AM THE ONLY ONE HERE.
WHAT ABOUT THE MAP ...?
MAP
No map available for this area.
IS THIS A GAME OR WHAT!?
JIJI (BZZT)

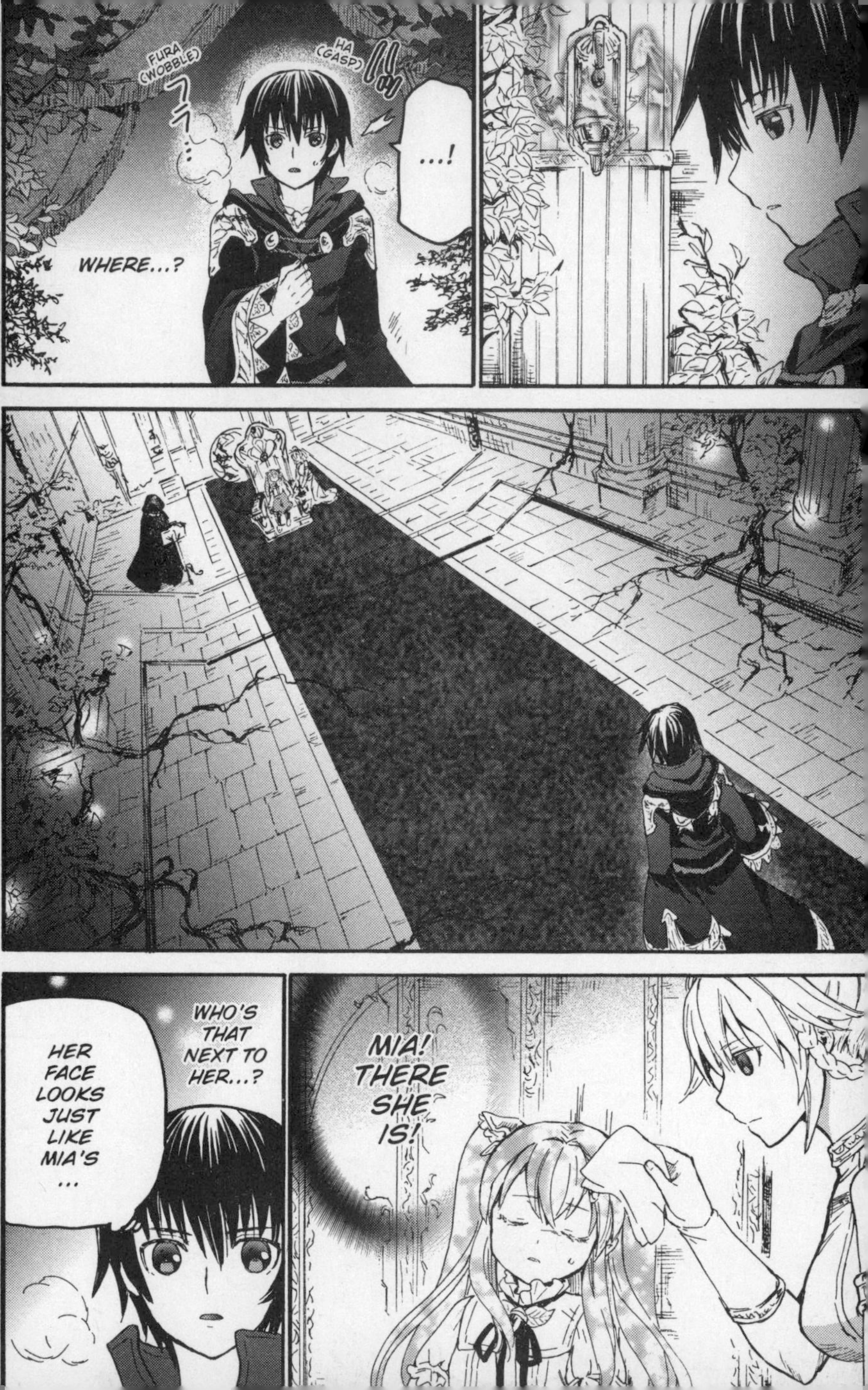
HA (GASP)
...!
FURA (WOBBLE)
WHERE...?
MIA! THERE SHE IS!
WHO'S THAT NEXT TO HER...?
HER FACE LOOKS JUST LIKE MIA'S ...

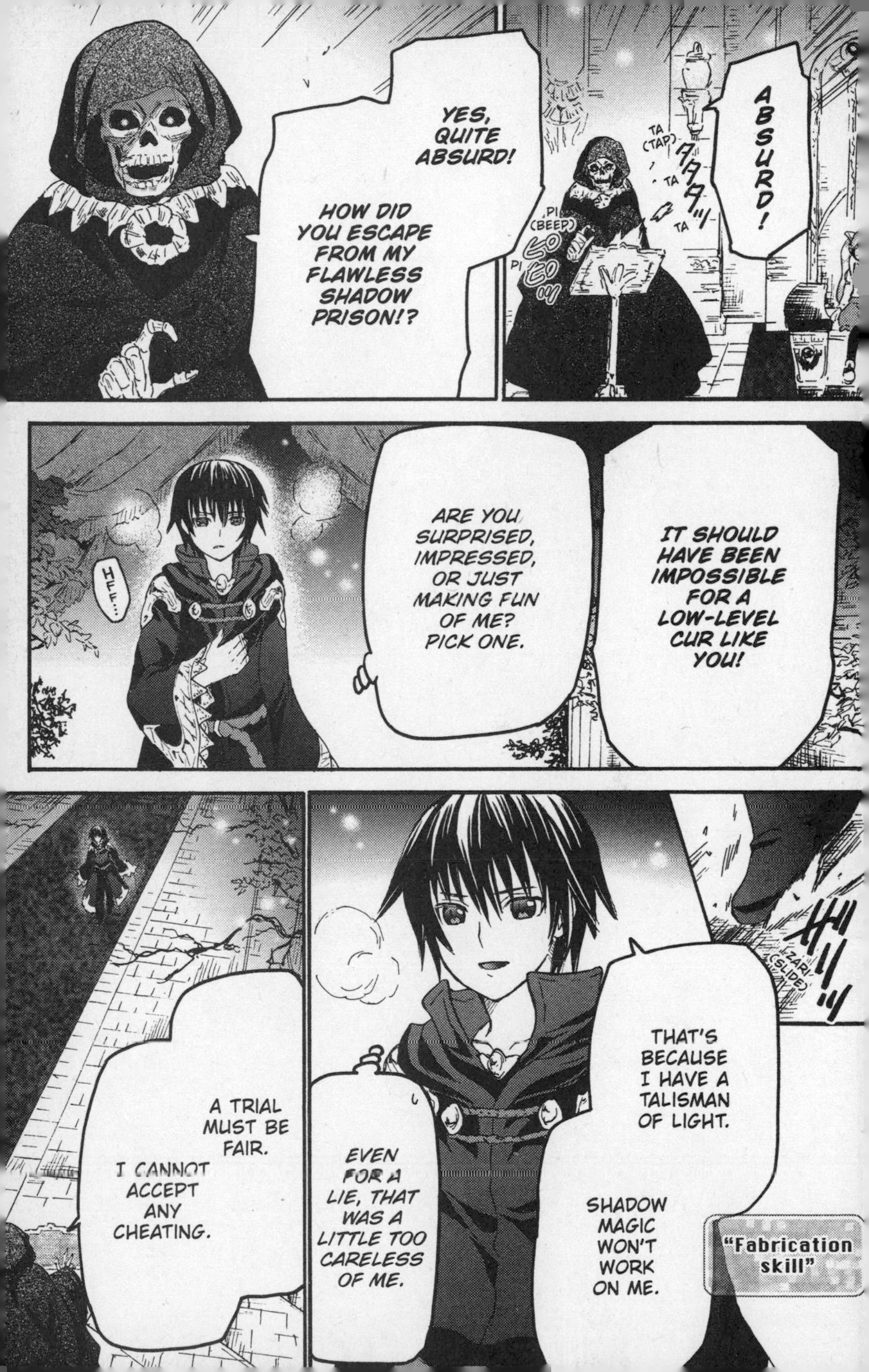
ABSURD!
TA (TAP) TA TA
PI (BEEP) PI
YES, QUITE ABSURD!
HOW DID YOU ESCAPE FROM MY FLAWLESS SHADOW PRISON!?
IT SHOULD HAVE BEEN IMPOSSIBLE FOR A LOW-LEVEL CUR LIKE YOU!
ARE YOU SURPRISED, IMPRESSED, OR JUST MAKING FUN OF ME? PICK ONE.
HFF...
ZARI (SLIDE)
THAT'S BECAUSE I HAVE A TALISMAN OF LIGHT.
SHADOW MAGIC WON'T WORK ON ME.
“Fabrication skill”
EVEN FOR A LIE, THAT WAS A LITTLE TOO CARELESS OF ME.
A TRIAL MUST BE FAIR.
I CANNOT ACCEPT ANY CHEATING.

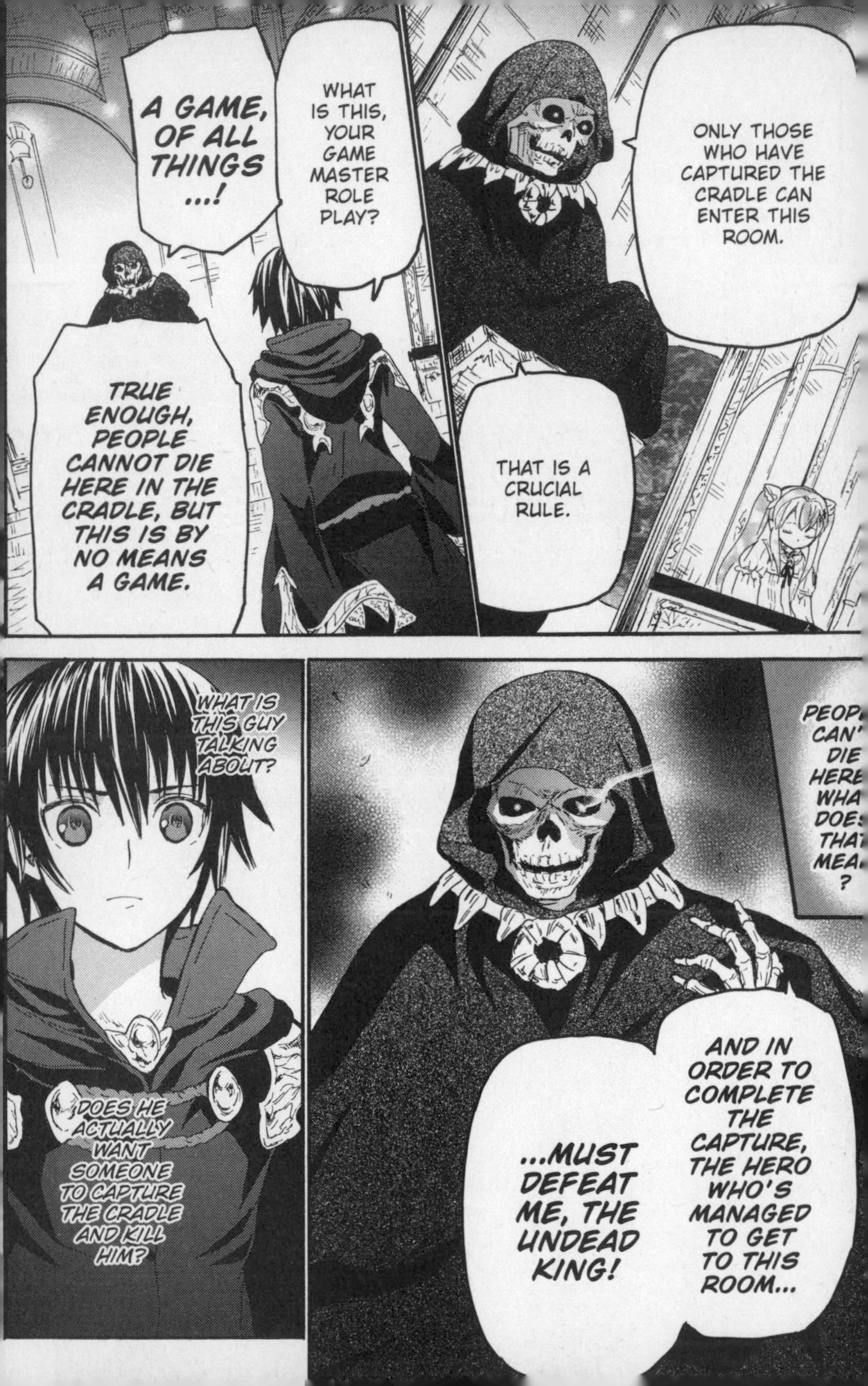
ONLY THOSE WHO HAVE CAPTURED THE CRADLE CAN ENTER THIS ROOM.
THAT IS A CRUCIAL RULE.
WHAT IS THIS, YOUR GAME MASTER ROLE PLAY?
A GAME, OF ALL THINGS ...!
TRUE ENOUGH, PEOPLE CANNOT DIE HERE IN THE CRADLE, BUT THIS IS BY NO MEANS A GAME.
AND IN ORDER TO COMPLETE THE CAPTURE, THE HERO WHO'S MANAGED TO GET TO THIS ROOM...
...MUST DEFEAT ME, THE UNDEAD KING!
WHAT IS THIS GUY TALKING ABOUT?
DOES HE ACTUALLY WANT SOMEONE TO CAPTURE THE CRADLE AND KILL HIM?

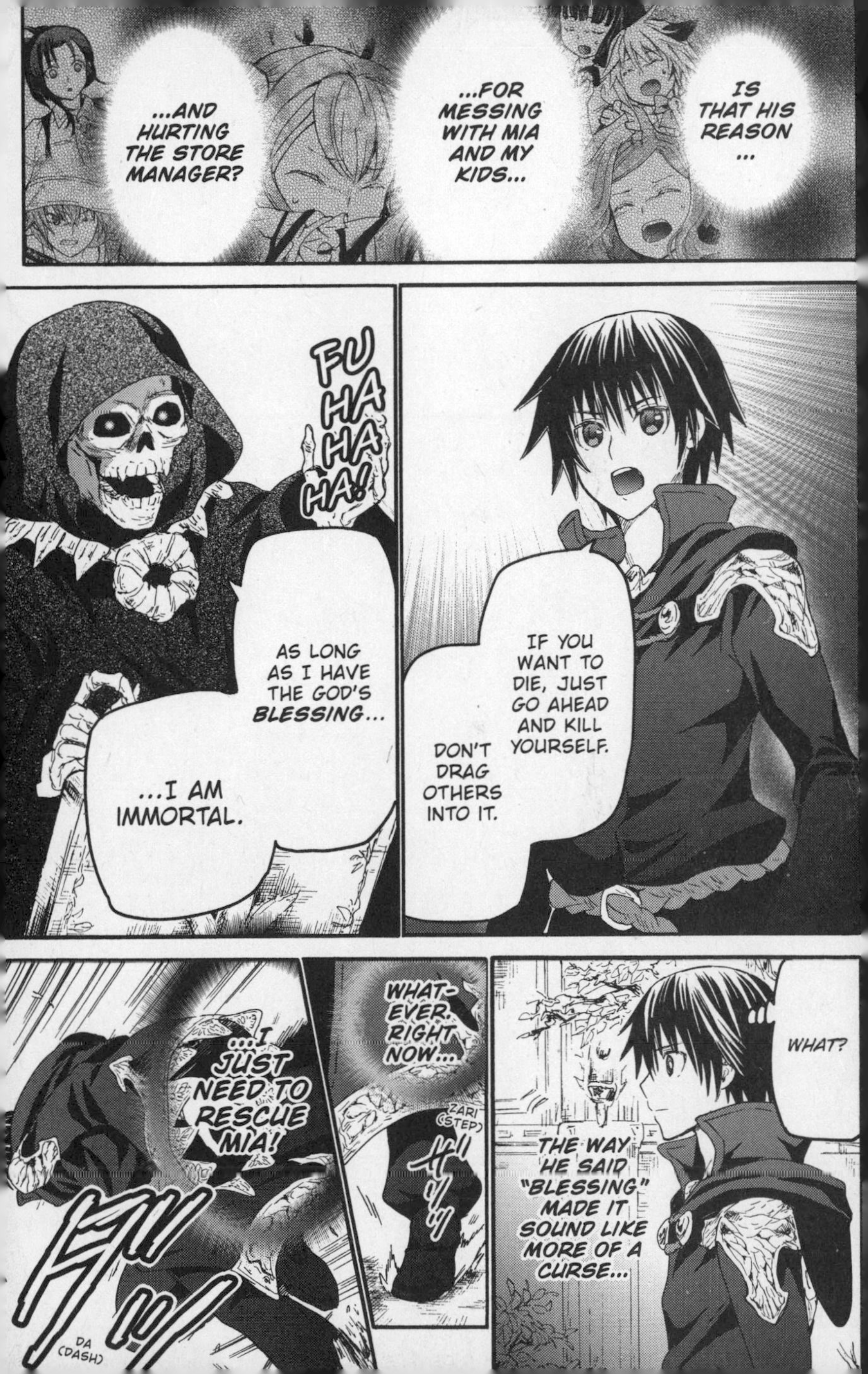
IS THAT HIS REASON ...
...FOR MESSING WITH MIA AND MY KIDS...
...AND HURTING THE STORE MANAGER?
IF YOU WANT TO DIE, JUST GO AHEAD AND KILL YOURSELF.
DON'T DRAG OTHERS INTO IT.
FU HA HA HA HA!
AS LONG AS I HAVE THE GOD'S BLESSING...
...I AM IMMORTAL.
WHAT?
THE WAY HE SAID "BLESSING" MADE IT SOUND LIKE MORE OF A CURSE...
WHAT-EVER. RIGHT NOW...
ZARI (STEP)
...I JUST NEED TO RESCUE MIA!
DA (DASH)

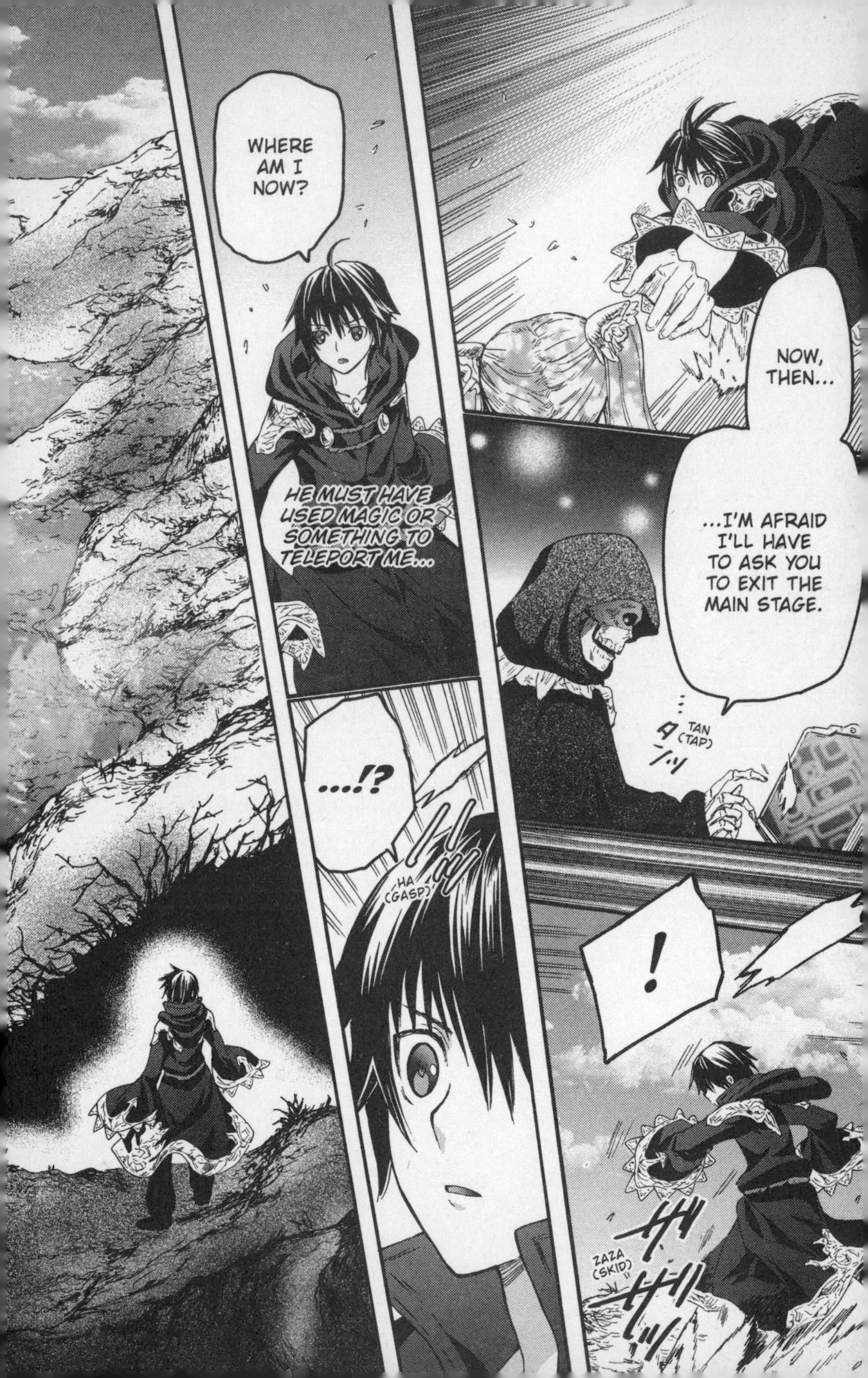
NOW, THEN...
...I'M AFRAID I'LL HAVE TO ASK YOU TO EXIT THE MAIN STAGE.
TAN (TAP)
!
ZAZA (SKID)
WHERE AM I NOW?
HE MUST HAVE USED MAGIC OR SOMETHING TO TELEPORT ME...
...!?
HA (GASP)

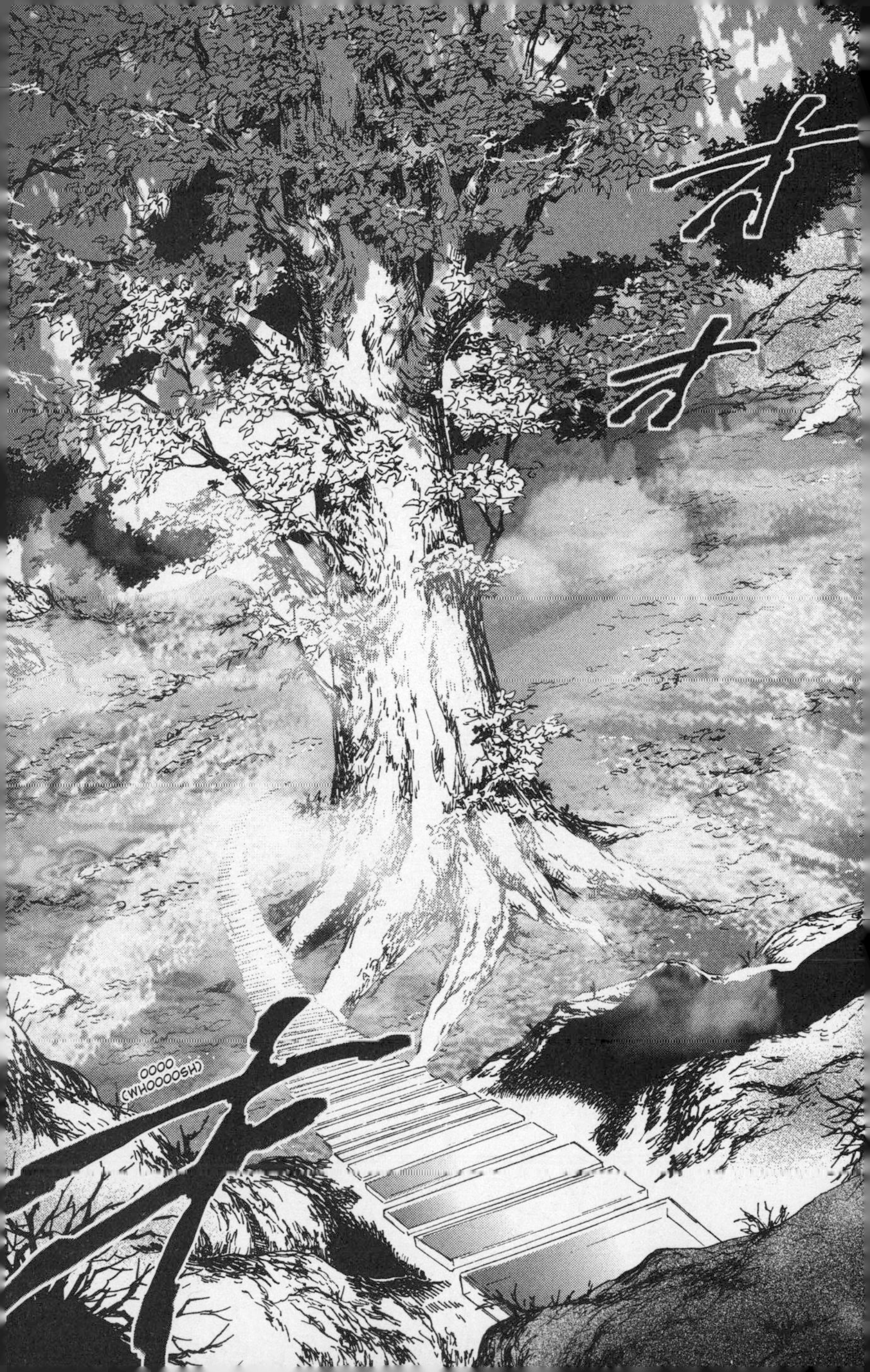
オオオ
OOOO
(WHOOOOSH)

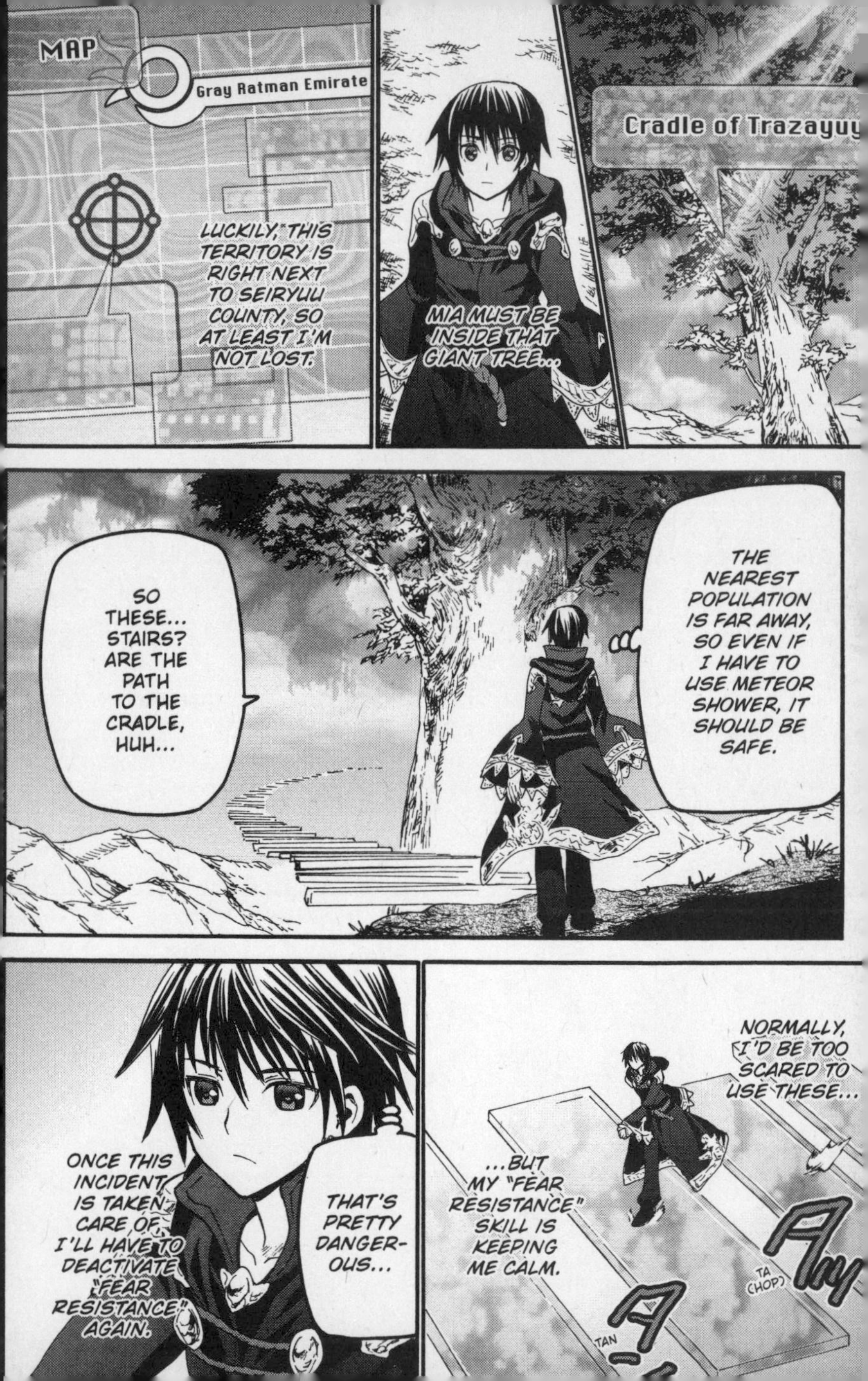
Cradle of Trazayuy
MIA MUST BE INSIDE THAT GIANT TREE...
MAP
Gray Ratman Emirate
LUCKILY, THIS TERRITORY IS RIGHT NEXT TO SEIRYUU COUNTY, SO AT LEAST I'M NOT LOST.
THE NEAREST POPULATION IS FAR AWAY, SO EVEN IF I HAVE TO USE METEOR SHOWER, IT SHOULD BE SAFE.
SO THESE... STAIRS? ARE THE PATH TO THE CRADLE, HUH...
NORMALLY, I'D BE TOO SCARED TO USE THESE...
...BUT MY "FEAR RESISTANCE" SKILL IS KEEPING ME CALM.
TA (HOP)
TAN
THAT'S PRETTY DANGER-OUS...
ONCE THIS INCIDENT IS TAKEN CARE OF, I'LL HAVE TO DEACTIVATE "FEAR RESISTANCE" AGAIN.

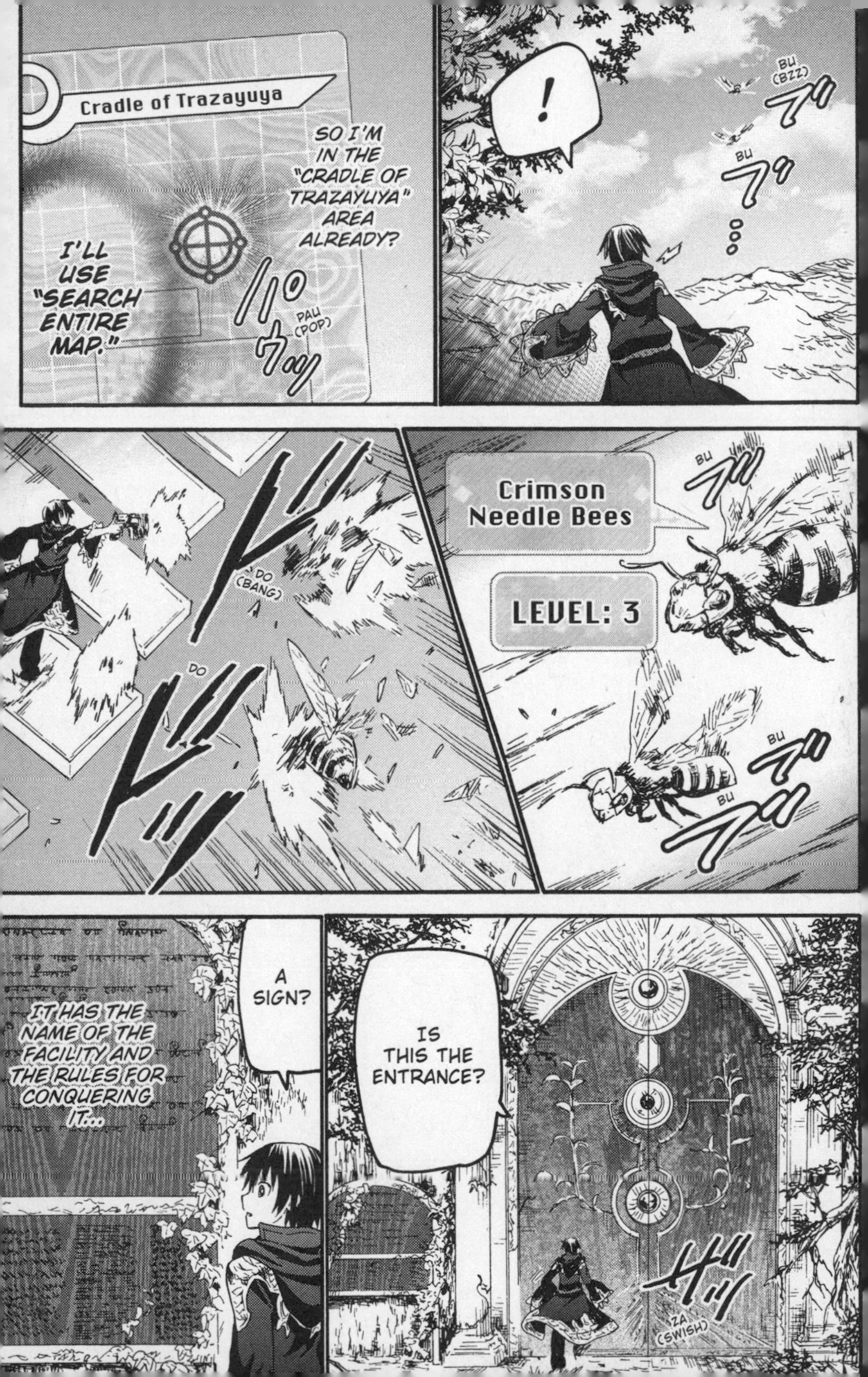
!
BU (BZZ)
BU
SO I'M IN THE "CRADLE OF TRAZAYUYA" AREA ALREADY?
Cradle of Trazayuya
PAU (POP)
I'LL USE "SEARCH ENTIRE MAP."
BU
Crimson Needle Bees
LEVEL: 3
BU
BU
DO (BANG)
DO
IS THIS THE ENTRANCE?
ZA (SWISH)
A SIGN?
IT HAS THE NAME OF THE FACILITY AND THE RULES FOR CONQUERING IT...

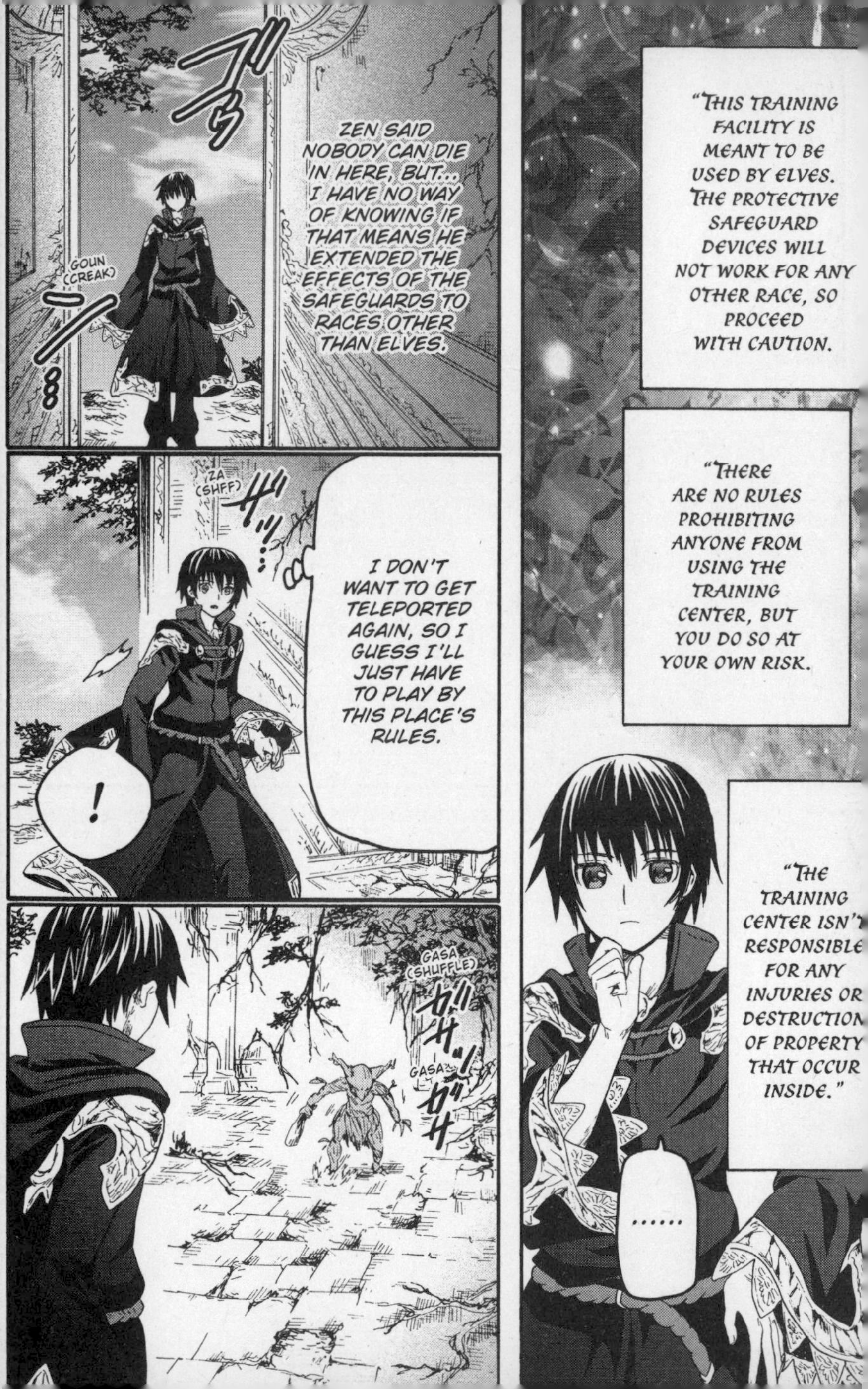
"THIS TRAINING FACILITY IS MEANT TO BE USED BY ELVES. THE PROTECTIVE SAFEGUARD DEVICES WILL NOT WORK FOR ANY OTHER RACE, SO PROCEED WITH CAUTION.
"THERE ARE NO RULES PROHIBITING ANYONE FROM USING THE TRAINING CENTER, BUT YOU DO SO AT YOUR OWN RISK.
"THE TRAINING CENTER ISN'T RESPONSIBLE FOR ANY INJURIES OR DESTRUCTION OF PROPERTY THAT OCCUR INSIDE."
......
ZEN SAID NOBODY CAN DIE IN HERE, BUT... I HAVE NO WAY OF KNOWING IF THAT MEANS HE EXTENDED THE EFFECTS OF THE SAFEGUARDS TO RACES OTHER THAN ELVES.
GOUN (CREAK)
I DON'T WANT TO GET TELEPORTED AGAIN, SO I GUESS I'LL JUST HAVE TO PLAY BY THIS PLACE'S RULES.
ZA (SHFF)
!
GASA (SHUFFLE)
GASA

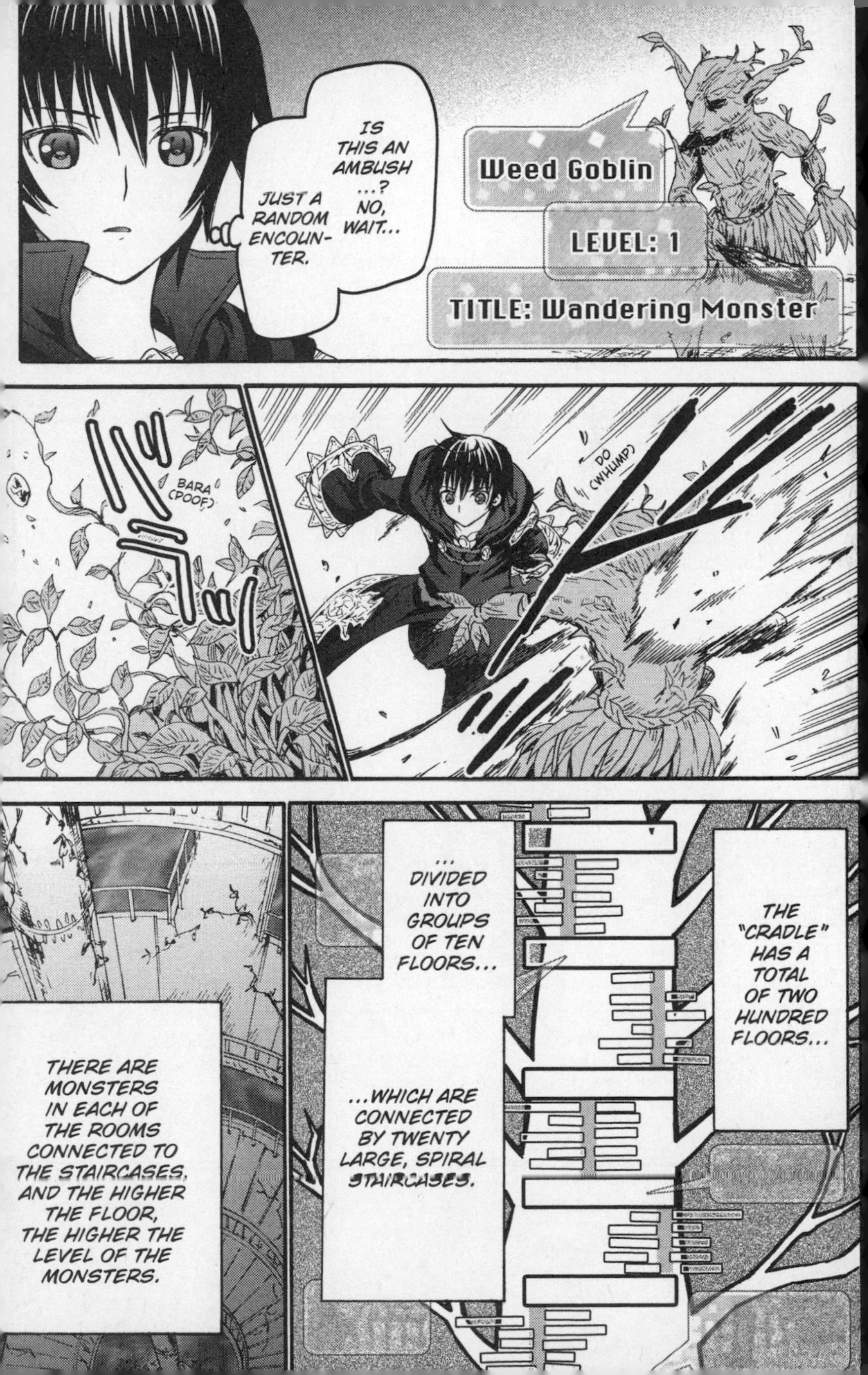
Weed Goblin
LEVEL: 1
TITLE: Wandering Monster
IS THIS AN AMBUSH...? NO, WAIT...
JUST A RANDOM ENCOUN-TER.
DO (WHUMP)
BARA (POOF)
THE "CRADLE" HAS A TOTAL OF TWO HUNDRED FLOORS...
...DIVIDED INTO GROUPS OF TEN FLOORS...
...WHICH ARE CONNECTED BY TWENTY LARGE, SPIRAL STAIRCASES.
THERE ARE MONSTERS IN EACH OF THE ROOMS CONNECTED TO THE STAIRCASES, AND THE HIGHER THE FLOOR, THE HIGHER THE LEVEL OF THE MONSTERS.

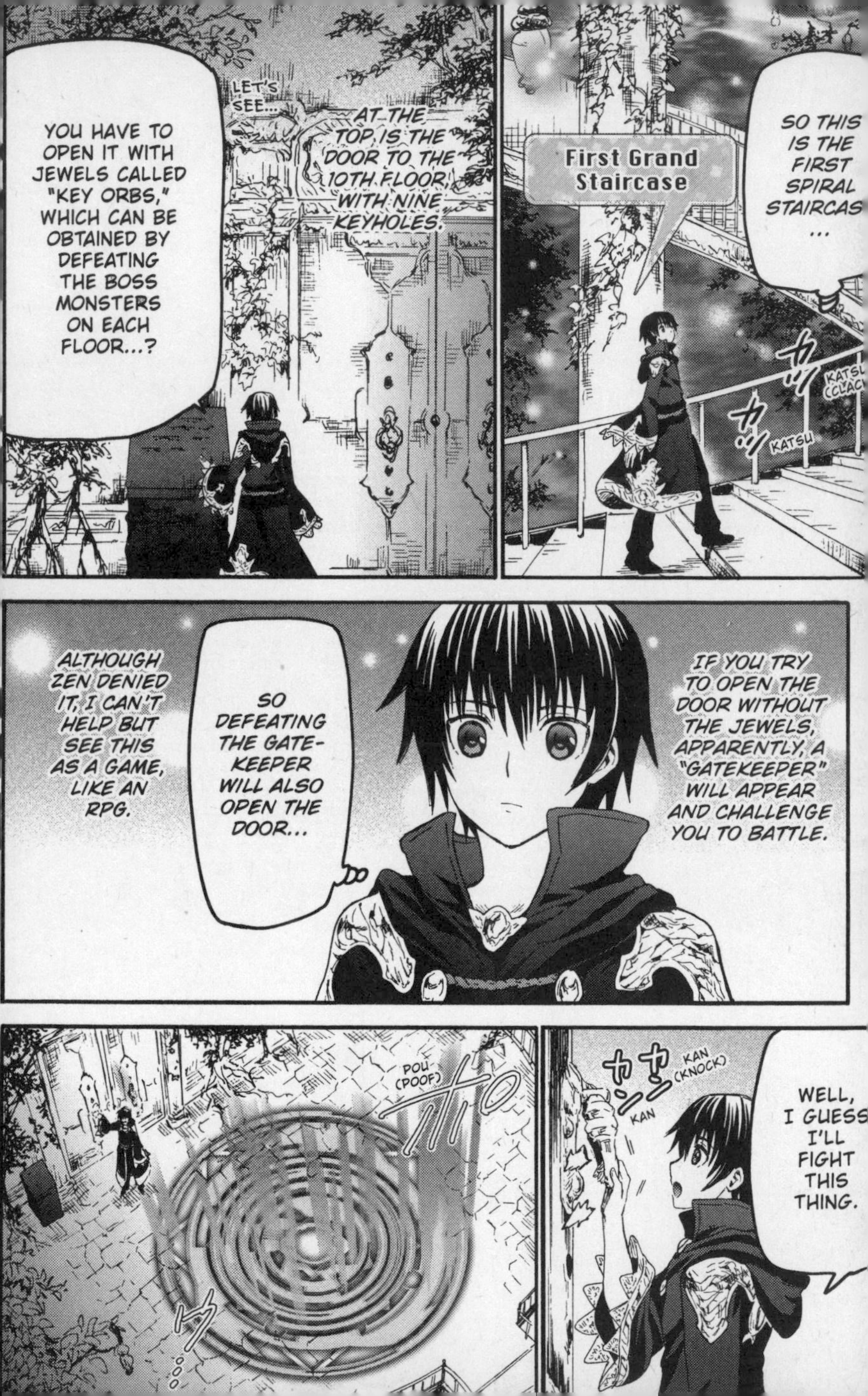
First Grand Staircase
SO THIS IS THE FIRST SPIRAL STAIRCAS...
KATSU (CLAC
KATSU
LET'S SEE...
AT THE TOP IS THE DOOR TO THE 10TH FLOOR, WITH NINE KEYHOLES.
YOU HAVE TO OPEN IT WITH JEWELS CALLED "KEY ORBS," WHICH CAN BE OBTAINED BY DEFEATING THE BOSS MONSTERS ON EACH FLOOR...?
IF YOU TRY TO OPEN THE DOOR WITHOUT THE JEWELS, APPARENTLY, A "GATEKEEPER" WILL APPEAR AND CHALLENGE YOU TO BATTLE.
SO DEFEATING THE GATE-KEEPER WILL ALSO OPEN THE DOOR...
ALTHOUGH ZEN DENIED IT, I CAN'T HELP BUT SEE THIS AS A GAME, LIKE AN RPG.
WELL, I GUESS I'LL FIGHT THIS THING.
KAN (KNOCK)
KAN
POU (POOF)

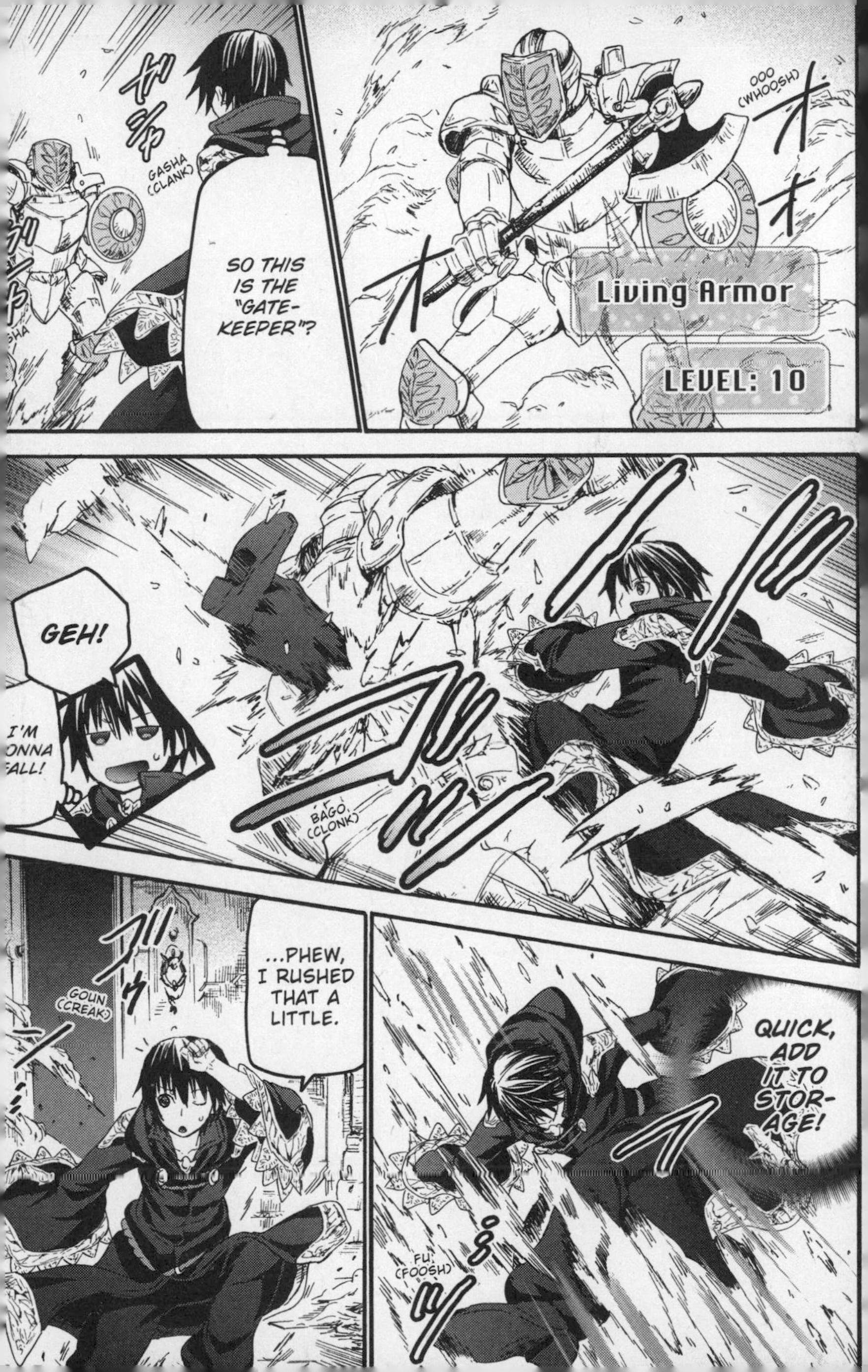

OOO (WHOOSH)
Living Armor
LEVEL: 10
GASHA (CLANK)
SO THIS IS THE "GATE-KEEPER"?
SHA
GEH!
I'M ONNA FALL!
BAGO (CLONK)
QUICK, ADD IT TO STORAGE!
FU (FOOSH)
GOUN (CREAK)
...PHEW, I RUSHED THAT A LITTLE.

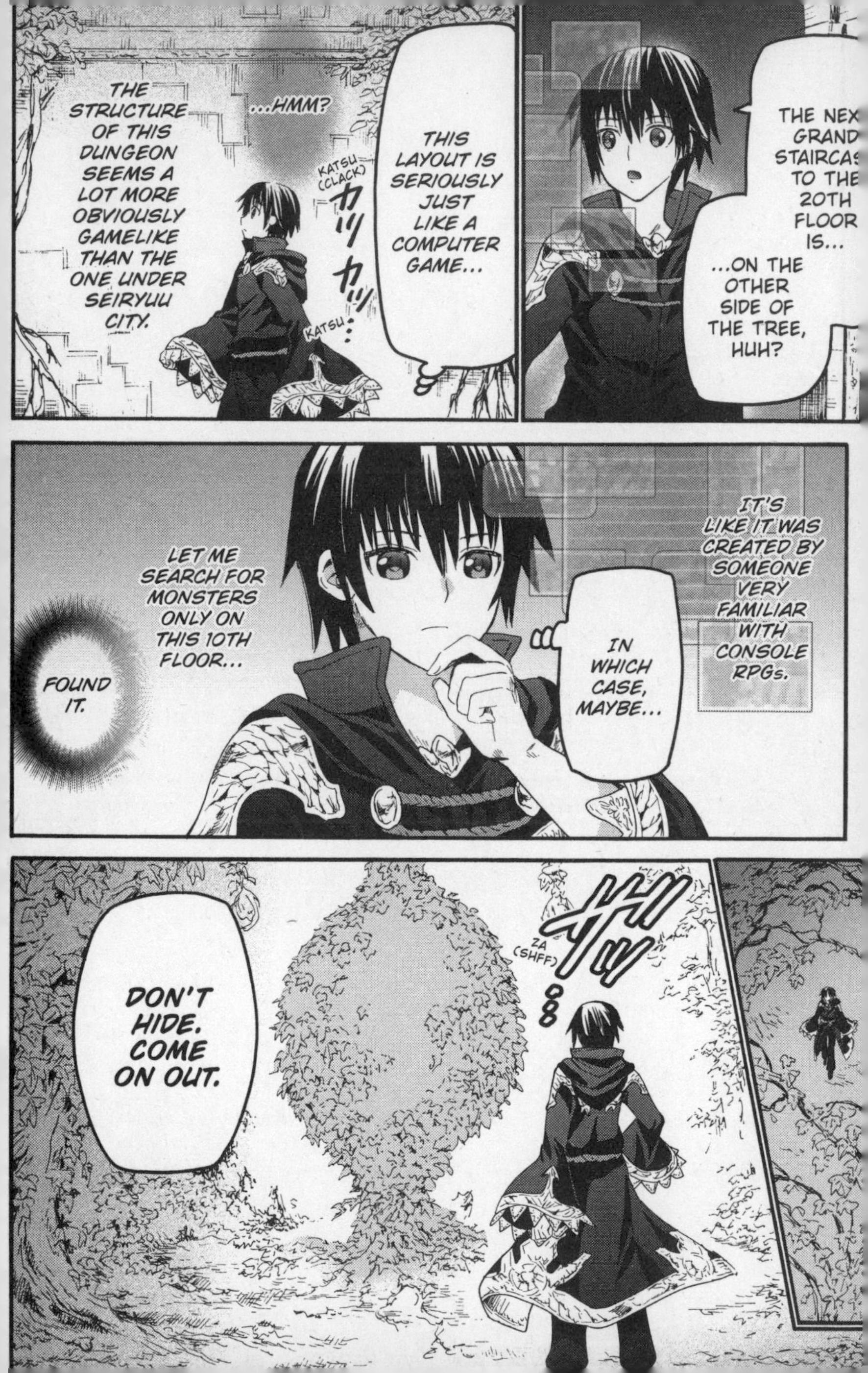
THE NEX GRAND STAIRCAS TO THE 20TH FLOOR IS...
...ON THE OTHER SIDE OF THE TREE, HUH?
THIS LAYOUT IS SERIOUSLY JUST LIKE A COMPUTER GAME...
KATSU (CLACK)
カッ
カッ
KATSU
...HMM?
THE STRUCTURE OF THIS DUNGEON SEEMS A LOT MORE OBVIOUSLY GAMELIKE THAN THE ONE UNDER SEIRYUU CITY.
IT'S LIKE IT WAS CREATED BY SOMEONE VERY FAMILIAR WITH CONSOLE RPGs.
IN WHICH CASE, MAYBE...
LET ME SEARCH FOR MONSTERS ONLY ON THIS 10TH FLOOR...
FOUND IT.
ザッ
ZA (SHFF)
DON'T HIDE. COME ON OUT.

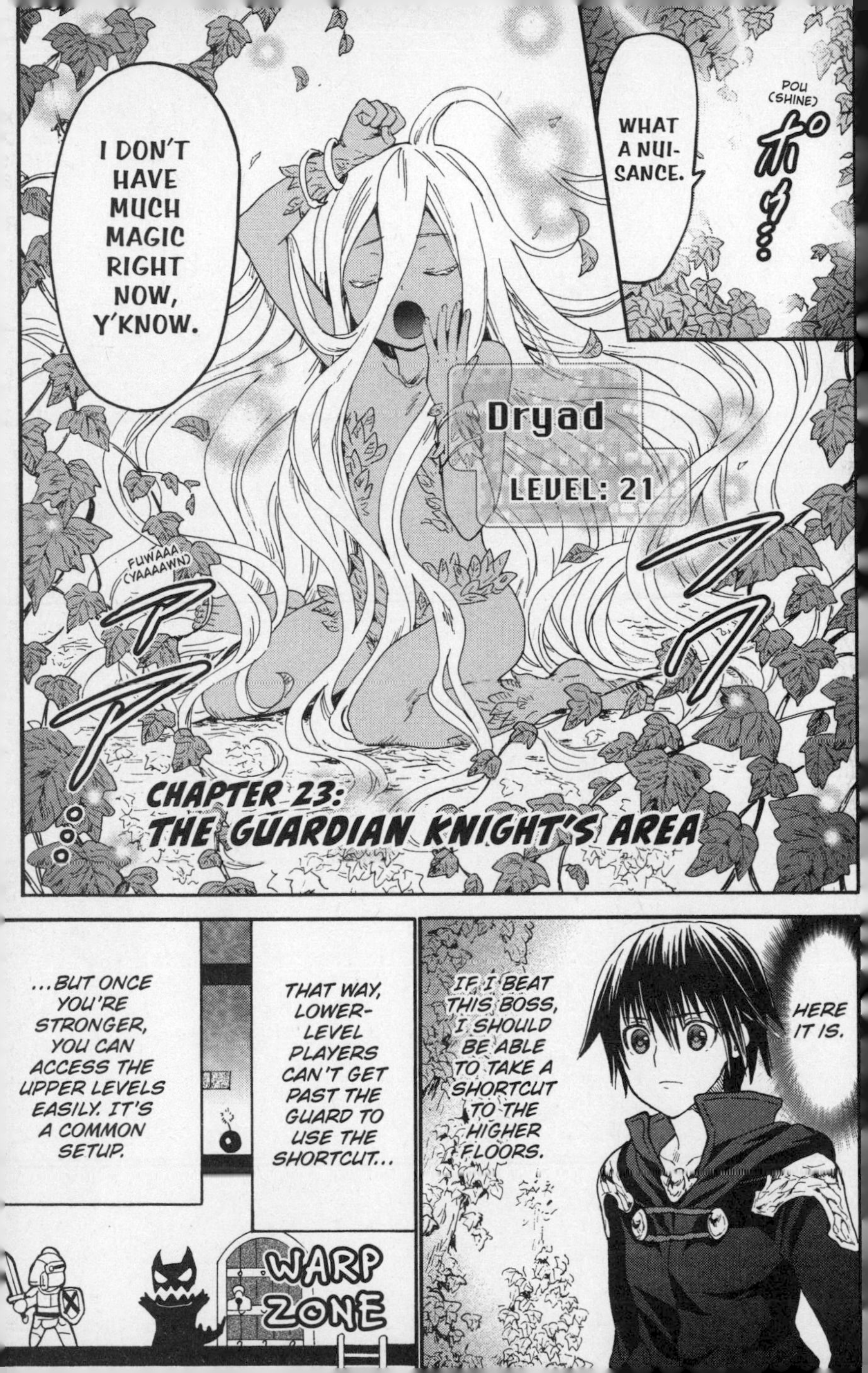
WHAT A NUI-SANCE.
POU (SHINE)
I DON'T HAVE MUCH MAGIC RIGHT NOW, Y'KNOW.
Dryad
LEVEL: 21
FUWAAA (YAAAAWN)
CHAPTER 23: THE GUARDIAN KNIGHT'S AREA
HERE IT IS.
IF I BEAT THIS BOSS, I SHOULD BE ABLE TO TAKE A SHORTCUT TO THE HIGHER FLOORS.
THAT WAY, LOWER-LEVEL PLAYERS CAN'T GET PAST THE GUARD TO USE THE SHORTCUT...
...BUT ONCE YOU'RE STRONGER, YOU CAN ACCESS THE UPPER LEVELS EASILY. IT'S A COMMON SETUP.
WARP ZONE

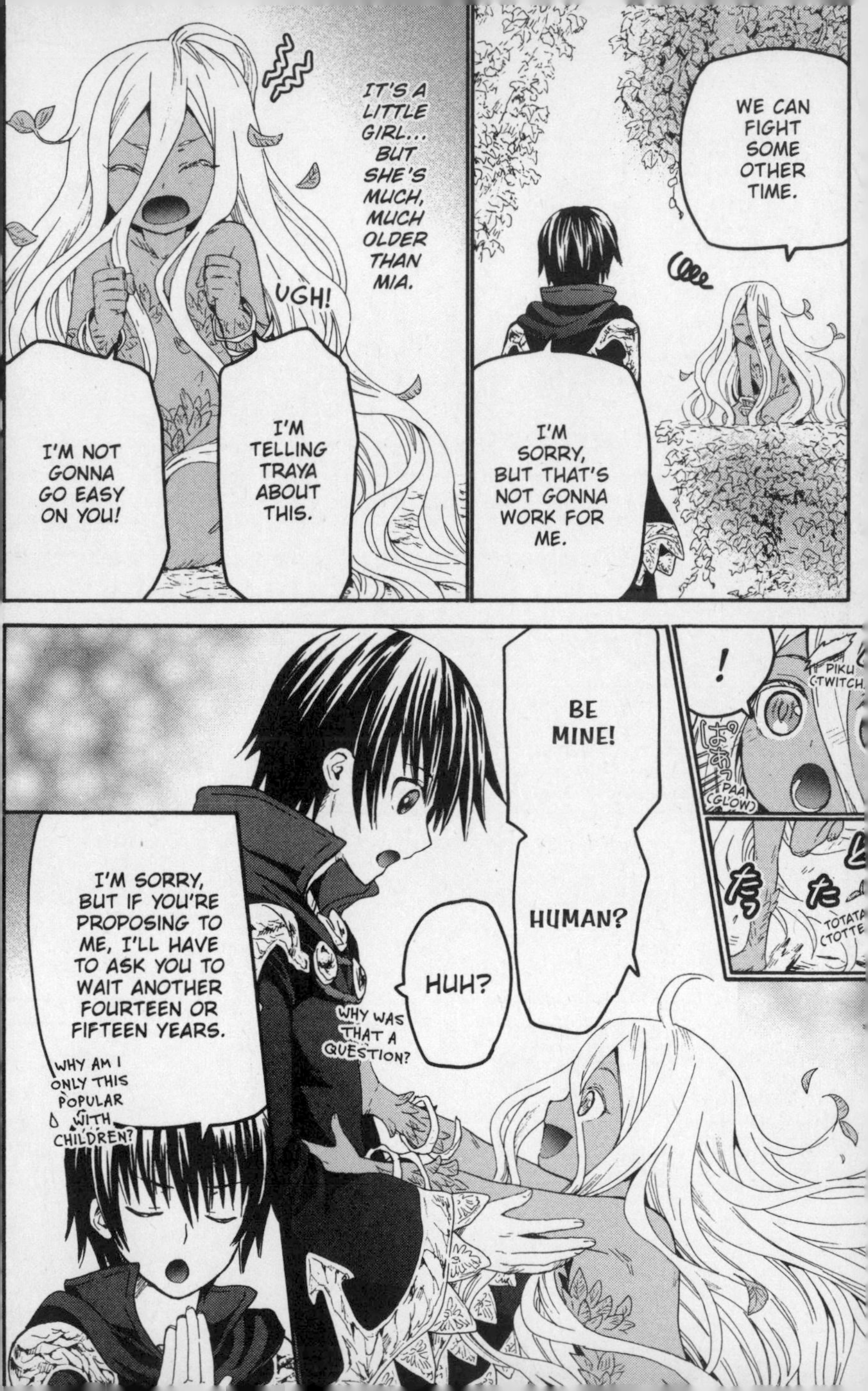
WE CAN FIGHT SOME OTHER TIME.
I'M SORRY, BUT THAT'S NOT GONNA WORK FOR ME.
IT'S A LITTLE GIRL... BUT SHE'S MUCH, MUCH OLDER THAN MIA.
UGH!
I'M TELLING TRAYA ABOUT THIS.
I'M NOT GONNA GO EASY ON YOU!
!
PIKU (TWITCH)
ぱあっ
PAA (GLOW)
TOTATA
BE MINE!
HUMAN?
HUH?
WHY WAS THAT A QUESTION?
I'M SORRY, BUT IF YOU'RE PROPOSING TO ME, I'LL HAVE TO ASK YOU TO WAIT ANOTHER FOURTEEN OR FIFTEEN YEARS.
WHY AM I ONLY THIS POPULAR WITH CHILDREN?

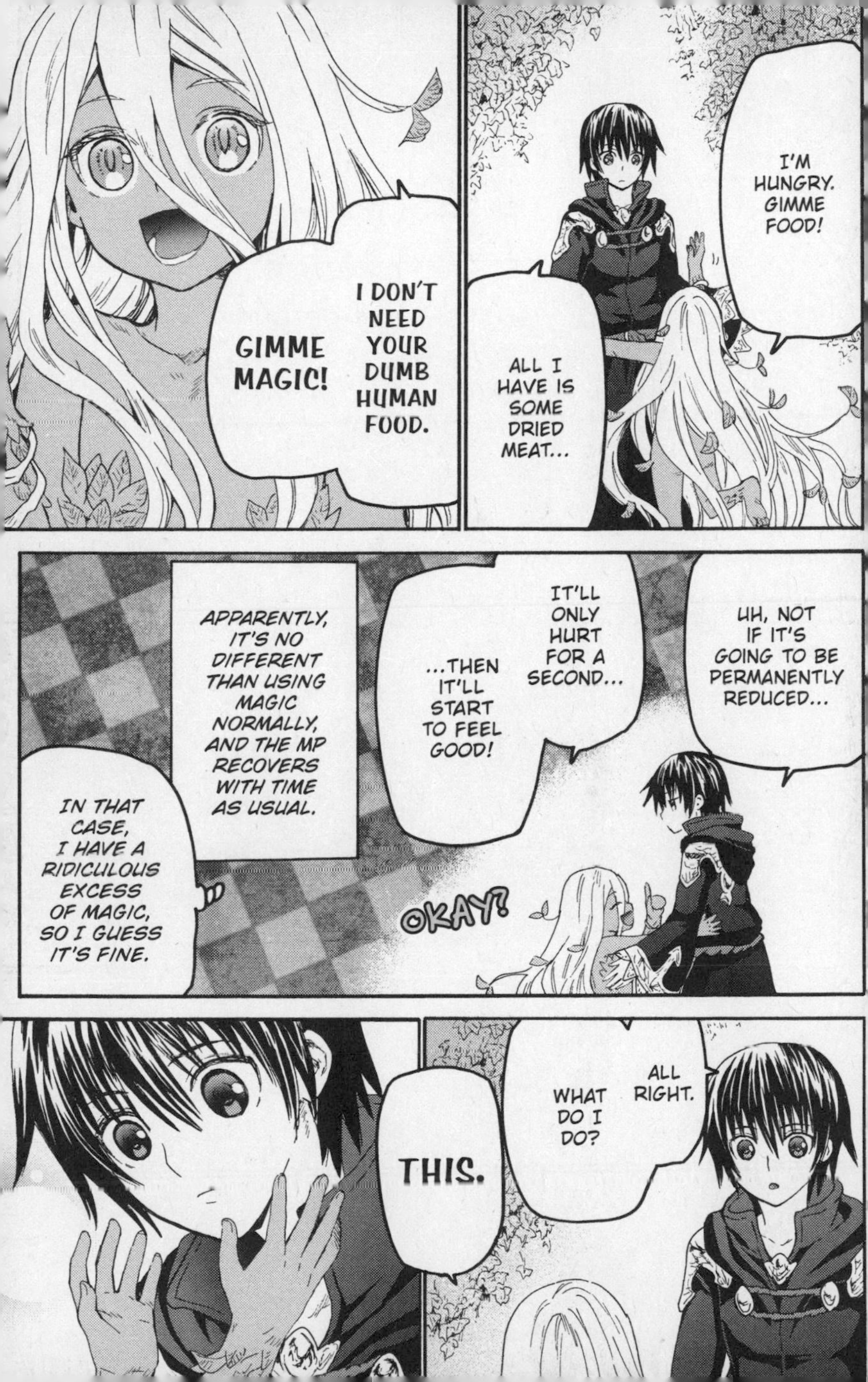
I'M HUNGRY. GIMME FOOD!
ALL I HAVE IS SOME DRIED MEAT...
I DON'T NEED YOUR DUMB HUMAN FOOD.
GIMME MAGIC!
UH, NOT IF IT'S GOING TO BE PERMANENTLY REDUCED...
IT'LL ONLY HURT FOR A SECOND...
...THEN IT'LL START TO FEEL GOOD!
OKAY?
APPARENTLY, IT'S NO DIFFERENT THAN USING MAGIC NORMALLY, AND THE MP RECOVERS WITH TIME AS USUAL.
IN THAT CASE, I HAVE A RIDICULOUS EXCESS OF MAGIC, SO I GUESS IT'S FINE.
ALL RIGHT.
WHAT DO I DO?
THIS.

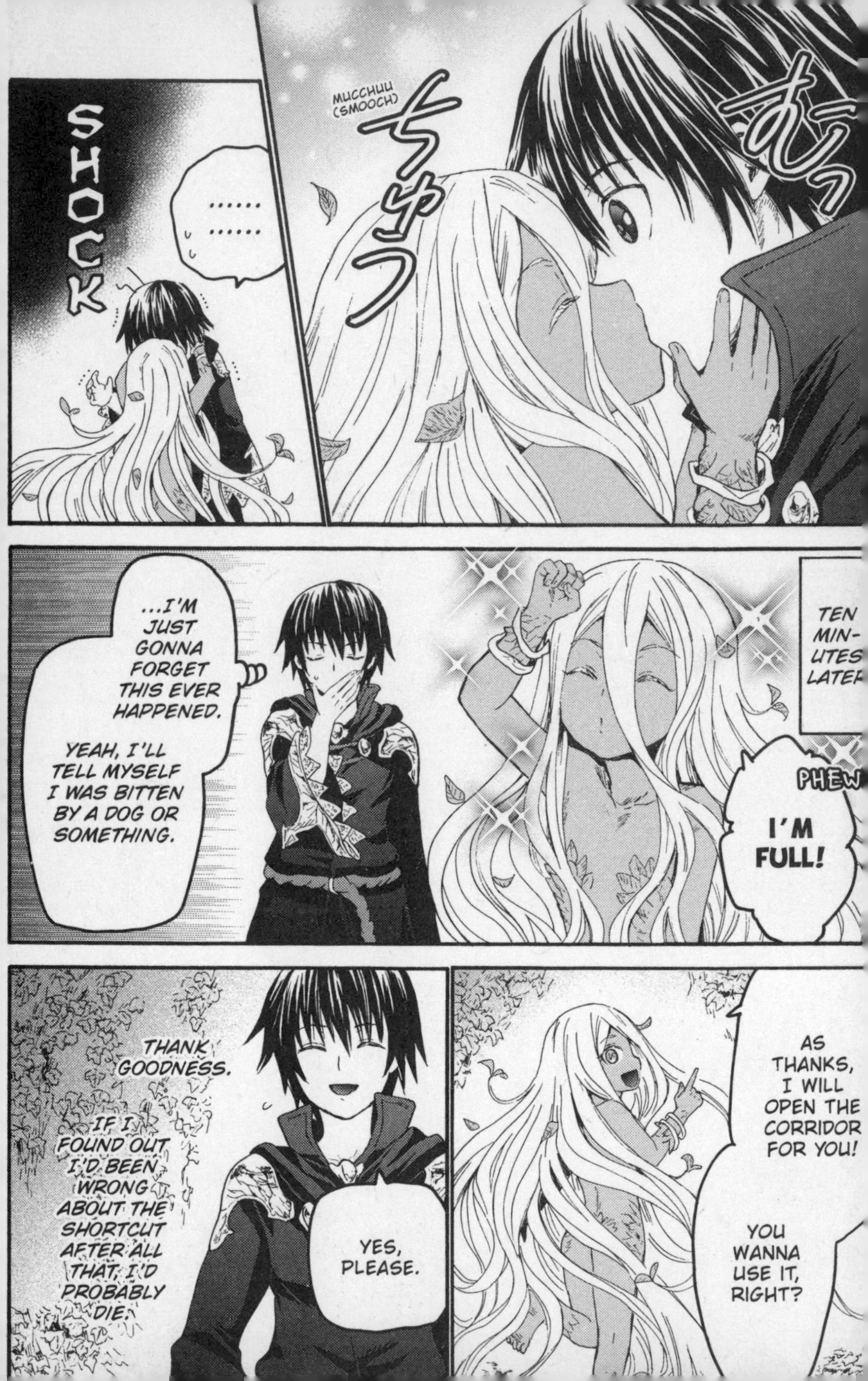
MUCCHUU (SMOOCH)
......
......
SHOCK
TEN MIN-UTES LATER
PHEW
I'M FULL!
...I'M JUST GONNA FORGET THIS EVER HAPPENED.
YEAH, I'LL TELL MYSELF I WAS BITTEN BY A DOG OR SOMETHING.
AS THANKS, I WILL OPEN THE CORRIDOR FOR YOU!
YOU WANNA USE IT, RIGHT?
YES, PLEASE.
THANK GOODNESS.
IF I FOUND OUT I'D BEEN WRONG ABOUT THE SHORTCUT AFTER ALL THAT, I'D PROBABLY DIE.

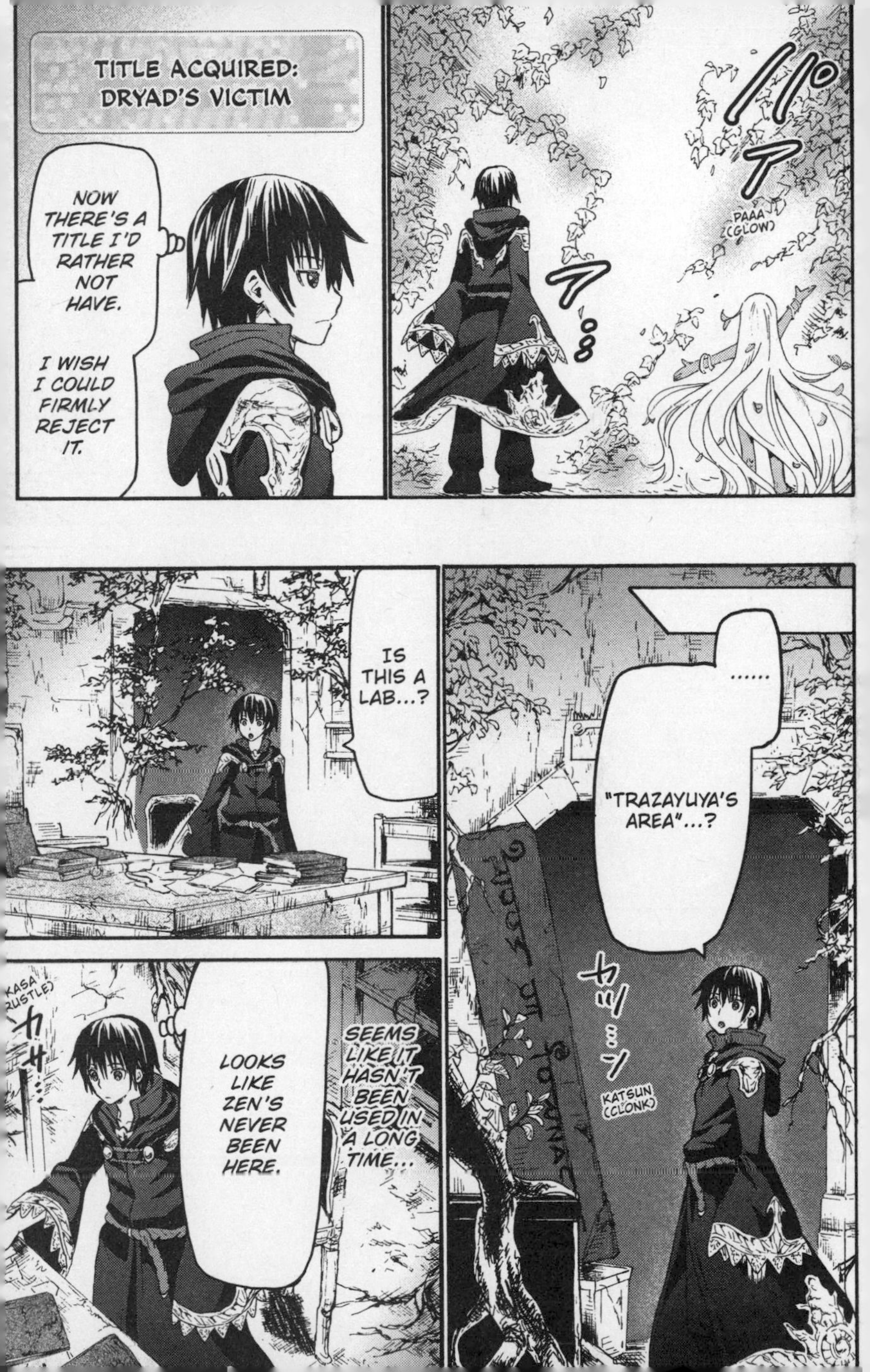
PAAA (GLOW)
TITLE ACQUIRED: DRYAD'S VICTIM
NOW THERE'S A TITLE I'D RATHER NOT HAVE.
I WISH I COULD FIRMLY REJECT IT.
......
"TRAZAYUYA'S AREA"...?
KATSUN (CLONK)
IS THIS A LAB...?
SEEMS LIKE IT HASN'T BEEN USED IN A LONG TIME...
LOOKS LIKE ZEN'S NEVER BEEN HERE.
KASA (RUSTLE)

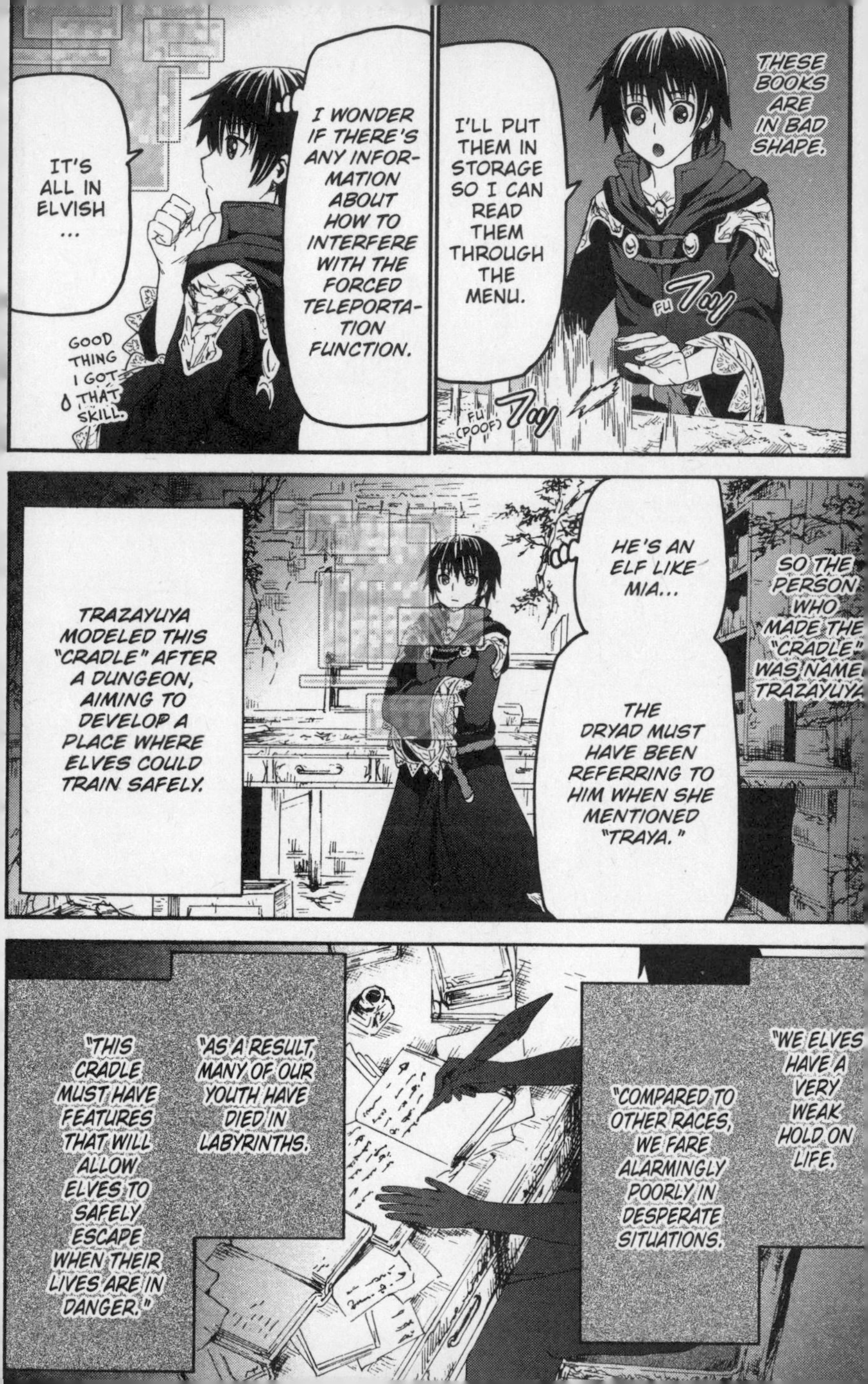
THESE BOOKS ARE IN BAD SHAPE.
I'LL PUT THEM IN STORAGE SO I CAN READ THEM THROUGH THE MENU.
FU
FU (POOF)
I WONDER IF THERE'S ANY INFORMATION ABOUT HOW TO INTERFERE WITH THE FORCED TELEPORTATION FUNCTION.
IT'S ALL IN ELVISH...
GOOD THING I GOT THAT SKILL.
SO THE PERSON WHO MADE THE "CRADLE" WAS NAME TRAZAYUYA
HE'S AN ELF LIKE MIA...
THE DRYAD MUST HAVE BEEN REFERRING TO HIM WHEN SHE MENTIONED "TRAYA."
TRAZAYUYA MODELED THIS "CRADLE" AFTER A DUNGEON, AIMING TO DEVELOP A PLACE WHERE ELVES COULD TRAIN SAFELY.
"WE ELVES HAVE A VERY WEAK HOLD ON LIFE.
"COMPARED TO OTHER RACES, WE FARE ALARMINGLY POORLY IN DESPERATE SITUATIONS.
"AS A RESULT, MANY OF OUR YOUTH HAVE DIED IN LABYRINTHS.
"THIS CRADLE MUST HAVE FEATURES THAT WILL ALLOW ELVES TO SAFELY ESCAPE WHEN THEIR LIVES ARE IN DANGER."

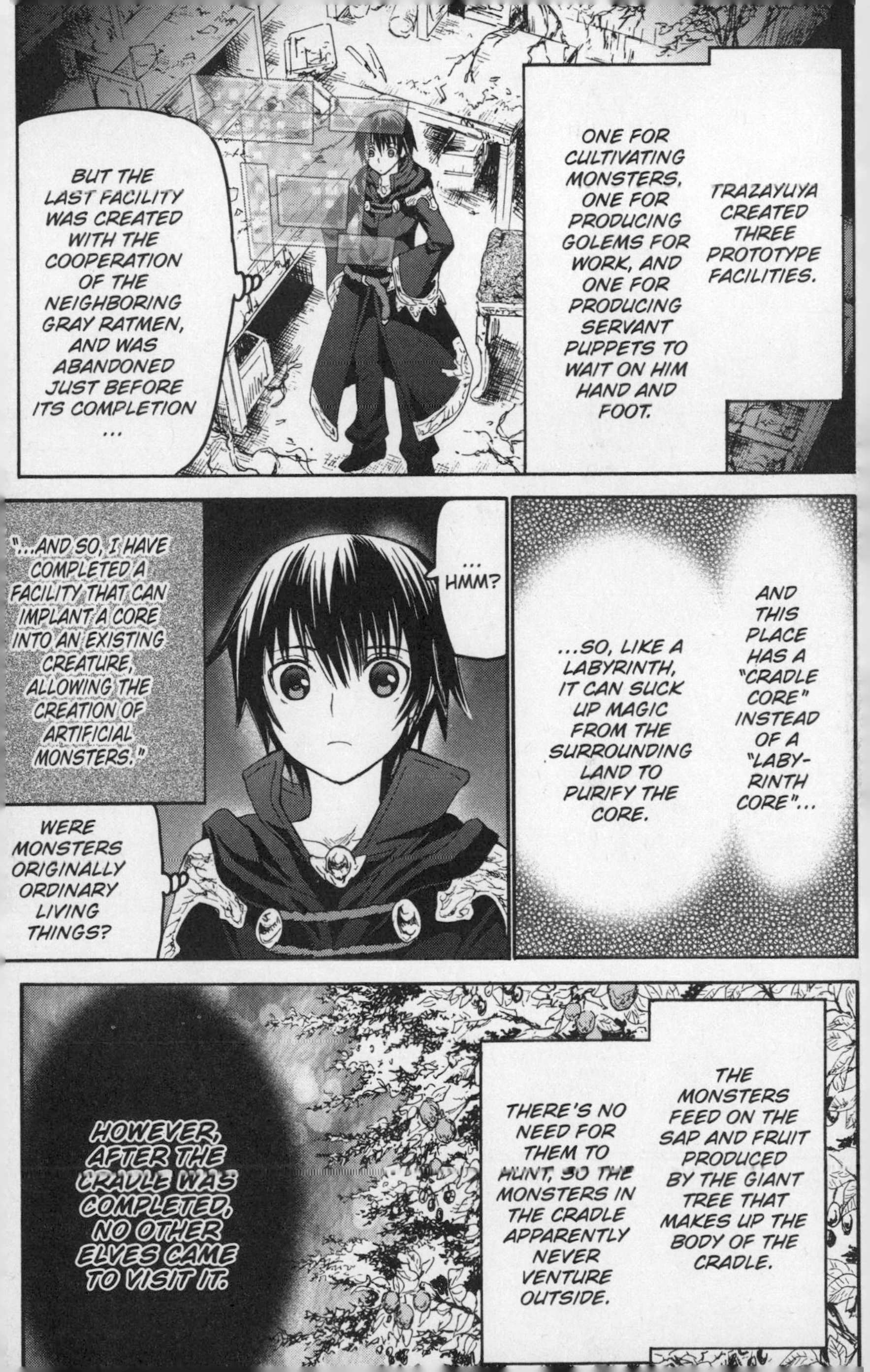
TRAZAYUYA CREATED THREE PROTOTYPE FACILITIES.
ONE FOR CULTIVATING MONSTERS, ONE FOR PRODUCING GOLEMS FOR WORK, AND ONE FOR PRODUCING SERVANT PUPPETS TO WAIT ON HIM HAND AND FOOT.
BUT THE LAST FACILITY WAS CREATED WITH THE COOPERATION OF THE NEIGHBORING GRAY RATMEN, AND WAS ABANDONED JUST BEFORE ITS COMPLETION ...
AND THIS PLACE HAS A "CRADLE CORE" INSTEAD OF A "LABY-RINTH CORE"...
...SO, LIKE A LABYRINTH, IT CAN SUCK UP MAGIC FROM THE SURROUNDING LAND TO PURIFY THE CORE.
... HMM?
"...AND SO, I HAVE COMPLETED A FACILITY THAT CAN IMPLANT A CORE INTO AN EXISTING CREATURE, ALLOWING THE CREATION OF ARTIFICIAL MONSTERS."
WERE MONSTERS ORIGINALLY ORDINARY LIVING THINGS?
THE MONSTERS FEED ON THE SAP AND FRUIT PRODUCED BY THE GIANT TREE THAT MAKES UP THE BODY OF THE CRADLE.
THERE'S NO NEED FOR THEM TO HUNT, SO THE MONSTERS IN THE CRADLE APPARENTLY NEVER VENTURE OUTSIDE.
HOWEVER, AFTER THE CRADLE WAS COMPLETED, NO OTHER ELVES CAME TO VISIT IT.

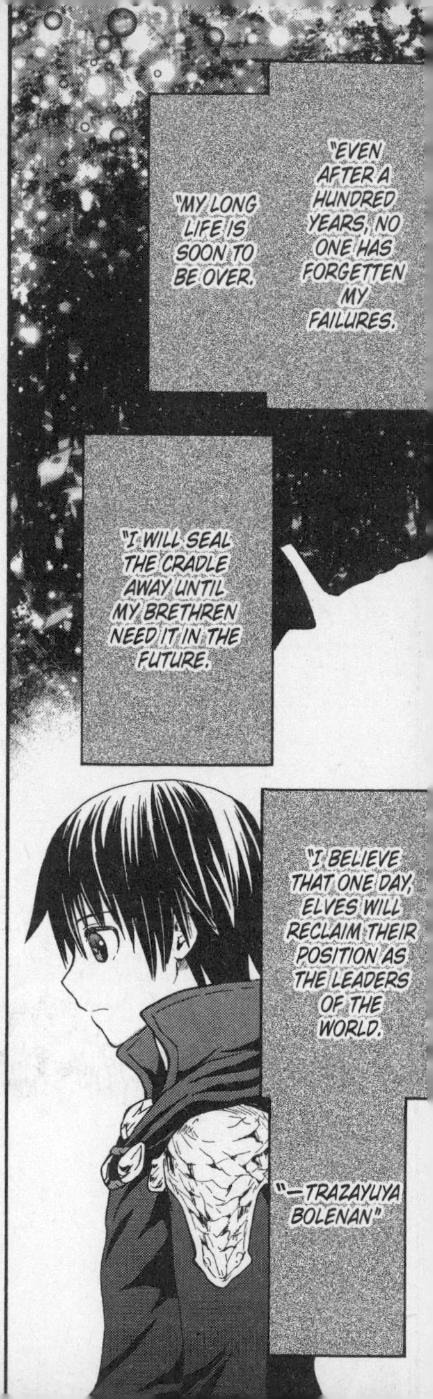
"EVEN AFTER A HUNDRED YEARS, NO ONE HAS FORGETTEN MY FAILURES.
"MY LONG LIFE IS SOON TO BE OVER.
"I WILL SEAL THE CRADLE AWAY UNTIL MY BRETHREN NEED IT IN THE FUTURE.
"I BELIEVE THAT ONE DAY, ELVES WILL RECLAIM THEIR POSITION AS THE LEADERS OF THE WORLD.
"—TRAZAYUYA BOLENAN"

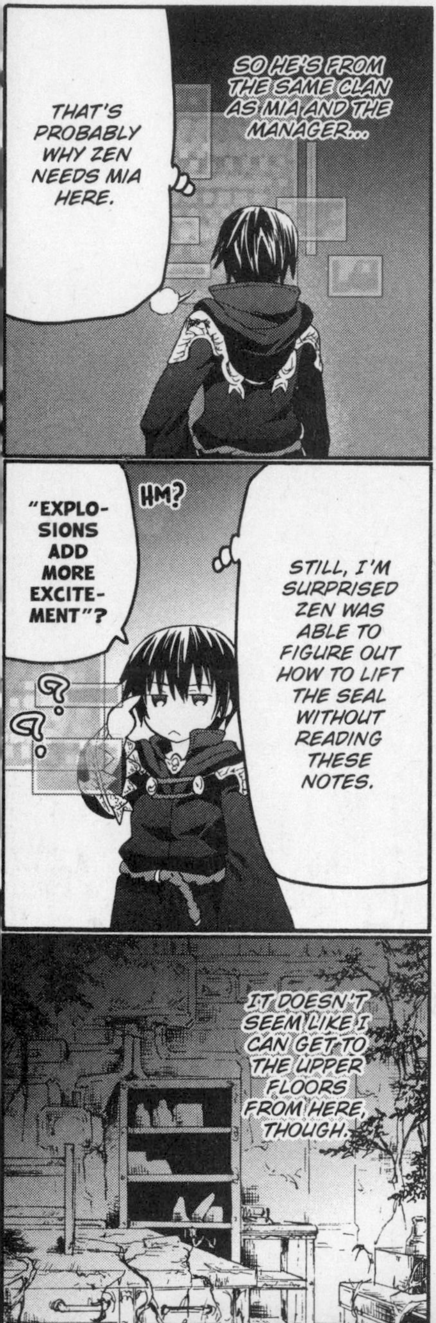
SO HE'S FROM THE SAME CLAN AS MIA AND THE MANAGER...
THAT'S PROBABLY WHY ZEN NEEDS MIA HERE.
STILL, I'M SURPRISED ZEN WAS ABLE TO FIGURE OUT HOW TO LIFT THE SEAL WITHOUT READING THESE NOTES.
HM?
"EXPLOSIONS ADD MORE EXCITEMENT"?
IT DOESN'T SEEM LIKE I CAN GET TO THE UPPER FLOORS FROM HERE, THOUGH.

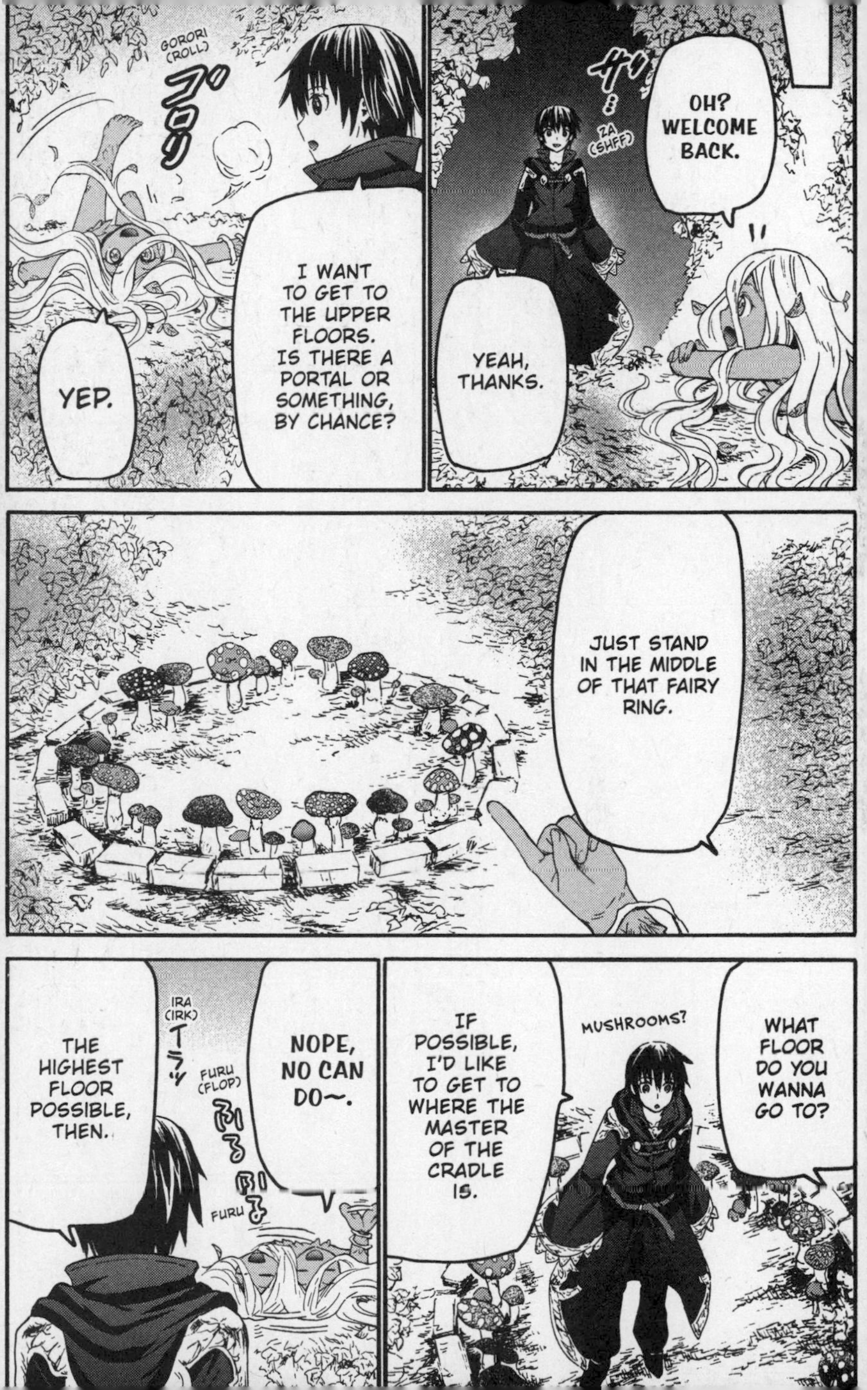
OH? WELCOME BACK.
ザッ
ZA (SHFF)
YEAH, THANKS.
GORORI (ROLL)
ゴロリ
I WANT TO GET TO THE UPPER FLOORS. IS THERE A PORTAL OR SOMETHING, BY CHANCE?
YEP.
JUST STAND IN THE MIDDLE OF THAT FAIRY RING.
WHAT FLOOR DO YOU WANNA GO TO?
MUSHROOMS?
IF POSSIBLE, I'D LIKE TO GET TO WHERE THE MASTER OF THE CRADLE IS.
NOPE, NO CAN DO~.
FURU (FLOP)
ふるふる
FURU
IRA (IRK)
イラッ
THE HIGHEST FLOOR POSSIBLE, THEN.

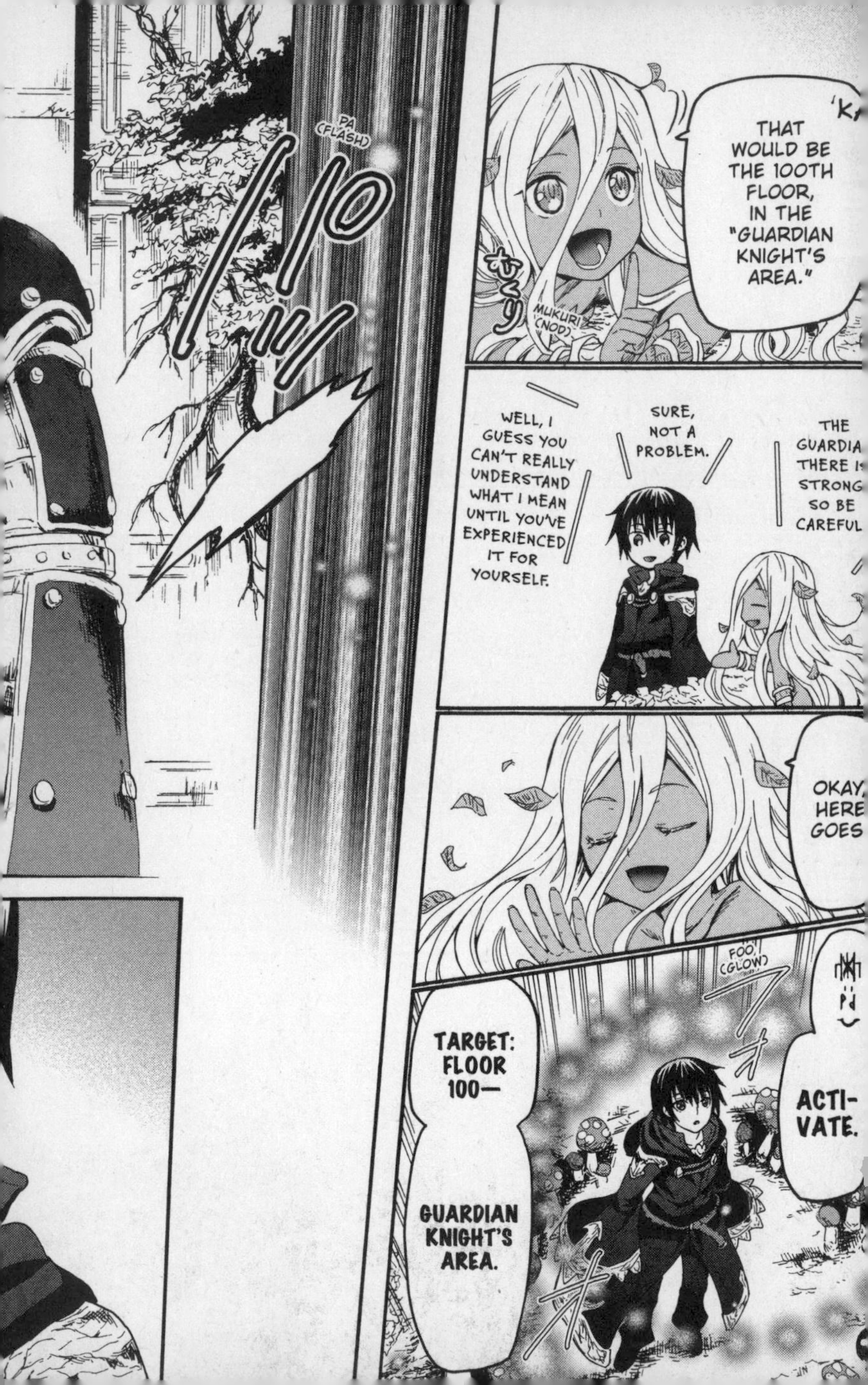
'K
THAT WOULD BE THE 100TH FLOOR, IN THE "GUARDIAN KNIGHT'S AREA."
MUKURI (NOD)
THE GUARDIA THERE IS STRONG SO BE CAREFUL
SURE, NOT A PROBLEM.
WELL, I GUESS YOU CAN'T REALLY UNDERSTAND WHAT I MEAN UNTIL YOU'VE EXPERIENCED IT FOR YOURSELF.
OKAY, HERE GOES
ACTI-VATE.
FOO (GLOW)
TARGET: FLOOR 100—
GUARDIAN KNIGHT'S AREA.
PA (FLASH)

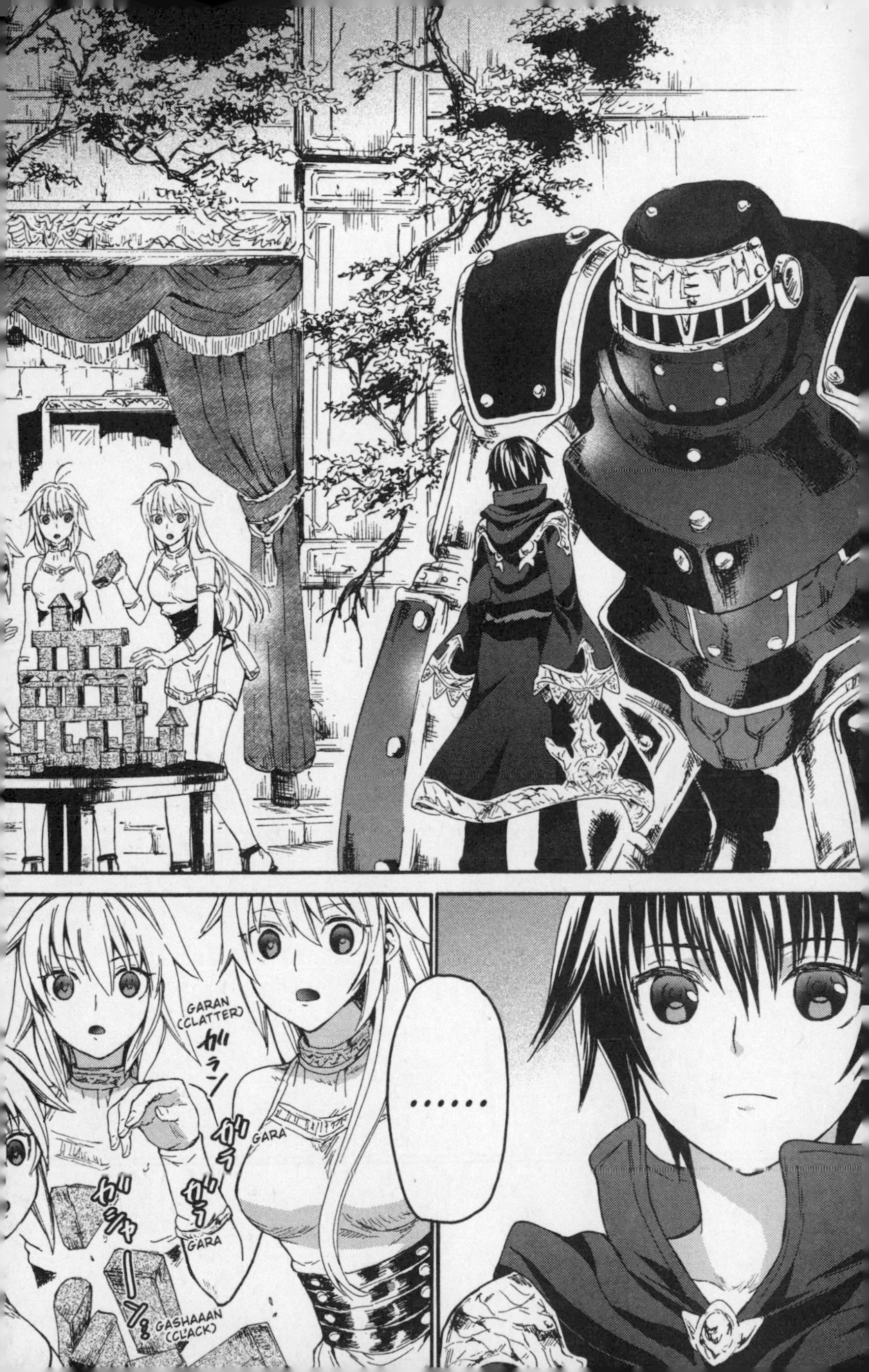
EMETH
......
GARAN (CLATTER)
ガラン
GARA
ガラ
GARA
ガラ
GASHAAAN (CL'ACK)
ガシャーン

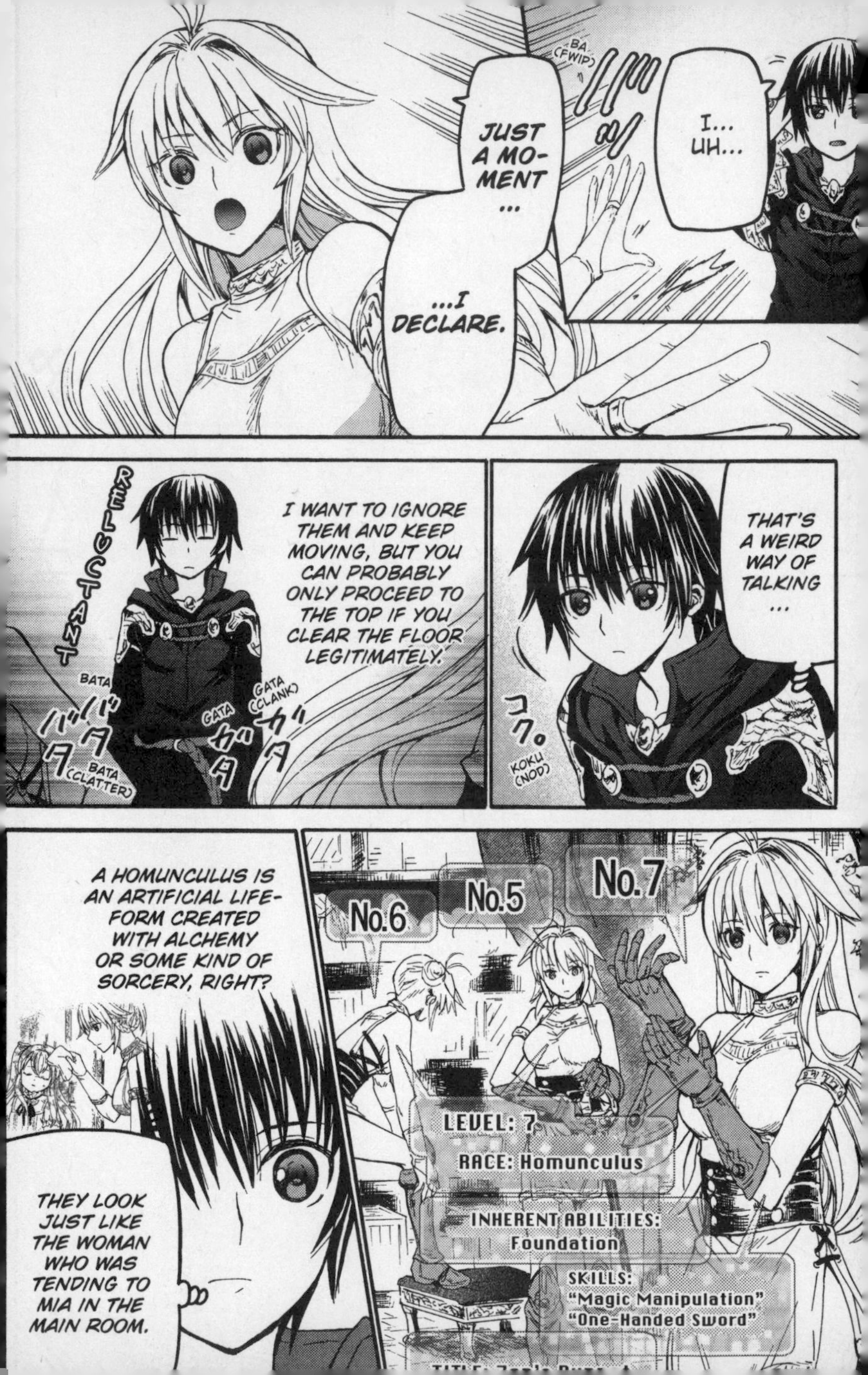

I... UH...
BA (FWIP)
JUST A MO- MENT ...
...I DECLARE.
THAT'S A WEIRD WAY OF TALKING ...
KOKU (NOD)
I WANT TO IGNORE THEM AND KEEP MOVING, BUT YOU CAN PROBABLY ONLY PROCEED TO THE TOP IF YOU CLEAR THE FLOOR LEGITIMATELY.
RELUCTANT
GATA (CLANK)
GATA
BATA
BATA (CLATTER)
No.7
No.5
No.6
LEVEL: 7
RACE: Homunculus
INHERENT ABILITIES: Foundation
SKILLS: "Magic Manipulation" "One-Handed Sword"
A HOMUNCULUS IS AN ARTIFICIAL LIFE-FORM CREATED WITH ALCHEMY OR SOME KIND OF SORCERY, RIGHT?
THEY LOOK JUST LIKE THE WOMAN WHO WAS TENDING TO MIA IN THE MAIN ROOM.

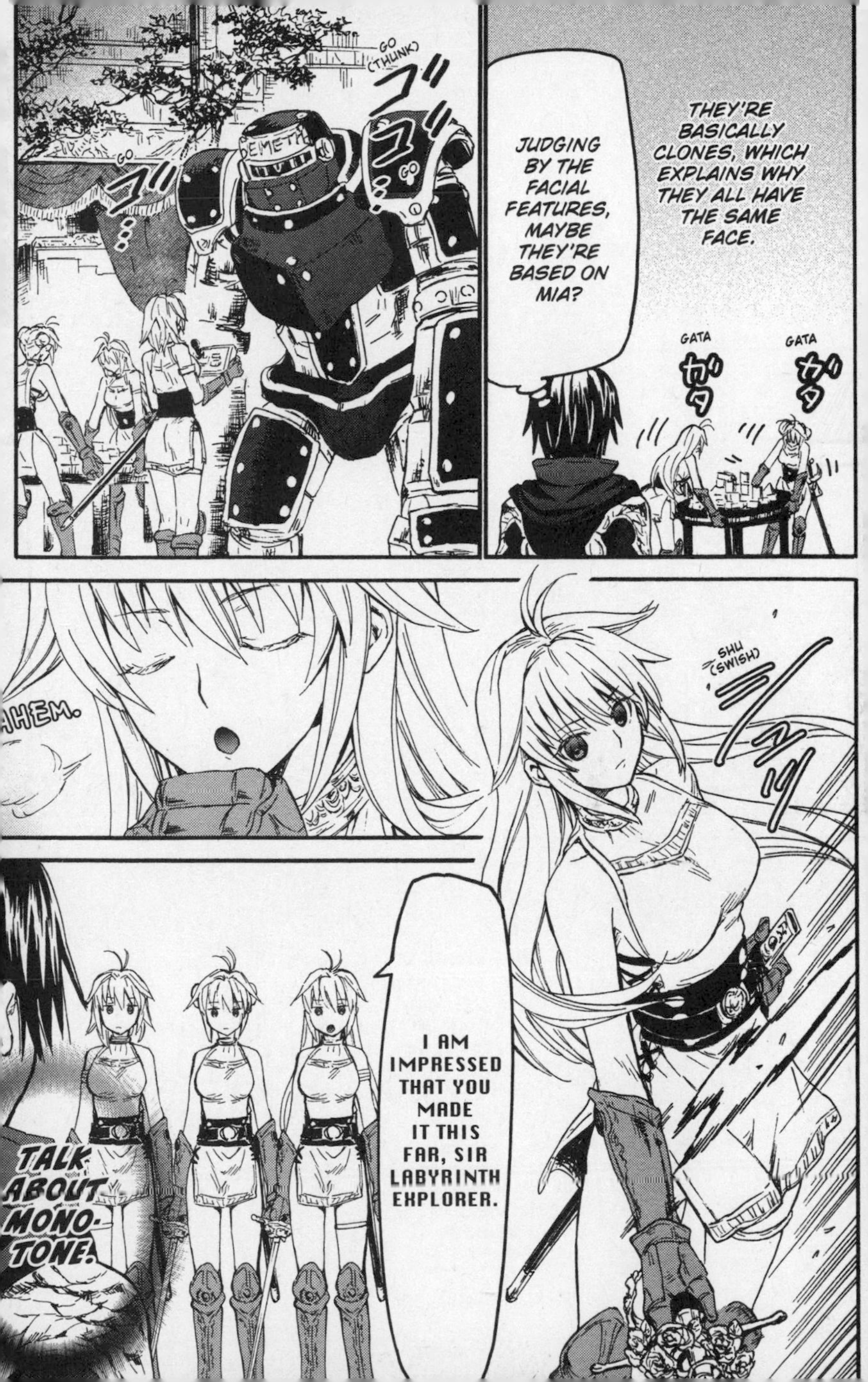

THEY'RE BASICALLY CLONES, WHICH EXPLAINS WHY THEY ALL HAVE THE SAME FACE.
JUDGING BY THE FACIAL FEATURES, MAYBE THEY'RE BASED ON MIA?
GATA
GATA
GO (THUNK)
GO
GO
SHU (SWISH)
AHEM.
I AM IMPRESSED THAT YOU MADE IT THIS FAR, SIR LABYRINTH EXPLORER.
TALK ABOUT MONOTONE.

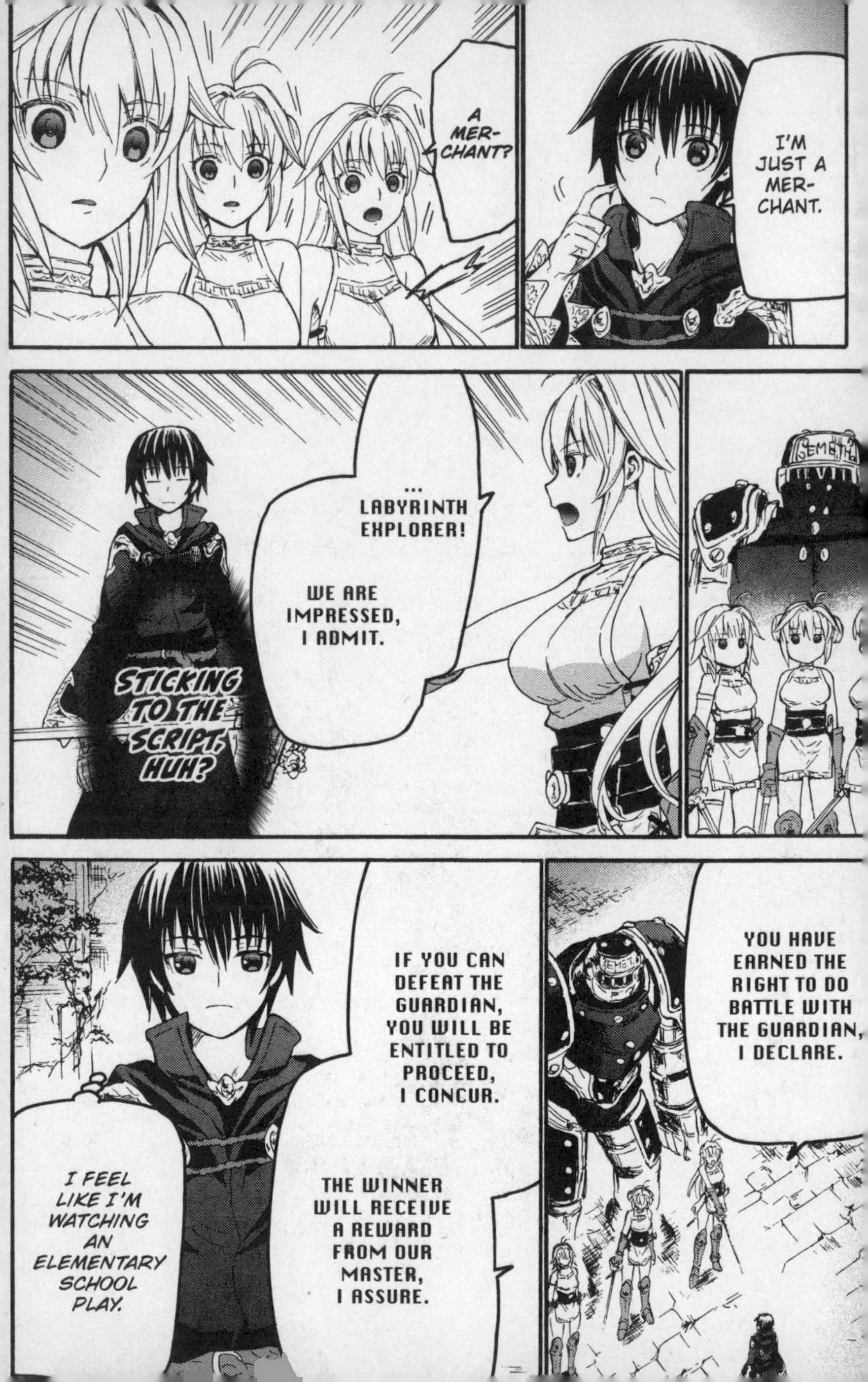
I'M JUST A MERCHANT.
A MERCHANT?
... LABYRINTH EXPLORER!
WE ARE IMPRESSED, I ADMIT.
STICKING TO THE SCRIPT, HUH?
YOU HAVE EARNED THE RIGHT TO DO BATTLE WITH THE GUARDIAN, I DECLARE.
IF YOU CAN DEFEAT THE GUARDIAN, YOU WILL BE ENTITLED TO PROCEED, I CONCUR.
THE WINNER WILL RECEIVE A REWARD FROM OUR MASTER, I ASSURE.
I FEEL LIKE I'M WATCHING AN ELEMENTARY SCHOOL PLAY.

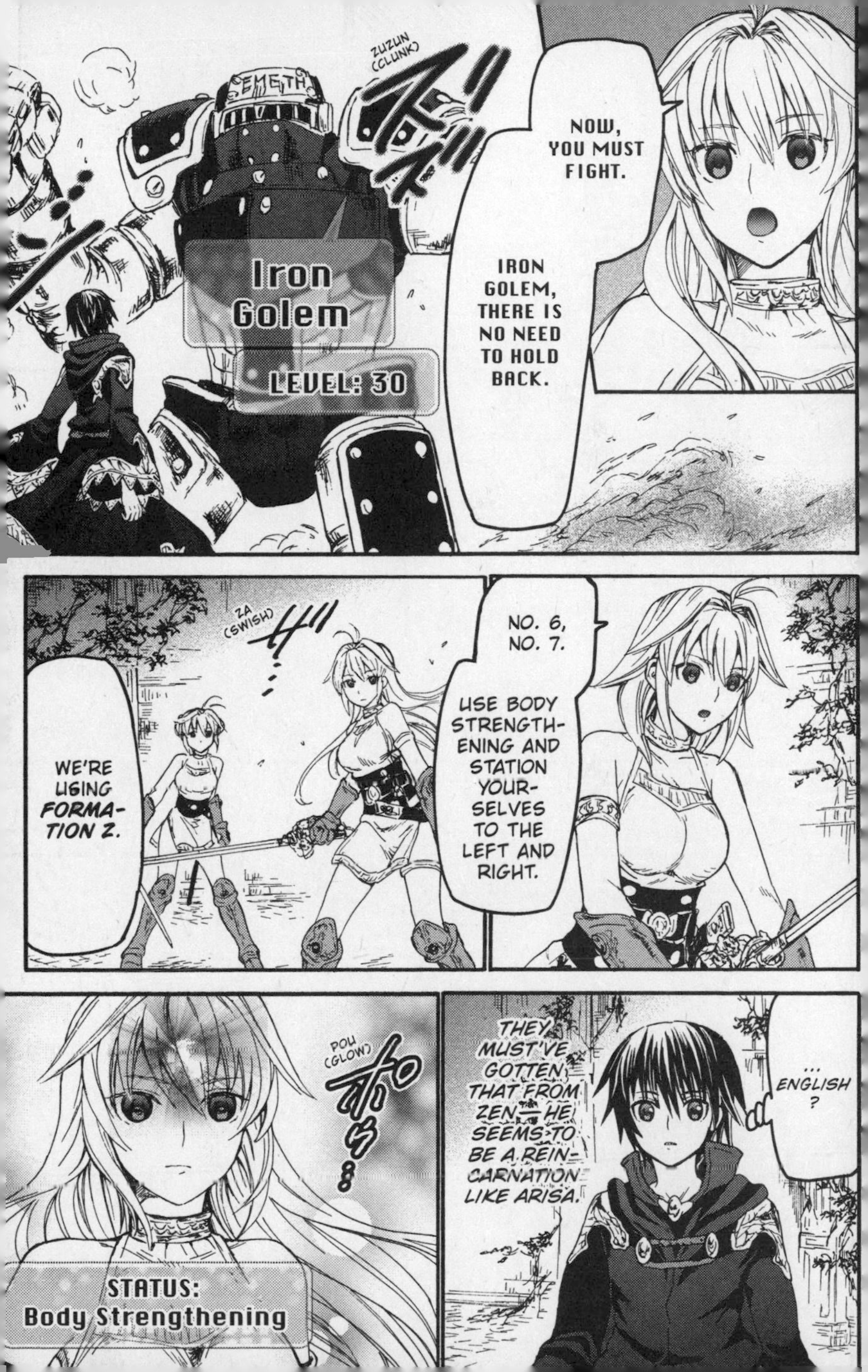
NOW, YOU MUST FIGHT.
IRON GOLEM, THERE IS NO NEED TO HOLD BACK.
ZUZUN (CLUNK)
EMETH
Iron Golem
LEVEL: 30
NO. 6, NO. 7.
USE BODY STRENGTHENING AND STATION YOURSELVES TO THE LEFT AND RIGHT.
ZA (SWISH)
WE'RE USING FORMATION Z.
... ENGLISH?
THEY MUST'VE GOTTEN THAT FROM ZEN—HE SEEMS TO BE A REINCARNATION LIKE ARISA.
POU (GLOW)
STATUS: Body Strengthening

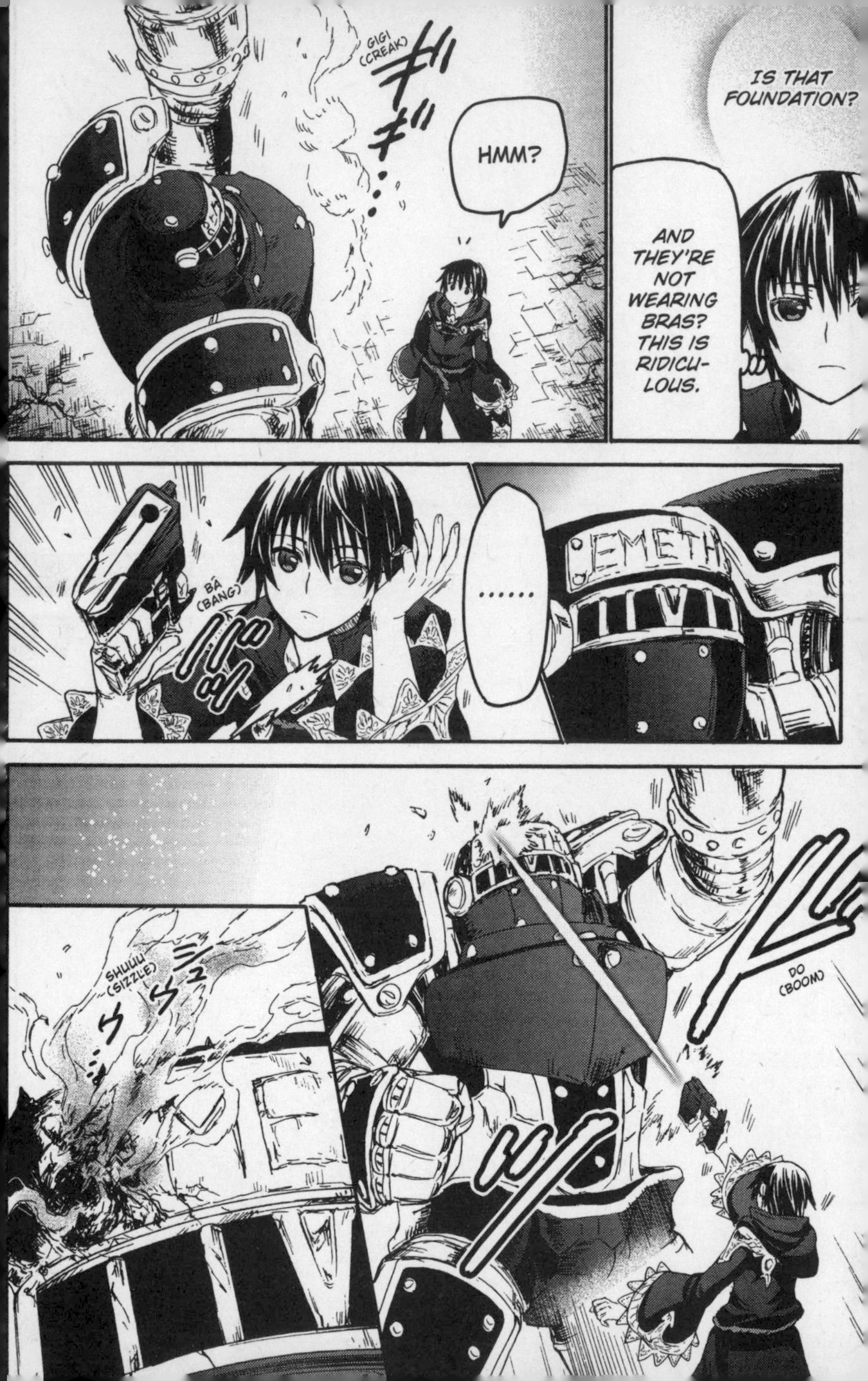
IS THAT FOUNDATION?
AND THEY'RE NOT WEARING BRAS? THIS IS RIDICULOUS.
GIGI (CREAK)
HMM?
......
BA (BANG)
DO (BOOM)
SHUUU (SIZZLE)

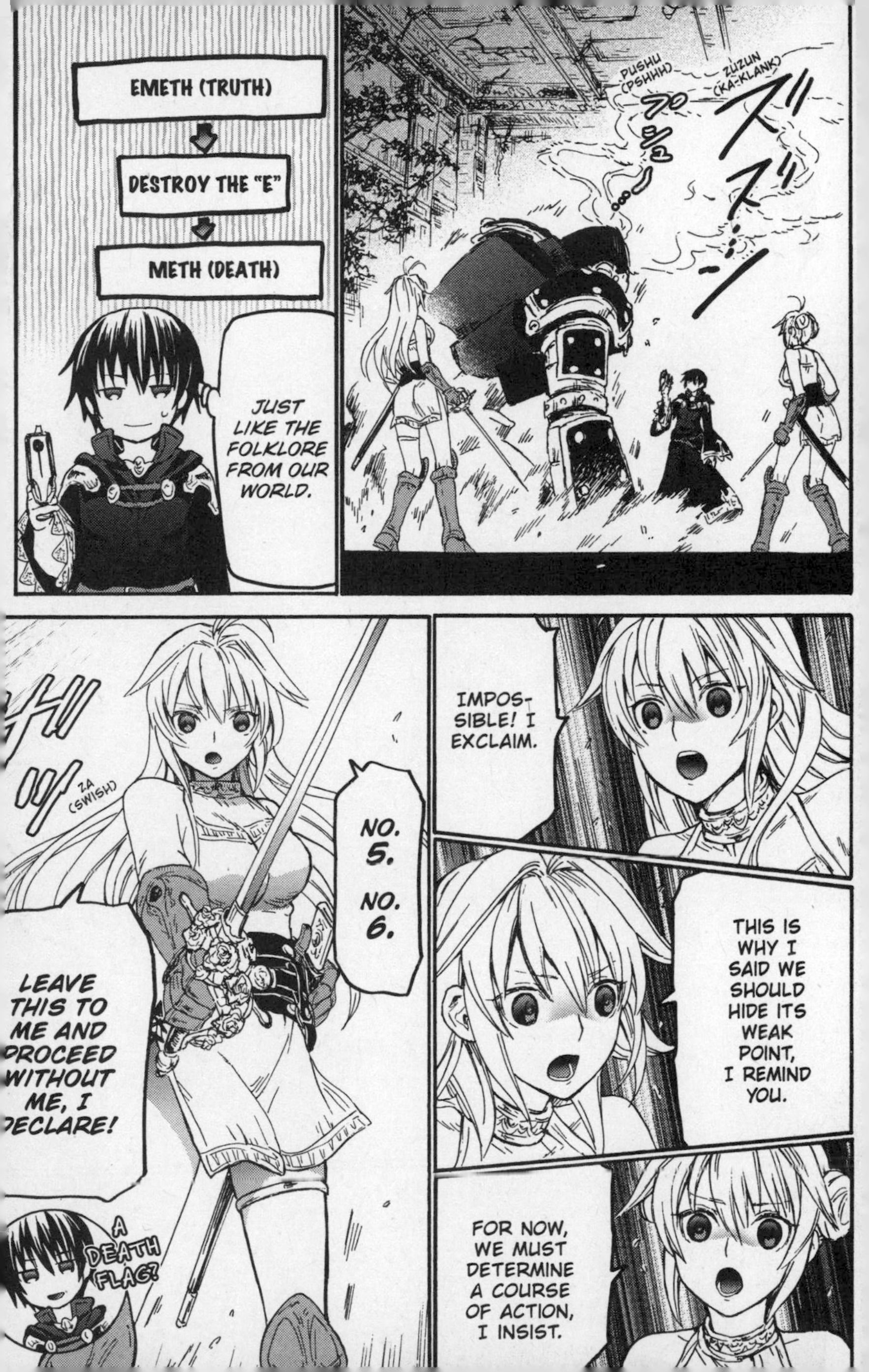
ZUZUN (KA-KLANK)
PUSHU (PSHHH)
EMETH (TRUTH)
DESTROY THE "E"
METH (DEATH)
JUST LIKE THE FOLKLORE FROM OUR WORLD.
IMPOSSIBLE! I EXCLAIM.
THIS IS WHY I SAID WE SHOULD HIDE ITS WEAK POINT, I REMIND YOU.
FOR NOW, WE MUST DETERMINE A COURSE OF ACTION, I INSIST.
ZA (SWISH)
NO. 5. NO. 6.
LEAVE THIS TO ME AND PROCEED WITHOUT ME, I DECLARE!
A DEATH FLAG?

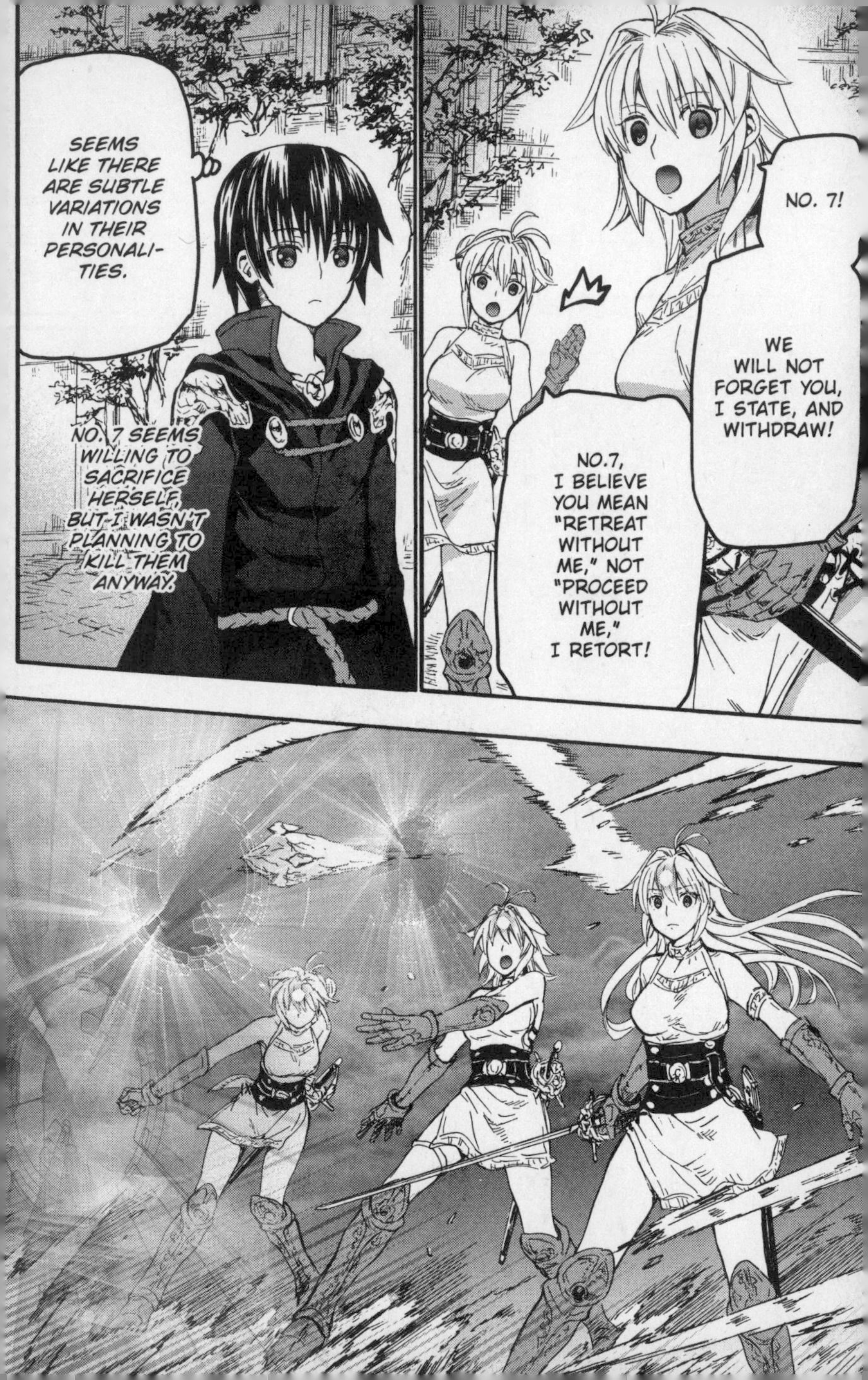
NO. 7!
WE WILL NOT FORGET YOU, I STATE, AND WITHDRAW!
NO.7, I BELIEVE YOU MEAN "RETREAT WITHOUT ME," NOT "PROCEED WITHOUT ME," I RETORT!
SEEMS LIKE THERE ARE SUBTLE VARIATIONS IN THEIR PERSONALI-TIES.
NO. 7 SEEMS WILLING TO SACRIFICE HERSELF, BUT I WASN'T PLANNING TO KILL THEM ANYWAY.

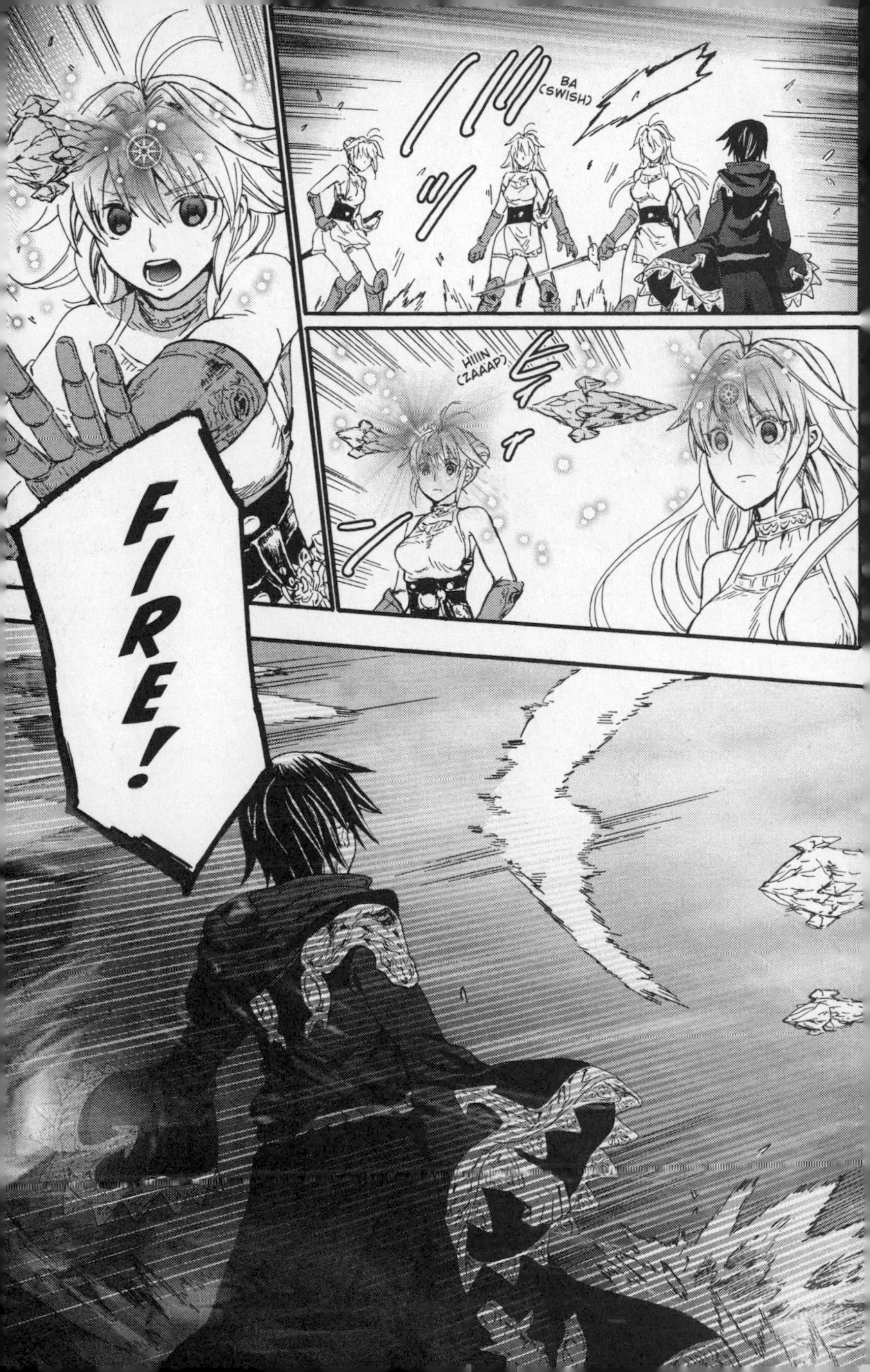
BA
(SWISH)
HIIIN
(ZAAAP)
FIRE!

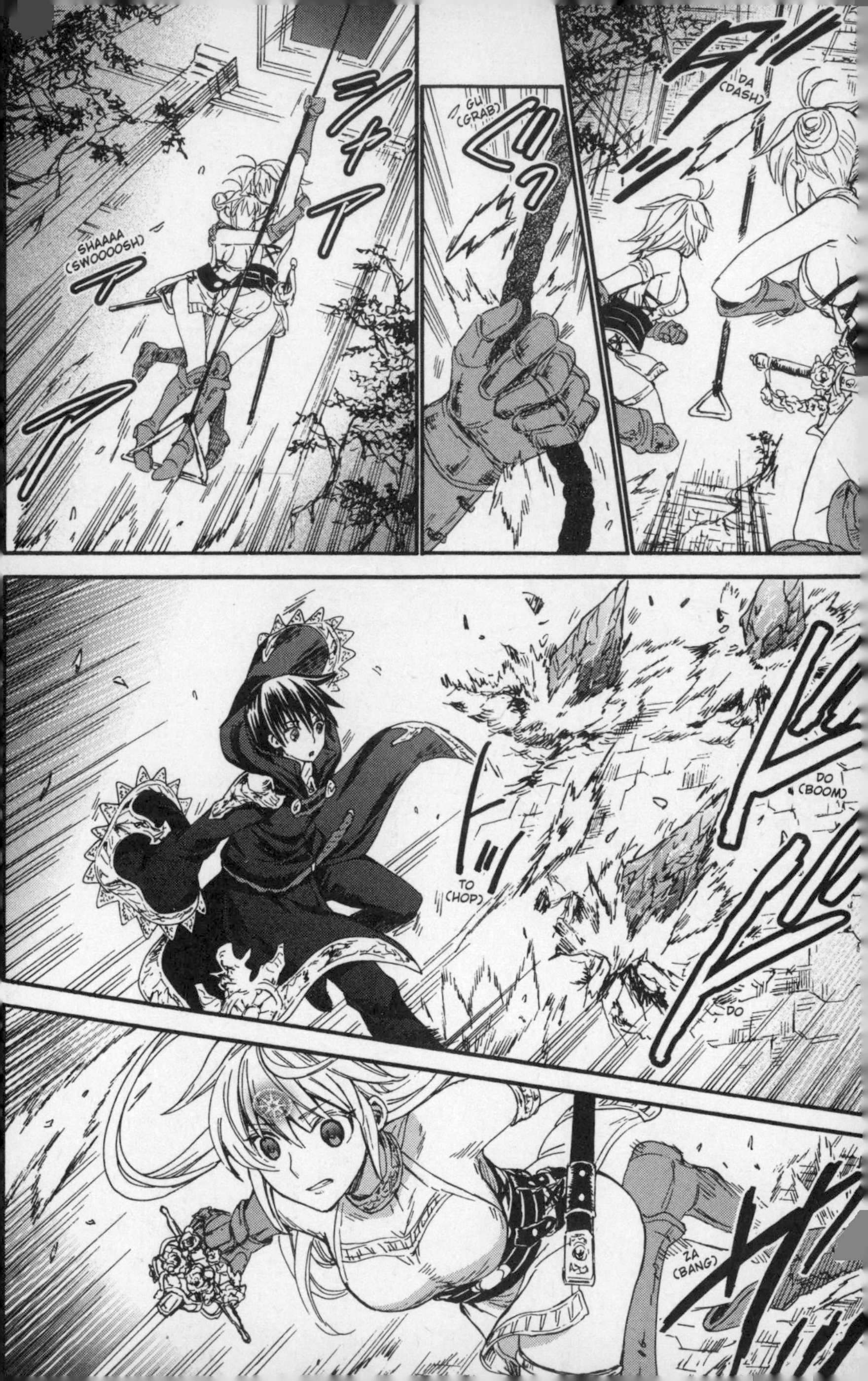
DA (DASH)
GU (GRAB)
SHAAAA (SWOOOOSH)
DO (BOOM)
TO (HOP)
DO
ZA (BANG)

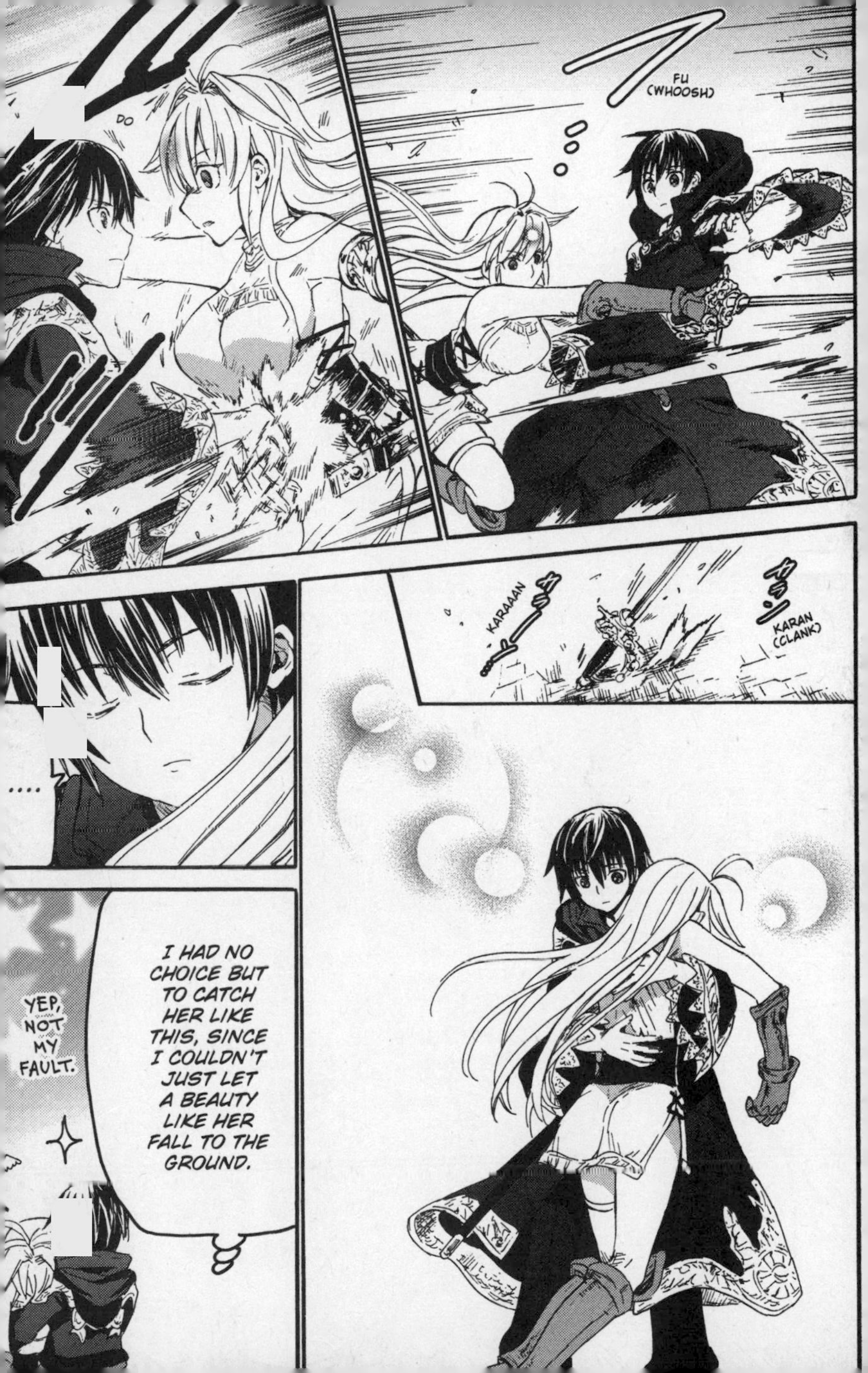
FU (WHOOSH)
DO
KARAN (CLANK)
KARAAAN
....
I HAD NO CHOICE BUT TO CATCH HER LIKE THIS, SINCE I COULDN'T JUST LET A BEAUTY LIKE HER FALL TO THE GROUND.
YEP, NOT MY FAULT.

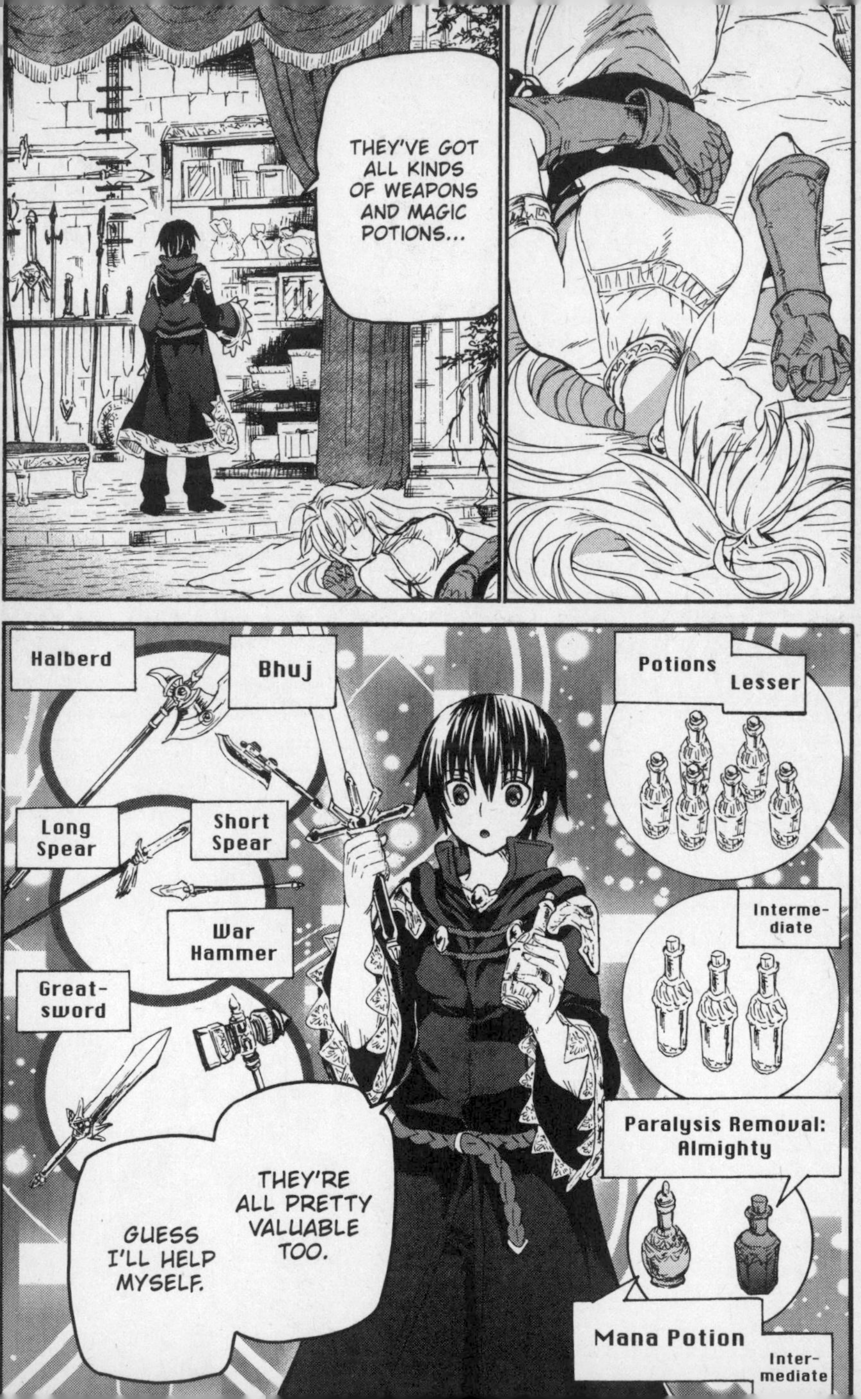
THEY'VE GOT ALL KINDS OF WEAPONS AND MAGIC POTIONS...
Potions Lesser
Intermediate
Paralysis Removal: Almighty
Mana Potion
Intermediate
Bhuj
Halberd
Short Spear
Long Spear
War Hammer
Great-sword
THEY'RE ALL PRETTY VALUABLE TOO.
GUESS I'LL HELP MYSELF.

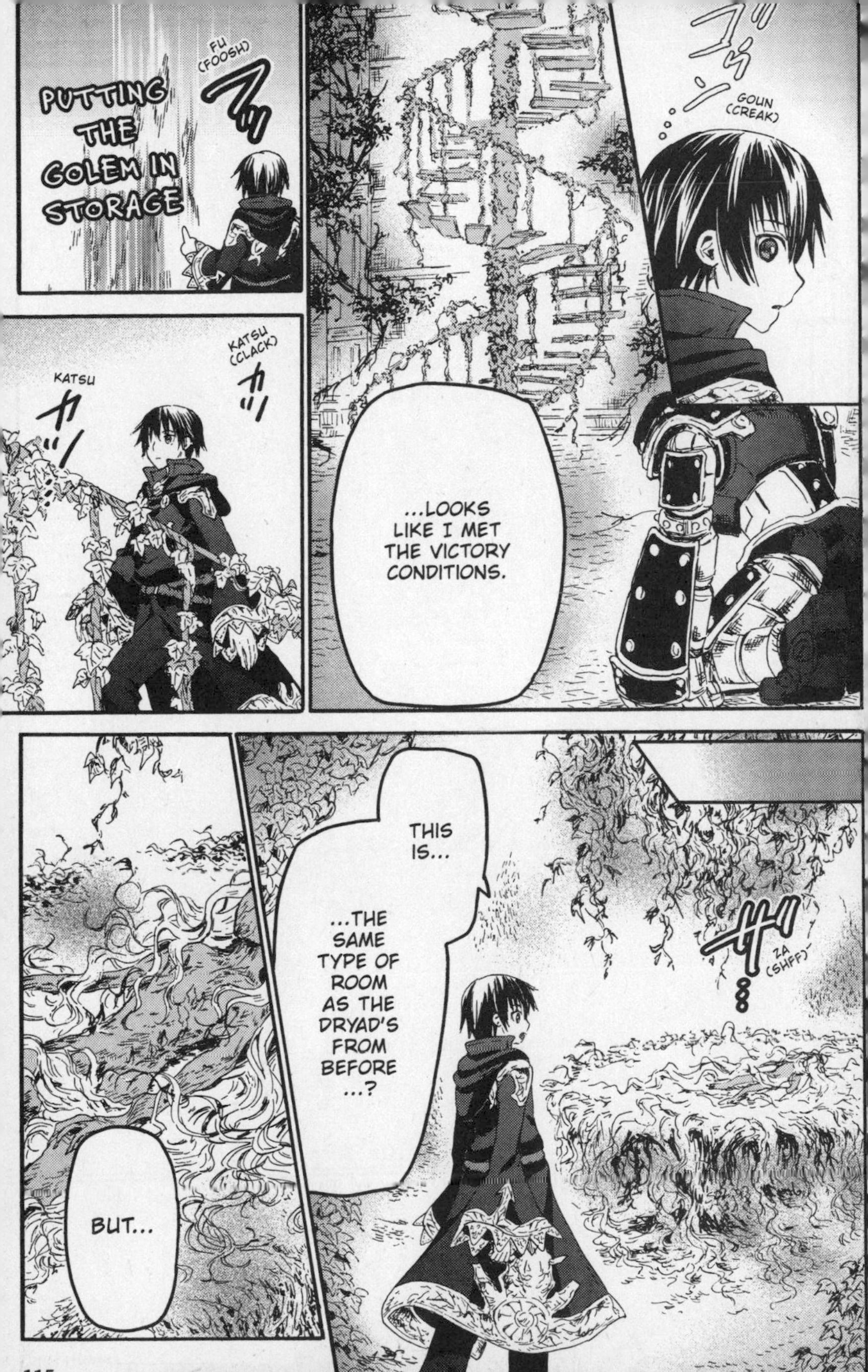
GOUN (CREAK)
...LOOKS LIKE I MET THE VICTORY CONDITIONS.
FU (FOOSH)
PUTTING THE GOLEM IN STORAGE
KATSU (CLACK)
KATSU
ZA (SHFF)
THIS IS...
...THE SAME TYPE OF ROOM AS THE DRYAD'S FROM BEFORE ...?
BUT...

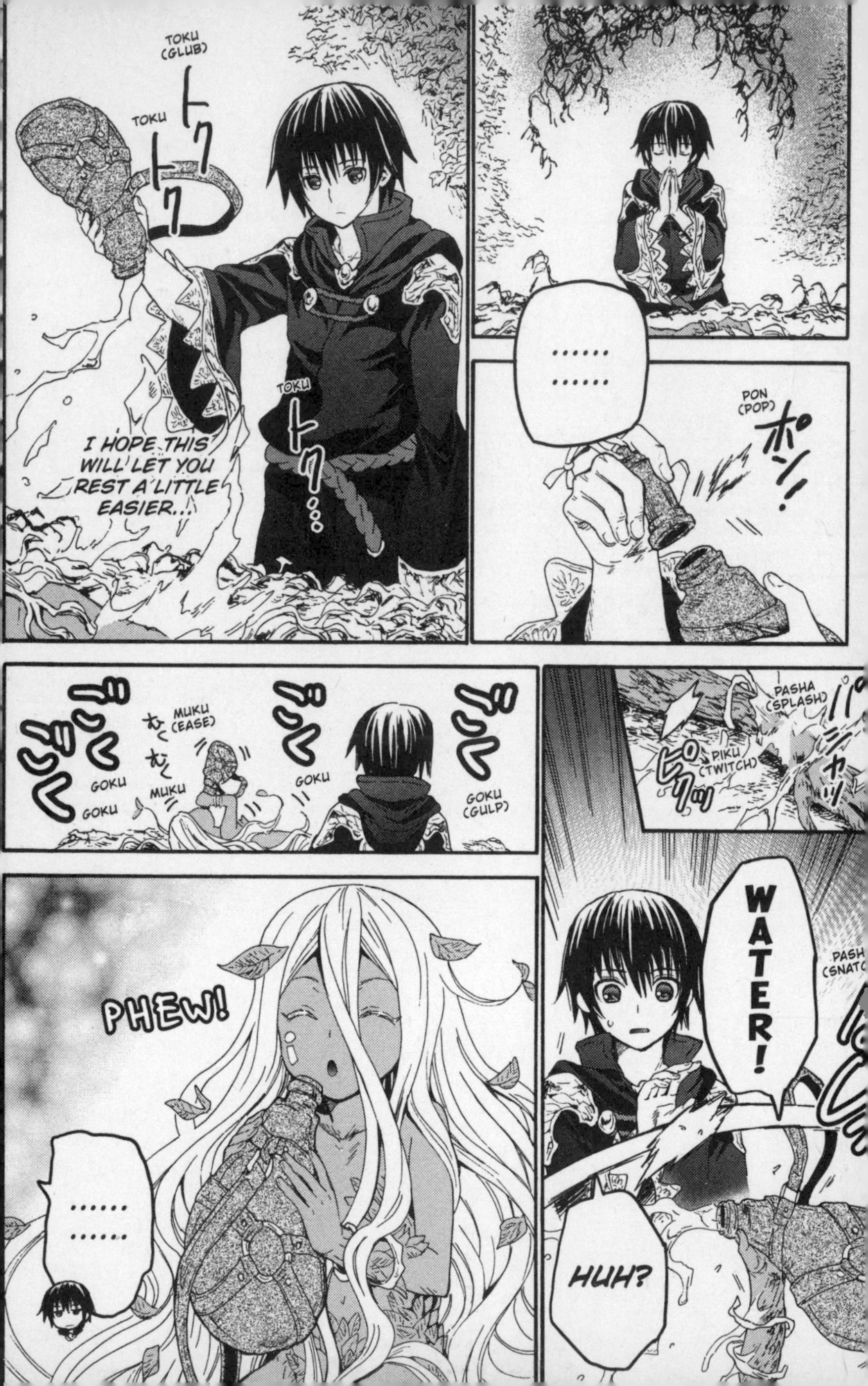

....
PON (POP)
ポン!!
TOKU (GLUB)
トク
TOKU
トク
TOKU
トク...
I HOPE THIS WILL LET YOU REST A LITTLE EASIER...
PASHA (SPLASH)
パシャッ
PIKU (TWITCH)
ピクッ
GOKU (GULP)
ごく
GOKU
ごく
MUKU (EASE)
むく
MUKU
むく
GOKU GOKU
ごくごく
WATER!
PASH (SNATC
HUH?
PHEW!
....

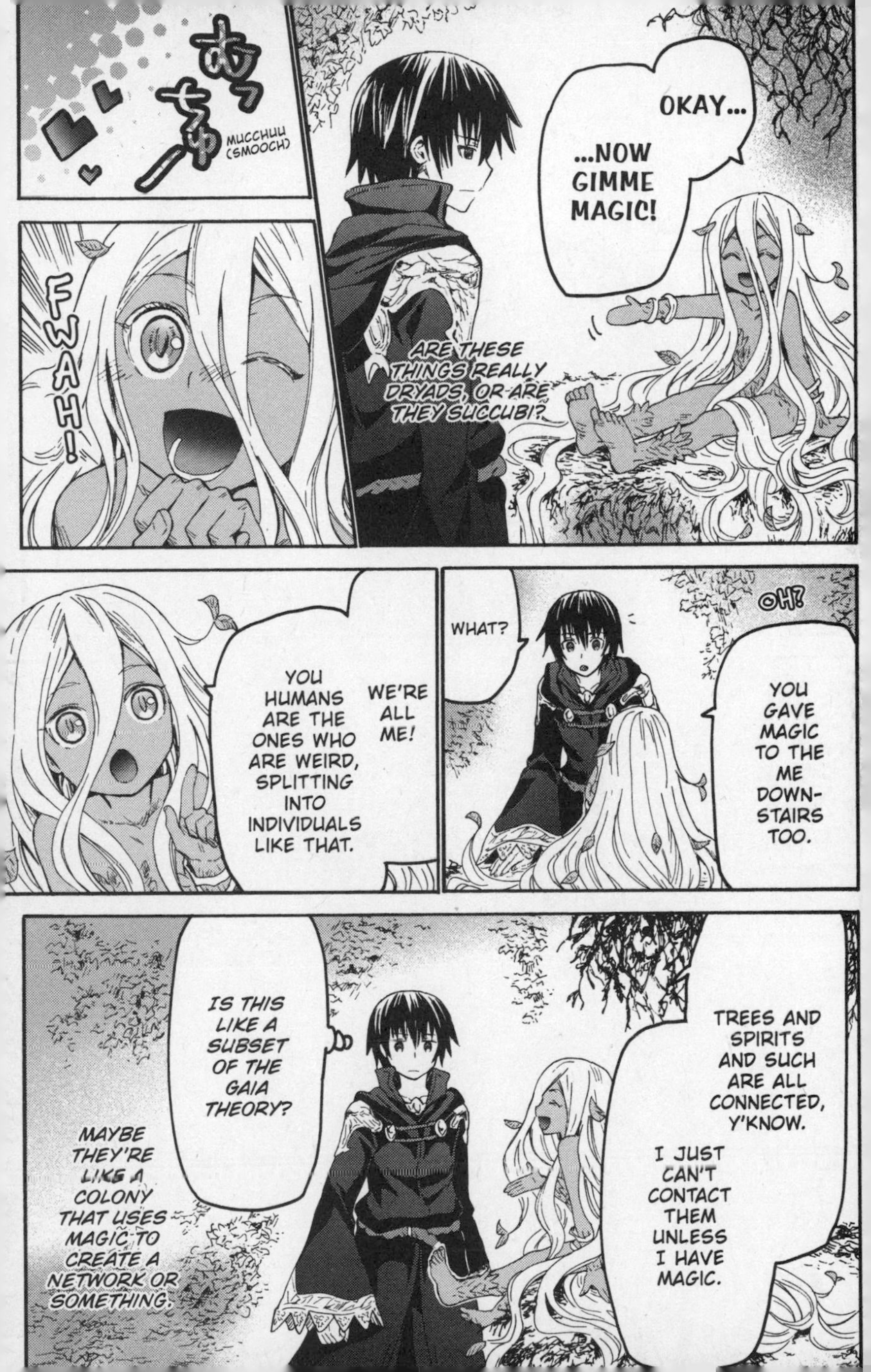
OKAY...
...NOW GIMME MAGIC!
ARE THESE THINGS REALLY DRYADS, OR ARE THEY SUCCUBI?
あっちゅ
MUCCHUU (SMOOCH)
FWAH!
OH?
YOU GAVE MAGIC TO THE ME DOWN-STAIRS TOO.
WHAT?
WE'RE ALL ME!
YOU HUMANS ARE THE ONES WHO ARE WEIRD, SPLITTING INTO INDIVIDUALS LIKE THAT.
TREES AND SPIRITS AND SUCH ARE ALL CONNECTED, Y'KNOW.
I JUST CAN'T CONTACT THEM UNLESS I HAVE MAGIC.
IS THIS LIKE A SUBSET OF THE GAIA THEORY?
MAYBE THEY'RE LIKE A COLONY THAT USES MAGIC TO CREATE A NETWORK OR SOMETHING.

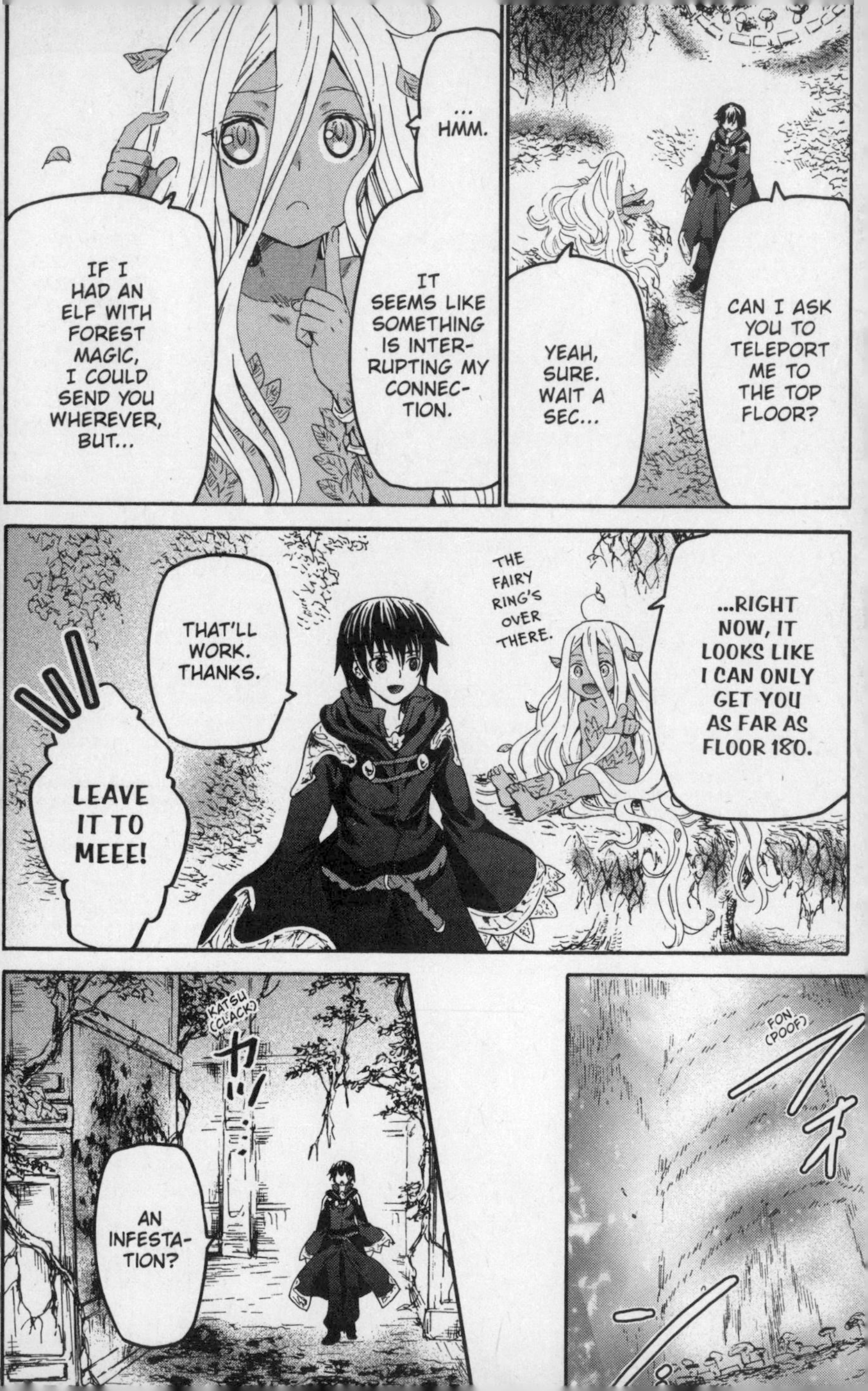
CAN I ASK YOU TO TELEPORT ME TO THE TOP FLOOR?
YEAH, SURE. WAIT A SEC...
... HMM.
IT SEEMS LIKE SOMETHING IS INTERRUPTING MY CONNECTION.
IF I HAD AN ELF WITH FOREST MAGIC, I COULD SEND YOU WHEREVER, BUT...
...RIGHT NOW, IT LOOKS LIKE I CAN ONLY GET YOU AS FAR AS FLOOR 180.
THE FAIRY RING'S OVER THERE.
THAT'LL WORK. THANKS.
LEAVE IT TO MEEE!
FON (POOF)
KATSU (CLACK)
AN INFESTATION?

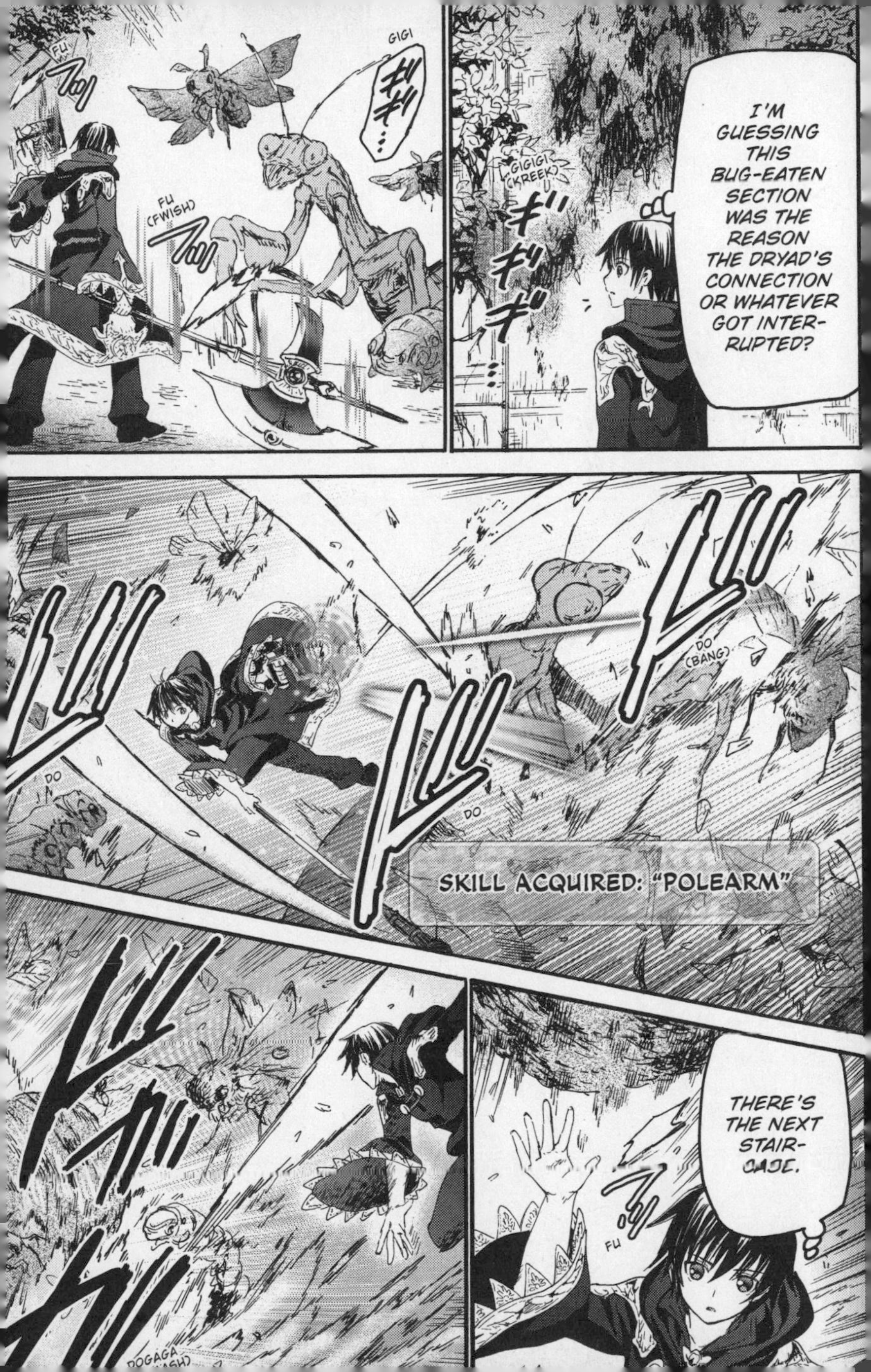
I'M GUESSING THIS BUG-EATEN SECTION WAS THE REASON THE DRYAD'S CONNECTION OR WHATEVER GOT INTER-RUPTED?
GIGIGI (KREEK)
GIGI
FU
FU (FWISH)
DO (BANG)
DO
DO
SKILL ACQUIRED: "POLEARM"
THERE'S THE NEXT STAIR-CASE.
FU
DOGAGA

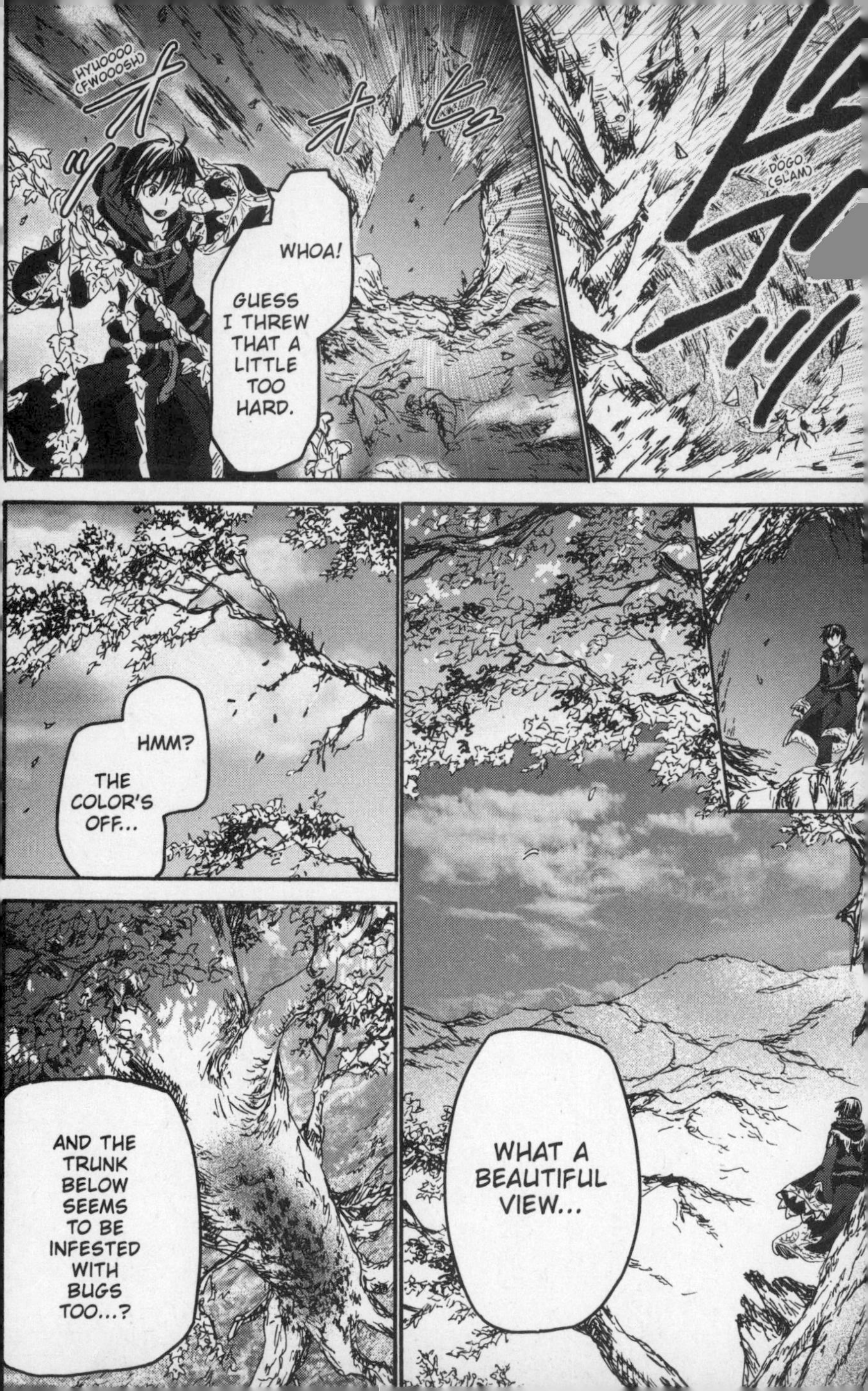
DOGO (SLAM)
HYUOOOO (FWOOOSH)
WHOA!
GUESS I THREW THAT A LITTLE TOO HARD.
WHAT A BEAUTIFUL VIEW...
HMM?
THE COLOR'S OFF...
AND THE TRUNK BELOW SEEMS TO BE INFESTED WITH BUGS TOO...?

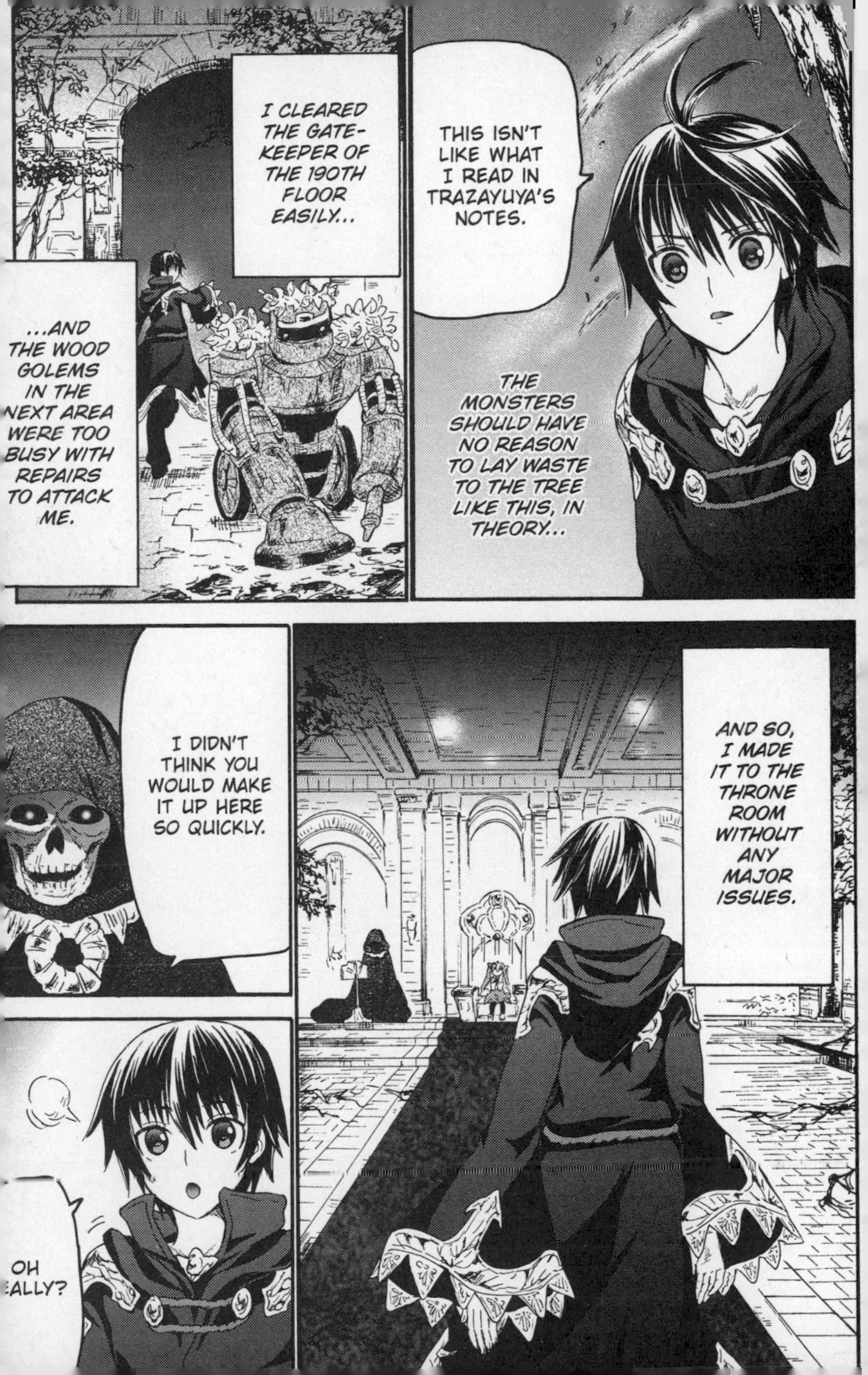
THIS ISN'T LIKE WHAT I READ IN TRAZAYUYA'S NOTES.
THE MONSTERS SHOULD HAVE NO REASON TO LAY WASTE TO THE TREE LIKE THIS, IN THEORY...
I CLEARED THE GATE-KEEPER OF THE 190TH FLOOR EASILY...
...AND THE WOOD GOLEMS IN THE NEXT AREA WERE TOO BUSY WITH REPAIRS TO ATTACK ME.
AND SO, I MADE IT TO THE THRONE ROOM WITHOUT ANY MAJOR ISSUES.
I DIDN'T THINK YOU WOULD MAKE IT UP HERE SO QUICKLY.
OH EALLY?

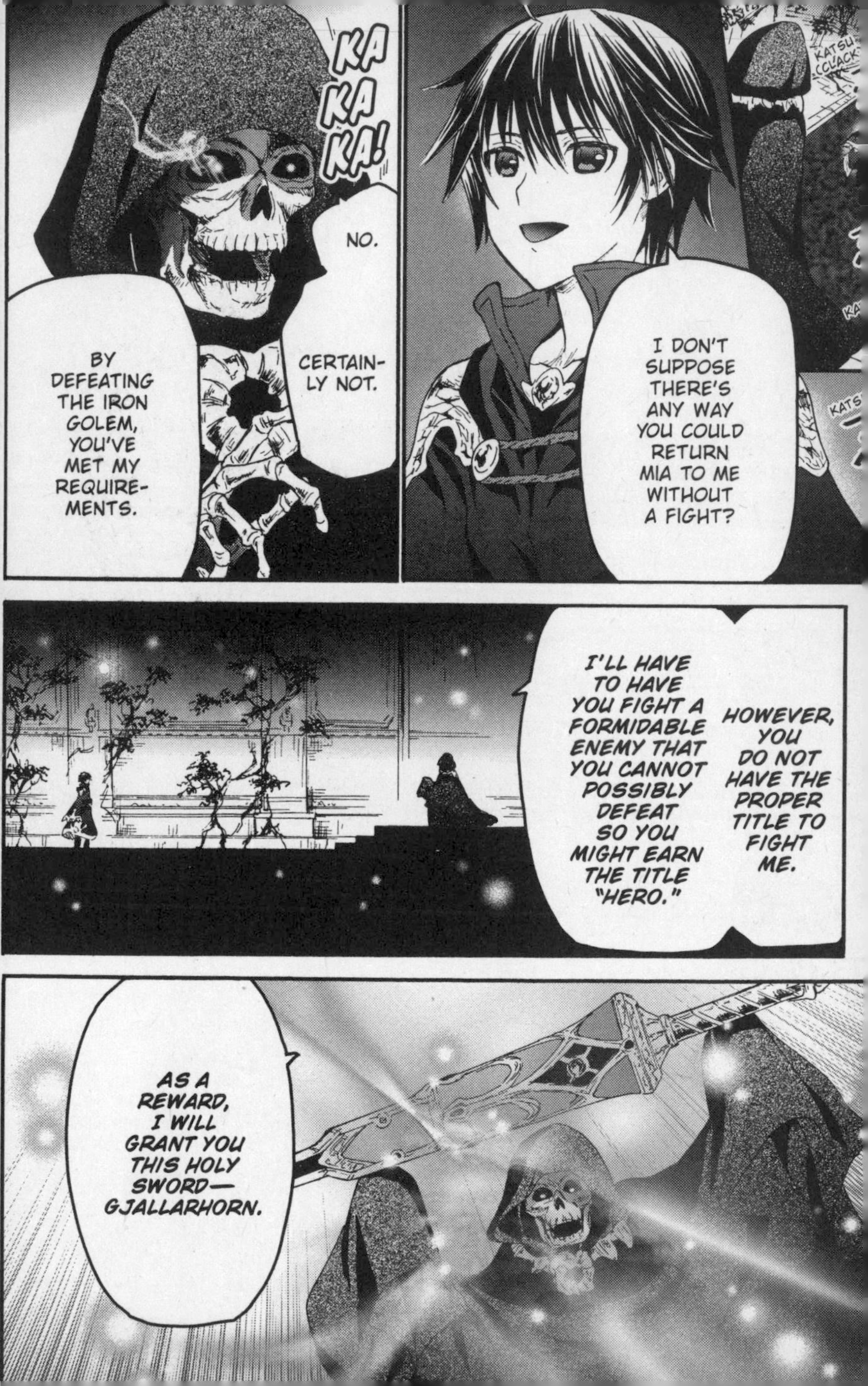
KATSU CLACK
I DON'T SUPPOSE THERE'S ANY WAY YOU COULD RETURN MIA TO ME WITHOUT A FIGHT?
KA KA KA!
NO.
CERTAIN-LY NOT.
BY DEFEATING THE IRON GOLEM, YOU'VE MET MY REQUIRE-MENTS.
HOWEVER, YOU DO NOT HAVE THE PROPER TITLE TO FIGHT ME.
I'LL HAVE TO HAVE YOU FIGHT A FORMIDABLE ENEMY THAT YOU CANNOT POSSIBLY DEFEAT SO YOU MIGHT EARN THE TITLE "HERO."
AS A REWARD, I WILL GRANT YOU THIS HOLY SWORD— GJALLARHORN.

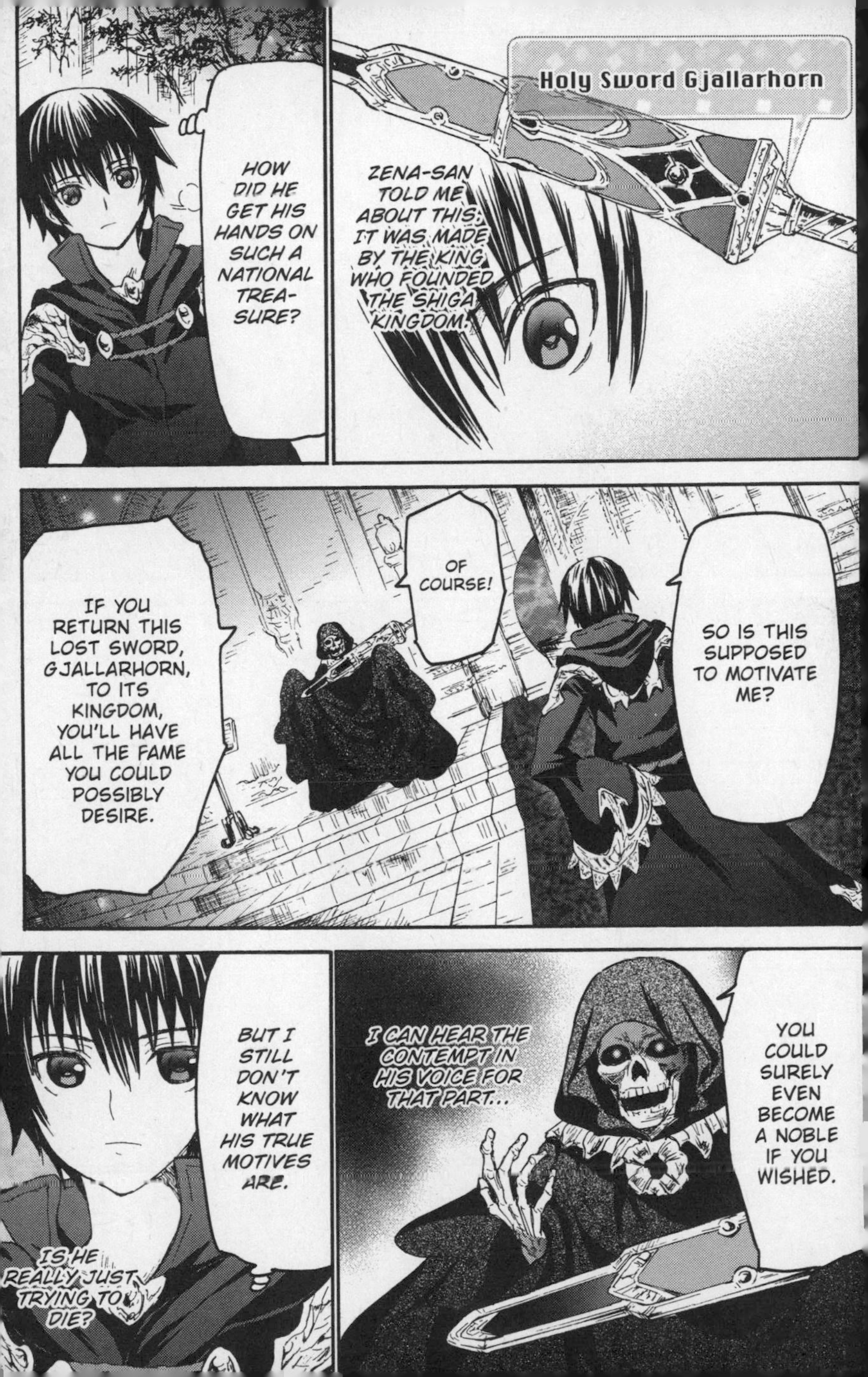
Holy Sword Gjallarhorn
ZENA-SAN TOLD ME ABOUT THIS. IT WAS MADE BY THE KING WHO FOUNDED THE SHIGA KINGDOM.
HOW DID HE GET HIS HANDS ON SUCH A NATIONAL TREA-SURE?
SO IS THIS SUPPOSED TO MOTIVATE ME?
OF COURSE!
IF YOU RETURN THIS LOST SWORD, GJALLARHORN, TO ITS KINGDOM, YOU'LL HAVE ALL THE FAME YOU COULD POSSIBLY DESIRE.
YOU COULD SURELY EVEN BECOME A NOBLE IF YOU WISHED.
I CAN HEAR THE CONTEMPT IN HIS VOICE FOR THAT PART...
BUT I STILL DON'T KNOW WHAT HIS TRUE MOTIVES ARE.
IS HE REALLY JUST TRYING TO DIE?

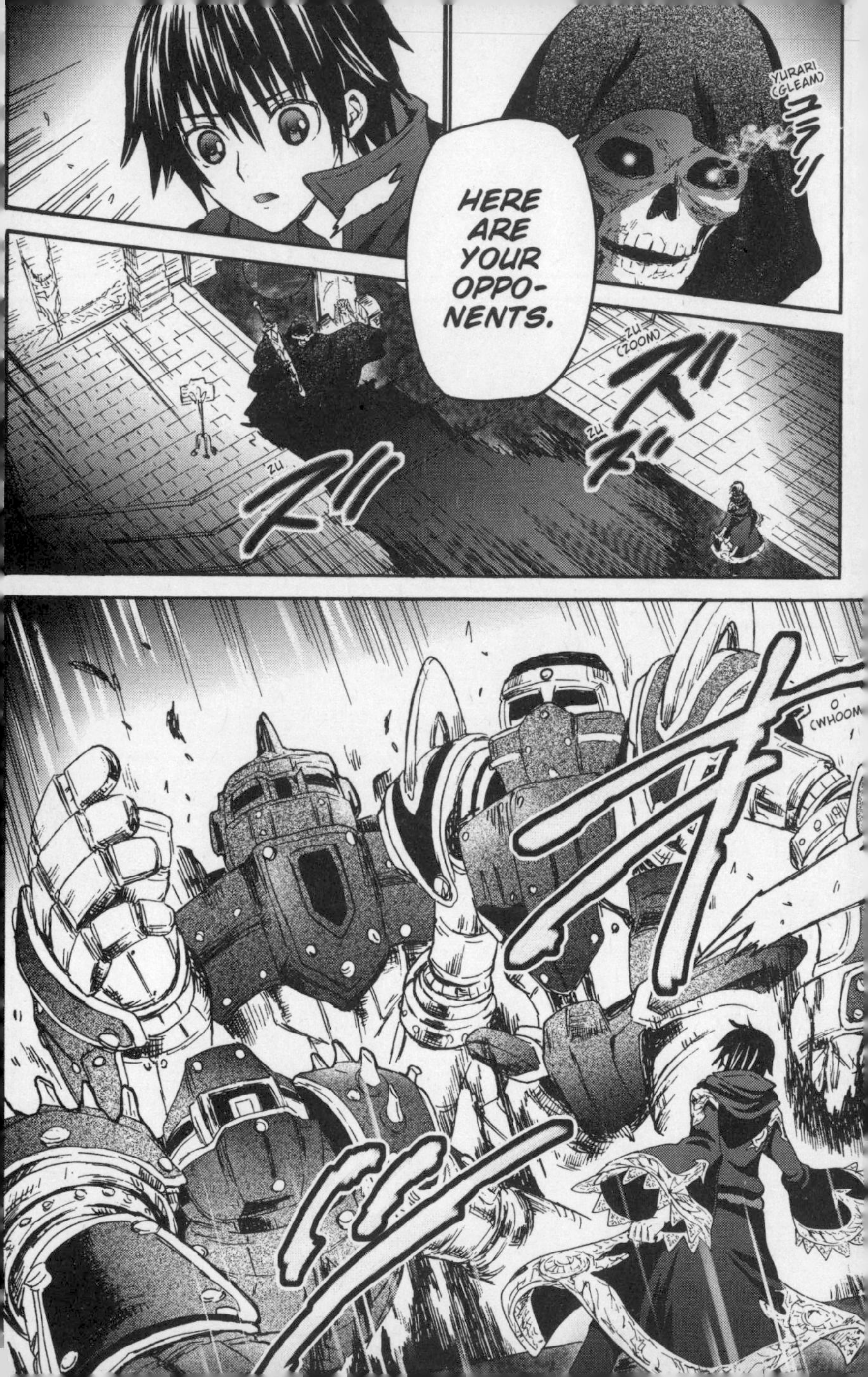
YURARI (GLEAM)
HERE ARE YOUR OPPO-NENTS.
ZU (ZOOM)
ZU
ZU
O (WHOOM

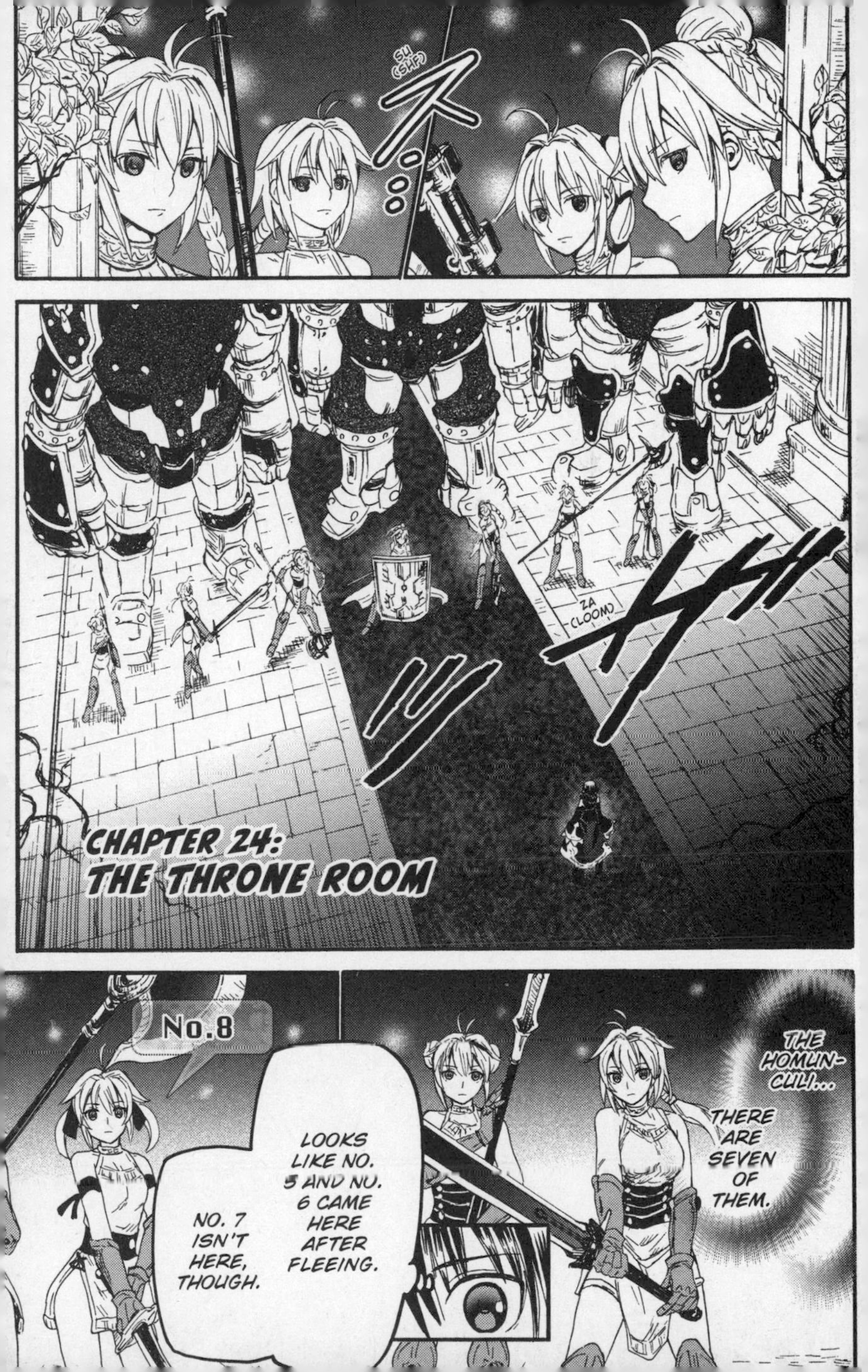
SU (SHF)
ZA (LOOM)
CHAPTER 24: THE THRONE ROOM
THE HOMUN-CULI...
THERE ARE SEVEN OF THEM.
No.8
LOOKS LIKE NO. 5 AND NO. 6 CAME HERE AFTER FLEEING.
NO. 7 ISN'T HERE, THOUGH.

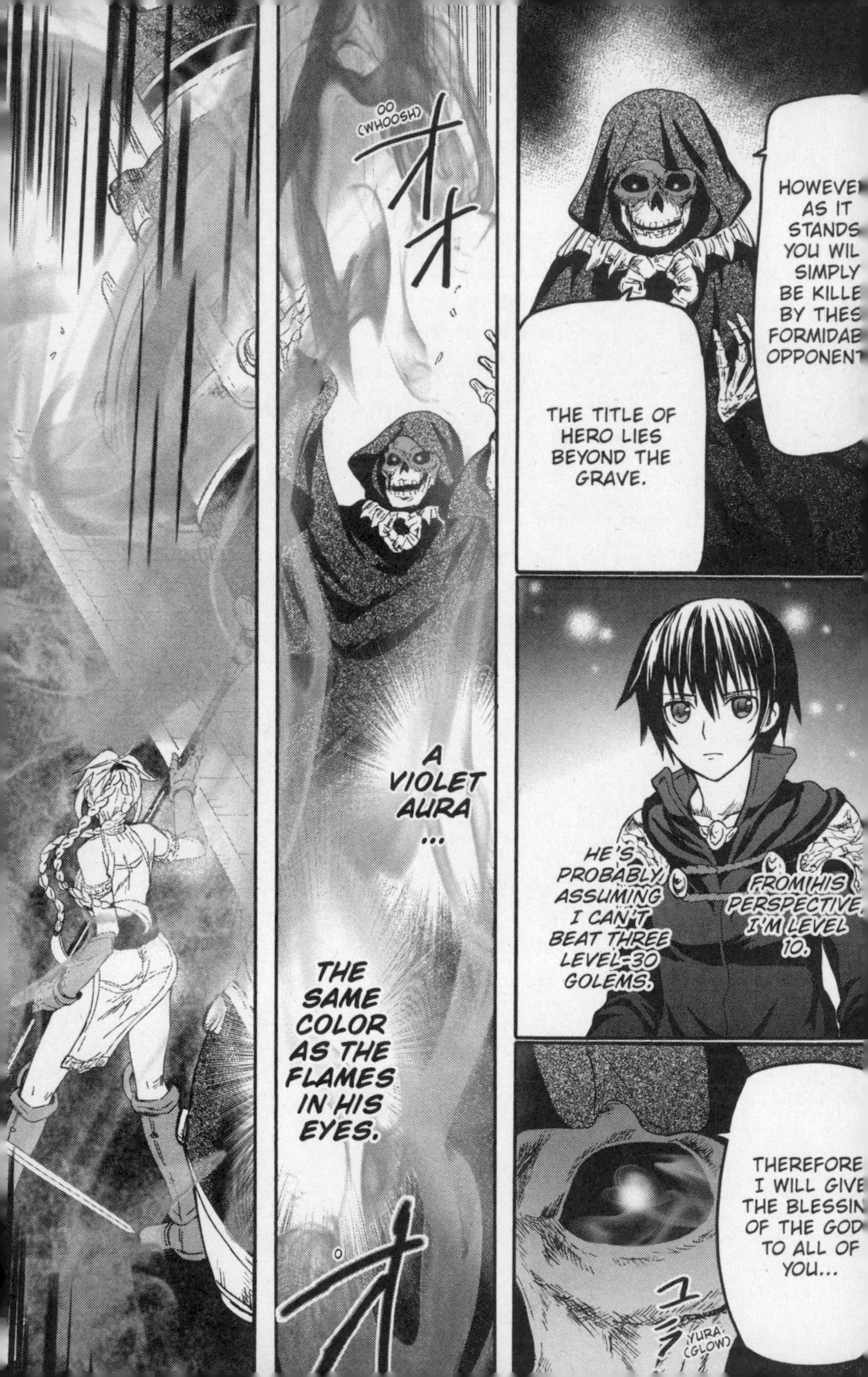
HOWEVE AS IT STANDS YOU WIL SIMPLY BE KILLE BY THES FORMIDAB OPPONENT
THE TITLE OF HERO LIES BEYOND THE GRAVE.
FROM HIS PERSPECTIVE, I'M LEVEL 10.
HE'S PROBABLY ASSUMING I CAN'T BEAT THREE LEVEL-30 GOLEMS.
THEREFORE I WILL GIVE THE BLESSIN OF THE GOD TO ALL OF YOU...
YURA (GLOW)
OO (WHOOSH)
A VIOLET AURA...
THE SAME COLOR AS THE FLAMES IN HIS EYES.

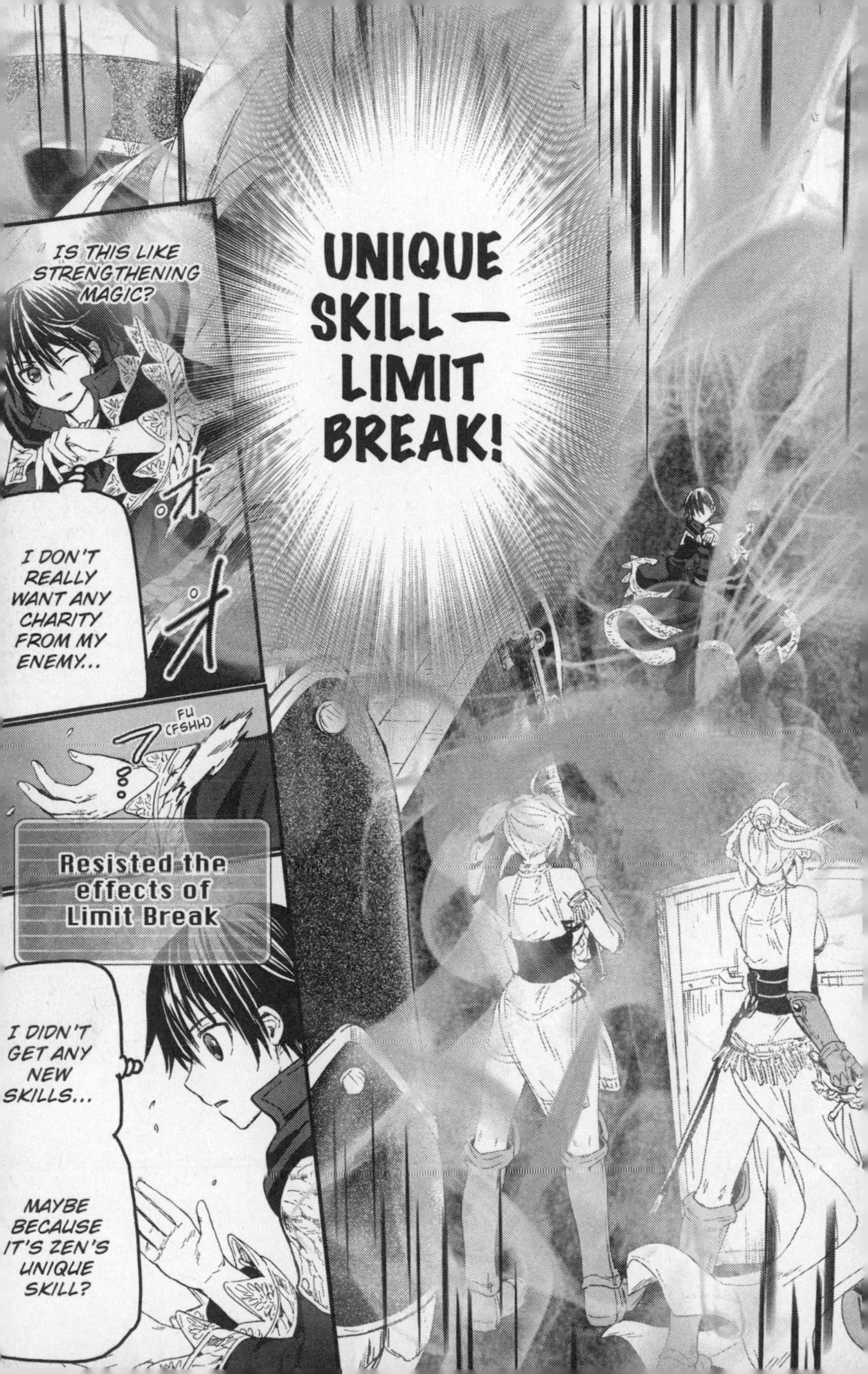
UNIQUE SKILL— LIMIT BREAK!
IS THIS LIKE STRENGTHENING MAGIC?
I DON'T REALLY WANT ANY CHARITY FROM MY ENEMY...
FU (FSHH)
Resisted the effects of Limit Break
I DIDN'T GET ANY NEW SKILLS...
MAYBE BECAUSE IT'S ZEN'S UNIQUE SKILL?

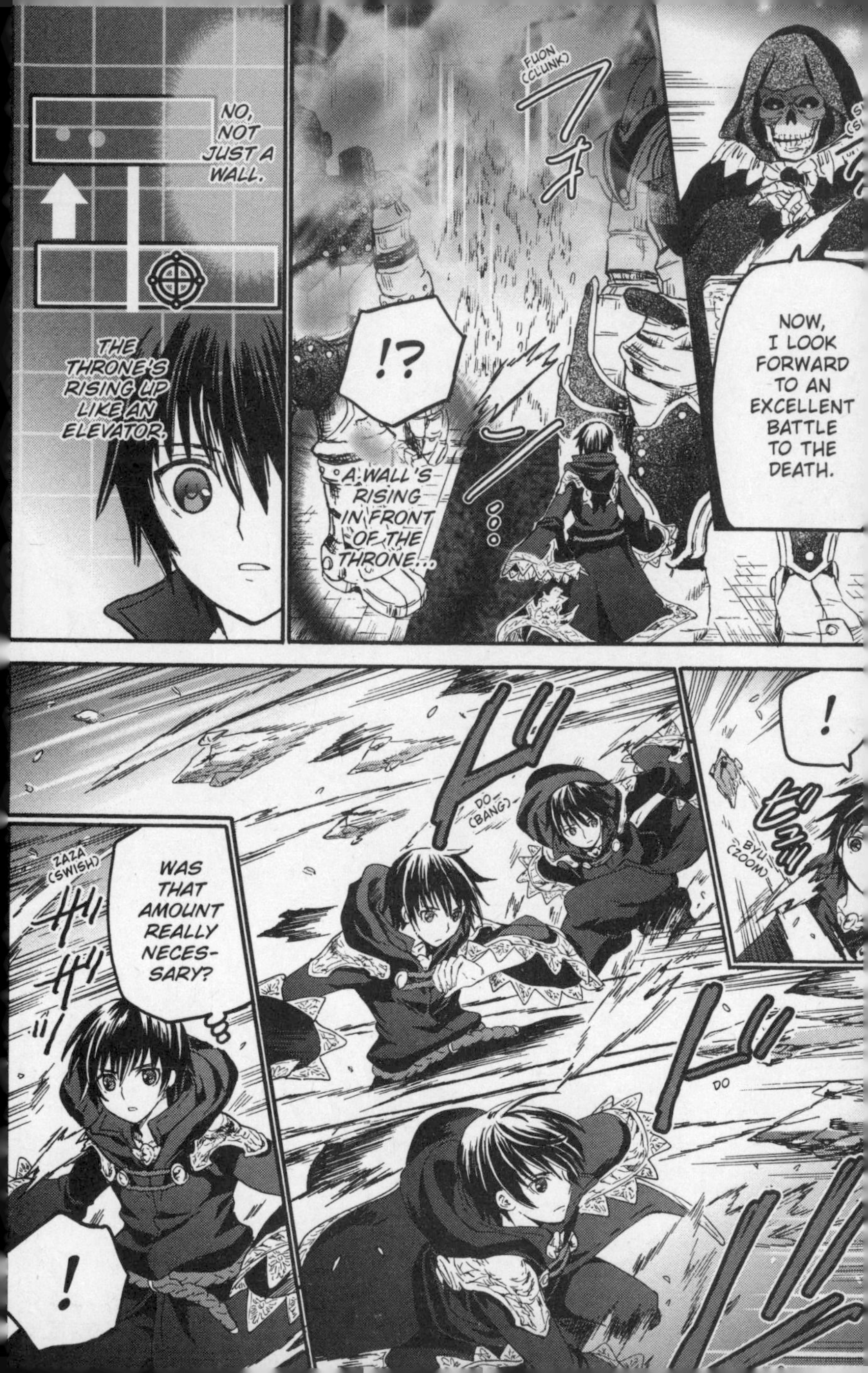
NOW, I LOOK FORWARD TO AN EXCELLENT BATTLE TO THE DEATH.
FUON (CLUNK)
!?
A WALL'S RISING IN FRONT OF THE THRONE...
...
NO, NOT JUST A WALL.
THE THRONE'S RISING UP LIKE AN ELEVATOR.
!
BYU (ZOOM)
DO (BANG)
DO
ZAZA (SWISH)
WAS THAT AMOUNT REALLY NECES-SARY?
!

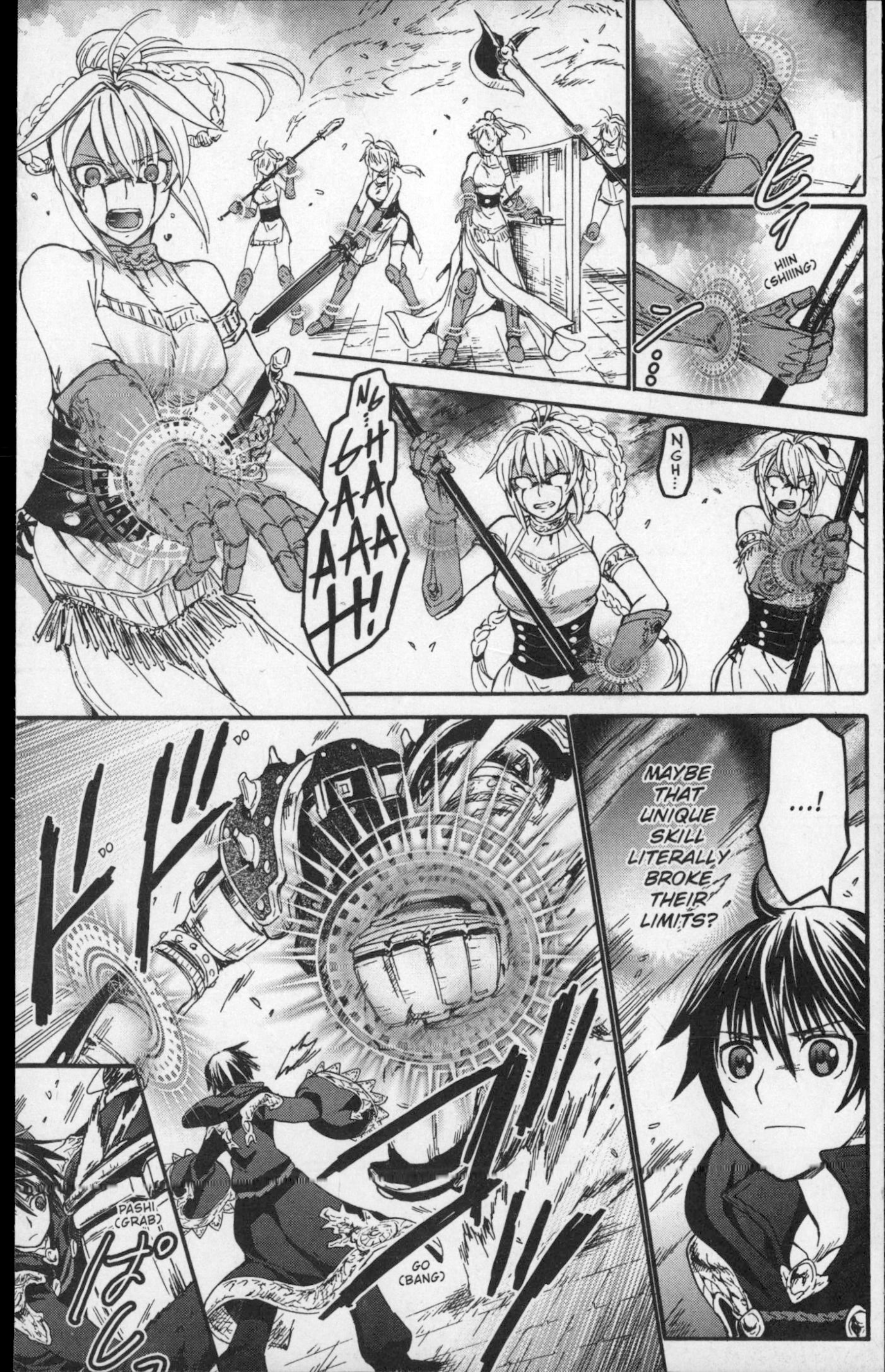
HIIN (SHIIING)
NGH...
NG... SHAAAAAAH!
MAYBE THAT UNIQUE SKILL LITERALLY BROKE THEIR LIMITS?
...!
DO
DO
GO (BANG)
PASHI (GRAB)

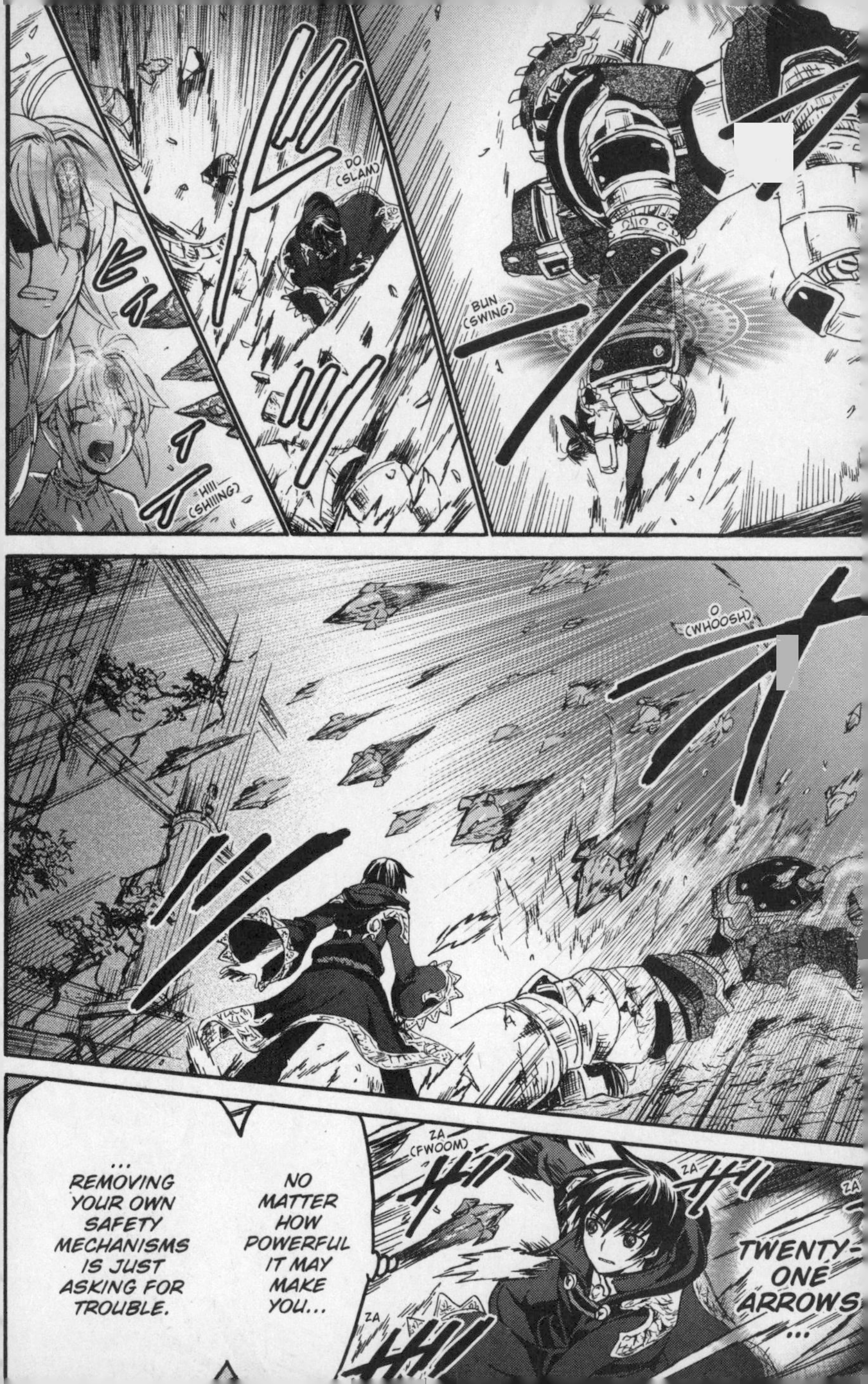
BUN (SWING)
DO (SLAM)
HIII (SHIIING)
O (WHOOSH)
TWENTY-ONE ARROWS...
ZA
ZA
ZA (FWOOM)
ZA
NO MATTER HOW POWERFUL IT MAY MAKE YOU...
...REMOVING YOUR OWN SAFETY MECHANISMS IS JUST ASKING FOR TROUBLE.

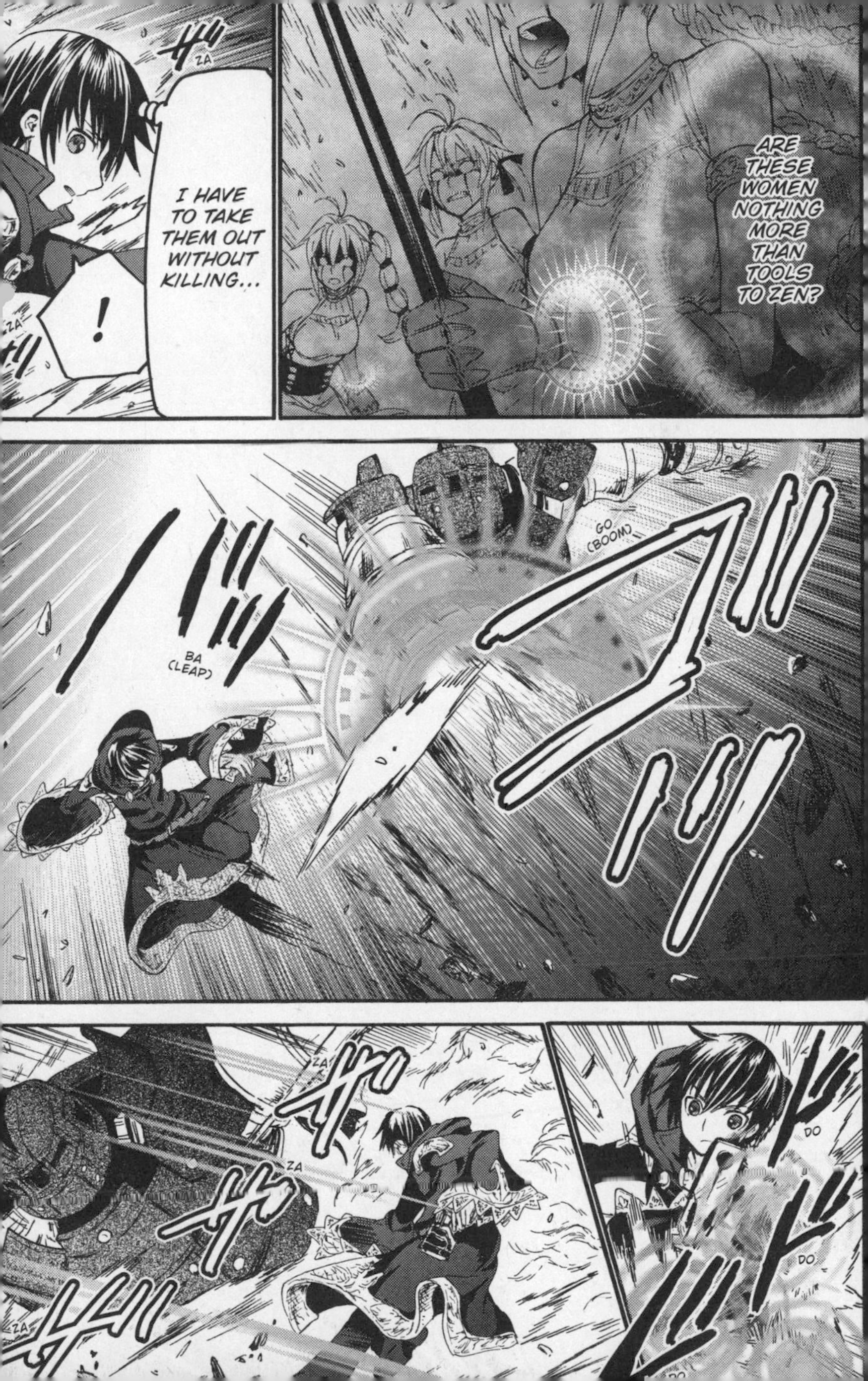
ARE THESE WOMEN NOTHING MORE THAN TOOLS TO ZEN?
ZA
I HAVE TO TAKE THEM OUT WITHOUT KILLING...
!
ZA
GO (BOOM)
BA (LEAP)
DO
DO
ZA
ZA
ZA

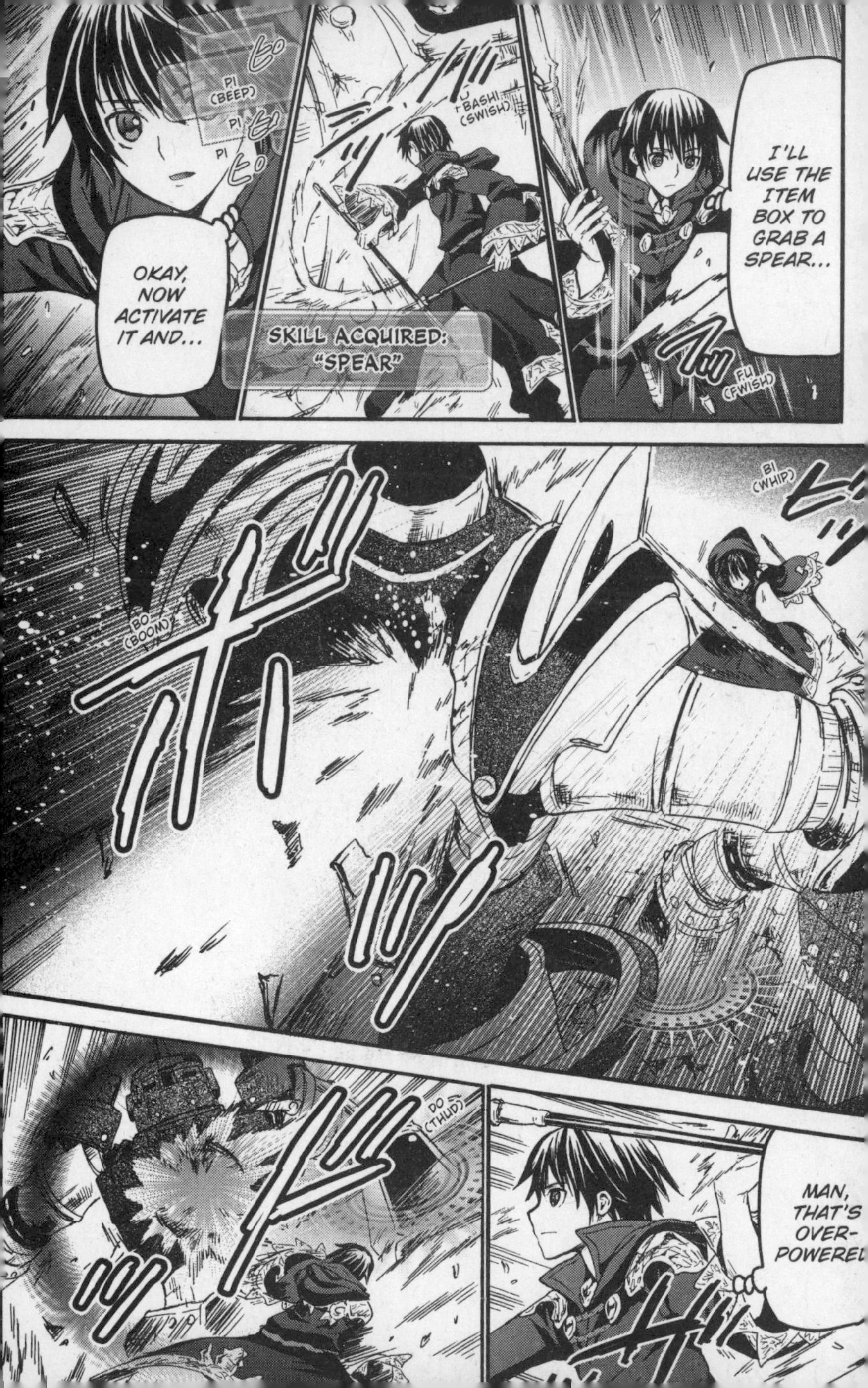
I'LL USE THE ITEM BOX TO GRAB A SPEAR...
FU (FWISH)
BASHI (SWISH)
SKILL ACQUIRED: "SPEAR"
PI (BEEP)
PI
PI
OKAY, NOW ACTIVATE IT AND...
BI (WHIP)
BO (BOOM)
MAN, THAT'S OVER-POWERED
DO (THUD)

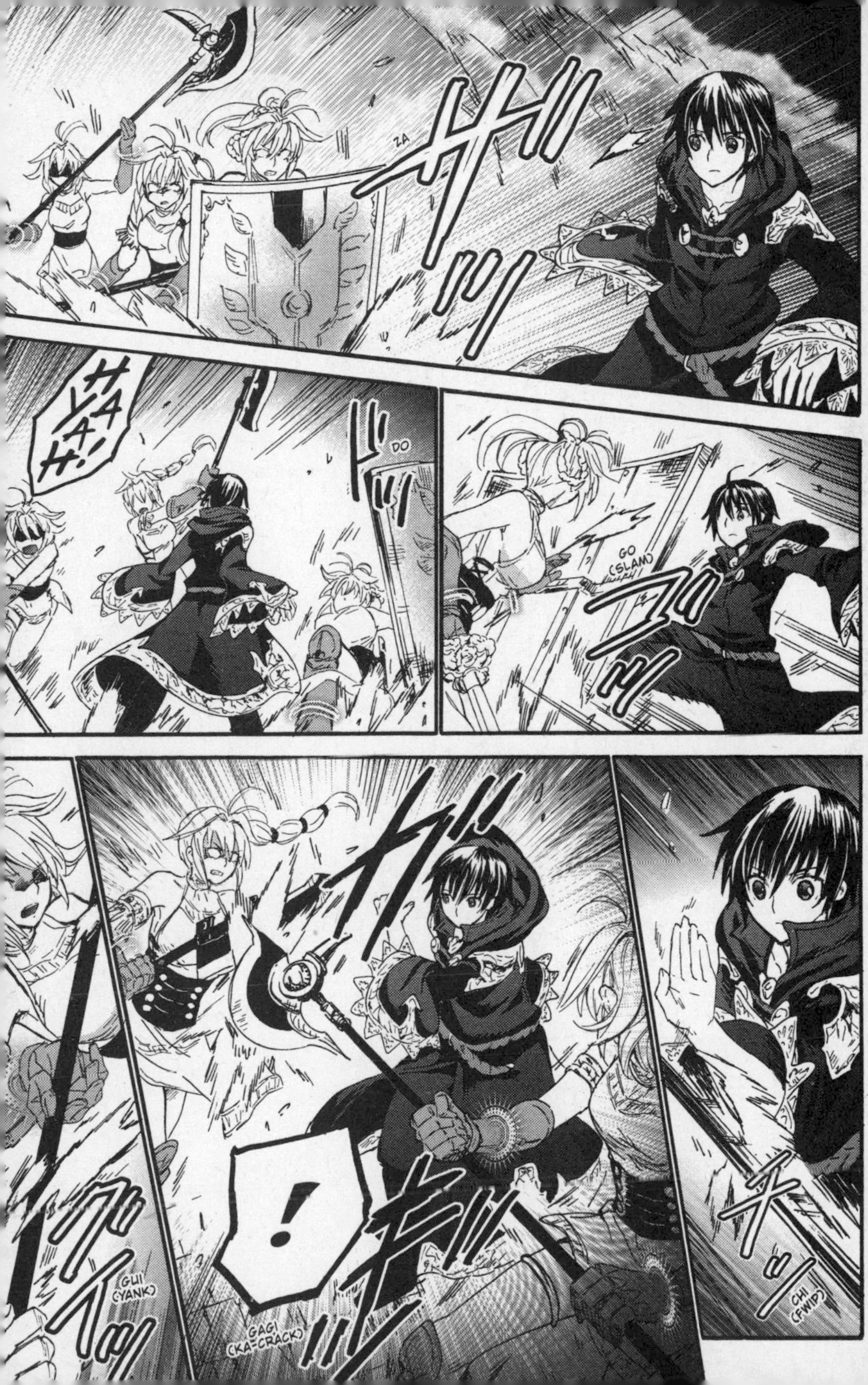
ZA
GO (SLAM)
DO
HYAAH!
CHI (FWIP)
!
GAGI (KA-CRACK)
GUI (YANK)

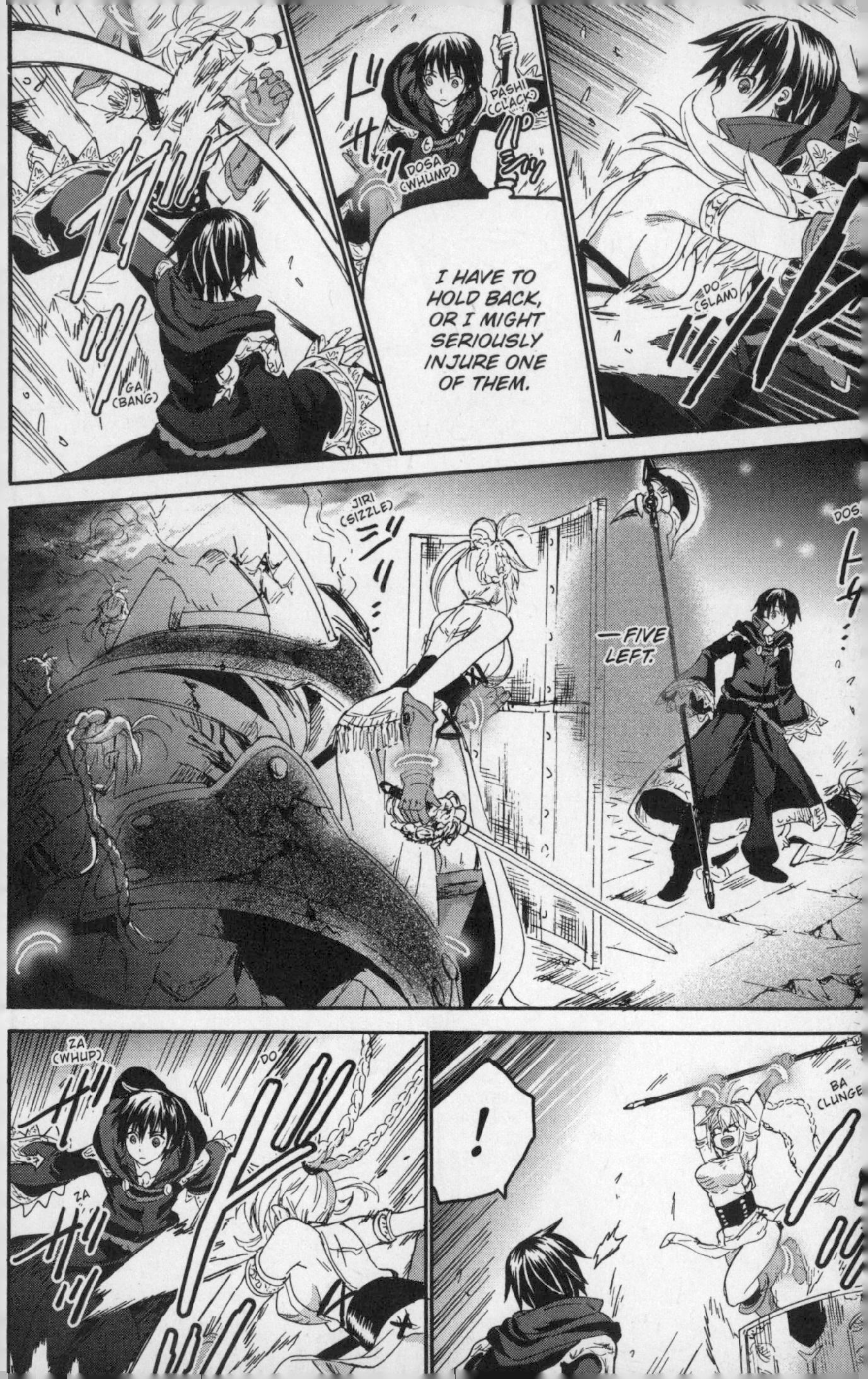
DO (SLAM)
PASHI (CLACK)
DOSA (WHUMP)
I HAVE TO HOLD BACK, OR I MIGHT SERIOUSLY INJURE ONE OF THEM.
GA (BANG)
—FIVE LEFT.
JIRI (SIZZLE)
BA (LUNGE)
!
DO
ZA (WHUP)
ZA

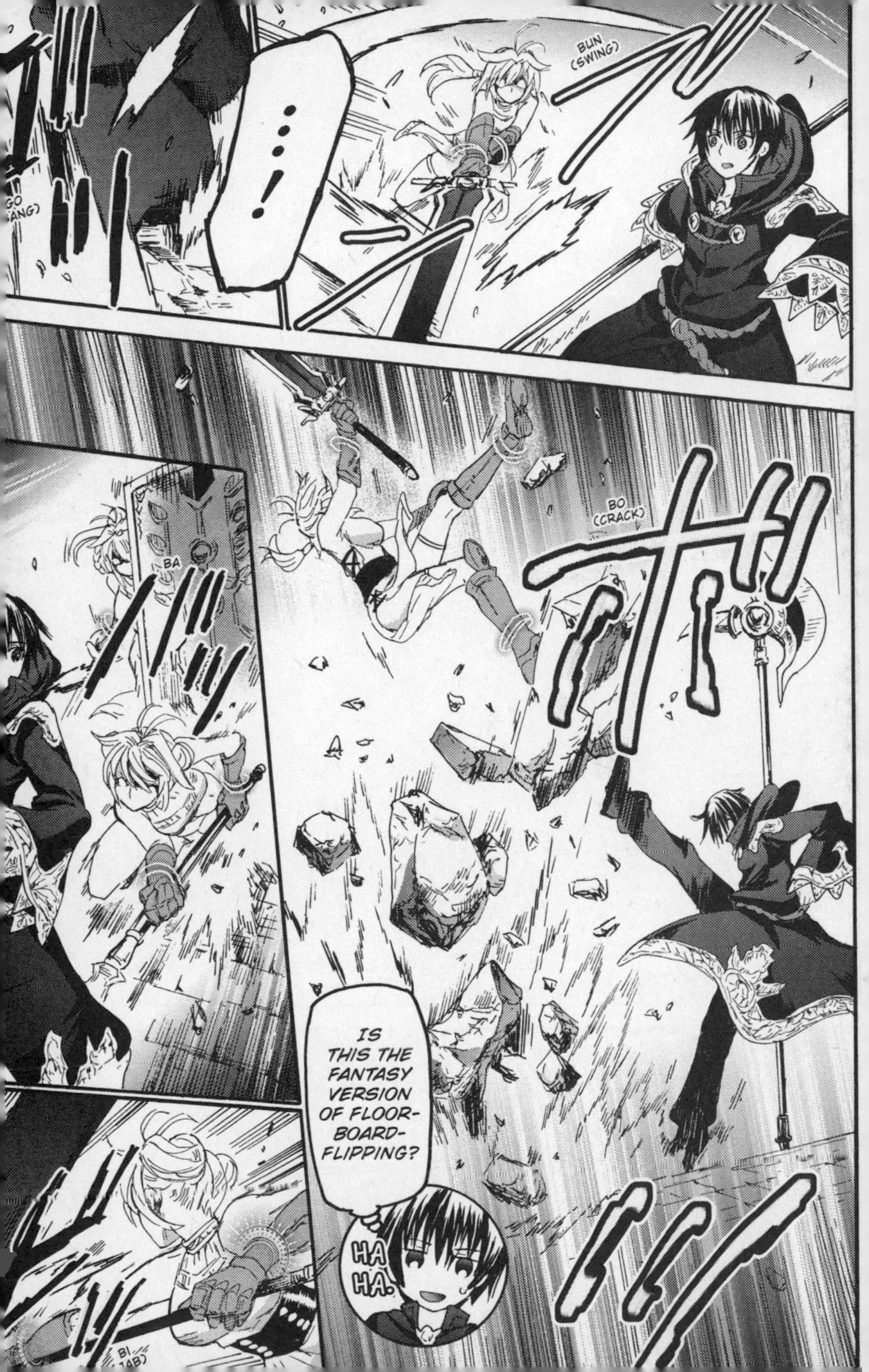

BUN (SWING)
...!
GO
BO (CRACK)
IS THIS THE FANTASY VERSION OF FLOOR-BOARD-FLIPPING?
HA HA.
BA
BI-

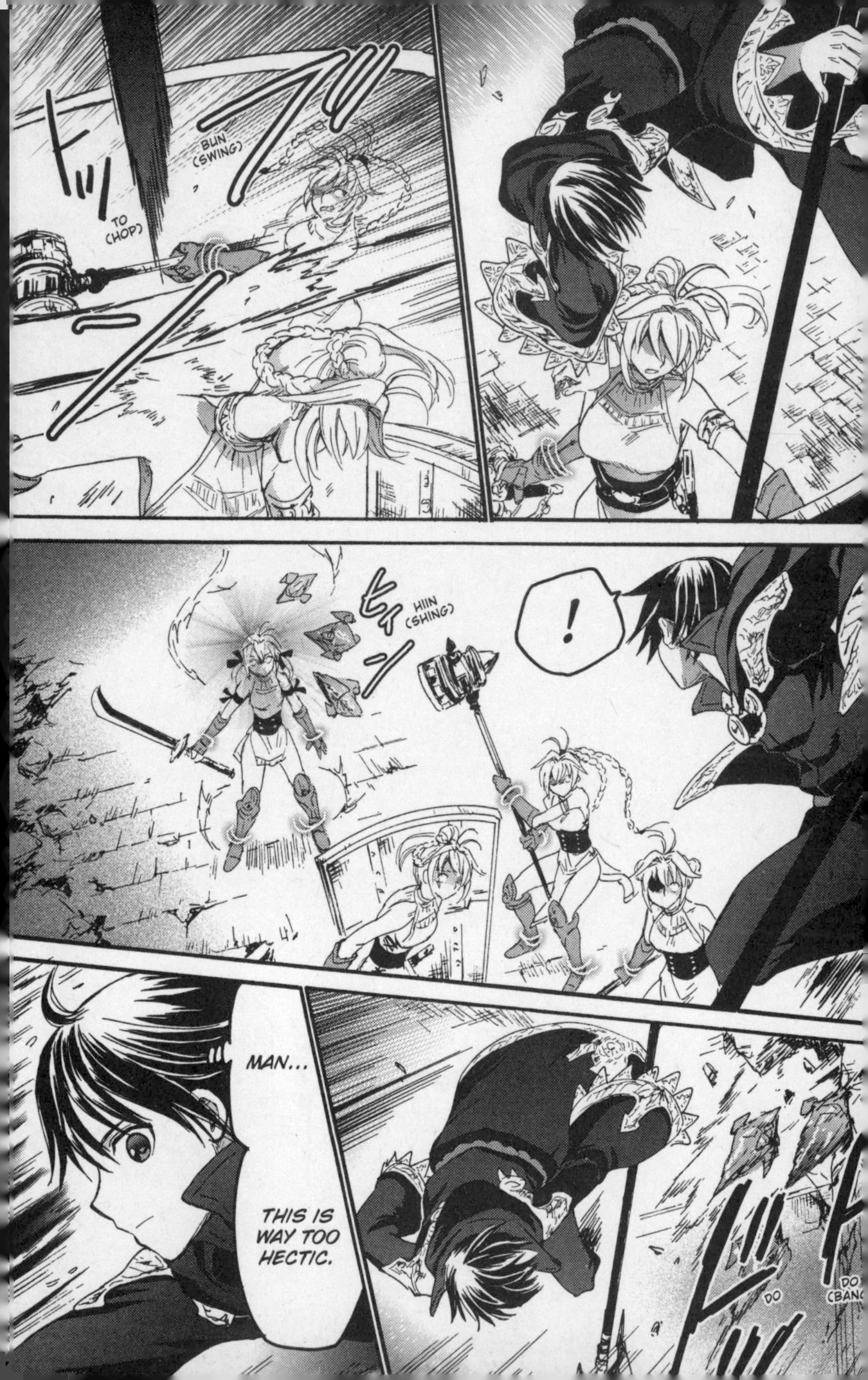
BUN (SWING)
TO (HOP)
!
HIIN (SHING)
DO
DO (BANG
MAN...
THIS IS WAY TOO HECTIC.

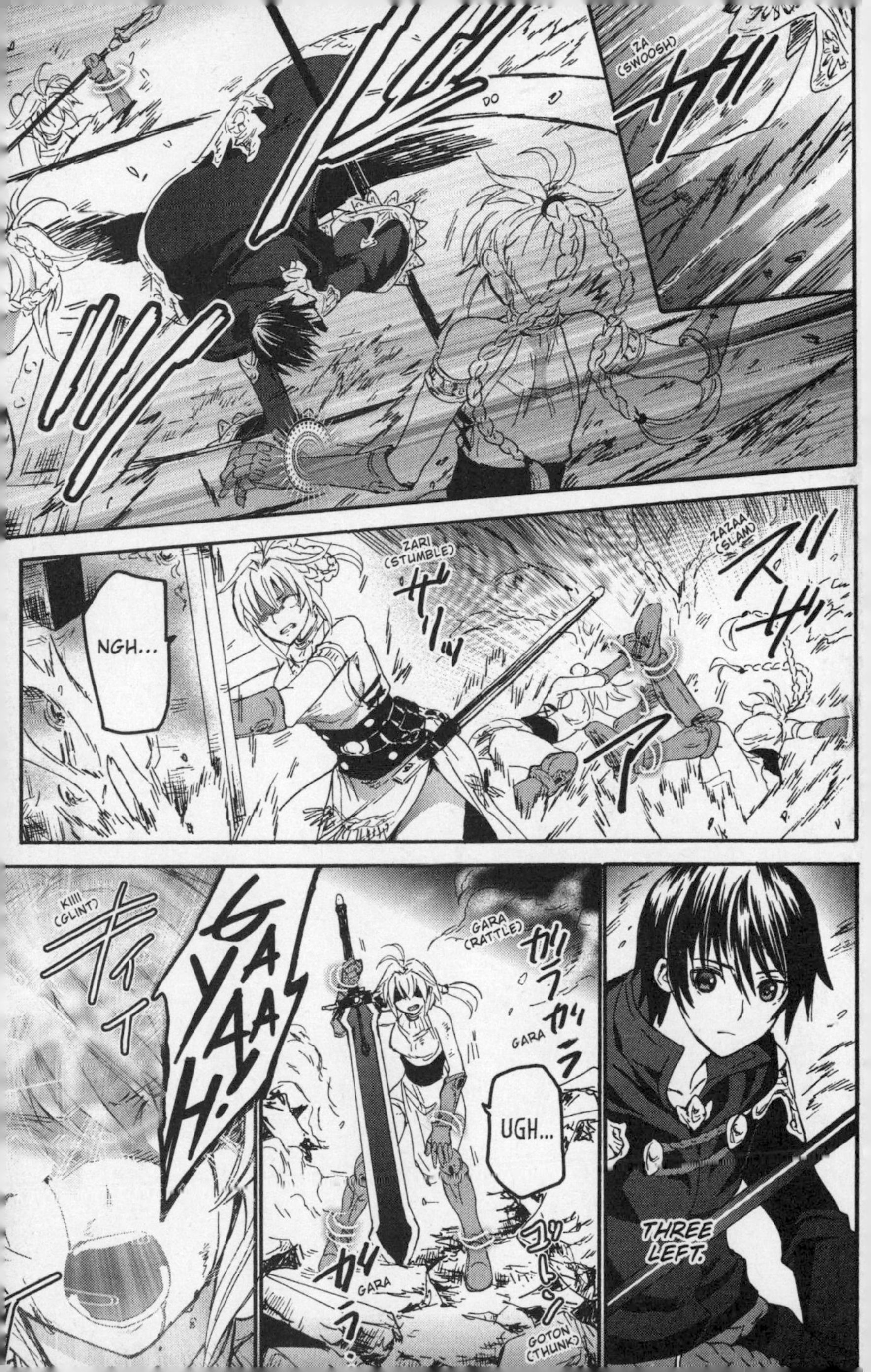
ZA
(SWOOSH)
DO
ZAZAA
(SLAM)
ZARI
(STUMBLE)
NGH...
THREE LEFT.
GARA
(RATTLE)
GARA
UGH...
GOTON
(THUNK)
GARA
KIIII
(GLINT)
GAYAAAH!

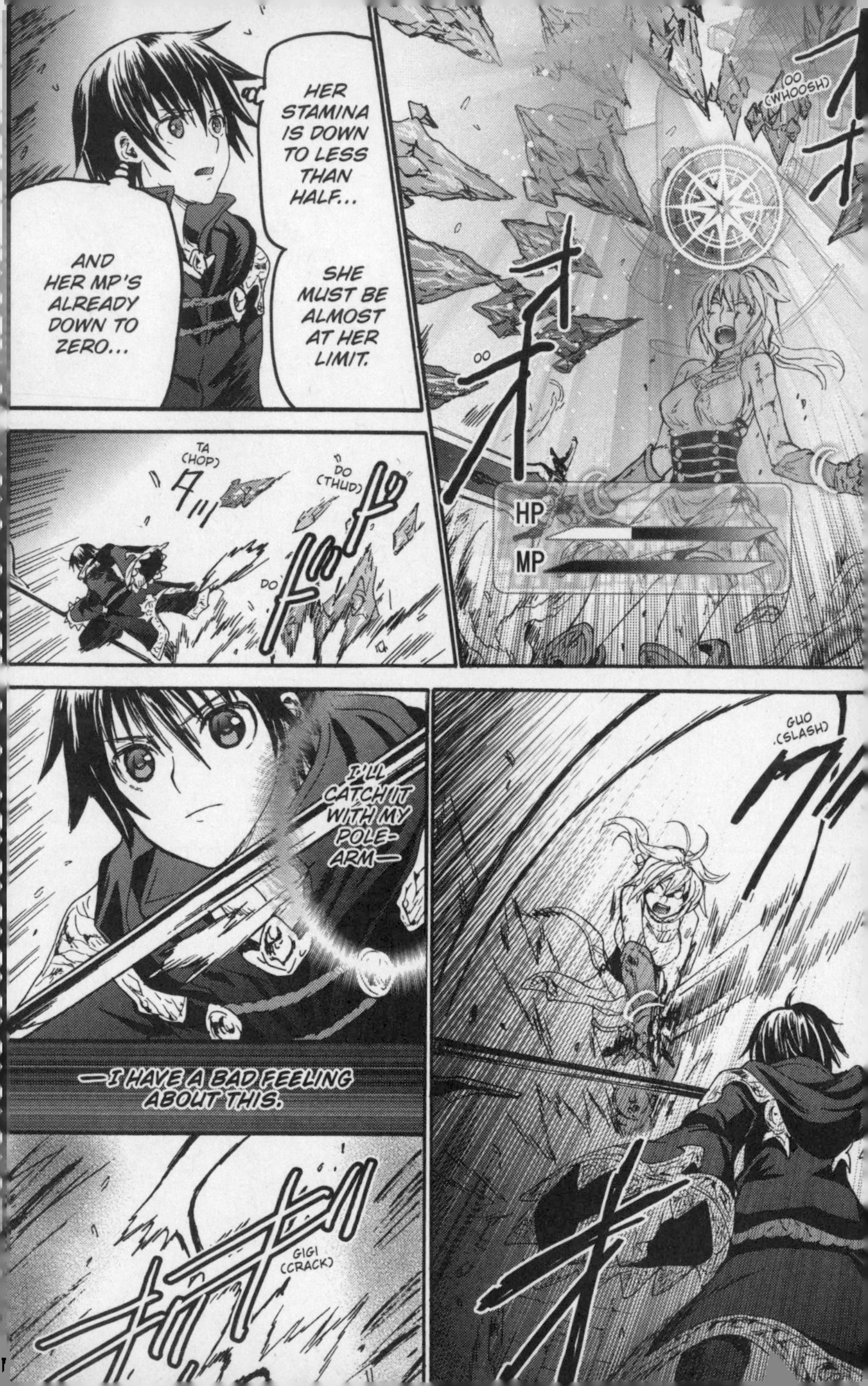
OO (WHOOSH)
OO
HP
MP
HER STAMINA IS DOWN TO LESS THAN HALF...
SHE MUST BE ALMOST AT HER LIMIT.
AND HER MP'S ALREADY DOWN TO ZERO...
DO (THUD)
DO
TA (HOP)
GUO (SLASH)
I'LL CATCH IT WITH MY POLE-ARM—
—I HAVE A BAD FEELING ABOUT THIS.
GIGI (CRACK)

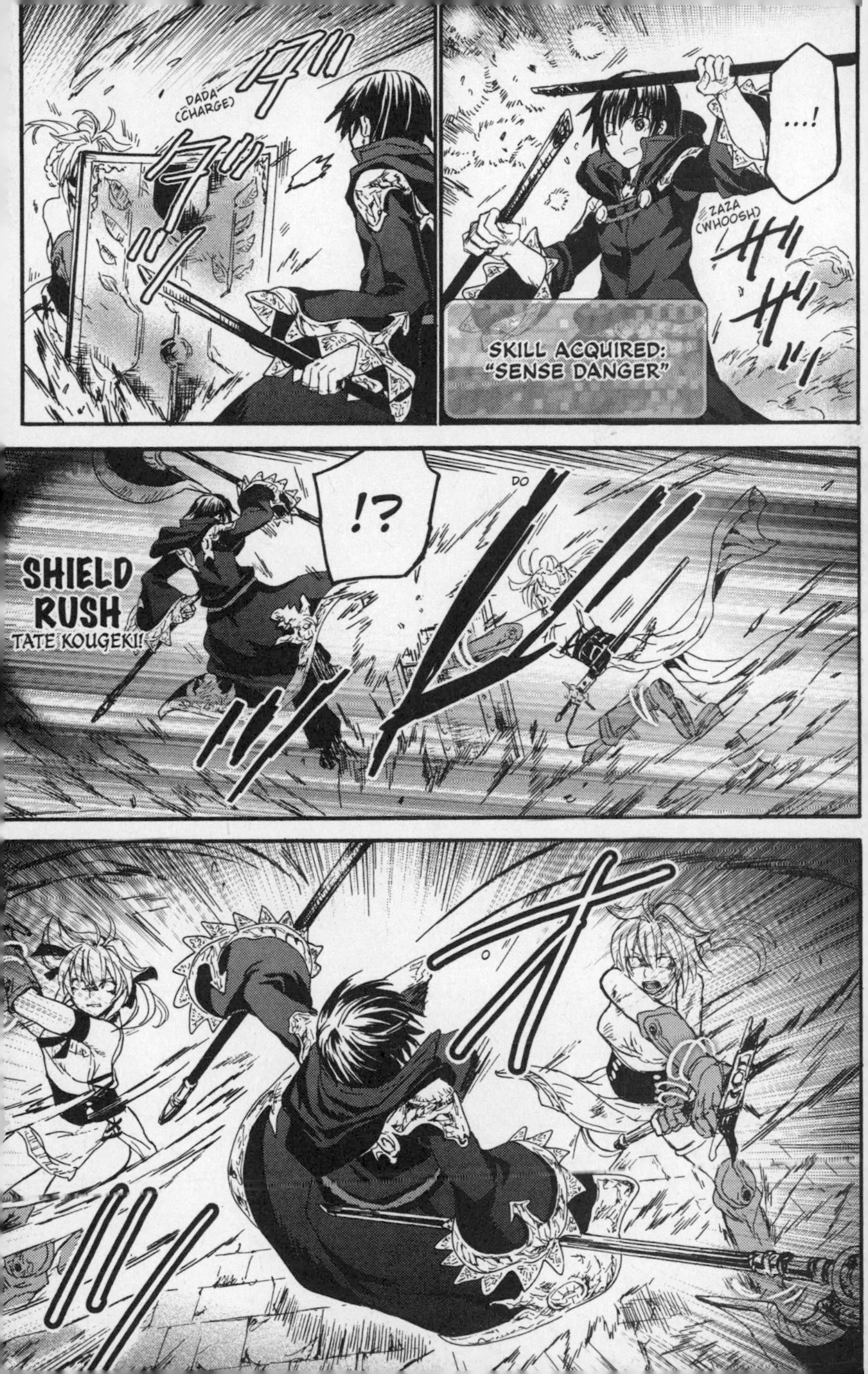
...!
ZAZA (WHOOSH)
SKILL ACQUIRED: “SENSE DANGER”
DADA (CHARGE)
DO
!?
SHIELD RUSH
TATE KOUGEKI!

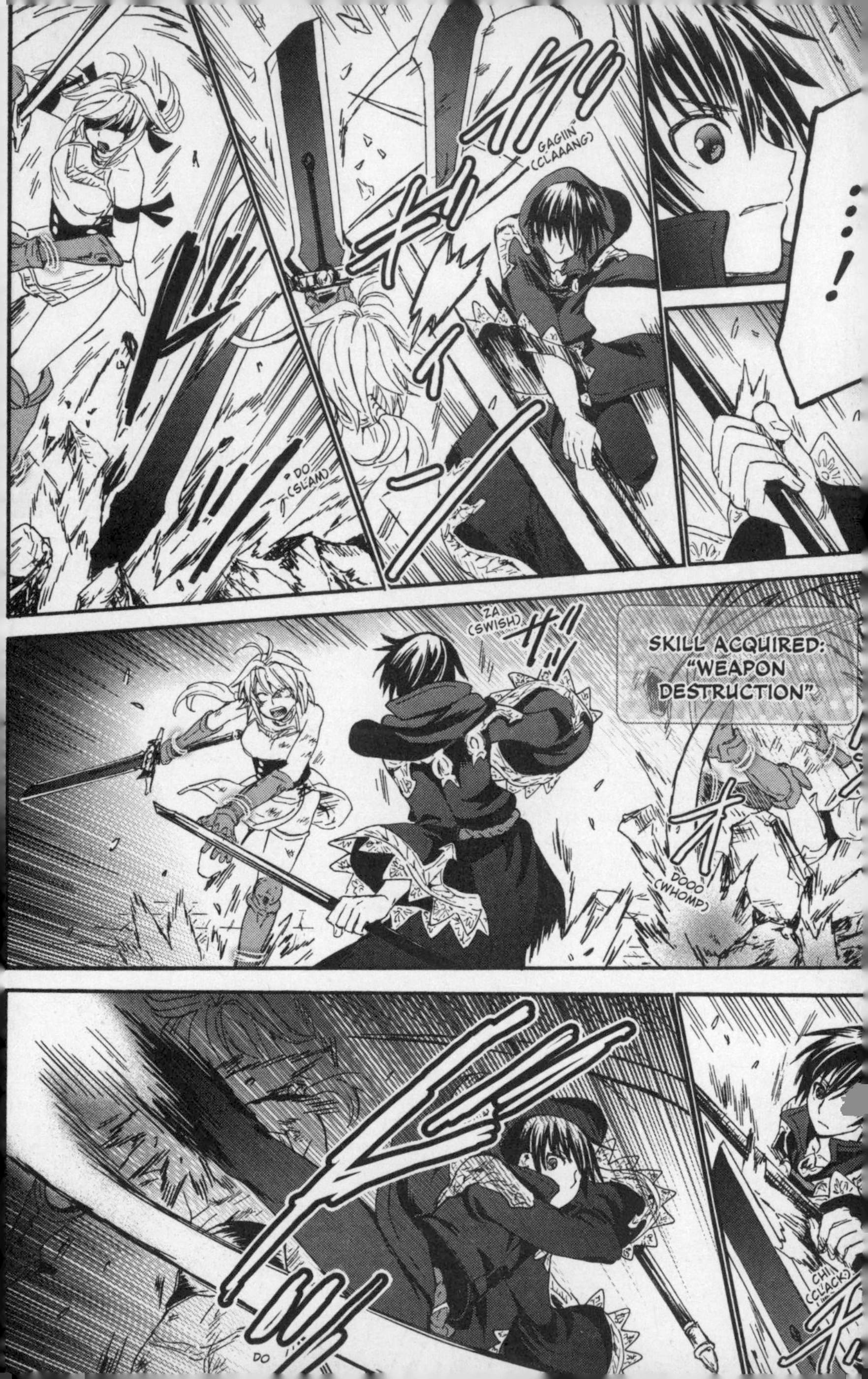
...!
GAGIIN (CLAAANG)
DO (SLAM)
SKILL ACQUIRED: "WEAPON DESTRUCTION"
ZA (SWISH)
DOOO (WHOMP)
CHI (CLACK)
DO

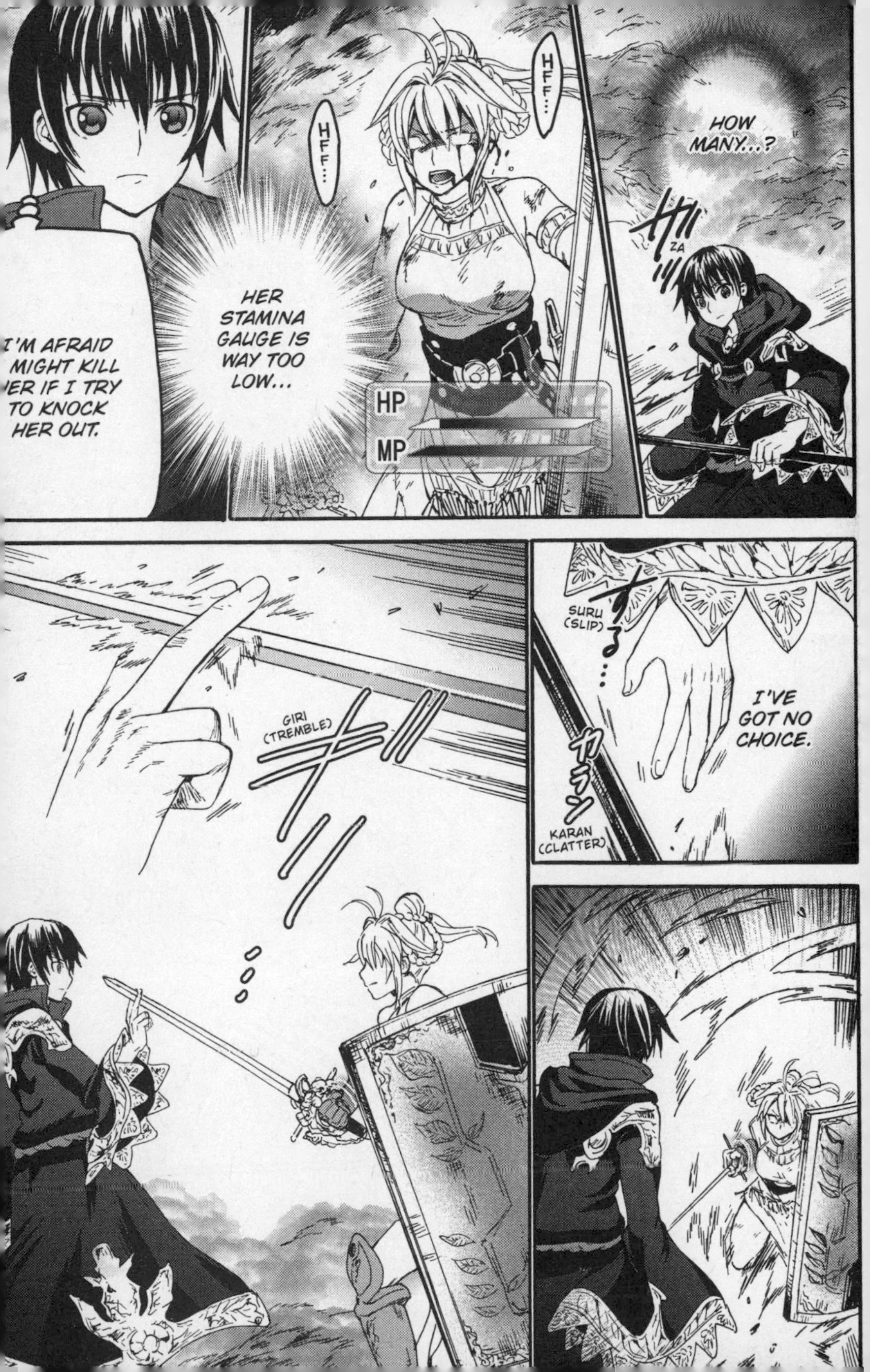
HOW MANY...?
ZA
HFF...
HFF...
HER STAMINA GAUGE IS WAY TOO LOW...
HP
MP
I'M AFRAID
MIGHT KILL
ER IF I TRY
TO KNOCK
HER OUT.
SURU (SLIP)
I'VE GOT NO CHOICE.
KARAN (CLATTER)
GIRI (TREMBLE)

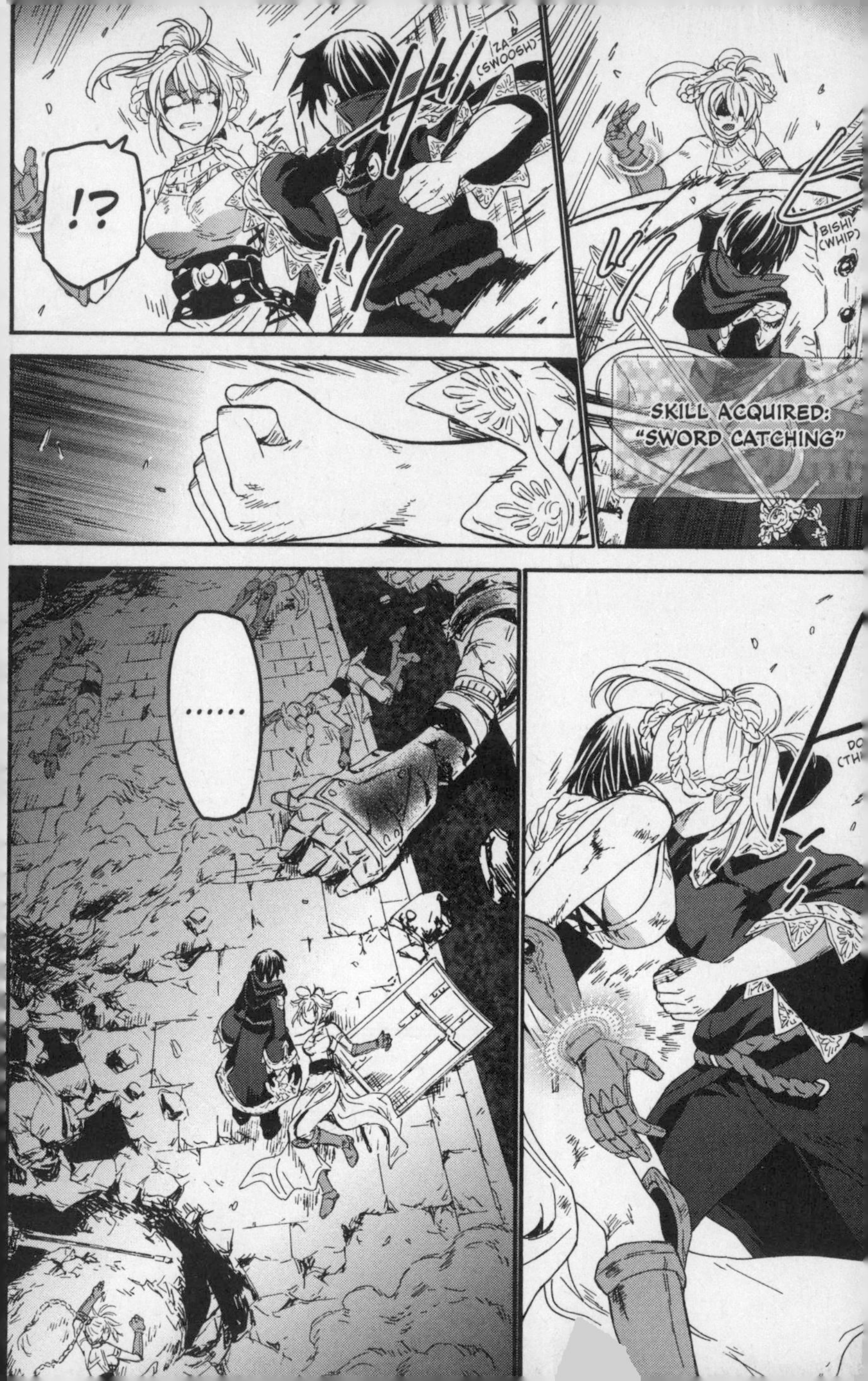
BISHI (WHIP)
SKILL ACQUIRED: "SWORD CATCHING"
ZA (SWOOSH)
!?
......

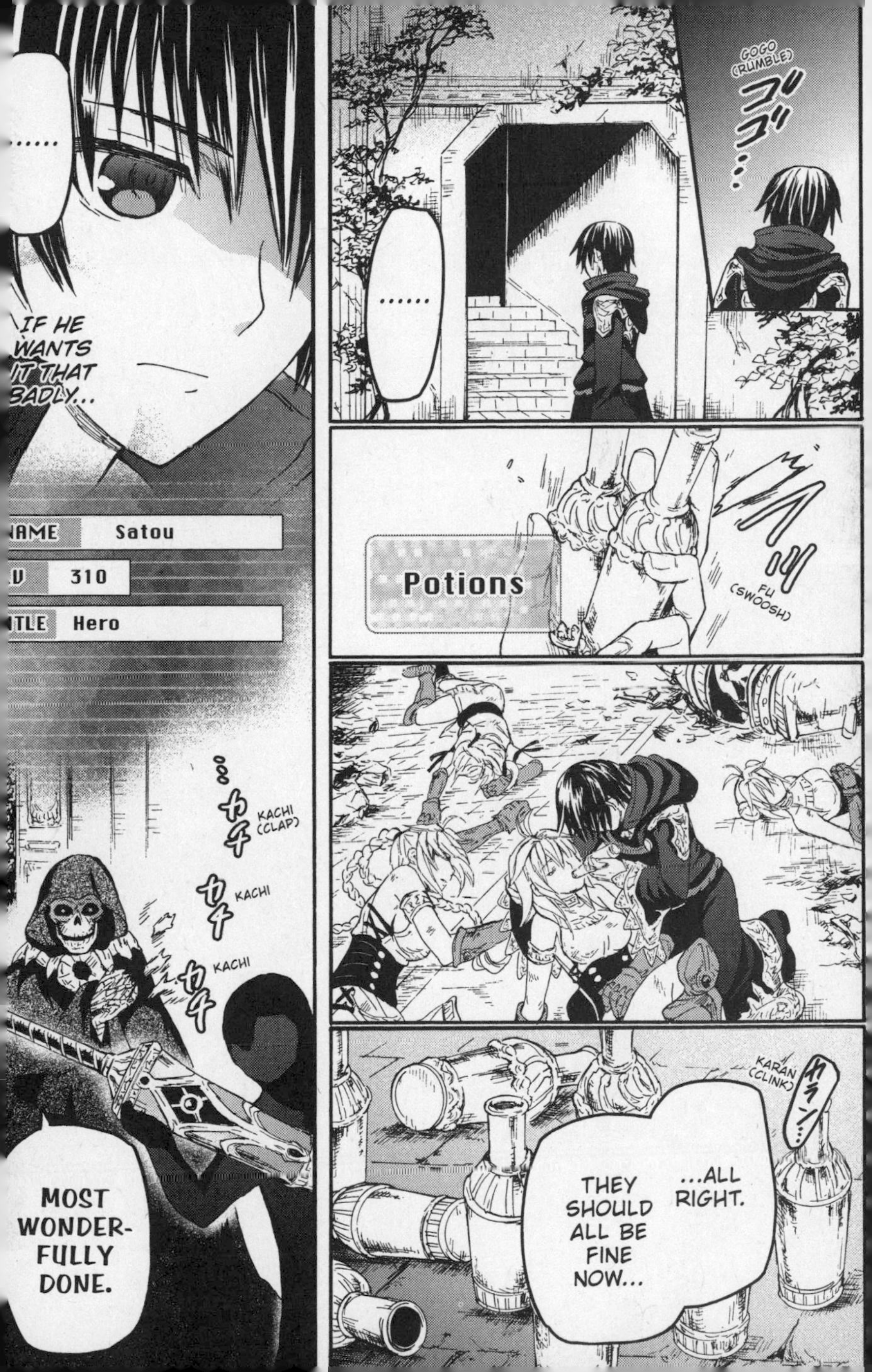
GOGO (RUMBLE)
......
FU (SWOOSH)
Potions
KARAN (CLINK)
...ALL RIGHT.
THEY SHOULD ALL BE FINE NOW...
......
IF HE WANTS IT THAT BADLY...
NAME Satou
V 310
TLE Hero
KACHI (CLAP)
KACHI
KACHI
MOST WONDER-FULLY DONE.

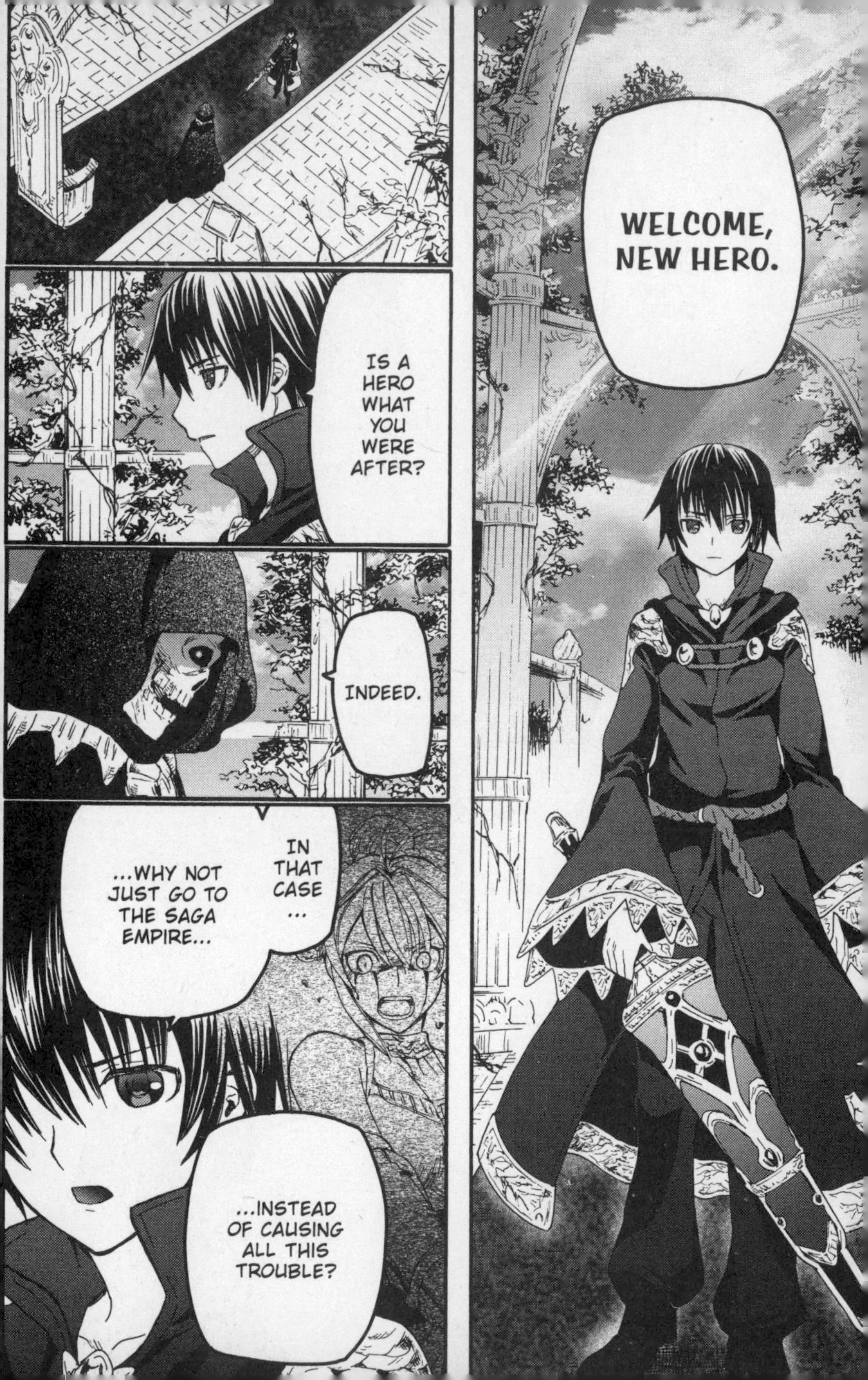
WELCOME, NEW HERO.
IS A HERO WHAT YOU WERE AFTER?
INDEED.
IN THAT CASE ...
...WHY NOT JUST GO TO THE SAGA EMPIRE...
...INSTEAD OF CAUSING ALL THIS TROUBLE?

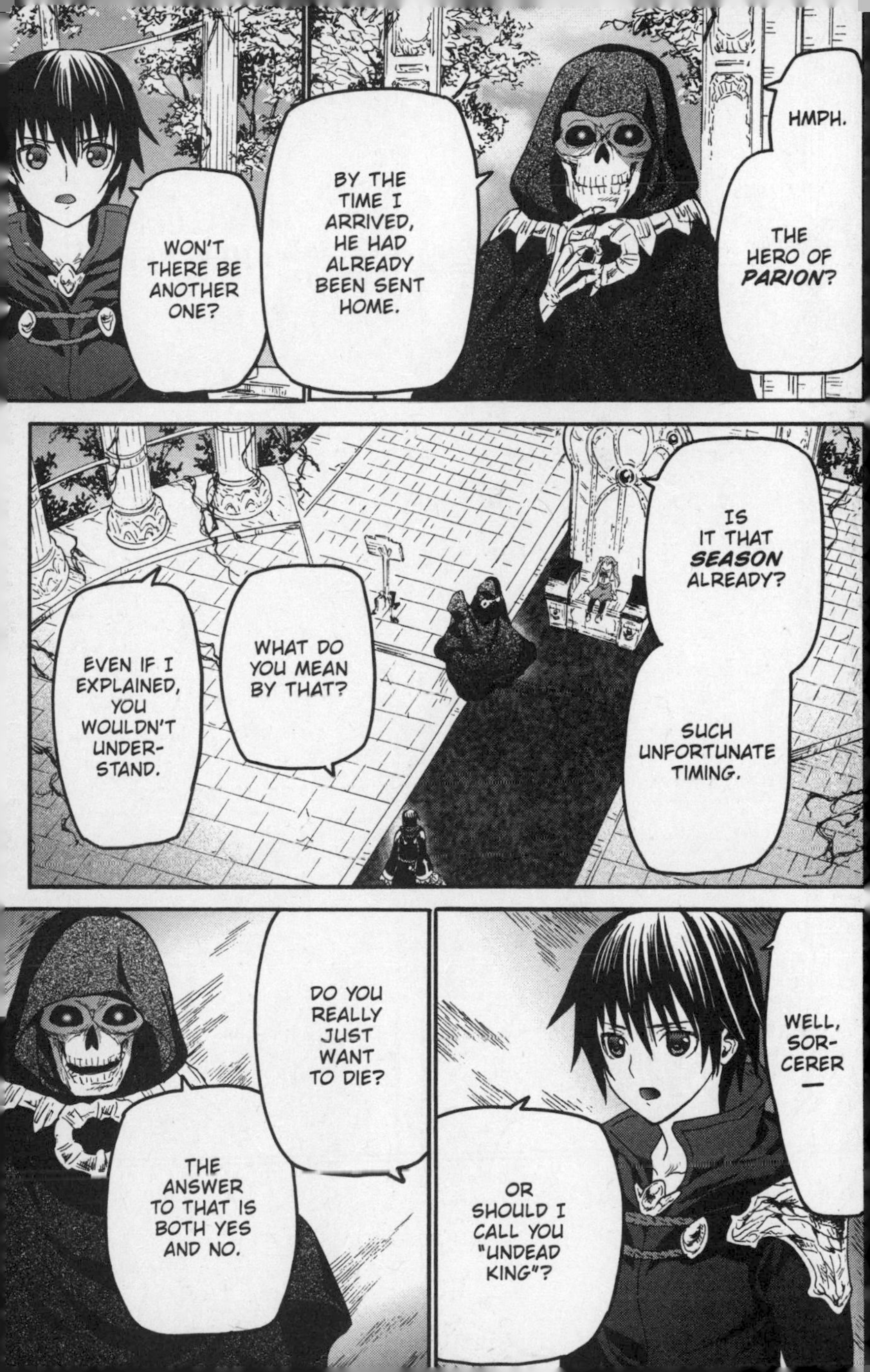
HMPH.
THE HERO OF *PARION*?
BY THE TIME I ARRIVED, HE HAD ALREADY BEEN SENT HOME.
WON'T THERE BE ANOTHER ONE?
IS IT THAT *SEASON* ALREADY?
SUCH UNFORTUNATE TIMING.
WHAT DO YOU MEAN BY THAT?
EVEN IF I EXPLAINED, YOU WOULDN'T UNDER-STAND.
WELL, SOR-CERER—
OR SHOULD I CALL YOU "UNDEAD KING"?
DO YOU REALLY JUST WANT TO DIE?
THE ANSWER TO THAT IS BOTH YES AND NO.

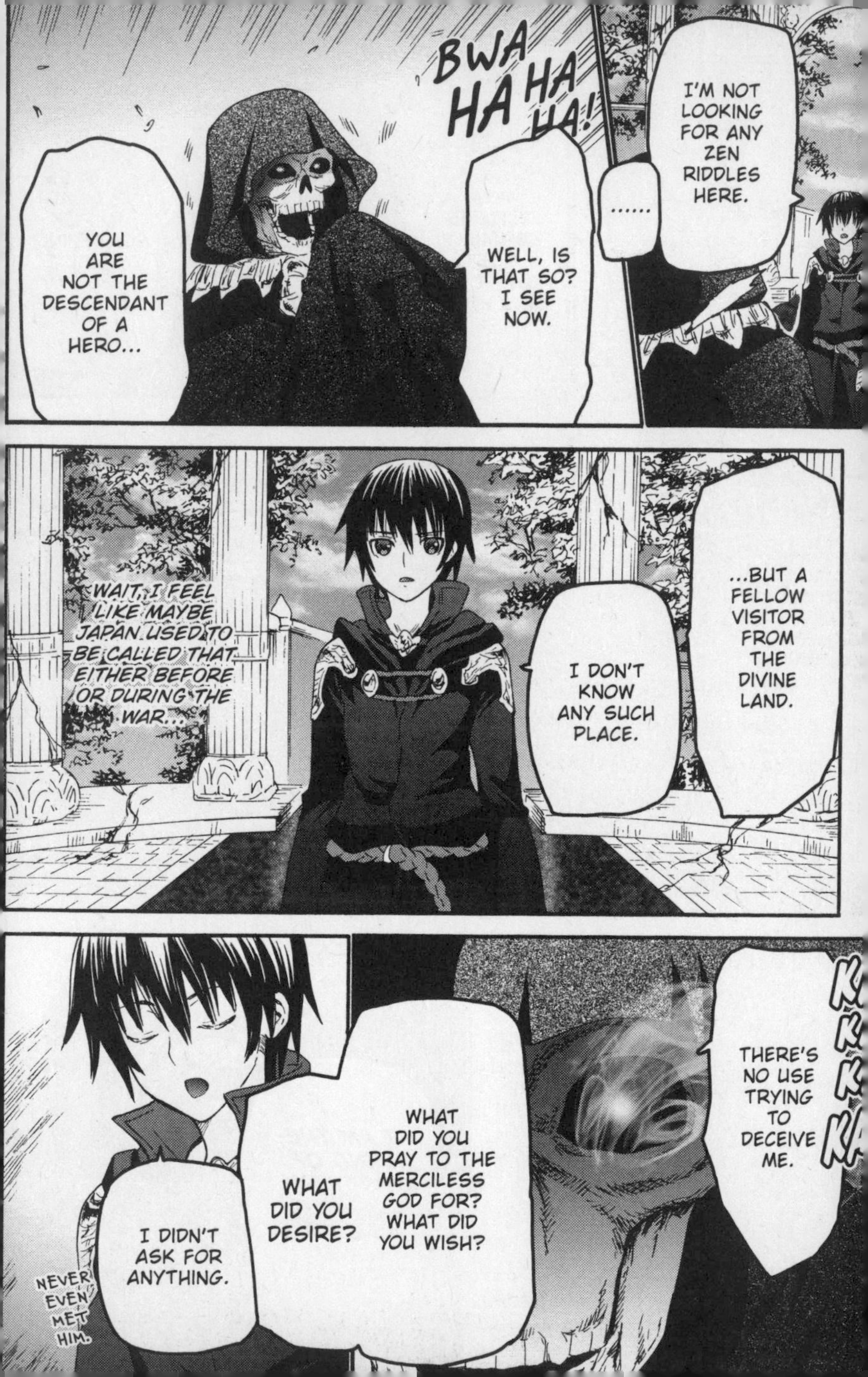
I'M NOT LOOKING FOR ANY ZEN RIDDLES HERE.
......
BWA HA HA HA!
WELL, IS THAT SO? I SEE NOW.
YOU ARE NOT THE DESCENDANT OF A HERO...
...BUT A FELLOW VISITOR FROM THE DIVINE LAND.
I DON'T KNOW ANY SUCH PLACE.
WAIT, I FEEL LIKE MAYBE JAPAN USED TO BE CALLED THAT EITHER BEFORE OR DURING THE WAR...
KA KA KA KA
THERE'S NO USE TRYING TO DECEIVE ME.
WHAT DID YOU PRAY TO THE MERCILESS GOD FOR? WHAT DID YOU WISH?
WHAT DID YOU DESIRE?
I DIDN'T ASK FOR ANYTHING.
NEVER EVEN MET HIM.

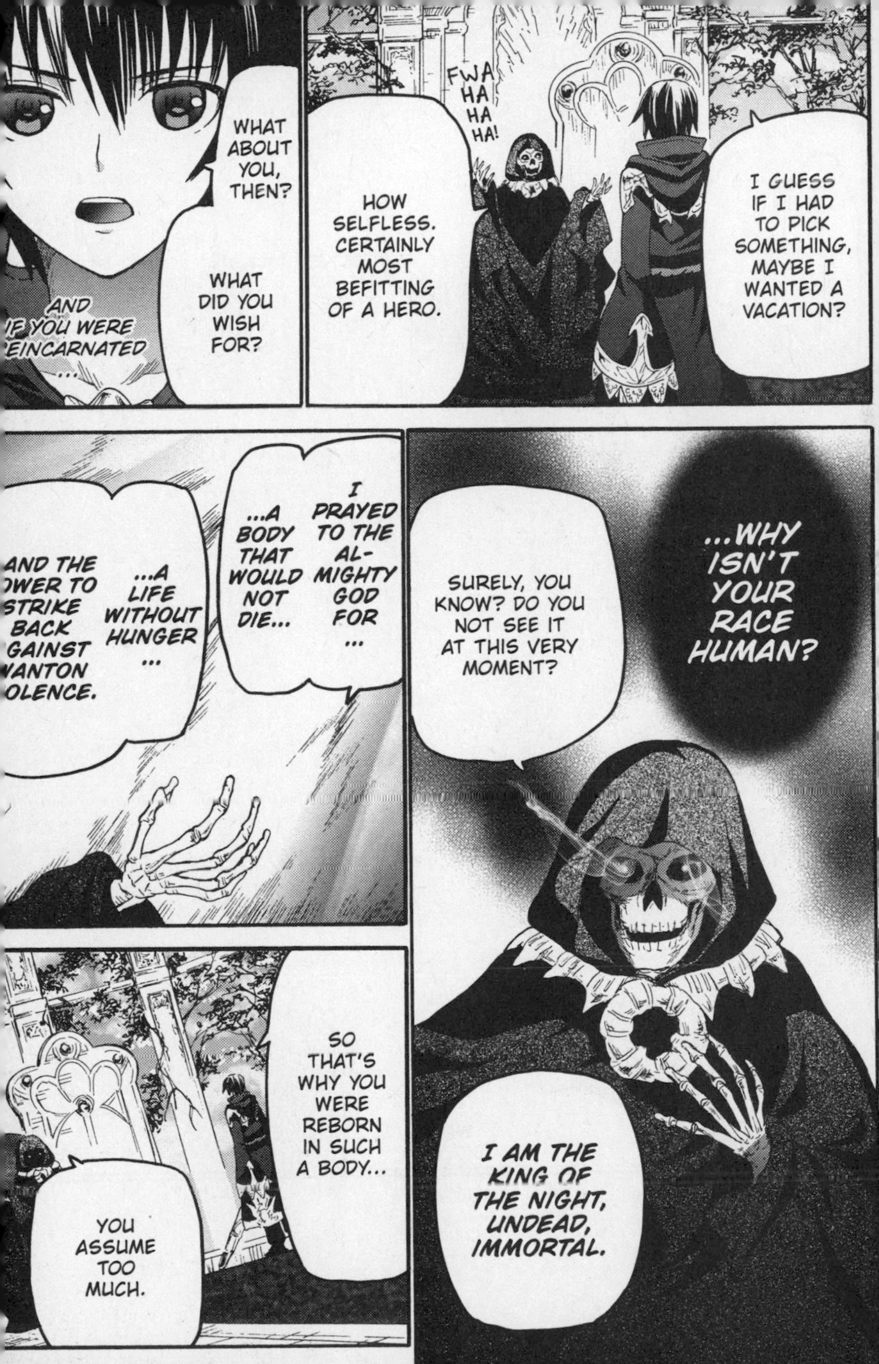
I GUESS IF I HAD TO PICK SOMETHING, MAYBE I WANTED A VACATION?
FWA HA HA HA!
HOW SELFLESS. CERTAINLY MOST BEFITTING OF A HERO.
WHAT ABOUT YOU, THEN?
WHAT DID YOU WISH FOR?
AND IF YOU WERE EINCARNATED ...
...WHY ISN'T YOUR RACE HUMAN?
SURELY, YOU KNOW? DO YOU NOT SEE IT AT THIS VERY MOMENT?
I AM THE KING OF THE NIGHT, UNDEAD, IMMORTAL.
I PRAYED TO THE AL-MIGHTY GOD FOR ...
...A BODY THAT WOULD NOT DIE...
...A LIFE WITHOUT HUNGER ...
AND THE OWER TO STRIKE BACK GAINST ANTON OLENCE.
SO THAT'S WHY YOU WERE REBORN IN SUCH A BODY...
YOU ASSUME TOO MUCH.

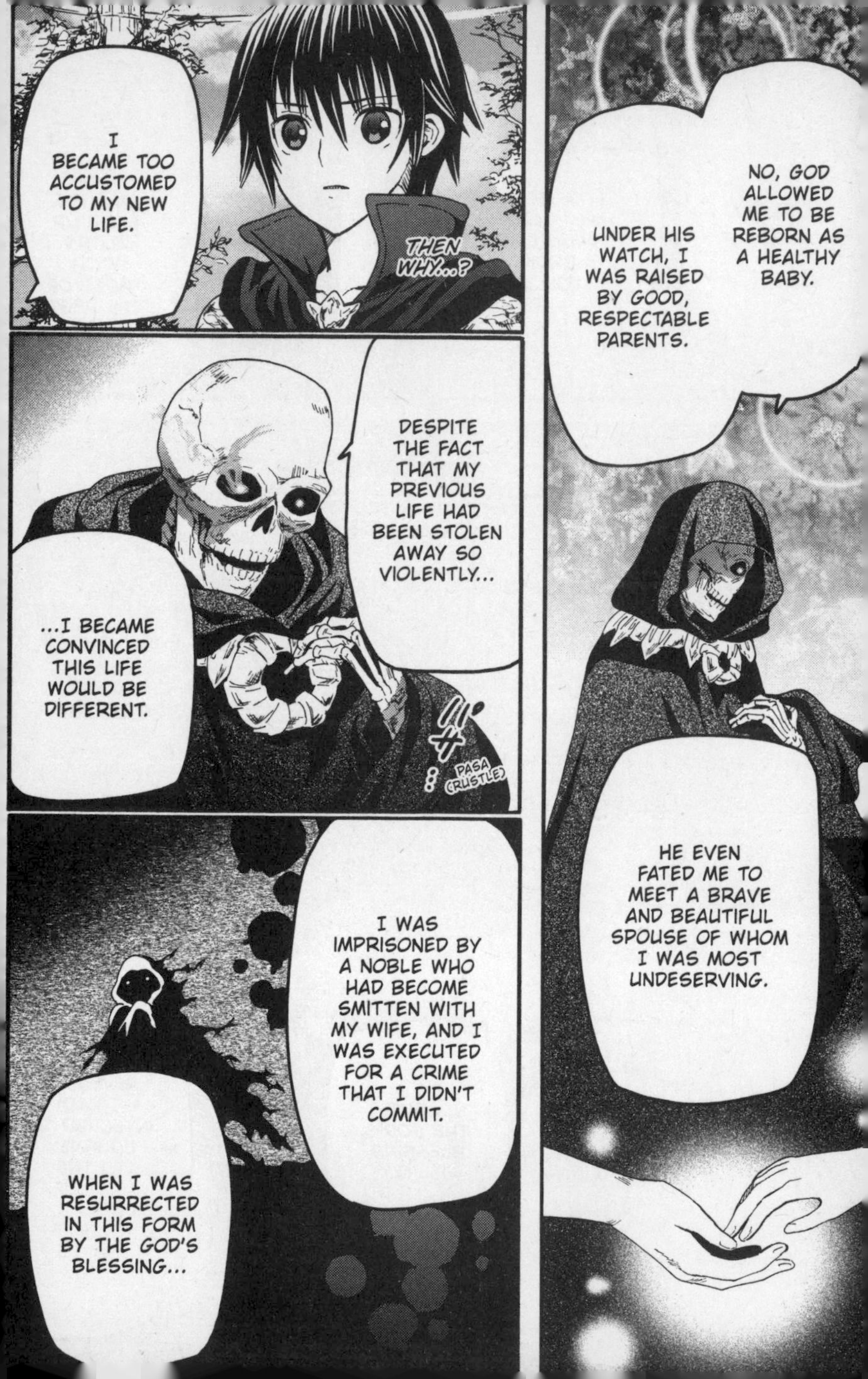
NO, GOD ALLOWED ME TO BE REBORN AS A HEALTHY BABY.
UNDER HIS WATCH, I WAS RAISED BY GOOD, RESPECTABLE PARENTS.
HE EVEN FATED ME TO MEET A BRAVE AND BEAUTIFUL SPOUSE OF WHOM I WAS MOST UNDESERVING.
I BECAME TOO ACCUSTOMED TO MY NEW LIFE.
THEN WHY...?
DESPITE THE FACT THAT MY PREVIOUS LIFE HAD BEEN STOLEN AWAY SO VIOLENTLY...
...I BECAME CONVINCED THIS LIFE WOULD BE DIFFERENT.
PASA (RUSTLE)
I WAS IMPRISONED BY A NOBLE WHO HAD BECOME SMITTEN WITH MY WIFE, AND I WAS EXECUTED FOR A CRIME THAT I DIDN'T COMMIT.
WHEN I WAS RESURRECTED IN THIS FORM BY THE GOD'S BLESSING...

...THE FIRST THINGS I SAW WERE THE HEADS OF MY PARENTS, LINED UP ALONG WITH THOSE OF THE REST OF MY FAMILY.

AND UNDERNEATH THEM, THE BODY OF MY WIFE, THROWN AWAY LIKE A BROKEN DOLL...

I HAVE NO NEED OF YOUR PITY.

I REVIVED THE BODIES OF MY FAMILY AS UNDEAD MONSTERS, AS WELL AS THOSE OF MANY OTHERS WHO'D DIED UNDER SIMILAR CIRCUMSTANCES...

...AND I TURNED MY FANGS ON THE NOBLES WHO HELD ALL THE POWER AT THAT TIME, DESTROYING EVERYTHING.

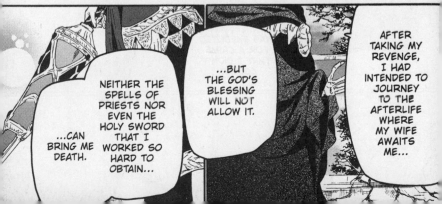

AFTER TAKING MY REVENGE, I HAD INTENDED TO JOURNEY TO THE AFTERLIFE WHERE MY WIFE AWAITS ME...

...BUT THE GOD'S BLESSING WILL NOT ALLOW IT.

NEITHER THE SPELLS OF PRIESTS NOR EVEN THE HOLY SWORD THAT I WORKED SO HARD TO OBTAIN...

...CAN BRING ME DEATH.

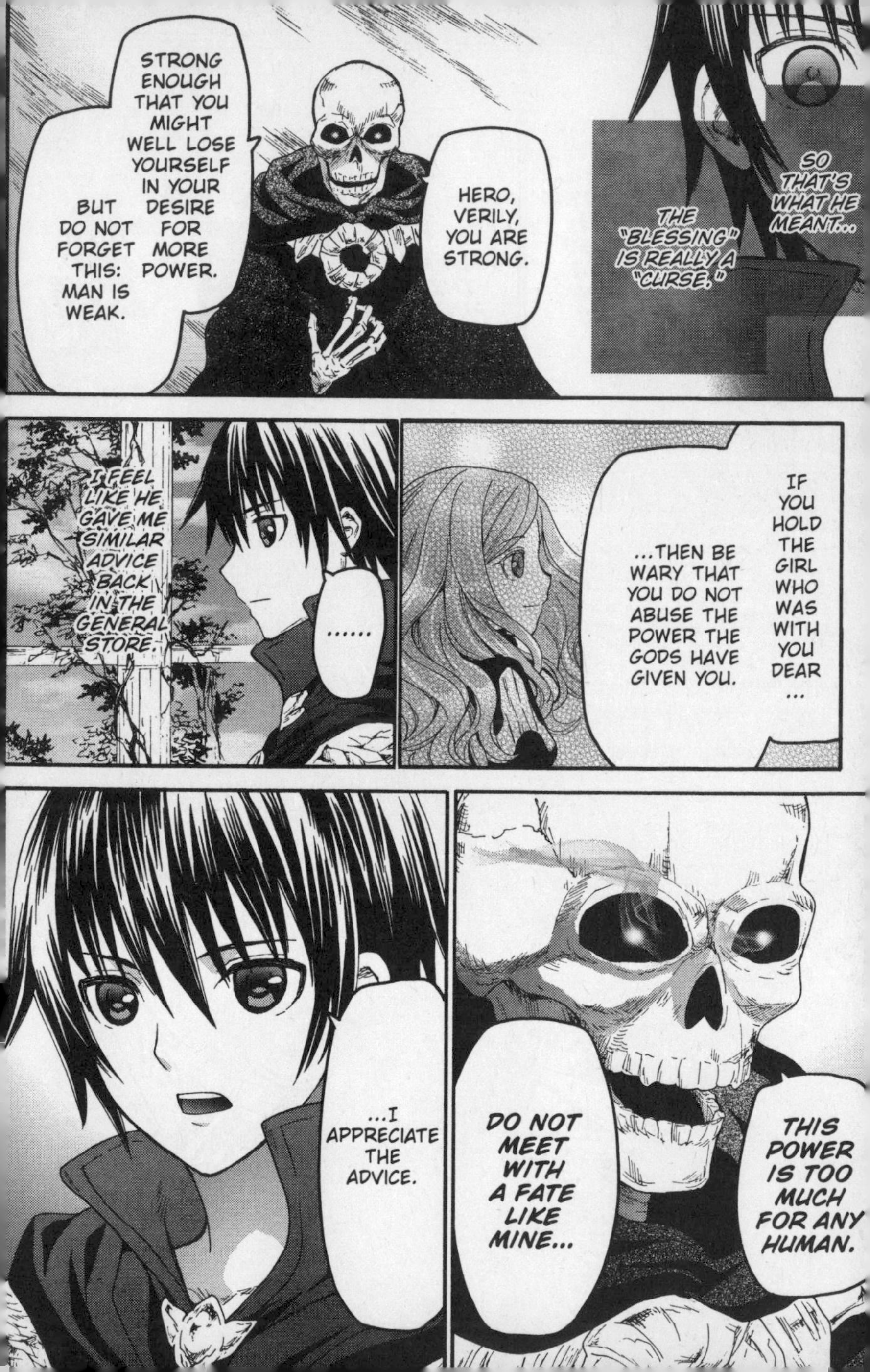
SO THAT'S WHAT HE MEANT...
THE "BLESSING" IS REALLY A "CURSE."
HERO, VERILY, YOU ARE STRONG.
STRONG ENOUGH THAT YOU MIGHT WELL LOSE YOURSELF IN YOUR DESIRE FOR MORE POWER.
BUT DO NOT FORGET THIS: MAN IS WEAK.
IF YOU HOLD THE GIRL WHO WAS WITH YOU DEAR...
...THEN BE WARY THAT YOU DO NOT ABUSE THE POWER THE GODS HAVE GIVEN YOU.
I FEEL LIKE HE GAVE ME SIMILAR ADVICE BACK IN THE GENERAL STORE.
......
THIS POWER IS TOO MUCH FOR ANY HUMAN.
DO NOT MEET WITH A FATE LIKE MINE...
...I APPRECIATE THE ADVICE.

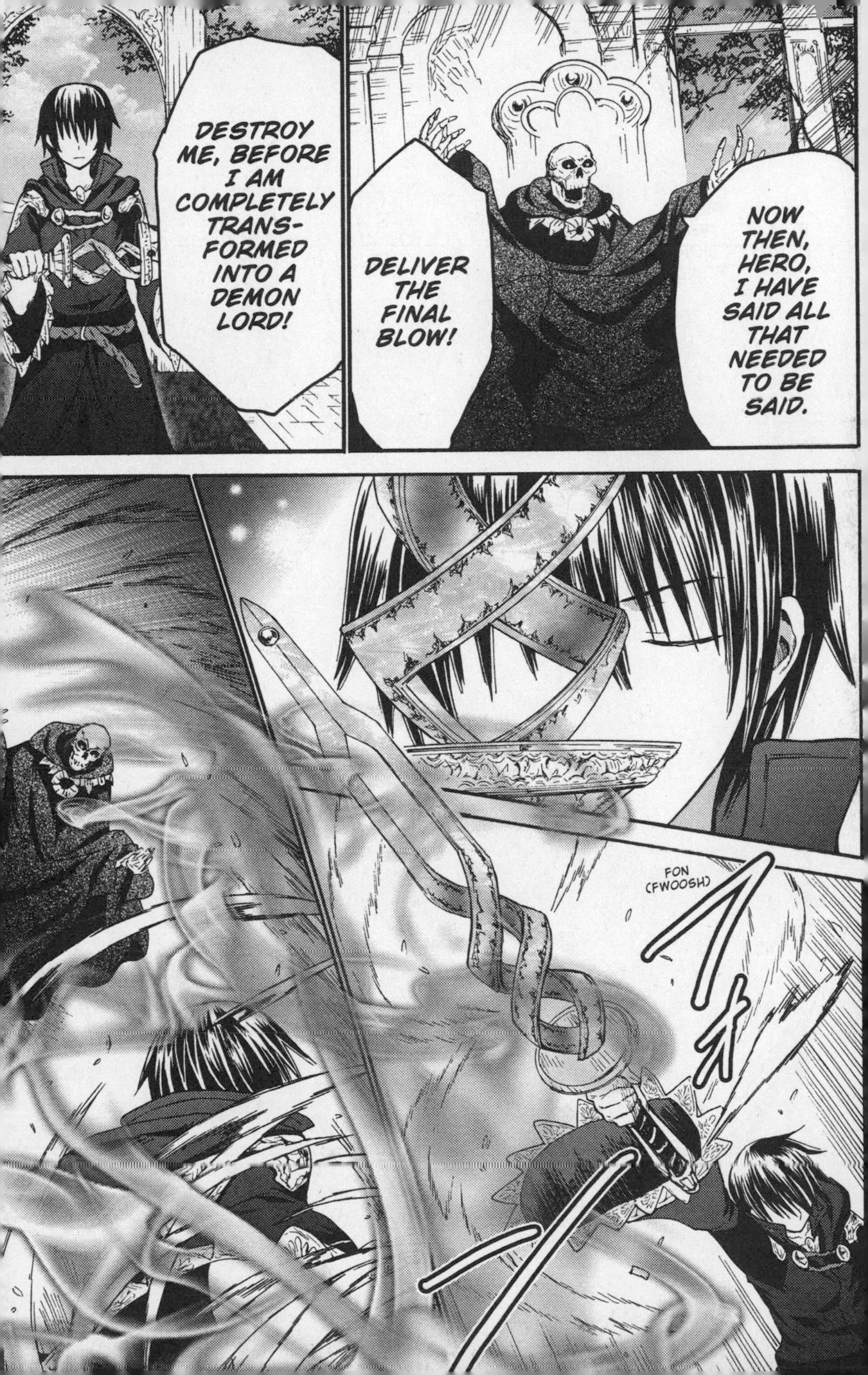
NOW THEN, HERO, I HAVE SAID ALL THAT NEEDED TO BE SAID.
DELIVER THE FINAL BLOW!
DESTROY ME, BEFORE I AM COMPLETELY TRANS-FORMED INTO A DEMON LORD!
FON (FWOOSH)

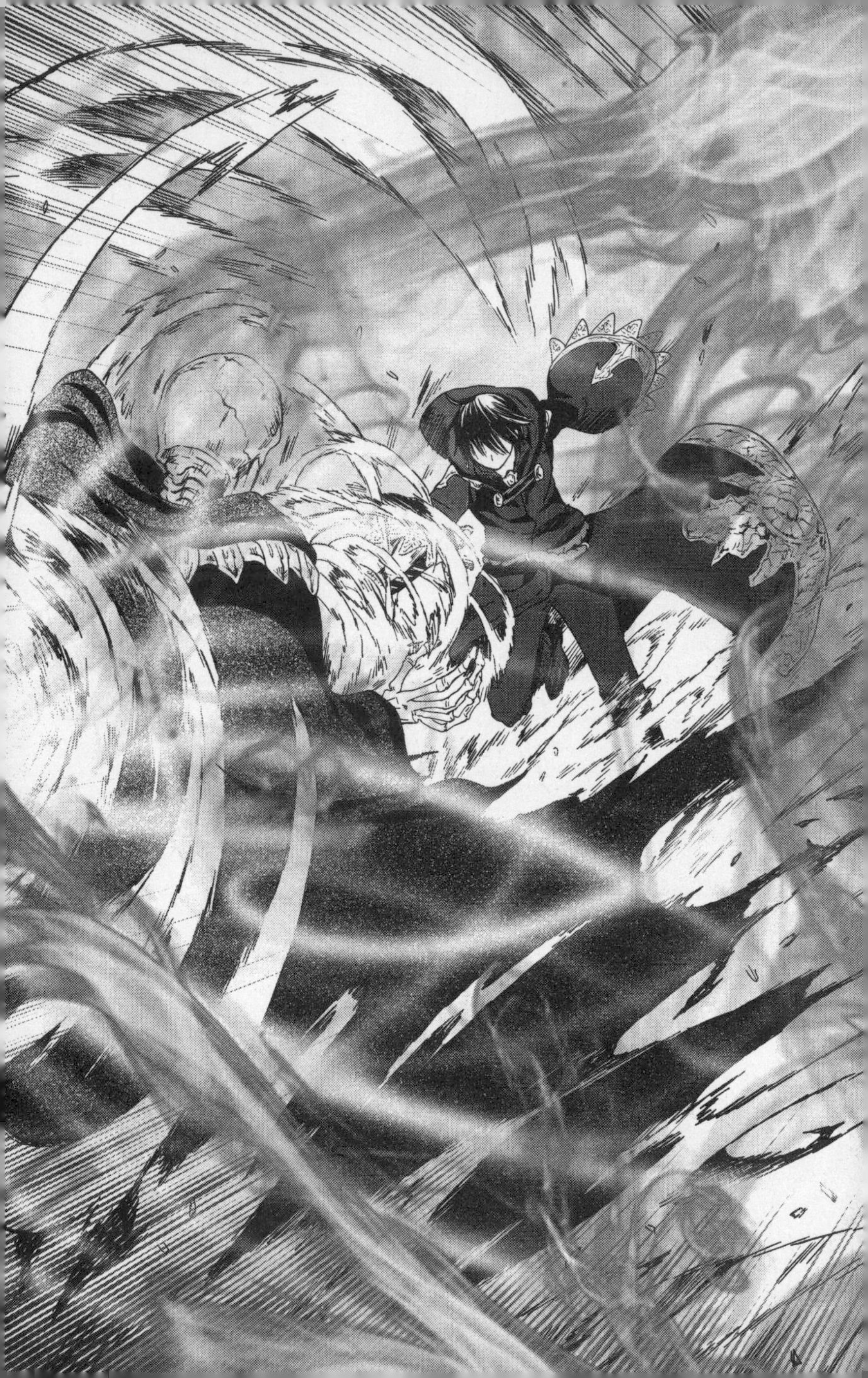

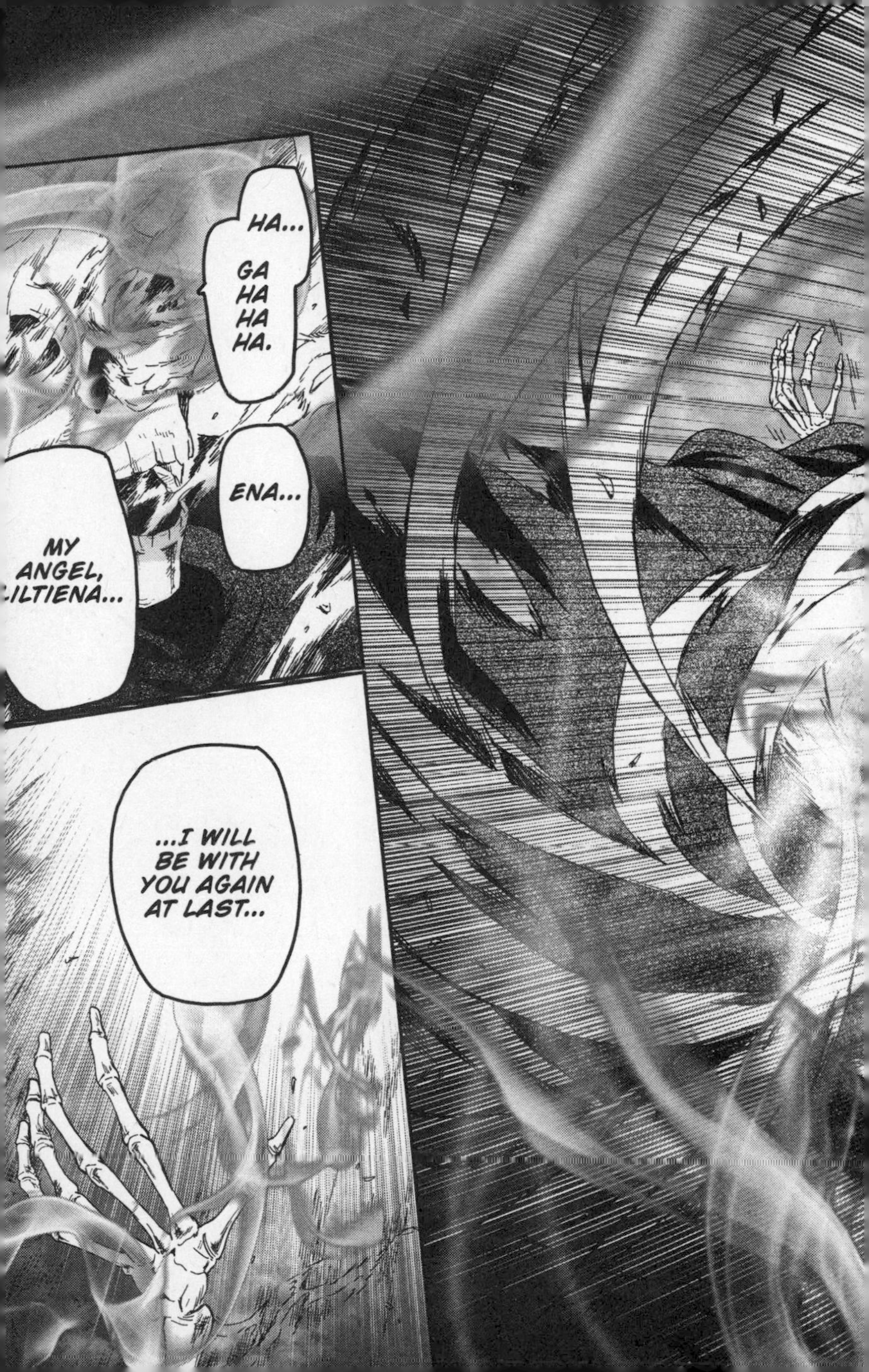
HA...
GA HA HA HA.
ENA...
MY ANGEL, ILTIENA...
...I WILL BE WITH YOU AGAIN AT LAST...

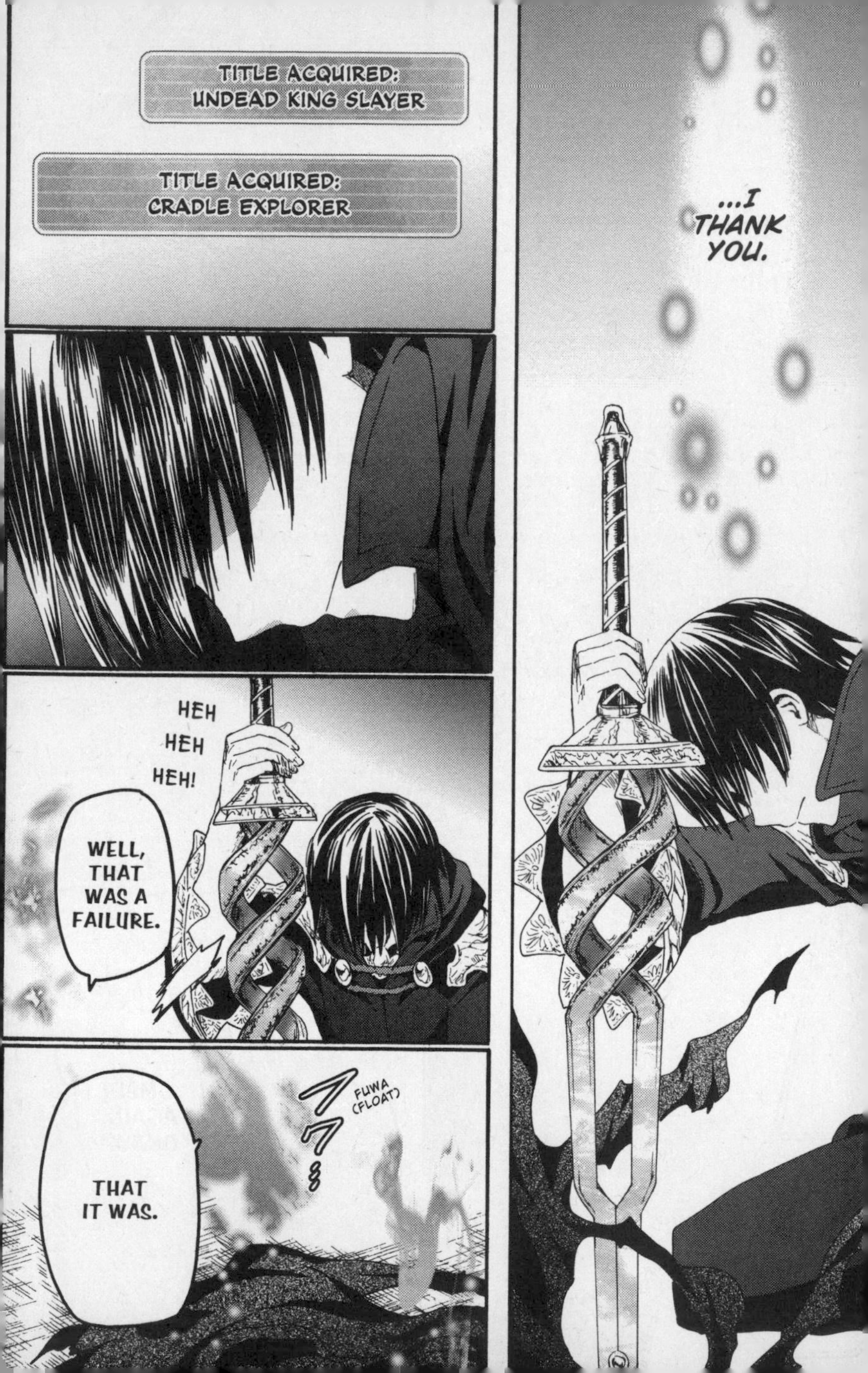
...I THANK YOU.
TITLE ACQUIRED: UNDEAD KING SLAYER
TITLE ACQUIRED: CRADLE EXPLORER
HEH HEH HEH!
WELL, THAT WAS A FAILURE.
FUWA (FLOAT)
THAT IT WAS.

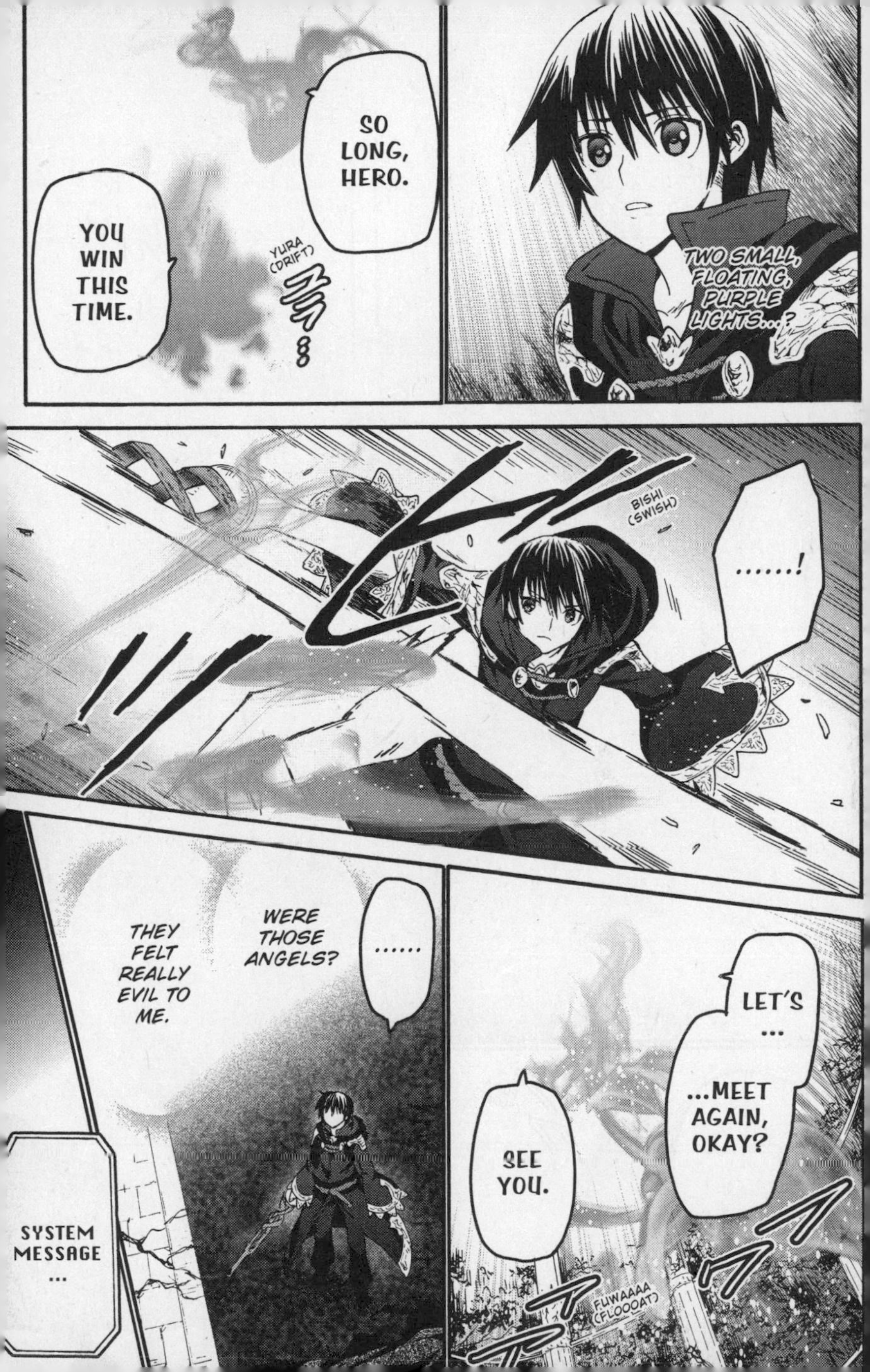
TWO SMALL, FLOATING, PURPLE LIGHTS...?
SO LONG, HERO.
YURA (DRIFT)
YOU WIN THIS TIME.
BISHI (SWISH)
......!
LET'S ...
...MEET AGAIN, OKAY?
SEE YOU.
FUWAAAA (FLOOOAT)
......
WERE THOSE ANGELS?
THEY FELT REALLY EVIL TO ME.
SYSTEM MESSAGE ...

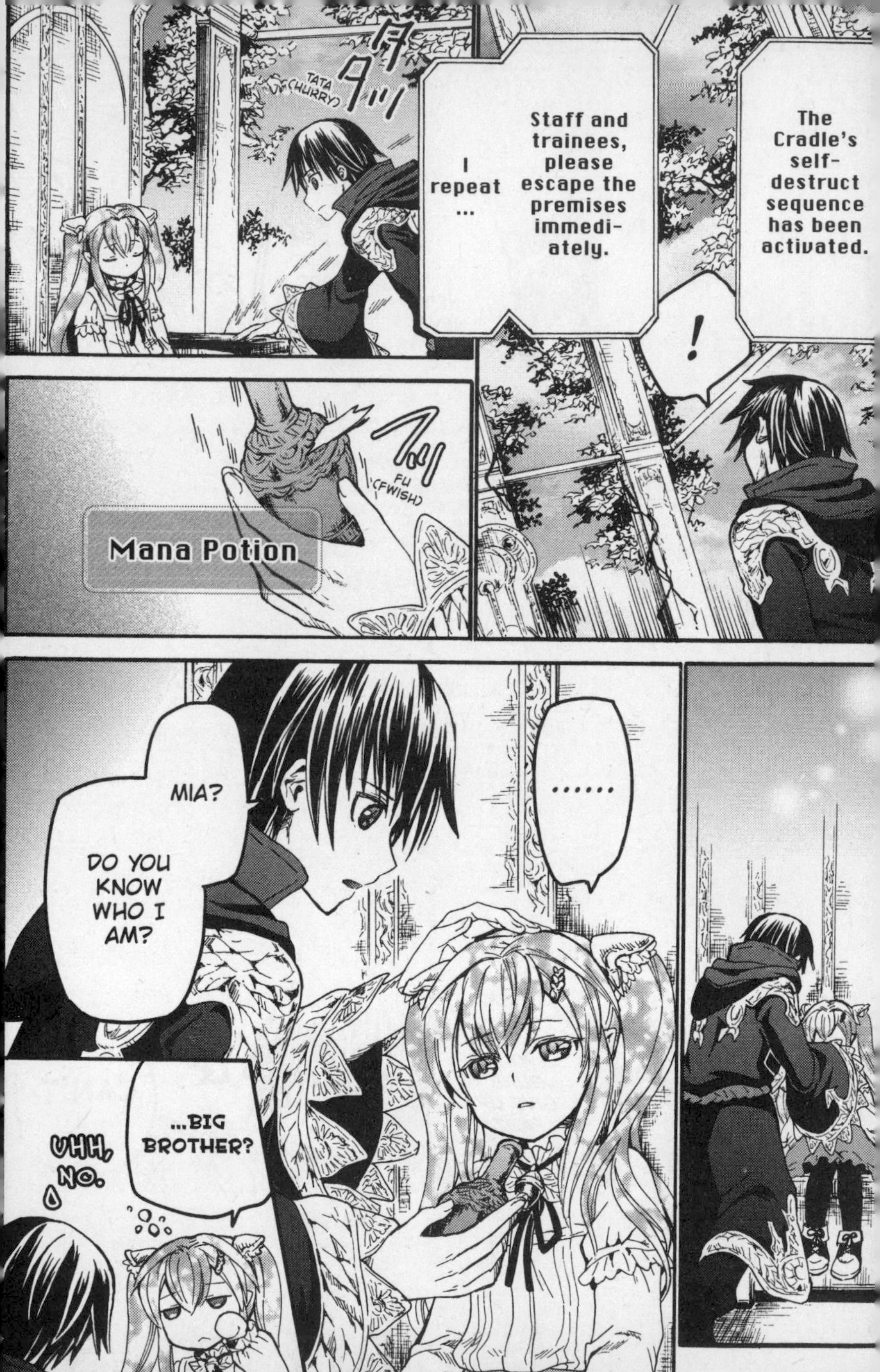
The Cradle's self-destruct sequence has been activated.
Staff and trainees, please escape the premises immediately.
I repeat ...
TATA (HURRY)
!
FU (FWISH)
Mana Potion
......
MIA?
DO YOU KNOW WHO I AM?
...BIG BROTHER?
UHH, NO.

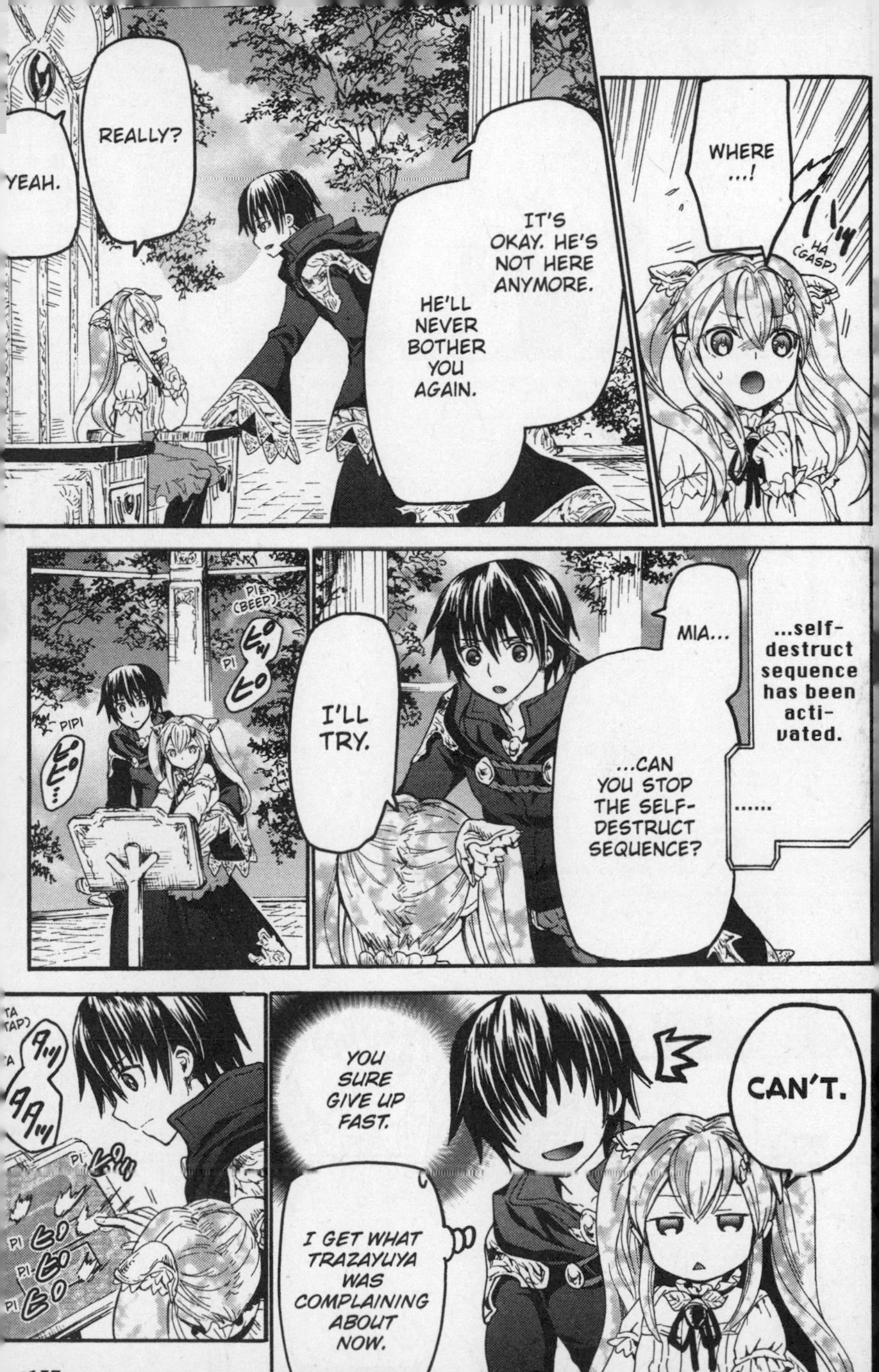

WHERE ...!
HA (GASP)
IT'S OKAY. HE'S NOT HERE ANYMORE.
HE'LL NEVER BOTHER YOU AGAIN.
REALLY?
YEAH.
...self-destruct sequence has been activated.
MIA...
......
...CAN YOU STOP THE SELF-DESTRUCT SEQUENCE?
I'LL TRY.
PI (BEEP)
PI
PIPI
CAN'T.
YOU SURE GIVE UP FAST.
I GET WHAT TRAZAYUYA WAS COMPLAINING ABOUT NOW.
PI
PI
PI
PI

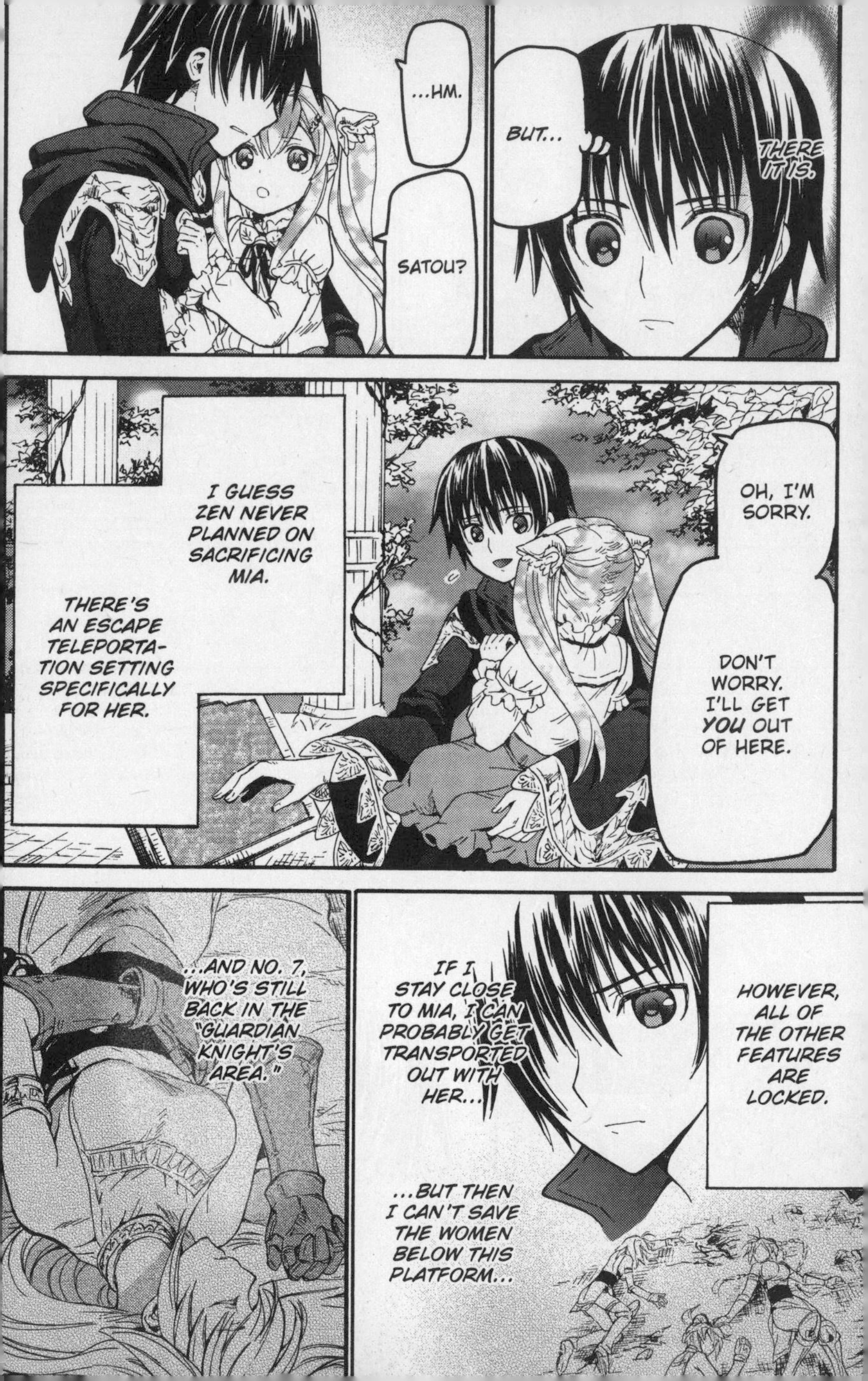
THERE IT IS.
BUT...
...HM.
SATOU?
OH, I'M SORRY.
DON'T WORRY. I'LL GET *YOU* OUT OF HERE.
I GUESS ZEN NEVER PLANNED ON SACRIFICING MIA.
THERE'S AN ESCAPE TELEPORTATION SETTING SPECIFICALLY FOR HER.
HOWEVER, ALL OF THE OTHER FEATURES ARE LOCKED.
IF I STAY CLOSE TO MIA, I CAN PROBABLY GET TRANSPORTED OUT WITH HER...
...BUT THEN I CAN'T SAVE THE WOMEN BELOW THIS PLATFORM...
...AND NO. 7, WHO'S STILL BACK IN THE "GUARDIAN KNIGHT'S AREA."

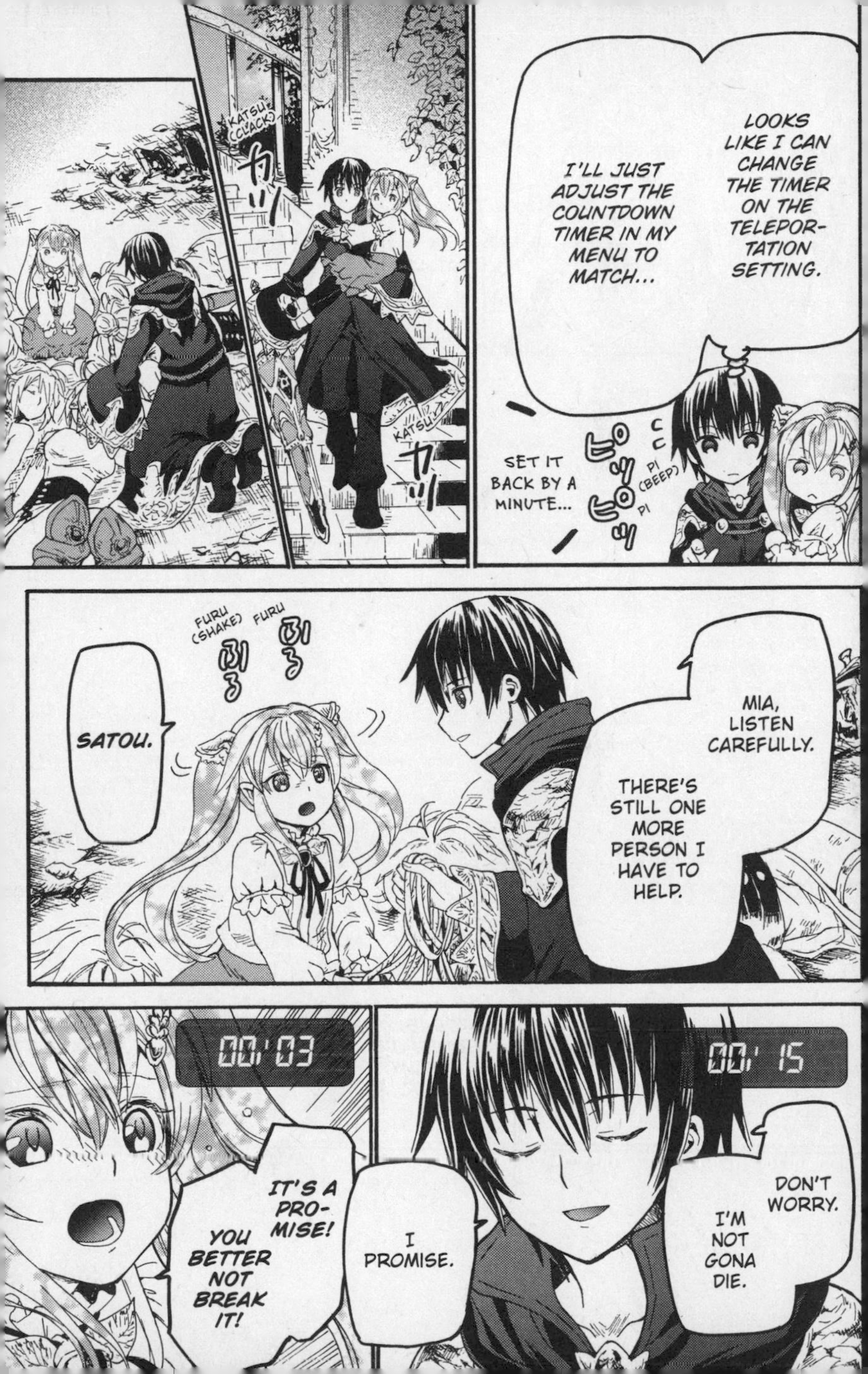
LOOKS LIKE I CAN CHANGE THE TIMER ON THE TELEPOR-TATION SETTING.
I'LL JUST ADJUST THE COUNTDOWN TIMER IN MY MENU TO MATCH...
PI (BEEP) PI
ピッ ピッ
SET IT BACK BY A MINUTE...
KATSU (CLACK)
カッ
KATSU
カッ
MIA, LISTEN CAREFULLY.
THERE'S STILL ONE MORE PERSON I HAVE TO HELP.
FURU (SHAKE) FURU
ふる ふる
SATOU.
00' 15
DON'T WORRY.
I'M NOT GONA DIE.
I PROMISE.
00' 03
IT'S A PRO-MISE!
YOU BETTER NOT BREAK IT!

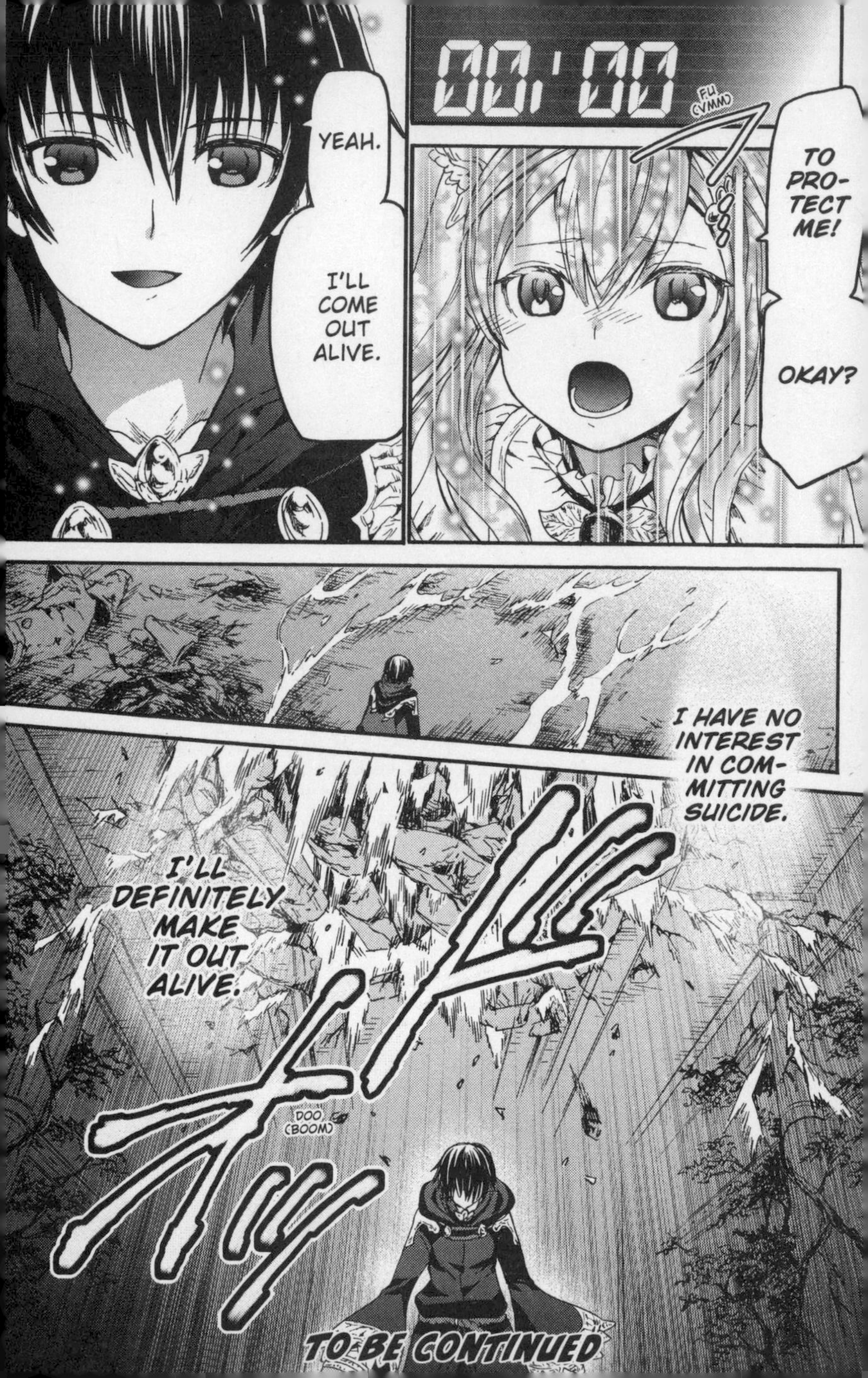
TO PRO-TECT ME!
OKAY?
FU (VMM)
00:00
YEAH.
I'LL COME OUT ALIVE.
I HAVE NO INTEREST IN COM-MITTING SUICIDE.
I'LL DEFINITELY MAKE IT OUT ALIVE.
DOO (BOOM)
TO BE CONTINUED

FAIRY RING

A Dryad's
teleportation device.

Creates glowing,
green spores that
form a tunnel of light
around the center.

INTERPRETATION SKILL LV. 0

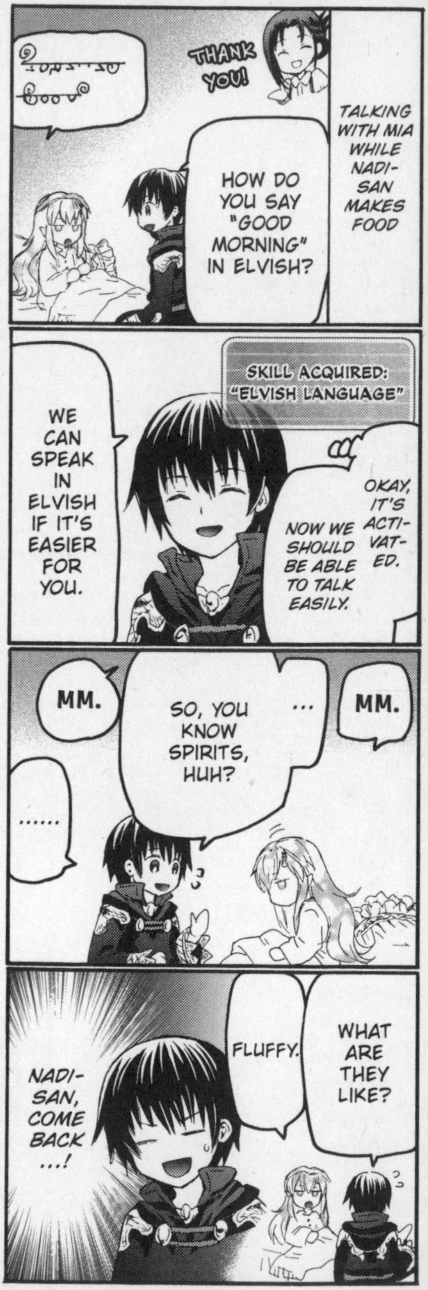
TALKING WITH MIA WHILE NADI-SAN MAKES FOOD
THANK YOU!
HOW DO YOU SAY "GOOD MORNING" IN ELVISH?
SKILL ACQUIRED: "ELVISH LANGUAGE"
OKAY, IT'S ACTIVATED.
NOW WE SHOULD BE ABLE TO TALK EASILY.
WE CAN SPEAK IN ELVISH IF IT'S EASIER FOR YOU.
MM.
...
SO, YOU KNOW SPIRITS, HUH?
MM.
......
WHAT ARE THEY LIKE?
FLUFFY.
NADI-SAN, COME BACK ...!

TOUGH WORLD

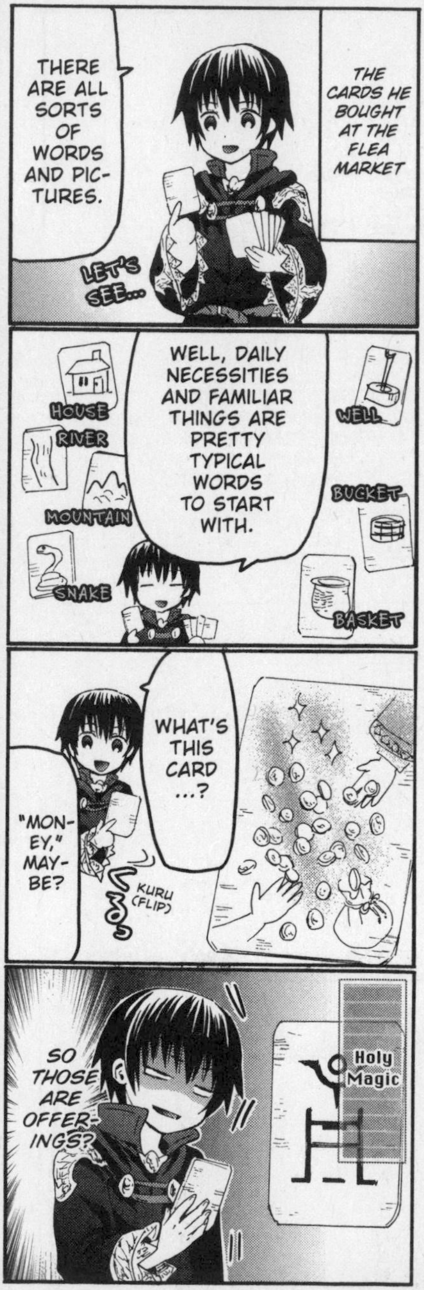
THE CARDS HE BOUGHT AT THE FLEA MARKET
THERE ARE ALL SORTS OF WORDS AND PICTURES.
LET'S SEE...
WELL
BUCKET
BASKET
WELL, DAILY NECESSITIES AND FAMILIAR THINGS ARE PRETTY TYPICAL WORDS TO START WITH.
HOUSE
RIVER
MOUNTAIN
SNAKE
WHAT'S THIS CARD ...?
KURU (FLIP)
"MONEY," MAYBE?
Holy Magic
SO THOSE ARE OFFERINGS?

CAUSE & EFFECT (*ONLY A JOKE)

PAS-SING THE TIME WITH BLO-CKS
I WOULD LIKE TO ATTEMPT A LARGER STRUC-TURE, I REMARK.
PERHAPS WE SHOULD COLLECT MORE WOODEN BLOCKS, I PRO-POSE.
THERE IS NO SHORTAGE OF MATERIAL IN THE CRADLE, I CONCUR.
LET US MAKE MANY BLOCKS, I ENTHUSE.
GIKO (SAW)
GIKO
BUTSU (WHUNK)
THE NEXT DAY
HMM.
IT SEEMS LIKE SOME-THING'S INTERRUPT-ING MY CONNEC-TION.
HMM?

We've reached Volume 4.

Things are pretty chaotic here, and I haven't quite gotten used to it yet.

I'm starting to feel like I'm lagging behind, but I think it's important to move at my own pace.

I hope we can meet again in the next volume.

Thank you very much.

–Ayamegumu

...Special Thanks

- Manuscript production collaborators
Kaname Yukishiro-sama
Satoru Ezaki-sama
Yuna Kobayashi-sama
Hacchan-sama

- Editors
Toyohara-sama
Hagiwara-sama
Kuwazuru-sama
Arakawa-sama

- Binding
coil-sama

- Supervision
Hiro Ainana-sama
shri-sama

- Everyone who helped with the production and publication of this book

And you!

DEATH MARCHING TO THE PARALLEL WORLD RHAPSODY

TO THE
PARALLEL WORLD

Original Story: Hiro Ainana
Art: AYAMEGUMU
Character Design: shri

Translation: Jenny McKeon ◆ Lettering: Rochelle Gancio

DEATH MARCHING TO THE PARALLEL WORLD RHAPSODY Vol. 4
©AYAMEGUMU 2016
©HIRO AINANA, shri 2016
First published in Japan in 2016 by KADOKAWA CORPORATION, Tokyo. English translation rights arranged with KADOKAWA CORPORATION, Tokyo through TUTTLE-MORI AGENCY, INC., Tokyo.

English translation © 2017 by Yen Press, LLC

Yen Press
1290 Avenue of the Americas
New York, NY 10104

Visit us at yenpress.com
facebook.com/yenpress
twitter.com/yenpress
yenpress.tumblr.com
instagram.com/yenpress

First Yen Press Edition: December 2017

Yen Press is an imprint of Yen Press, LLC.
The Yen Press name and logo are trademarks of Yen Press, LLC.

Printed in the United States of America